The Way We Lived

Volume II
1865–Present

The Way We Lived

Essays and Documents
in American Social History
Fifth Edition

Frederick M. Binder
City University of New York, College of Staten Island

David M. Reimers
New York University

Houghton Mifflin Company   Boston   New York

Publisher: Charles Hartford
Editor-in-Chief: Jean L. Woy
Development Editor: Leah R. Strauss
Associate Project Editor: Lindsay Frost
Editorial Assistant: Teresa Huang
Senior Production/Design Coordinator: Jodi O'Rourke
Senior Manufacturing Coordinator: Marie Barnes
Senior Marketing Manager: Sandra McGuire

Printed in the U.S.A.

Library of Congress Catalog Number: 2002109365

ISBN: 0-618-30586-6

23456789-FFG-08 07 06 05 04

Contents

Part II *Modern American Society,*
1920–Present   **133**

Contents

Preface

History courses have traditionally emphasized the momentous events of our past. Wars and laws, technological advances and economic crises, ideas and ideologies, and the roles of famous heroes and infamous villains have been central to these studies. Yet what made events momentous is the impact they had on society at large, on people from all walks of life. Modern scholars' growing attention to social history is in part a recognition that knowledge of the experiences, values, and attitudes of these people is crucial to gaining an understanding of our past.

America's history as reflected in the everyday lives of its people provides the focus of these volumes. In preparing a work of selected readings, we have had to make choices as to which episodes from our past to highlight. Each of those included, we believe, was significant in the shaping of our society. Each of the essays is followed by original documents that serve several purposes. They provide examples of the kinds of source materials used by social historians in their research; they help to illuminate and expand upon the subject dealt with in the essays; and they bring the reader into direct contact with the people of the past—people who helped shape, and people who were affected by, the "momentous events."

Our introduction to each essay and its accompanying documents is designed to set the historical scene and to call attention to particular points in the selections, raising questions for students to ponder as they read. A list of suggested readings follows after each of the major divisions of the text. We trust that these volumes will prove to be what written history at its best can be—interesting and enlightening.

We are pleased to note that favorable comments by faculty and students as well as the large number of course adoptions attest to the success of our first four editions. Quite naturally, we thus have no desire in our fifth edition to alter the basic focus, style, and organization of *The Way We Lived*. Many of those essays that our readers and we consider to have been the earlier editions' best remain intact. However, it is our belief that the new selections, reflecting recent scholarship, will identify and clarify significant issues in American social history even more effectively than those they replaced. In choosing new essays and documents for inclusion, we have sought to present a broader view of historical events.

Thus, in Volume I, we have replaced our essay on the Middle Passage with one tracing the evolution of slavery from captivity in Africa to the horrors of the sea voyage to the New World, and finally to its existence in the

American colonies. Similarly, the new essay on immigration begins in Ireland and follows a particular group of emigrants from their native homes to their settlement in New York City and adaptation to life in the United States. We are particularly pleased to include an essay that demonstrates that, following the Civil War, there were Southern blacks who took an active role in shaping their own destinies and who were not, as often depicted, merely the passive recipients of federal aid and charitable assistance. Also, for the first time this edition includes documents relating to the Spanish colonization of New Mexico and to New Orleans under French rule.

In Volume II, a new essay about women in wheat country offers a view of the life of women in the late 19th century in Kansas, asking probing questions about the nature of rural America as it pertains to women. Another new essay, from David Kennedy's prize-winning book on the Great Depression, gives the reader a sweeping view of the impact of the Depression on Americans. Kennedy quite properly calls it "The ordeal of the American people." Also new to the fifth edition is an essay that focuses on the desegregation of Little Rock's Central High School, painting in detail the difficulties, including violence, faced by the black children who desegregated the school.

We would like to thank the following reviewers for their excellent and helpful comments: Charles A. Keller, Fairmont State College; Kriste Lindenmyer, University of Maryland—Baltimore County; Leonard D. Ortiz, University of Kansas; and Victoria W. Wolcott, University of Rochester.

It is our hope that students will find as much pleasure in reading this new edition as we have had in creating it.

F. M. B.

D. M. R.

PART I

The Emergence of an Urban, Industrial Society
1865—1920

Chapter 1

Reconstruction: Triumphs and Tragedies

The Howard School, founded in 1869 by African American citizens of Fayetteville, North Carolina.

In the past, depictions of the era of Reconstruction have often portrayed the African Americans of the South as, on the one hand, recipients of assistance from federal government agencies and Northern missionary societies and, on the other hand, victims of legislative and extralegal measures to deny them their rights as citizens. Recognition that blacks themselves took an active role in shaping their own destiny has occurred relatively recently. Mark Andrew Huddle's essay "To Educate a Race" tells the story of the African American residents of the textile-manufacturing center of Fayetteville, North Carolina, and their largely successful efforts to establish elementary and secondary schools as well as teacher training institutions. What characteristics of Fayetteville's black community and its leaders were of particular significance in contributing to its successes? In what ways did the actions of both Southern and Northern whites lead Fayetteville's African Americans to look "to themselves for their own elevation"?

Although even the most tenacious Southerners recognized that slavery was finished and that the South needed a new system of labor, few white Southerners could accept the freedmen as social and political equals. From 1865 to 1866, Southern politicians established Black Codes to ensure white supremacy. Huddle's essay reveals that Fayetteville's African Americans did not passively sit back and submit to efforts by the white community to restrict their freedom and efforts at self-improvement. The first document provides evidence that such assertiveness was not limited to the North Carolina town. It is a letter from a freed slave to his former master. It speaks eloquently of the conditions and humiliations that he had endured in the past and also of the better life that he had built for himself. How would you describe the general tone of the letter?

Black Codes represented efforts to maintain white dominance through legislative acts. The onset of Radical Reconstruction brought an end to this tactic. In its place, to serve the same purpose, there arose secret societies, most notably the Ku Klux Klan, which employed terror and intimidation to achieve the goal of keeping the freedmen down. The second document is an excerpt from the initiation ritual of the Knights of the White Camelia, a secret society founded in New Orleans in 1867, and very much a clone of the Ku Klux Klan. You will note that the candidate for membership is required to take an oath "to cherish" the society's "grand principles." From your reading, what do you perceive these "principles" to have been?

While the Civil War still raged, Frederick Douglass had delivered a speech that revealed his recognition that, despite the abolition of slavery and the ultimate end of the war, the attainment of equal rights for blacks would involve further struggle. The final document is an excerpt from that speech. Compare Douglass's position and arguments regarding the issues of racial superiority and inferiority, and the right to vote with those expressed by the Knights of the White Camelia.

The struggle Douglass envisioned did indeed occur and lasted for many more years than he might have expected. Beginning in the 1890s, the freedmen lost the rights and opportunities they had won during the ten years following the Civil War, as Southern whites began systematically to disfranchise African Americans and to institutionalize segregationist and discriminatory practices. Although blacks never accepted these conditions as permanent, over half a century would pass before their march toward full equality resumed with the promise of significant success.

ESSAY

To Educate a Race
Mark Andrew Huddle

In 1877 Gov. Zebulon Vance urged an education reform program upon a skeptical North Carolina legislature. Central to Vance's plan was the establishment of state-funded normal schools for the training of teachers. The first normal school for the training of white teachers was to be overseen at a special summer course to be operated at the University of North Carolina at Chapel Hill. Scholars were to be trained in a variety of disciplines and indoctrinated in the latest educational theories and practices. Interestingly, at a time when only the rudiments of public instruction existed for white North Carolinians, Governor Vance also included a call for the creation of a "state colored normal school."

In consideration of the poor condition of African American education in the immediate aftermath of the Civil War and the need for state control of any such ventures, Governor Vance called on the representatives to fund not just a summer session, but a "long-term school" in which prospective black teachers might be instructed in "appropriate" educational techniques and philosophies as well as the subjects that they would teach. The act that eventually passed the legislature in 1877 set aside $2,000 for the funding of such an institution, and a special committee of the state board of education met in June of that year to act on the governor's personal recommendation that the school be located at Fayetteville, North Carolina.

The choice of Fayetteville as the site for the school was in no way random. Soon after the passage of Governor Vance's bill, the state board of education was besieged with offers from municipalities from across the state that were interested in providing a home for the first state normal school for African Americans. A meeting of the board of education on April 10, 1877, drew more than thirty African American representatives from fifteen counties. Fayetteville sent the formidable African Methodist Episcopal Zion (AMEZ) bishop James Walker Hood to that meeting, and his efforts on behalf of the town resulted in a visit to Fayetteville by Governor Vance and state superintendent of public instruction John C. Scarborough in June 1877. Both Vance and Scarborough were favorably impressed with what they saw and recommended to the board that Fayetteville serve as the site for the school.

Source: Mark Andrew Huddle, "To Educate a Race: The Making of the First State Colored Normal School, Fayetteville, North Carolina, 1865–1877," *North Carolina Historical Review* 74 (April 1997): 135–60. Reprinted with permission of the North Carolina Office of Archives and History.

In actuality, historical precedent worked in Fayetteville's favor in the competition for the normal school. A sophisticated education effort in the town's black community had been under way since 1865. Noted African American educators Cicero and Robert Harris administered respectively the elementary Phillips School and the secondary Sumner School from 1866 until 1869, when the two schools were consolidated to form the Howard School. During the late 1860s, Fayetteville's African American schools owed much of their financial support to the northern-based American Missionary Association (AMA) and to the federal Freedmen's Bureau. It is distinctive that these schools were controlled by the African American community of Fayetteville, a community that had emerged from the war organized and with an agenda that emphasized the importance of education. In this tumultuous period, these blacks were able to maintain a remarkable independence of action in achieving their community goals. African American agency was the determining factor in the success of the Fayetteville experiment and its eventual designation as the State Colored Normal School. . . .

[L]ong before the American Missionary Association (AMA) and Freedmen's Bureau began their work to establish a school among the freed people, Fayetteville had a large, organized African American community. There is significant evidence that a portion of this community was literate and that a number of free blacks actively engaged in the clandestine education of elements within the slave population. Historian John Hope Franklin has argued that among free blacks the apprenticeship system offered opportunities for the attainment of basic literacy. This desire for education certainly played a role in the urban setting of Fayetteville. From 1822 to 1824 the noted black educator and Presbyterian minister, John Chavis, whose academy in Raleigh was responsible for educating both whites and free blacks, taught at Fayetteville. There is also evidence that in 1850 a number of white elites established a short-lived day school for the training of free blacks. Finally, 1860 census data shows that approximately 11 percent of the adult (age twenty-one years and above) free black and mulatto population could read and/or write.

It is certain that a number of free blacks at Fayetteville secretly labored to teach basic reading and writing skills to slaves. When Robert Harris, a man most responsible for the success of the Howard School and the establishment of the State Colored Normal School, applied to the AMA for a teaching commission in 1864, the only experience of which he could boast was the work that he and his brother had done among the slave population at Fayetteville in the 1840s. Wrote Harris: "I have had no experience in [t]eaching except in privately teaching slaves in the south where I lived in my youth." Harris's older brother, William, also reported having taught for two years among the slaves of Fayetteville. In sum, the educational impulse was well established in Fayetteville's African American community by the end of the Civil War, when that community began a systematic effort to establish a school, train teachers, and reach out to freed people in the vicinity. All of these efforts preceded the establishment of the State Colored Normal School in 1877.

The Civil War proved particularly destructive for Fayetteville. . . . General Sherman and his troops occupied Fayetteville on March 11[, 1865]. On that same day, the general issued Special Field Order No. 28, which ordered the destruction of "all railroad property, all shops, factories, tanneries, &c., and all mills save one water-mill of sufficient capacity to grind meal for the people of Fayetteville." The demolition of the railroad was not limited to the town limits but was directed to take place "as far up as the lower Little River." The cavalry was also ordered to demolish the armory and everything pertaining to it. In addition to this destruction, there was considerable pillaging: livestock was seized, and Sherman's "bummers" were said to have visited every home in the city. One wealthy Fayetteville citizen reported property losses of nearly $100,000.

Fayetteville's black community was not spared in the ensuing turmoil. In October 1865, a local African American reported to newspaper correspondent John Dennett that every black home had been ransacked during Sherman's occupation. A black man seen on the streets "with a good suit of clothes, or a new pair of shoes, was halted at once and made to exchange" with a Union soldier. As a result, Dennett, reported, Fayetteville's African Americans "no longer believed that every man of Northern birth must be their friends and they more clearly [looked] to themselves for their own elevation."

Union soldiers were not the only threat to Fayetteville blacks. According to Dennett's informant, soon after Sherman's withdrawal from the city, whites moved quickly to reestablish control of the town and reinstitute elements of the antebellum slave code. Public whipping was reinstated as punishment for blacks who broke the law. Blacks were banned from meeting together for worship; they were even barred from carrying walking sticks within the city limits. Fayetteville's African American population did not simply submit to these indignities: black leaders let it be known that, if members of the white community did not desist from their attacks, they would request that a garrison of black soldiers be stationed in the town. The freed people were obviously aware of the chastening effect that such a contingent would have on the unreconstructed element in Fayetteville. In any case, the town's white leaders decided to make an accommodation with local blacks and requested that a representative of the Freedmen's Bureau be stationed in the town to serve as an arbiter for any disputes that might arise between the two groups.

In this uncertain environment, Fayetteville blacks struggled to build a community, and the center for this organizing process was Evans Chapel. One of the first of many thorny issues that had to be resolved concerned the question of denominational affiliation. The post-emancipation South witnessed the dual phenomena of northern missionaries flooding into the section to work among the freed people and the black disengagement from white southern churches. In the black mind, freedom was commensurate with independent institutions; and, along with schools, the churches had been and would continue to be the focal point of the African American community. With all of these African American souls available for salvation, northern and southern denominations engaged in an intense competition to bring the former slaves into their respective organizations.

Among the several denominations leading the first wave into the South were the African Methodist Episcopal (AME) and African Methodist Episcopal Zion (AMEZ) Churches. These northern black missionaries saw themselves as uniquely suited to work among the freed people. Both denominations were united by race and common experience with their charges; what these smaller churches lacked in resources they made up for in missionary zeal. While the AME held the organizational upper hand among blacks throughout much of the South, in North Carolina the AMEZ was supreme. . . .

The AMEZ and other black denominations resisted white charity, arguing that such largess perpetuated perceptions of white superiority among the former slaves. The church became the focus of African American life and culture as the freed people came to have their children christened, their marriages sanctified, and their funerals officiated. Black churches sponsored outings—both religious and secular—and provided necessary social services that contributed to an evolving sense of community. In a more abstract sense, these institutions provided a sense of belonging that was so important as the social organization of the slave system disappeared.

The missionary impulse had its most profound effect in the area of education. Emancipation brought opportunity to the freed people; however, without education—particularly the ability to read and write—the former slaves were unprepared to take advantage of all that could be available to them. For the missionaries, the most important part of education was teaching the freed people to read, which gave each individual personal access to the stories and lessons of the Bible. The AMEZ and other black churches took an active role in planning and implementing education programs: church buildings were used as schoolhouses, and congregations raised money to support teachers and students alike. The churches were not alone in their efforts to assist the former slaves.

Along with northern denominations that came to work among the freed people came northern benevolent societies. . . . One of the most prominent of these benevolent societies was the American Missionary Association, an abolitionist missionary organization founded in 1846 and headquartered in New York City.

The first AMA support at Fayetteville was for the educational efforts of a white Congregationalist minister, the Reverend David Dickson. In

December 1865, shortly after the failure of an attempt by Fayetteville's African American community to establish a school at Evans Chapel, the AMA dispatched Dickson and his wife, Mary, to North Carolina. Although Dickson was quite active in Fayetteville for a mere five months, his correspondence records the complex environment that fostered the founding and growth of the African American school there. The missionary's first official act was to meet with the Freedmen's Bureau agent, Major H. C. Lawrence, who, in turn, introduced him to Fayetteville's mayor and white elite. Dickson reported that he received considerable encouragement from the town's white leaders, and he later commented that the "better class of people here are in favor of having the Negro instructed." Fayetteville's white elite generally supported the combined efforts of the Freedmen's Bureau and the AMA to educate blacks. This is not to argue that the town's white populace was somehow more enlightened than the inhabitants of the rest of the Cape Fear region, where racial conflicts were severe. Early in the postwar period Fayetteville's white and black communities seem to have reached an uneasy accommodation that acknowledged a tenuous white acceptance of a literate work force in the process of economic reconstruction. Much of the AMA correspondence from the period confirms the general acceptance by local whites of black schooling. The local press periodically published articles that extolled the virtues of African American education and emphasized the need for southern white control of that process. Although occasionally Dickson lamented his treatment at the hand of those he characterized as lower-class whites, the level of white-against-black violence appears to have been lower than in other parts of North Carolina and throughout the South.

David Dickson's letters also reveal Fayetteville's African American community to be proud and well organized. In one letter the missionary vividly describes the 1866 Emancipation Day celebrations, during which blacks throughout the region met at Evans Chapel to march past the former slave market in remembrance of circumstances not long past.

More significantly, the Reverend Mr. Dickson's correspondence illustrates the explosive growth of the Fayetteville school. In the "Report of Freemen's Schools for the Southern District of North Carolina, January, 1866," the clergyman reported that in the one month in which he had served at Fayetteville, the student population had jumped from seventy-five "scholars" to 245. Although the number of students fluctuated from season to season, especially at planting and harvest times, the African American school exhibited steady growth. By the middle of February, Dickson was forced to hire two black assistants and expand the school's offerings to include two day-sessions and one night-school. His report to the AMA for February 1866 noted 272 students enrolled in these classes.

David Dickson's tenure among Fayetteville's freed people was cut short in April 1866. After suffering a "bilious attack," the clergyman was forced to undergo a period of convalescence. Mary Dickson attempted to carry on her husband's work. But when an attack of dysentery further weakened the AMA missionary, a local physician recommended that the Dicksons leave Fayetteville immediately. Rev. David Dickson died while in transit to Philadelphia.

The AMA moved quickly to replace David Dickson. Local blacks took an active role in this process and lobbied for a black replacement. The ideal choice was Robert W. Harris, who had been born in 1840 to free black parents in Fayetteville. . . .

In Virginia, Robert Harris [had] quickly established himself not only as a talented teacher but also as an advocate for the rights of the former slaves. In March 1866, he boldly offered the readers of the *American Missionary* his prescription for racial uplift in the South, calling on "northern capitalists" to purchase large tracts of land, which could be divided into small plots and sold to the freed people at cost. He also declared that the condition of black southerners was dependent upon the continued activism of a victorious North. Yet, he demonstrated a great deal of tact when dealing with local whites, a talent learned through hard experience. He was especially respected by AMA officials for his zealous temperance activities. All of these factors played a role in the decision by the AMA to consider Harris for the Fayetteville vacancy in the autumn of 1866.

Another important element in the decision to send Robert Harris to North Carolina was the active participation of Fayetteville's African American community in the process. The AMA queried local black leader John S. Leary about conditions in the town. He assured officials that a school would flourish there and went on to stress the importance of a "native teacher" in the success of any such venture. Leary then took an active role both in arranging for the leasing of two buildings for the school and in securing a commitment from the Freedmen's Bureau for financial assistance.

Robert Harris arrived in Fayetteville in late November 1866. His first act as AMA superintendent of schools was to name his younger brother, Cicero, as his assistant. Next, he divided his students into primary and intermediate grade levels based on their educational attainments. Cicero Harris was given responsibility for the primary grades, which were designated as the "Phillips School"; Robert Harris assumed control of the intermediate levels, which were called the "Sumner School." In his first report from the North Carolina field, Harris declared a total enrollment of 321 students in the school.

Despite the uncertainties of these years, the African American school at Fayetteville exhibited tremendous growth well into the 1870s. Although enrollment tended to fluctuate wildly depending on the season, the institution boasted as many as six hundred students. . . .

Initially, the school was in session from September to May. However, by 1869 the Harris brothers were seeking financial support to keep the school open throughout the summer months. Citing the "urgings of the people" and the need to prepare a group of young people to fill teaching responsibilities in the small, rural schools of the region, Robert Harris felt compelled to keep the doors open. According to the educator, his school was so inextricably "connected with the educational, religious, social and industrial affairs of the people that we cannot be spared."

The curriculum at Fayetteville emphasized practicality. The majority of instruction in the school focused on reading and writing. Students were also taught arithmetic with an emphasis on the types of problem-solving skills that would be useful when negotiating for one's labor. As the educational apparatus became more sophisticated, the curriculum boasted geography and science classes, the latter of which revolved around the school's acquisition of a telescope in 1869.

The Harrises' school provided special attention to the moral development of its students. This aspect of the curriculum reflected the close ties of the school to the AMEZ Church. Not only were classes often held in the church—the only structure large enough to house the student body—but the Harris brothers also taught the Sunday school at Evans Chapel. They used their ties to the Congregationalist-based American Missionary Association to procure religious tracts for distribution among their pupils. . . .

Another facet of this moral education was temperance. One of the first primers used by Robert Harris was entitled *The Temperance Almanac,* which contained stories concerning the evils of overindulgence and the glories of overcoming the "demon rum." In December 1868, Harris announced the organization of a "Band of Hope." Members pledged themselves to abstain from alcohol, tobacco, and profane language. Children, in particular, were singled out for membership; and a periodical titled the *Youth's Temperance Banner* was the reading material of choice in the Fayetteville Band of Hope. Members' rules also included a prohibition against marble-playing "for keeps," a practice that Robert Harris equated with gambling. Between December 1868 and January 1872, the Harrises' Band of Hope had as many as 136 members.

The success of black education efforts at Fayetteville stemmed in part from the willingness of the white community to countenance those efforts. An integral element in this tenuous accommodation was the unusually high esteem accorded to both the local Freedmen's Bureau agent and the contingent of federal troops stationed in the town. The local newspaper often expressed the appreciation of white Fayetteville to bureau officials who "labored in . . . responsible and gentlemanly fashion." According to the Fayetteville *News,* "No negro felt any injustice, and no white man felt annoyed or troubled with the officious interference which has occasioned elsewhere so much complaint." On one notable occasion, the *News* rose to the defense of the federals when they were accused by the Raleigh *Progress* of using an altercation at a local house of prostitution to foment a "war of the races." The *News* blasted the *Progress* for its "bad taste and lack of dignity" and further remarked that "the best feelings prevail between the citizens and soldiers here."

It would be inaccurate to portray postbellum Fayetteville as some sort of racial Shangri-La.* There were bitter, sometimes violent, conflicts. In May 1866, the *News* reported that a mob "got up by mullattoe scamps" had attempted to free a black male from the town jail. Local whites, especially "all returned soldiers," were admonished to arm themselves. The news story concluded with the warning that "[p]repared we have nothing to fear; unprepared we might lose some of our best citizens." In February 1867, a black man, Archie Beebe, was arrested for attacking a white woman, Mrs. Elvina Massey. While being transported to jail after an arraignment, Beebe and the sheriff's deputies protecting him were attacked by an angry white mob. In the ensuing melee, Beebe was murdered. The *News* commented on the event: "It is one of those instances where awful justice speaks from the mouth of the people and the bloody mark of vengeance is stamped by man's hand."

With the onset of radical Reconstruction in the spring of 1867, the community became increasingly politicized, and black-white relations were placed under increasing strain. The center for black political activity, not surprisingly, was the Evans Chapel AMEZ Church, which was also flourishing under the adroit leadership of the Reverend James Walker Hood. The Republican Party held its first organizational meeting in Cumberland County at the chapel on April 4, 1867. Addressing the gathering were Rev. J. W. Hood and John S. Leary; Cicero Harris also took an active role in the proceedings. Noticeably absent from that meeting (and all subsequent political gatherings) was Robert Harris. Although the educator often commented on local politics in his private correspondence, his public pronouncements on political issues were exceedingly rare.

As a native of Fayetteville, Harris no doubt recognized the political and social complexities in the town. The success of his school was contingent upon the goodwill of local whites and his own personal standing among them. The local white elite generally favored the educational work among the freed people—if the efforts were controlled by the "Southern states." While Harris's ties to the northern-based AMA and the federal Freedmen's Bureau were public knowledge, he was quick to downplay these affiliations by shifting the focus of any query toward his North Carolina upbringing. It is testimony to Robert Harris's diplomatic skills that his school never fell into disfavor with the white community. His studious avoidance of politics was matched only by his strenuous efforts to bring stability and self-sufficiency to the school. . . .

---

*An imaginary land of beauty, peace, and harmony described in James Hilton's novel *Lost Horizon* (Eds.)

The most important accomplishment in Robert Harris's bid for independence and institutional stability was the construction of a new building to permanently house the Phillips and Sumner Schools under one roof. Soon after arriving in Fayetteville, the educator began soliciting assistance from the Freedmen's Bureau and the AMA to build a new structure for the school. In September 1867, he queried the bureau's superintendent of education, F. A. Fiske, as to whether there was "any hope for a school-house in Fayetteville?" Fiske replied in the affirmative; and, in November, Harris informed AMA officials that members of the community had purchased two lots for the school and that a deed for the property had been forwarded to the Freedmen's Bureau offices for approval. In March 1868, Cicero Harris was able to report that a contract to build a "large and commodious school-building" had been awarded and that construction would soon commence. . . . The building was dedicated in early April 1869; and the Howard School, named after Freedmen's Bureau chief Gen. O. O. Howard, opened for its first official session the following September.

Robert Harris's most enduring legacy to North Carolina education was in the training of teachers. . . . In the beginning, it was necessity that forced Harris beyond providing basic literacy to Fayetteville's freed people. The crush of students descending on the school placed great strains on the teachers, and Harris's repeated requests for northern teachers went unheeded by AMA officials. In one of his first reports, the educator acknowledged that he had employed two local blacks as temporary instructors. While both of these women, Mary Payne and Caroline Bryant, were literate, neither met with his complete approval. Still, the large number of scholars at the Phillips and Sumner Schools forced Harris to continue the practice of hiring locals. In December 1867, he announced that he had hired two of his most promising students as assistants in the primary school. Interestingly, these teachers did not receive commissions, and their salaries were to be paid by local subscription. The success of this system was soon readily apparent, and Harris's regular requests for northern teachers ceased.

The impact of training the most talented students for the classroom was felt most in the small rural schools in Cumberland and surrounding counties. In the immediate postwar period, the records of the Freedmen's Bureau include numerous requests for teachers and material support throughout the region. There were so many requests, in fact, that many outlying schools began using Robert Harris as an intermediary between themselves and the bureau. A great source of anxiety for rural teachers was the insecurity caused by the rapid turnover of the Freedmen's Bureau agents. A remedy for this uncertainty was to give Harris the responsibility for placing teachers in appropriate schools and seeing to their needs. In June 1868, he reported that there was a great demand for teachers in rural Cumberland and Moore Counties. Harris was soon placing his most promising students in teaching positions at Beaver Creek, Lower Rockfish, Black River, and Manchester in

Cumberland County and at Jonesboro in Moore County. By January, his operation had spread to Harnett and Bladen Counties, and as many as fifteen schools fell under his purview. Thus, by supplying teachers to black schools in neighboring towns and counties, Robert Harris's Fayetteville institution was functioning as a normal school a full decade before the State of North Carolina officially established it as the South's first "state colored normal school."

By the end of 1870, the Freedmen's Bureau ceased providing educational assistance to the former slaves. The last trickle of aid to the Howard School from the American Missionary Association ended in 1872. By then the school had established its independence and a well-defined sense of mission. Robert Harris continued to train young black men and women as educators until his death in 1879. . . .

The State Colored Normal School has had a lasting legacy in North Carolina history. . . . In 1939 the State Colored Normal School was renamed as Fayetteville State Teachers College, and in 1963 as Fayetteville State College. Since 1969, when it joined the University of North Carolina system, the school has operated as Fayetteville State University. The institution has come a long way from the anxious days of Reconstruction. The long-term vision of Fayetteville's African American community—in both slavery and in freedom, passed down through the generations—continues to have a profound influence on that city, North Carolina, and the nation.

DOCUMENTS

A Letter
"To My Old Master," c. 1865

TO MY OLD MASTER, COLONEL P. H. ANDERSON,
BIG SPRING, TENNESSEE

Sir: I got your letter, and was glad to find that you had not forgotten Jourdon, and that you wanted me to come back and live with you again, promising to do better for me than anybody else can. I have often felt uneasy about you. I thought the Yankees would have hung you long before this, for harboring Rebs they found at your house. I suppose they never heard about your going to Colonel Martin's to kill the Union soldier that was left by his company in their stable. Although you shot at me twice be-

SOURCE: L. Maria Child, *The Freedmen's Book* (1865).

fore I left you, I did not want to hear of your being hurt, and am glad you are still living. It would do me good to go back to the dear old home again, and see Miss Mary and Miss Martha and Allen, Esther, Green, and Lee. Give my love to them all, and tell them I hope we will meet in the better world, if not in this. I would have gone back to see you all when I was working in the Nashville Hospital, but one of the neighbors told me that Henry intended to shoot me if he ever got a chance.

I want to know particularly what the good chance is you propose to give me. I am doing tolerably well here. I get twenty-five dollars a month, with victuals and clothing; have a comfortable home for Mandy—the folks call her Mrs. Anderson—and the children—Milly, Jane, and Grundy—go to school and are learning well. The teacher says Grundy has a head for a preacher. They go to Sunday school, and Mandy and me attend church regularly. We are kindly treated. Sometimes we overhear others saying, "Them colored people were slaves" down in Tennessee. The children feel hurt when they hear such remarks; but I tell them it was no disgrace in Tennessee to belong to Colonel Anderson. Many darkeys would have been proud, as I used to be, to call you master. Now if you will write and say what wages you will give me, I will be better able to decide whether it would be to my advantage to move back again.

As to my freedom, which you say I can have, there is nothing to be gained on that score, as I got my free papers in 1864 from the Provost-Marshal-General of the Department of Nashville. Mandy says she would be afraid to go back without some proof that you were disposed to treat us justly and kindly; and we have concluded to test your sincerity by asking you to send us our wages for the time we served you. This will make us forget and forgive old scores, and rely on your justice and friendship in the future. I served you faithfully for thirty-two years, and Mandy twenty years. At twenty-five dollars a month for me, and two dollars a week for Mandy, our earnings would amount to eleven thousand six hundred and eighty dollars. Add to this the interest for the time our wages have been kept back, and deduct what you paid for our clothing, and three doctor's visits to me, and pulling a tooth for Mandy, and the balance will show what we are in justice entitled to. Please send the money by Adam's Express, in care of V. Winters, Esq., Dayton, Ohio. If you fail to pay us for faithful labors in the past, we can have little faith in your promises in the future. We trust the good Maker has opened your eyes to the wrongs which you and your fathers have done to me and my fathers, in making us toil for you for generations without recompense. Here I draw my wages every Saturday night; but in Tennessee there was never any pay-day for the Negroes any more than for the horses and cows. Surely there will be a day of reckoning for those who defraud the laborer of his hire.

In answering this letter, please state if there would be any safety for my Milly and Jane, who are now grown up, and both good-looking girls. You know how it was with poor Matilda and Catherine. I would rather stay here and starve—and die, if it come to that—than have my girls brought to shame by the violence and wickedness of their young masters. You will also please state if there has been any schools opened for the colored children in your neighborhood. The great desire of my life now is to give my children an education, and have them form virtuous habits.

Say howdy to George Carter, and thank him for taking the pistol from you when you were shooting at me.

FROM YOUR OLD SERVANT,

JOURDON ANDERSON

The Knights of the White Camelia, 1868

Questions

1. Do you belong to the white race? *Answer.*—I do.
2. Did you ever marry any woman who did not, or does not, belong to the white race? *Ans.*—No.
3. Do you promise never to marry any woman but one who belongs to the white race? *Ans.*—I do.
4. Do you believe in the superiority of your race? *Ans.*—I do.
5. Will you promise never to vote for anyone for any office of honor, profit, or trust who does not belong to your race? *Ans.*—I do.
6. Will you take a solemn oath never to abstain from casting your vote at any election in which a candidate of the Negro race shall be opposed to a white man attached to your principles, unless or prevented by severe illness or any other physical disability? *Ans.*—I will.
7. Are you opposed to allowing the control of the political affairs of this country to go in whole or in part into the hands of the African race, and will you do everything in your power to prevent it? *Ans.*—Yes.
8. Will you devote your intelligence, energy, and influence to the furtherance and propagation of the principles of our Order? *Ans.*—I will.
9. Will you, under all circumstances, defend and protect persons of the white race in their lives, rights, and property against all encroachments or invasions from any inferior race, and especially the African? *Ans.*—Yes.
10. Are you willing to take an oath forever to cherish these grand principles and to unite yourself with others who, like you, believing in

SOURCE: Walter L. Fleming, ed., *Documents Relating to Reconstruction* (Morgantown, W.Va.: 1904), No. 1.

their truth, have firmly bound themselves to stand by and defend them against all? *Ans.*—I am.

The commander shall then say: If you consent to join our Association, raise your right hand and I will administer to you the oath which we have all taken:

Oath

I do solemnly swear, in the presence of these witnesses, never to reveal, without authority, the existence of this Order, its objects, its acts, and signs of recognition; never to reveal or publish, in any manner whatsoever, what I shall see or hear in this Council; never to divulge the names of the members of the Order or their acts done in connection therewith. I swear to maintain and defend the social and political superiority of the white race on this continent; always and in all places to observe a marked distinction between the white and African races; to vote for none but white men for any office of honor, profit, or trust; to devote my intelligence, energy, and influence to instill these principles in the minds and hearts of others; and to protect and defend persons of the white race in their lives, rights, and property against the encroachments and aggressions of an inferior race.

I swear, moreover, to unite myself in heart, soul, and body with those who compose this Order; to aid, protect, and defend them in all places; to obey the orders of those who, by our statutes, will have the right of giving those orders; to respond at the peril of my life to a call, sign, or cry coming from a fellow member whose rights are violated; and to do everything in my power to assist him through life. And to the faithful performance of this oath, I pledge my life and sacred honor. . . .

Frederick Douglass Demands the Franchise, c. 1865

. . . I know that we are inferior to you in some things—virtually inferior. We walk about among you like dwarfs among giants. Our heads are scarcely seen above the great sea of humanity. The Germans are superior to us; the Irish are superior to us; the Yankees are superior to us (laughter); they can do what we cannot, that is, what we have not hitherto been allowed to do. But while I make this admission, I utterly deny that we are originally, or naturally, or practically, or in any way, or in any important sense, inferior to anybody on this globe. (Loud applause.) This charge of inferiority is an old dodge. It has been made available for oppression on many occasions. It is only about six centuries since the blue-eyed and

SOURCE: Frederick Douglass, "What the Black Man Wants," in *The Equality of All Men Before the Law* (Boston, 1865), 37–38.

fair-haired Anglo-Saxons were considered inferior by the haughty Normans, who once trampled upon them. If you read the history of the Norman Conquest, you will find that this proud Anglo-Saxon was once looked upon as of coarser clay than his Norman master, and might be found in the highways and byways of old England laboring with a brass collar on his neck, and the name of his master marked upon it. *You* were down then! (Laughter and applause.) You are up now. I am glad you are up, and I want you to be glad to help us up also. (Applause.)

I hold that the American people are bound, not only in self-defence, to extend this right to the freedmen of the South, but they are bound by their love of country, and by all their regard for the future safety of those Southern States, to do this—to do it as a measure essential to the preservation of peace there. But I will not dwell upon this. I put it to the American sense of honor. The honor of a nation is an important thing. It is said in the Scriptures, "What doth it profit a man if he gain the whole world, and lose his own soul?" It may be said, also, What doth it profit a nation if it gain the whole world, but lose its honor? I hold that the American government has taken upon itself a solemn obligation of honor, to see that this war—let it be long or let it be short, let it cost much or let it cost little—that this war shall not cease until every freedman at the South has the right to vote. (Applause.) It has bound itself to it. What have you asked the black men of the South, the black men of the whole country, to do? Why, you have asked them to incur the deadly enmity of their masters, in order to befriend you and to befriend this Government. You have asked us to call down, not only upon ourselves, but upon our children's children, the deadly hate of the entire Southern people. You have called upon us to turn our backs upon our masters, to abandon their cause and espouse yours; to turn against the South and in favor of the North; to shoot down the Confederacy and uphold the flag—the American flag. You have called upon us to expose ourselves to all the subtle machinations of their malignity for all time. And now, what do you propose to do when you come to make peace? To reward your enemies, and trample in the dust your friends? Do you intend to sacrifice the very men who have come to the rescue of your banner in the South, and incurred the lasting displeasure of their masters thereby? Do you intend to sacrifice them and reward your enemies? Do you mean to give your enemies the right to vote, and take it away from your friends? Is that wise policy? Is that honorable? Could American honor withstand such a blow? I do not believe you will do it. I think you will see to it that we have the right to vote. . . .

Chapter 2

The Last Frontier

Chinese workers building the transcontinental railroad.

From eastern North Dakota south to the Texas panhandle and west to the Rocky Mountains lay the Great Plains, a region at one time considered so bleak and uninhabitable that travelers referred to it as the "Great American Desert." In time, however, it would prove a source of immense wealth in minerals, grains, and livestock. This last American frontier—the land of the miner, the farmer, and the cowboy—by the late 1800s underwent a dramatic transformation paralleling change in the large cities and smoking factories of the urban, industrial East.

American literature and folklore have immortalized those who settled and tamed the Great Plains—the miners and their wide-open towns; the sod-house farmers; and, above all, the cowboys. But we all too often overlook the racial and ethnic diversity of those who built the West. Moreover, we forget what a critical role technology played in developing this region. The railroad, for example, was among the most important factors propelling the westward movement. In the essay "Linking a Continent and a Nation," Jack Chen highlights the role of Chinese immigrants in building the transcontinental railroad. How does Chen's description compare to popular depictions in western novels, in the movies, and on television?

The story of mining, like that of cattle raising and farming, was one of initial boom and prosperity for some, followed by bust for many. Like the other ventures, mining added to the nations's wealth—$1,242,872,032 in gold and $901,160,660 in silver were unearthed between 1860 and 1890. At the same time, it enriched the nation's folklore. In 1862, before he took the pen name Mark Twain, Samuel Clemens worked as a reporter for the Virginia City (Nevada) Enterprise. In the first document, taken from his book *Roughing It,* Clemens describes Virginia City, America's premier mining town and home of the world's richest vein of silver, the Comstock Lode.

Farmers also benefited from technology—steel plows to cut rough sod, windmills to pump water from deep in the ground, and barbed wire to fence off land on the treeless plains. There was also the lure of cheap or free land, thanks to the Homestead Act of 1862. This incentive pulled Americans from the East and immigrants from Europe. Farmers could tolerate the loneliness of rural life, but there were some hardships that they could not overcome. The second document, a memoir of a German woman who farmed in South Dakota in the 1880s, tells of her life there and her eventual decision to give up farming. Why did her family make this decision?

The last document, by Theodore Roosevelt, tells about a typical "cow town," Miles City, Montana. A romantic view of cowboys, it also reveals much about the ethnic diversity of the new Westerners. How does Roosevelt's picture complement the essay by Jack Chen?

ESSAY

Linking a Continent and a Nation

Jack Chen

Without the "Chinamen's" knowledge and respect for explosive powders, ability to work on the side of near vertical cliffs at dizzying heights and survive hardships which white

SOURCE: Jack Chen, *The Chinese of America: From the Beginning to the Present.* Copyright © 1980 by Jack Chen. Reprinted by permission of HarperCollins Publishers, Inc.

men could not endure, the Central Pacific would never have been completed when it was but much later.

R. W. HOWARD, *The Great Iron Trail*

The Chinese filled swamps, cut into mountains, dug tunnels, built bridges. As one historian notes, "The work was so obviously needed and all groups and areas vied with each other to build a railroad in their area, so that they would have welcomed the devil himself had he built a road. The lack of white laborers was too evident to cause even the most ardent anti-Chinese to resent their employment on such work.

ROBERT E. WYNNE, *Reaction to the Chinese in the Pacific Northwest and British Columbia*

The expansion of the railroad system in the United States was astonishingly swift. England had pioneered the building of railways and for a time was the acknowledged leader in the field, but from the moment the first locomotive was imported into the United States in 1829 the farsighted saw railways as the obvious solution for transport across the vast spaces of the American continent. By 1850, 9,000 miles of rails had been laid in the eastern states and up to the Mississippi. The California Gold Rush and the opening of the American West made talk about a transcontinental line more urgent. As too often happens, war spurred the realization of this project.

The West was won. California was a rich and influential state, but a wide unsettled belt of desert, plain, and mountains, separated it and Oregon from the rest of the states. As the economic separation of North and South showed, this situation was fraught with danger. It could lead to a political rift. In 1860, it was cheaper and quicker to reach San Francisco from Canton in China—a sixty-day voyage by sea—than from the Missouri River, six months away by wagon train. The urgent need was to link California firmly with the industrialized eastern states and their 30,000 miles of railways. A railway would cut the journey to a week. The threat of civil war loomed larger between North and South over the slavery issue. Abraham Lincoln's Republican administration saw a northern transcontinental railway as a means to outflank the South by drawing the western states closer to the North. In 1862, Congress voted funds to build the 2,500-mile-long railway. It required enormous resourcefulness and determination to get this giant project off the drawing boards. Not much imagination was required to see its necessity, but the actual building presented daunting difficulties. It was calculated that its cost would mount to $100 million, double the federal budget of 1861.

It was Theodore Judah, described by his contemporaries as "Pacific Railroad Crazy," who began to give substance to the dream. An eastern engineer who had come west to build the short Sacramento Valley Railroad, he undertook a preliminary survey and reported that he had found a feasible route crossing the Sierra by way of Dutch Flat. But the mainly small investors who supported his efforts could not carry through the whole immense undertaking. With rumors of civil war between North and South, San Francisco capitalists, mostly Southerners, boycotted the scheme as a northern plot, and pressed for a southern route. Then the "Big Four," Sacramento merchants, took up the challenge: Leland Stanford as president, C. P. Huntington as vice-president, Mark Hopkins as treasurer, and Charles Crocker, in charge of construction, formed the Central Pacific Railway Company. Judah was elbowed out.

The Big Four came as gold seekers in 1849 or soon after but found that there was more money to be made in storekeeping than in scrabbling in the rocks in the mountains. As Republicans, they held the state for the Union against the secessionists. Leland Stanford, the first president of the Central Pacific, was also the first Republican governor of California.

The beginnings were not auspicious. The Union Pacific [UP] was building from Omaha in the East over the plains to the Rockies, but supplies had to come in by water or wagon because the railways had not yet reached Omaha. The Civil War now raged and manpower, materials and funds were hard to get. The Indians were still contesting invasion of their lands. By 1864, however, with the Civil War ending, these problems were solved. The UP hired Civil War veterans, Irish immigrants fleeing famine and even Indian women, and the line began to move westward.

The Central Pacific, building eastward from Sacramento, had broken ground on January 8, 1863, but in 1864, beset by money and labor problems, it had built only thirty-one miles of track. It had an even more intractable manpower problem than the UP. California was sparsely populated, and the gold mines, homesteading, and other lucrative employments offered stiff competition for labor. Brought to the railhead, three out of every five men quit immediately and took off for the better prospects of the new Nevada silver strikes. Even Charles Crocker, boss of construction and raging like a mad bull in the railway camps, could not control them. In the winter of 1864, the company had only 600 men working on the line when it had advertised for 5,000. Up to then, only white labor had been recruited and California white labor was still motivated by the Gold Rush syndrome. They wanted quick wealth, not hard, regimented railway work. After two years only fifty miles of track had been laid.

James Strobridge, superintendent of construction, testified to the 1876 Joint Congressional Committee on Chinese Immigration: "[These] were unsteady men, unreliable. Some would not go to work at all. . . . Some would stay until pay day, get a little money, get drunk and clear out." Something drastic had to be done.

In 1858, fifty Chinese had helped to build the California Central Railroad from Sacramento to Marysville. In 1860, Chinese were working on the San Jose Railway and giving a good account of themselves, so it is surprising that there was so much hesitation about employing them on the Central Pacific's western end of the first transcontinental railway. Faced with a growing crisis of no work done and mounting costs, Crocker suggested hiring Chinese. Strobridge strongly objected: "I will not boss Chinese. I don't think they could build a railroad." Leland Stanford was also reluctant. He had advocated exclusion of the Chinese from California and was embarrassed to reverse himself. Crocker, Huntington, Hopkins, and Stanford, the Big Four of the Central Pacific, were all merchants in hardware, dried goods, and groceries in the little town of Sacramento. Originally, they knew nothing about railroad building, but they were astute and hard-headed businessmen. Crocker was insistent. Wasted time was wasted money. The CP's need for labor was critical. The men they already had were threatening a strike. Finally fifty Chinese were hired for a trial.

Building the Transcontinental Railroad

In February 1865, they marched up in self-formed gangs of twelve to twenty men with their own supplies and cooks for each mess. They ate a meal of rice and dried cuttlefish, washed and slept, and early next morning were ready for work filling dump carts. Their discipline and grading—preparing the ground for track laying—delighted Strobridge. Soon fifty more were hired, and finally some 15,000 had been put on the payroll. Crocker was enthusiastic: "They prove nearly equal to white men in the amount of labor they perform, and are much more reliable. No danger of strikes among them. We are training them to all kinds of labor: blasting, driving horses, handling rock as well as pick and shovel." Countering Strobridge's argument that the Chinese were "not masons," Crocker pointed out that the race that built the Great Wall could certainly build a railroad culvert. Up on the Donner Pass today the fine stonework embankments built by the Chinese are serving well after a hundred years.

Charles Nordhoff, an acute observer, reports Stobridge telling him "[The Chinese] learn all parts of the work easily." Nordhoff says he saw them "employed on every kind of work. . . . They do not drink, fight or strike; they do gamble, if it is not prevented; and it is always said of them that they are very cleanly in their habits. It is the custom, among them, after they have had their suppers every evening, to bathe with the help of small tubs. I doubt if the white laborers do as much." As well he might. Well-run boardinghouses in California in those days proudly advertised that they provided guests with a weekly bath.

Their wages at the start were $28 a month (twenty-six working days), and they furnished all their own food, cooking utensils, and tents. The headman of each gang, or sometimes an American employed as clerk by them, received all the wages and handed them out to the members of the work gang according to what had been earned. "Competent and wonderfully effective because tireless and unremitting in their industry," they worked from sun-up to sundown.

All observers remarked on the frugality of the Chinese. This was not surprising in view of the fact that, with a strong sense of filial duty, they came to America in order to save money and return as soon as possible to their homes and families in China. So they usually dressed poorly, and their dwellings were of the simplest [construction]. However, they ate well: rice and vermicelli (noodles) garnished with meats and vegetables, fish, dried oysters, cuttlefish, bacon and pork, and chicken on holidays, abalone meat, five kinds of dried vegetables, bamboo shoots, seaweed, salted cabbage, and mushrooms, four kinds of dried fruit, and peanut oil and tea. This diet shows a considerable degree of sophistication and balance compared to the beef, beans, potatoes, bread, and butter of the white laborers. Other supplies were purchased from the shop maintained by a Chinese merchant contractor in one of the railway cars that followed them as they carried the railway line forward. Here they could buy pipes, tobacco, bowls, chopsticks, lamps, Chinese-style shoes of cotton with soft cotton soles, and ready-made clothing imported from China.

On Sundays, they rested, did their washing, and gambled. They were prone to argue noisily, but did not become besotted with whiskey and make themselves unfit for work on Monday. Their sobriety was much appreciated by their employers.

Curtis, the engineer in charge, described them as "the best road-builders in the world." The once skeptical Strobridge, a smart, pushing Irishman, also now pronounced them "the best in the world." Leland Stanford described them in a report on October 10, 1865, to [President] Andrew Johnson:

> As a class, they are quiet, peaceable, patient, industrious, and economical. More prudent and economical [than white laborers] they are contented with less wages. We find them organized for mutual aid and assistance. Without them, it would be impossible to complete the western portion of this great national enterprise within the time required by the Act of Congress.

Crocker testified before the congressional committee that "if we found that we were in a hurry for a job of work, it was better to put on Chinese at once." All these men had originally resisted the employment of Chinese on the railway.

Four-fifths of the grading labor from Sacramento to Ogden was done by Chinese. In a couple of years more, of 13,500 workers on the payroll 12,000 were Chinese. They were nicknamed "Crocker's Pets."

Appreciating Chinese Skills

The Chinese crews won their reputation the hard way. They outperformed Cornish men brought in at extra wages to cut rock. Crocker testified,

> They would cut more rock in a week than the Cornish miners, and it was hard work, bone labor. [They] were skilled in using the hammer and drill, and they proved themselves equal to the very best Cornish miners in that work. They were very trusty, they were intelligent, and they lived up to their contracts.

Stanford held the Chinese workers in such high esteem that he provided in his will for the permanent employment of a large number on his estates. In the 1930s, some of their descendants were still living and working lands now owned by Stanford University.

The Chinese saved the day for Crocker and his colleagues. The terms of agreement with the government were that the railway companies would be paid from $16,000 to $48,000 for each mile of track laid. But there were only so many miles between the two terminal points of the projected line. The Union Pacific Company, working with 10,000 mainly Irish immigrants and Civil War veterans, had the advantage of building the line through Nebraska over the plains and made steady progress. The Central Pacific, after the first easy twenty-three miles between Newcastle and Colfax, had to conquer the granite mountains and gorges of the Sierra Nevada and Rockies before it could emerge onto the Nevada-Utah plains and make real speed and money. The line had to rise 7,000 feet in 100 miles over daunting terrain. Crocker and the Chinese proved up to the challenge. After reaching Cisco, there was no easy going. The line had to be literally carved out of the Sierra granite, through tunnels and on rock ledges cut on the sides of precipices.

Using techniques from China, they attacked one of the most difficult parts of the work: carrying the line over Cape Horn [promontory], with its sheer granite buttresses and steep shale embankments, 2,000 feet above the American River canyon. There was no foothold on its flanks. The indomitable Chinese, using age-old ways, were lowered from above in rope-held baskets, and there, suspended between earth and sky, they began to chip away with hammer and crowbar to form the narrow ledge that was later laboriously deepened to a shelf wide enough for the railway roadbed, 1,400 feet above the river.

Behind the advancing crews of Chinese builders came the money and supplies to keep the work going. This was an awesome exercise in logistics. The Big Four, unscrupulous, dishonest, and ruthless on a grand scale, were the geniuses of this effort. The marvel of engineering skill being created by Strobridge and his Chinese and Irish workers up in the Sierra was fed by a stream of iron rails, spikes, tools, blasting powder, locomotives, cars, and machinery. These materials arrived after an expensive and hazardous eight-month, 15,000-mile voyage from East Coast ports around Cape Horn to San Francisco, thence by river boat to Sacramento, and so to the railhead by road.

The weather, as well as the terrain, was harsh. The winter of 1865–1866 was one of the severest on record. Snow fell early, and storm after storm blanketed the Sierra Nevada. The ground froze solid. Sixty-foot drifts of snow had to be shoveled away before the graders could even reach the roadbed. Nearly half the work force of 9,000 men were set to clearing snow.

In these conditions, construction crews tackled the most formidable obstacle in their path: building the ten Summit Tunnels on the twenty-mile stretch between Cisco, ninety-two miles from Sacramento and Lake Ridge just west of Cold Stream Valley on the eastern slope of the summit. Work went on at all the tunnels simultaneously. Three shifts of eight hours each worked day and night.

The builders lived an eerie existence. In *The Big Four*, Oscar Lewis writes,

> Tunnels were dug beneath forty-foot drifts and for months, 3,000 workmen lived curious mole-like lives, passing from work to living quarters in dim passages far beneath the snow's surface. . . . [There] was constant danger, for as snows accumulated on the upper ridges, avalanches grew frequent, their approach heralded only by a brief thunderous roar. A second later, a work crew, a bunkhouse, an entire camp would go hurtling at a dizzy speed down miles of frozen canyon. Not until months later were the bodies recovered; sometimes groups were found with shovels or picks still clutched in their frozen hands.

On Christmas Day, 1866, the papers reported that "a gang of Chinamen employed by the railroad were covered up by a snow slide and four or five [note the imprecision] died before they could be exhumed." A whole camp of Chinese railway workers was enveloped during one night and had to be rescued by shovelers the next day.

No one has recorded the names of those who gave their lives in this stupendous undertaking. It is known that the bones of 1,200 men were shipped back to China to be buried in the land of their forefathers, but that was by no means the total score. The engineer John Gills recalled that "at Tunnel No. 10, some 15–20 Chinese [again, note the imprecision] were killed by a slide that winter. The year before, in the winter of 1864–65, two wagon road repairers had been buried and killed by a slide at the same location."

A. P. Partridge, who worked on the line, describes how 3,000 Chinese builders were driven out of the mountains by the early snow. "Most . . . came to Truckee and filled up all the old buildings and sheds. An old barn collapsed and killed four Chinese. A good many were frozen to death." One is astonished at the fortitude, discipline and dedication of the Chinese rail-road workers.

Many years later, looking at the Union Pacific section of the line, an old railwayman remarked, "There's an Irishman buried under every tie of that road." Brawling, drink, cholera, and malaria took a heavy toll. The construction crew towns on the Union Pacific part of the track, with their saloons, gambling dens, and bordellos, were nicknamed "hells on wheels." Jack Casement, in charge of construction there, had been a general in the Civil War and prided himself on the discipline of his fighting forces. His work crews worked with military precision, but off the job they let themselves go. One day, after gambling in the streets on payday (instigated by professional gamblers) had gotten too much out of hand, a visitor, finding the street suddenly very quiet, asked him where the gamblers had gone. Casement pointed to a nearby cemetery and replied, "They all died with their boots on." It was still the Wild West.

It is characteristic that only one single case of violent brawling was reported among the Chinese from the time they started work until they completed the job.

The Central Pacific's Chinese became expert at all kinds of work: grading, drilling, masonry, and demolition. Using black powder, they could average 1.18 feet daily through granite so hard that an incautiously placed charge could blow out backward. The Summit Tunnel work force was entirely composed of Chinese, with mainly Irish foremen. Thirty to forty worked on each face, with twelve to fifteen on the heading and the rest on the bottom removing material.

The Donner tunnels, totaling 1,695 feet, had to be bored through solid rock, and 9,000 Chinese worked on them. To speed the work, a new and untried explosive, nitroglycerin, was used. The tunnels were completed in November 1867, after thirteen months. But winter began before the way could be opened and the tracks laid. That winter was worse than the preceding one, but to save time it was necessary to send crews ahead to continue building the line even while the tunnels were being cut. Therefore, 3,000 men were sent with 400 carts and horses to Palisade Canyon, 300 miles in advance of the railhead. "Hay, grain and all supplies for men and horses had to be hauled by teams over the deserts for that great distance," writes Strobridge. "Water for men and animals was hauled at times 40 miles." Trees were felled and the logs laid side by side to form a "corduroy" roadway. On log sleds greased with lard, hundreds of Chinese manhandled three locomotives and forty wagons over the mountains. Strobridge later testified that it "cost nearly three times what it would have cost to have done it in the summertime when it should have been done. But we shortened the time seven years from what Congress expected when the act was passed."

Between 10,000 and 11,000 men were kept working on the line from 1866 to 1869. The Sisson and Wallace Company (in which Crocker's brother was a leading member) and the Dutch merchant Cornelius Koopmanschap of San Francisco procured these men for the line. Through the summer of 1866, Crocker's Pets—6,000 strong—swarmed over the upper canyons of the Sierra, methodically slicing cuttings and pouring rock and debris to make landfills and strengthen the foundations of trestle bridges. Unlike the Caucasian laborers, who drank unboiled stream water, the Chinese slaked their thirst with weak tea and boiled water kept in old whiskey kegs filled by their mess cooks. They kept themselves clean and healthy by daily sponge baths in tubs of hot water prepared by their cooks, and the work went steadily forward.

Crocker has been described as a "hulking, relentless driver of men." But his Chinese crews responded to his leadership and drive and were caught up in the spirit of the epic work on which they were engaged. They cheered and waved their cartwheel hats as the first through train swept down the eastern slopes of the Sierra to the meeting of the lines. They worked with devotion and self-sacrifice to lay that twenty-odd miles of track for the Central Pacific Company in 1866 over the most difficult terrain. The cost of those miles was enormous—$280,000 a mile—but it brought the builders in sight of the easier terrain beyond the Sierra and the Rockies. Here costs of construction by veteran crews were only half the estimated amount of federal pay.

By summer 1868, an army of 14,000 railway builders was passing over the mountains into the great interior plain. Nine-tenths of that work force was Chinese. More than a quarter of all Chinese in the country were building the railway.

When every available Chinese in California had been recruited for the work, the Central Pacific arranged with Chinese labor contractors in San Francisco to get men direct from China and send them up to the railhead. It was evidently some of these newcomers who fell for the Piute Indian's tall tales of snakes in the desert "big enough to swallow a man easily." Thereupon "four or five hundred Chinese took their belongings and struck out to return directly to Sacramento," reports the *Alta California*, "Crocker and Company had spent quite a little money to secure them and they sent men on horseback after them. Most of them came back again kind of quieted down, and after nothing happened and they never saw any of the snakes, they forgot about them." At least one Chinese quit the job for a similar reason. His daughter, married to a professor of Chinese art, told me that her father had worked on the railway but quit because "he was scared of the bears." He later went into domestic service.

By September 1868, the track was completed for 307 miles from Sacramento, and the crews were laying rails across the plain east of the Sierra. Parallel with the track layers went the telegraph installers, stringing their wires on the poles and keeping the planners back at headquarters precisely apprised of where the end of the track was.

The Great Railway Competition

On the plains, the Chinese worked in tandem with all the Indians Crocker could entice to work on the iron rails. They began to hear of the exploits of the Union Pacific's "Irish terriers" building from the east. One day, the Irish laid six miles of track, they were told. The Chinese of the Central Pacific topped this with seven. "No Chinaman is going to beat us," growled the Irish, and the next day, they laid seven and a half miles of track. They swore that they would outperform the competition no matter what it did.

Crocker taunted the Union Pacific that his men could lay ten miles of track a day. Durant, president of the rival line, laid a $10,000 wager that it could not be done. Crocker took no chances. He waited until the day before the last sixteen miles of track had to be laid and brought up all needed supplies for instant use. Then he unleashed his crews. On April 28, 1869, while Union Pacific checkers and newspaper reporters looked on, a combined gang of Chinese and eight picked Irish rail handlers laid ten miles and 1,800 feet more of track in twelve hours. This record was never surpassed until the advent of mechanized track laying. Each Irishman that day walked a total distance of ten miles, and their combined muscle handled sixty tons of rail.

So keen was the competition that when the two lines approached each other, instead of changing direction to link up, their builders careered on and on for 100 miles, building lines that would never meet. Finally, the government prescribed that the linkage point should be Promontory [Point], Utah.

Competition was keen, but there seems to be no truth in the story that the Chinese and Irish in this phase of work were trying to blow each other up with explosives. It is a fact, however, that when the two lines were very near each other, the Union Pacific blasters did not give the Central Pacific men timely warning when setting off a charge, and several Chinese were hurt. Then a Central Pacific charge went off unannounced and several Irishmen found themselves buried in dirt. This forced the foremen to take up the matter and an amicable settlement was arranged. There was no further trouble.

On May 10, 1869, the two lines were officially joined at Promontory [Point], north of Ogden in Utah. A great crowd gathered. A band played. An Irish crew and a Chinese crew were chosen to lay the last two rails side by side. The last tie was made of polished California laurel with a silver plate in its center proclaiming it "The last tie laid on the completion of the Pacific Railroad, May 10, 1869." But when the time came it was nowhere to be found. As consternation mounted, four Chinese approached with it on their shoulders and they laid it beneath the rails. A photographer stepped up and someone shouted to him "Shoot!" The Chinese only knew one meaning for that word. They fled. But order was restored and the famous ceremony began; Stanford drove a golden spike into the last tie with a silver hammer. The news flashed by telegraph to a waiting nation. But no Chinese appears in that famous picture of the toast celebrating the joining of the rails.

Crocker was one of the few who paid tribute to the Chinese that day: "I wish to call to your minds that the early completion of this railroad we have built has been in large measure due to the poor, despised class of laborers called the Chinese, to the fidelity and industry they have shown." No one even mentioned the name of Judah.

The building of the first transcontinental railway stands as a monument to the union of Yankee and Chinese-Irish drive and know-how. This was a formidable combination. They all complemented each other. Together they did in seven years what was expected to take at least fourteen.

In his book on the building of the railway, John Galloway, the noted transportation engineer, described this as "without doubt the greatest engineering feat of the nineteenth century," and that has never been disputed. David D. Colton, then vice-president of the Southern Pacific, was similarly generous in his praise of the Chinese contribution. He was asked, while giving evidence before the 1876 congressional committee, "Could you have constructed that road without Chinese labor?" He replied, "I do not think it could have been constructed so quickly, and with anything like the same amount of certainty as to what we were going to accomplish in the same length of time."

And, in answer to the question, "Do you think the Chinese have been a benefit to the State?" West Evans, a railway contractor, testified, "I do not see how we could do the work we have done, here, without them; at least I have done work that would not have been done if it had not been for the Chinamen, work that could not have been done without them."

It was heroic work. The Central Pacific crews had carried their railway 1,800 miles through the Sierra and Rocky mountains, over sagebrush desert and plain. The Union Pacific built only 689 miles, over much easier terrain. It had 500 miles in which to carry its part of the line to a height of 5,000 feet, with another fifty more miles in which to reach the high passes of the Black Hills. With newly recruited crews, the Central Pacific had to gain an altitude of 7,000 feet from the plain in just over 100 miles and make a climb of 2,000 feet in just 20 miles.

All this monumental work was done before the age of mechanization. It was pick and shovel, hammer and crowbar work, with baskets for earth carried slung from shoulder poles and put on one-horse carts.

For their heroic work, the Chinese workmen began with a wage of $26 a month, providing their own food and shelter. This was gradually raised to $30 to $35 a month. Caucasians were paid the same amount of money, but their food and shelter were provided. Because it cost $0.75 to $1.00 a day to feed a white unskilled worker, each Chinese saved the Central Pacific, at a minimum, two-thirds the price of a white laborer (1865 rates). Chinese worked as masons, dynamiters, and blacksmiths and at other skilled jobs that paid white workers from $3 to $5 a day. So, at a minimum, the company saved about $5 million by hiring Chinese workers.

Did this really "deprive white workers of jobs" as anti-Chinese agitators claimed? Certainly not. In the first place, experience had proved that white workers simply did not want the jobs the Chinese took on the railroad. In fact, the Chinese created jobs for white workers as straw bosses, foremen, railhandlers, teamsters, and supervisors.

The wages paid to the Chinese were, in fact, comparable to those paid unskilled or semiskilled labor in the East (where labor was relatively plentiful), and the Chinese were at first satisfied. Charles Nordhoff estimated that the frugal Chinese could save about $13 a month out of those wages. The *Alta California* estimated their savings at $20 a month and later, perhaps, as wages increased, they could lay aside even more. With a bit of luck, a year and a half to two years of work would enable them to return to China with $400 to buy a bit of land and be well-to-do farmers.

But the Chinese began to learn the American way of life. On one occasion in June 1867, 2,000 tunnelers went on strike, asking for $40 a month, an eight-hour day in the tunnels, and an end to beating by foremen. "Eight hours a day good for white man, all same good for Chinese," said their spokesman in the pidgin English common in the construction camps. But solidarity with the other workers was lacking, and after a week the strike was called off when the Chinese heard that Crocker was recruiting strikebreakers from the eastern states.

When the task was done, most of the Chinese railwaymen were paid off. Some returned to China with their hard-earned savings, and the epic story of building the Iron Horse's pathway across the continent must have regaled many a family gathering there. Some returned with souvenirs of the great work, chips of one of the last ties, which had been dug up and split up among them. Some settled in the little towns that had grown up along the line of the railway. Others took the railway to seek adventure further east and south. Most made their way back to California and took what jobs they could find in that state's growing industries, trades, and other occupations. Many used their traditional and newly acquired skills on the other transcontinental lines and railways that were being swiftly built in the West and Midwest. This was the start of the diaspora of the Chinese immigrants in America.

The Union and Central Pacific tycoons had done well out of the building of the line. Congressional investigation committees later calculated that, of $73 million poured into the Union Pacific coffers, no more than $50 million could be justified as true costs. The Big Four and their associates in the Central Pacific had done even better. They had made at least $63 million and owned most of the CP stock worth around $100 million and 9 million acres of land grants to boot.

Ironically, the great railway soon had disastrous results for the Chinese themselves. It now cost only $40 for an immigrant to cross the continent by rail and a flood of immigrants took advantage of the ease and cheapness of travel on the line the Chinese had helped to build. The labor shortage (and resulting high wages) in California turned into a glut. When the tangled affairs of the Northern Pacific line led to the stock market crash of Black Friday, September 19, 1873, and to financial panic, California experienced its first real economic depression. There was devastating unemployment, and the Chinese were made the scapegoats.

Building Other Lines

The expansion of the railroads was even faster in the following decade. In 1850, the United States had 9,000 miles of track. In 1860, it had 30,000. In 1890, it had over 70,000 miles. Three years later, it had five transcontinental lines.

The first transcontinental railway was soon followed by four more links: (1) the Southern Pacific–Texas and Pacific, completed in 1883 from San Francisco to Texas by way of Yuma, Tucson, and El Paso; (2) the Atcheson, Topeka, and Santa Fe, completed in 1885 from Kansas City to Los Angeles via Santa Fe and Albuquerque; (3) the Northern Pacific, completed in 1883 from Duluth, Minnesota, to Portland, Oregon; and (4) the Great Northern (1893). The skill of the Chinese as railroad builders was much sought after, and Chinese worked on all these lines. Some 15,000 worked on the Northern Pacific, laying tracks in Washington, Idaho, and Montana; 250 on the Houston and Texas line; 600 on the Alabama and Chattanooga line; 70 on the New Orleans line. Nearly 500 Chinese were recruited for the Union Pacific even after the lines were joined. Many worked in the Wyoming coal mines and during the summer months doubled as track laborers. They carried the Southern Pacific lines over the burning Mojave Desert. They helped link San Francisco with Portland in 1887.

The Canadian Pacific seized the chance to enlist veteran Chinese railwaymen from the Southern Pacific and Northern Pacific railroads and also brought Chinese workers direct from China. In 1880, some 1,500 were working on that line, increasing to 6,500 two years later. Casualties were heavy on this line. Hundreds lost their lives while working on it.

Chinese railwaymen helped on the Central and Southern Pacific's main line down the San Joaquin Valley in 1870 and 1871. They worked on the hookup to Los Angeles and the loop with seventeen tunnels over the Tehachapi Pass completed in 1876. On this line, 1,000 Chinese worked on the 6,975-foot San Fernando Tunnel, the longest in the West. This rail link between San Francisco and Los Angeles, tapping the rich Central Valley, played a major role in the development of California's agriculture, later its biggest industry. They worked on the line north from Sacramento along the Shasta route to Portland, which was reached in 1887. In 1869, the Virginia and Truckee line employed 450 Chinese, veterans of the Central Pacific, to grade its track. When the Virginia and Truckee's Carson and Colorado branch line was planned from Mound House to Benton, its tough manager Yerington arranged with the unions for the grading to be done by white labor to Dayton and by Chinese from Dayton on south. "If the entire line had to be graded by white labor, I would not think of driving a pick into the ground, but would abandon the undertaking entirely," he said.

Chinese laborers worked on the trans-Panamanian railway, which linked the Pacific and the Atlantic before the Panama Canal was completed. This railway played a major role in speeding up the economic development of the United States, but it was not built without sacrifice: hundreds of the Chinese builders died of fever and other causes during its construction.

This by no means completes the list of contributions of the Chinese railway workers. The transcontinental lines on which they worked "more than any other factor helped make the United States a united nation," writes the *Encyclopedia Britannica* ["Railways"]. They played a major role in building the communications network of iron roads that was the transport base of American industrial might in the twentieth century.

Speaking eloquently in favor of the Chinese immigrants, Oswald Garrison Villard said,

> I want to remind you of the things that Chinese labor did in opening up the Western portion of this country. . . . [They] stormed the forest fastnesses, endured cold and heat and the risk of death at hands of hostile Indians to aid in the opening up of our northwestern empire. I have a dispatch from the chief engineer of the Northwestern Pacific telling how Chinese laborers went out into eight feet of snow with the temperature far below zero to carry on the work when no American dared face the conditions.

And these men were from China's sun-drenched south, where it never snows.

In certain circles, there has been a conspiracy of silence about the Chinese railroadmen and what they did. When U.S. Secretary of Transportation John Volpe spoke at the "Golden Spike" centenary, not a single Chinese American was invited, and he made no mention in his speech of the Chinese railroad builders.

DOCUMENTS

Flush Times in Nevada,*
c. 1862

Six months after my entry into journalism that grand "flush times" of Silver-land began, and they continued with unabated splendor for three years. All difficulty about filling up the "local department" ceased, and the only trouble now was how to make the lengthened columns hold the world of incidents and happening that came to our literary net every day. Virginia had grown to be the "livest" town, for its age and population, that America had ever produced. The sidewalks swarmed with people—to such an extent, indeed, that it was generally no easy matter to stem the human tide. The streets themselves were just as crowded with quartz-wagons, freight-teams, and other vehicles. The procession was endless. So great was the pack, that buggies frequently had to wait half an hour for an opportunity to cross the principal street. Joy sat on every countenance, and there was a glad, almost fierce, intensity in every eye, that told of the money-getting schemes that held sway in every heart. Money was as plenty as dust; every individual considered himself wealthy, and a melancholy countenance was nowhere to be seen. There were military companies, fire companies, brass bands, banks, hotels, theaters, "hurdy-gurdy houses,"** wide-open gambling-palaces, political pow-wows, civic processions, street-fights, murders, inquests, riots, a whiskeymill every fifteen steps, a Board of Aldermen, a Mayor, a City Surveyor, a City Engineer, a Chief of the Fire Department, with First, Second, and Third Assistants, a Chief of Police, City Marshal, and a large police force, two Boards of Mining Brokers, a dozen breweries, and a half dozen jails and station-houses in full operation, and some talk of building a church. The "flush times" were in magnificent flower! Large fireproof brick buildings were going up in the principal streets, and the wooden suburbs were spreading out in all directions. Town lots soared up to prices that were amazing.

The great "Comstock lode" stretched its opulent length straight through the town from north to south, and every mine on it was in diligent process of development. One of these mines alone employed six hundred and seventy-five men, and in the matter of elections the adage was, "as the 'Gould & Curry' [mine] goes, so goes the city." Laboring-men's wages were four and six dollars a day, and they worked in three "shifts" or gangs, and the blasting and picking and shoveling went on without ceasing, night and day.

SOURCE: Samuel L. Clemens, *Roughing It* (New York: Harper and Brothers, 1890), 2:11–13, 16–19.

*The term *flush times* refers to the silver and gold boom in Nevada in the 1860s.(Eds.)
***Hurdy-gurdy houses* is a slang term for dance halls. (Eds.)

The "city" of Virginia roosted royally midway up the steep side of Mount Davidson, seven thousand two hundred feet above the level of the sea, and in the clear Nevada atmosphere was visible from a distance of fifty miles! It claimed a population of fifteen thousand to eighteen thousand, and all day long half of this little army swarmed the streets like bees and the other half swarmed the drifts and tunnels of the "Comstock," hundreds of feet down in the earth directly under those same streets. . . .

My salary was increased to forty dollars a week. But I seldom drew it. I had plenty of other resources, and what were two broad twenty-dollar gold pieces to a man who had his pockets full of such and a cumbersome abundance of bright half-dollars besides? (Paper money has never come into use on the Pacific coast.) Reporting was lucrative, and every man in the town was lavish with his money and his "feet."* The city and all the great mountainside were riddled with mining-shafts. There were more mines than miners. True, not ten of these mines were yielding rock worth hauling to a mill, but everybody said, "Wait till the shaft gets down where the ledge comes in solid, and then you will see!" So nobody was discouraged. These were nearly all "wildcat" mines, and wholly worthless, but nobody believed it then. The "Ophir," the "Gould Curry," the "Mexican," and other great mines on the Comstock lode in Virginia and Gold Hill were turning out huge piles of rich rock every day, and every man believed that his little wildcat claim was as good as any on the "main lead" and would infallibly be worth a thousand dollars a foot when he "got down where it came in solid." Poor fellow! he was blessedly blind to the fact that he would never see that day. So the thousand wildcat shafts burrowed deeper and deeper into the earth day by day, and all men were beside themselves with hope and happiness. How they labored, prophesied, exulted! Surely nothing like it was ever seen before since the world began. Every one of these wildcat mines—not mines, but holes in the ground over imaginary mines—was incorporated and had handsome engraved "stock" and the stock was salable, too. It was bought and sold with a feverish avidity on the boards every day. You could go up on the mountainside, scratch around and find a ledge (there was no lack of them), put up a "notice" with a grandiloquent name on it, start a shaft, get your stock printed, and with nothing whatever to prove that your mine was worth a straw, you could put your stock on the market and sell out for hundreds and even thousands of dollars. To make money, and make it fast, was as easy as it was to eat your dinner. Every man owned "feet" in fifty different wildcat mines and considered his fortune made. Think of a city with not one solitary poor man in it! One would suppose that when month after month went by and still not a wildcat mine (by wildcat I mean, in general terms, *any* claim not located on the mother vein, *i.e.*, the "Comstock") yielded a ton of rock worth crushing, the people

*Shares of stock in wildcat mines were measured in feet. (Eds.)

would begin to wonder if they were not putting too much faith in their prospective riches; but there was not a thought of such a thing. They burrowed away, bought and sold, and were happy.

New claims were taken daily, and it was the friendly custom to run straight to the newspaper offices, give the reporter forty or fifty "feet" and get him to go and examine the mine and publish a notice of it. They did not care a fig what you said about the property so [long as] you said something. Consequently we generally said a word or two to the effect that the "indications" were good, or that the ledge was "six feet wide," or that the rock "resembled the Comstock" (and so it did—but as a general thing the resemblance was not startling enough to knock you down!) . . .

There was *nothing* in the shape of a mining claim that was not salable. We received presents of "feet" every day. If we needed a hundred dollars or so, we sold some; if not we hoarded it away, satisfied that it would ultimately be worth a thousand dollars a foot. I had a trunk about half full of "stock." When a claim made a stir in the market and went up to a high figure, I searched through my pile to see if I had any of its stock—and generally found it.

Homesteading in South Dakota in the 1880s (1930)

On May 6, 1881, I left my beloved Fatherland and came to America. I still do not know why I left, for I was working for some very fine people with whom I had been for three years. They always said, "Stay here." I would have liked very much to go back once more but that did not come to pass. I was often homesick.

I already knew my husband in the old country. On May 26, 1881, I arrived at my sister's near Bloomington, Illinois. I worked for an English Methodist family. They were very fine people, and I often think of them. They have gone to "The Eternal Home" long ago.

October 20th, 1881, we were married in Bloomington, Illinois, at the parsonage of the Lutheran minister. My husband was working for $20.00 per month and free house rent. We lived in a little log cabin with one room and a small kitchen attached. Those were very beautiful times. We had two cows, hogs and chickens. But my husband was always desirous to have land of his own, and land in Illinois was too high in price for us to buy.

So when reservations were offered in South Dakota in 1883, my husband and his three brothers went to South Dakota and each staked a claim for 160 acres of land. It (South Dakota) has a very beautiful climate but lacks rain. We were there for 12 years. . . .

SOURCE: Family history of Caroline Reimers, author's possession, 1930

In 1888 we had the great snowstorm in South Dakota where so many school children lost their lives because the roofs were blown from the schoolhouses. The wind blew from 70 to 80 miles per hour and it was a dreadful storm.

In 1889 we had the great prairie-fire in which we lost everything, by fire, except our house and horses and cows. Everything else was burnt. That almost frightened us into leaving, for our children started to go to school a distance of two miles out in the prairie.

So we traded our land for two horses. There were no good years. We sold our best cows for $15.00, wheat for 35¢, corn for 15¢. We raised two bushels per acre. Those were hard years. But we always had enough to eat to satisfy our hunger.

We had no money, so we hitched our three horses to a moving wagon and started to Missouri, to my husband's brother in Marceline. It took us three weeks and a few days. . . .

A Montana Cowtown, 1899

A true "cow town" is worth seeing,—such a one as Miles City, for instance, especially at the time of the annual meeting of the great Montana Stock-raisers' Association. Then the whole place is full to overflowing, the importance of the meeting and the fun of the attendant frolics, especially the horse-races, drawing from the surrounding ranch country many hundreds of men of every degree, from the rich stock-owner worth his millions to the ordinary cowboy who works for forty dollars a month. It would be impossible to imagine a more typically American assemblage, for although there are always a certain number of foreigners, usually English, Irish, or German, yet they have become completely Americanized; and on the whole it would be difficult to gather a finer body of men, in spite of their numerous shortcomings. The ranch-owners differ more from each other than do the cowboys; and the former certainly compare very favorably with similar classes of capitalists in the East. Anything more foolish than the demagogic outcry against "cattle kings" it would be difficult to imagine. Indeed, there are very few businesses so absolutely legitimate as stock-raising and so beneficial to the nation at large; and a successful stock-grower must not only be shrewd, thrifty, patient, and enterprising, but he must also possess qualities of personal bravery, hardihood, and self-reliance to a degree not demanded in the least by any mercantile occupation in a community long settled. Stockmen are in the West the pioneers of civilization, and their daring and

SOURCE: Theodore Roosevelt, *Ranch Life and the Hunting-Trail* (New York: Century Co., 1899), 7, 10–11. Reprinted University Microfilms, Ann Arbor, Michigan, 1966.

adventurousness make the after settlement of the region possible. The whole country owes them a great debt. . . .

The bulk of the cowboys themselves are South-westerners; but there are also many from the Eastern and the Northern States, who, if they begin young, do quite as well as the Southerners. The best hands are fairly bred to the work and follow it from their youth up. Nothing can be more foolish than for an Easterner to think he can become a cowboy in a few months' time. Many a young fellow comes out hot with enthusiasm for life on the plains, only to learn that his clumsiness is greater than he could have believed possible; that the cowboy business is like any other and has to be learned by serving a painful apprenticeship; and that this apprenticeship implies the endurance of rough fare, hard living, dirt, exposure of every kind, no little toil, and month after month of the dullest monotony. For cowboy work there is need of special traits and special training, and young Easterners should be sure of themselves before trying it. The struggle for existence is very keen in the far West, and it is no place for men who lack the ruder, coarser virtues and physical qualities, no matter how intellectual or how refined and delicate their sensibilities. Such are more likely to fail there than in older communities. Probably during the past few years more than half of the young Easterners who have come West with a little money to learn the cattle business have failed signally and lost what they had in the beginning. The West, especially the far West, needs men who have been bred on the farm or in the workshop far more than it does clerks or college graduates.

Some of the cowboys are Mexicans, who generally do the actual work well enough, but are not trustworthy; moreover, they are always regarded with extreme disfavor by the Texans in an outfit, among whom the intolerant caste spirit is very strong. Southern-born whites will never work under them, and look down upon all colored or half-caste races. One spring I had with my wagon a Pueblo Indian, an excellent rider and roper, but a drunken, worthless, lazy devil; and in the summer of 1886 there were with us a Sioux half-breed, a quiet, hard-working, faithful fellow, and a mulatto, who was one of the best cow-hands in the whole round-up.

Chapter 3

Indian Schools: "Americanizing" the Native American

Native American girls at the Carlisle School for Indians, Carlisle, Pa.

The white settlers' movement onto the Great Plains devastated Native American tribes who had roamed the area for centuries. As on previous frontiers farther east, the Indians resisted the encroachment with some initial success, their most notable victory the defeat of General George Custer at the Little Bighorn River in 1876. However, the whites' superior manpower and technology, fueled by their desire to fulfill a "manifest destiny" to develop the entire continent, overcame the Native Americans, and in the end the whites removed virtually all of them to reservations.

During the 1870s and 1880s, even while the last Indian wars raged, the federal government passed legislation and instituted policies designed to solve the "Indian problem" by "Americanizing" them—assimilating them into American society. The federal government encouraged them, sometimes forcefully, to exchange their lands, held by the tribe as a whole, for individual holdings that they were expected to farm. Equally important, the government sought to educate their children away from their traditional cultures and provide them with the skills, knowledge, and attitudes deemed necessary for the new way of life that the dominant white culture dictated.

By 1881 the federal government operated 106 Indian day and boarding schools to accomplish these objectives. Although most of the schools were on or adjacent to reservation land, white educators placed their greatest faith in non-reservation boarding schools far removed from parental and tribal influences. Robert A. Trennert's essay, "Educating Indian Girls at Nonreservation Boarding Schools, 1878–1920," provides a detailed view of this policy in action. What do you think the advocates of Indian education meant by "assimilation"? To what does the author attribute the failure of the government's Indian-school policies during this period?

The first document consists of excerpts from the "Rules for Indian Schools" set forth by the Bureau of Indian Affairs (1890). What attitudes toward their mission and toward Native American youth would these instructions likely engender in the minds of the teachers who read them? In what ways does each of the rules cited contribute to the broad objectives of the government's Indian-education policies? What can you conclude about the immediate and long-term objectives of Indian education?

Although the government expressed its land and educational policies in positive terms, these principles in fact reflected the prevailing belief that the Native American culture was inferior. At the turn of the century, many social scientists had adapted Darwin's biological theories of evolution to explain social development, drawing conclusions totally rejected by their counterparts today. Specifically, they developed a theoretical hierarchy of superior and inferior races that placed northern Europeans at the top and Indians, blacks, and southern and eastern Europeans, among others, at the bottom. The second document, a 1905 report of the Board of Indian Commissioners, typifies the attitudes underlying governmental policies until the 1930s. This report sheds light on the basis for Indian policy and reveals much of the rationale for the immigration-restriction and racial-segregation laws of the era. In the final document, a Native American recalls her first days as a student in a government boarding school. How effective do you believe the treatment she received was in achieving the goal of weaning her away from her Indian culture, of "Americanizing" her? What evidence can you provide to demonstrate that educational policies and practices regarding Native American and other minority cultures have changed since the nineteenth and early twentieth centuries?

ESSAY

Educating Indian Girls at Nonreservation Boarding Schools, 1878–1920

Robert A. Trennert

During the latter part of the nineteenth century the Bureau of Indian Affairs made an intensive effort to assimilate the Indian into American society. One important aspect of the government's acculturation program was Indian education. By means of reservation day schools, reservation boarding schools, and off-reservation industrial schools, the federal government attempted to obliterate the cultural heritage of Indian youths and replace it with the values of Anglo-American society. One of the more notable aspects of this program was the removal of young Indian women from their tribal homes to government schools in an effort to transform them into a government version of the ideal American woman. This program of assimilationist education, despite some accomplishments, generally failed to attain its goals. This study is a review of the education of Indian women at the institutions that best typified the government program—the off-reservation industrial training schools. An understanding of this educational system provides some insight into the impact of the acculturation effort on the native population. Simultaneously, it illustrates some of the prevalent national images regarding both Indians and women.

The concept of educating native women first gained momentum among eighteenth-century New England missionaries who recommended that Indian girls might benefit from formal training in housekeeping. This idea matured to the point that, by the 1840s, the federal government had committed itself to educating Indian girls in the hope that women trained as good housewives would help their mates assimilate. A basic premise of this educational effort rested on the necessary elimination of Indian culture. Although recent scholarship has suggested that the division of labor between the sexes within Indian societies was rather equitable, mid-nineteenth-century Americans accepted a vision of Native American women as slaves toiling endlessly for their selfish, slovenly husbands and fathers in an atmosphere of immorality, degradation, and lust. Any cursory glance at contemporary literature provides striking evidence of this belief. Joel D. Steele, for example, in his 1876 history of the American nation described Indian society in the following terms: "The Indian was a barbarian. . . . Labor he considered degrading, and fit only for women. His squaw, therefore, built his

SOURCE: Robert A Trennert, "Educating Indian Girls at Nonreservation Boarding Schools, 1878–1920," *Western Historical Quarterly* 13 (July 1982): 169–90. Copyright by the Western History Association. Reprinted by permission.

wigwam, cut his wood, and carried his burdens when he journeyed. While he hunted or fished, she cleared the land . . . and dressed skins."

Government officials and humanitarian reformers shared Steele's opinion. Secretary of the Interior Carl Schurz, a noted reformer, stated in 1881 that "the Indian woman has so far been only a beast of burden. The girl, when arrived at maturity, was disposed of like an article of trade. The Indian wife was treated by her husband alternately with animal fondness, and with the cruel brutality of the slave driver." Neither Steele nor Schurz was unique in his day; both expressed the general opinion of American society. From this perspective, if women were to be incorporated into American society, their sexual role and social standing stood in need of change.

The movement to educate Indian girls reflected new trends in women's education. Radical changes in the economic and social life of late nineteenth-century America set up a movement away from the traditional academy education of young women. Economic opportunity created by the industrial revolution combined with the decline of the family as a significant economic unit produced a demand for vocational preparation for women. The new school discipline of "domestic science," a modern homemaking technique, developed as a means to bring stability and scientific management to the American family and provide skills to the increasing number of women entering the work force. In the years following the Civil War, increased emphasis was placed on domestic and vocational education as schools incorporated the new discipline into their curriculum. Similar emphasis appeared in government planning for the education of Indian women as a means of their forced acculturation. However, educators skirted the question of whether native women should be trained for industry or homemaking.

During the 1870s, with the tribes being confined to reservations, the government intensified its efforts to provide education for Indian youth of both sexes. The establishment of the industrial training schools at the end of the decade accelerated the commitment to educate Indian women. These schools got their start in 1878 when Captain Richard Henry Pratt, in charge of a group of Indian prisoners at Fort Marion, Florida, persuaded the government to educate eighteen of the younger male inmates at Hampton Normal Institute, an all-black school in Virginia, run by General Samuel C. Armstrong. Within six months Pratt and Armstrong were pleased enough with the results of their experiment to request more students. Both men strongly believed that girls should be added to the program, and Armstrong even went so far as to stipulate that Hampton would take more Indian students only on condition that half be women. At first Indian Commissioner Ezra A. Hayt rejected the proposal, primarily because he questioned the morality of allowing Indian women to mix with black men, but Armstrong's argument that "without educated women there is no civilization" finally prevailed. Thus, when Pratt journeyed west in the fall of 1878 to recruit more students, he fully expected half to be women.

Pratt was permitted to enlist fifty Indian students on his trip up the Missouri River. Mrs. Pratt went along to aid with the enlistment of girls. Although they found very little problem in recruiting a group of boys, they had numerous difficulties locating girls. At Fort Berthold, for instance, the Indians objected to having their young women taken away from home. Pratt interpreted this objection in terms of his own ethnocentric beliefs, maintaining that Indian tribes made their "squaws" do all the work. "They are too valuable in the capacity of drudge during the years they should be at school to be spared to go," he reported. Ultimately it required the help of local missionaries to secure four female students. Even then there were unexpected problems. As Pratt noted, "One of the girls [age ten] was especially bright and there was a general desire to save her from the degradation of her Indian surroundings. The mother [age twenty-six] said that education and civilization would make her child look upon her as a savage, and that unless she could go with her child and learn too, the child could not come." Pratt included both mother and daughter. Not all the missionaries and government agents, however, shared Pratt's enthusiasm. At Cheyenne River and other agencies a number of officials echoed the sentiments of Commissioner Hayt regarding the morality of admitting girls to a black school, and they succeeded in blocking recruitment. As a result, only nine girls were sent to Hampton.

Although the educational experiences of the first Indian girls to attend Hampton have not been well documented, a few things are evident. The girls were kept under strict supervision and were separated from the boys except during times of classroom instruction. In addition, the girls were kept apart from black pupils. Most of the academic work was focused on learning the English language, and the girls also received instruction in household skills. The small number of girls, of course, made it difficult to implement a general educational plan. Moreover, considerable opposition remained to educating Indian women at Hampton. Many prominent reformers expected confrontations, or even worse, love affairs, between black and red. Others expressed concern that Indian students in an all-black setting would not receive sufficient incentive and demanded they have the benefit of direct contact with white citizens.

Captain Pratt himself wanted to separate the Indians and blacks, and despite the fact that no racial trouble surfaced at Hampton, he pressured the government to create a school solely for Indians. Indian contact with blacks did not fit in with his plans for native education, and he reminded Secretary Schurz that Indians could become useful citizens only "through living among our people." The government consented, and in the summer of 1879 Pratt was authorized to open a school at Carlisle Barracks, Pennsylvania, "provided both boys and girls are educated in said school." Thus, while

Hampton continued to develop its own Indian program, it was soon accompanied by Carlisle and other all-Indian schools.

Under the guidance of General Armstrong at Hampton and Captain Pratt at Carlisle, a program for Indian women developed over a period of several years. Although these men differed on the question of racial mixing, they agreed on what Indian girls should be learning. By 1880, with fifty-seven Indian girls at Carlisle and about twenty at Hampton, the outlines of the program began to emerge. As rapidly as possible the girls were placed in a system that put maximum emphasis on domestic chores. Academic learning clearly played a subordinate role. The girls spent no more than half a day in the classroom and devoted the rest of their time to domestic work. At Carlisle the first arrivals were instructed in "the manufacture and mending of garments, the use of the sewing machine, laundry work, cooking, and the routine of household duties pertaining to their sex."

Discipline went hand in hand with work experience. Both Pratt and Armstrong possessed military backgrounds and insisted that girls be taught strict obedience. General Armstrong believed that obedience was completely foreign to the native mind and that discipline was a corollary to civilization. Girls, he thought, were more unmanageable than boys because of their "inherited spirit of independence." To instill the necessary discipline, the entire school routine was organized in martial fashion, and every facet of student life followed a strict timetable. Students who violated the rules were punished, sometimes by corporal means, but more commonly by ridicule. Although this discipline was perhaps no more severe than that in many non-Indian schools of the day, it contrasted dramatically with tribal educational patterns that often mixed learning with play. Thus, when Armstrong offered assurances that children accepted "the penalty gratefully as part of his [her] education in the good road," it might be viewed with a bit of skepticism.

Another integral part of the program centered on the idea of placing girls among white families to learn by association. The "outing" system, as it was soon called, began almost as quickly as the schools received students. Through this system Pratt expected to take Indian girls directly from their traditional homes and in three years make them acceptable for placement in public schools and private homes. By 1881 both Carlisle and Hampton were placing girls in white homes, most of which were located in rural Pennsylvania or New England. Here the girls were expected to become independent, secure a working knowledge of the English language, and acquire useful domestic skills. Students were usually sent to a family on an individual basis, although in a few cases several young women were placed in the same home. Emily Bowen, an outing program sponsor in Woodstock, Connecticut, reveals something of white motives for participation in the service. Miss Bowen, a former teacher, heard of Pratt's school in 1880 and became convinced that God had called upon her to "lift up the lowly." Hesitating to endure the dangers of the frontier, she volunteered instead to take eight Indian girls into her home to "educate them to return and be a blessing to their people." Bowen proposed to teach the girls "practical things, such as housework, sewing, and all that is necessary to make home comfortable and pleasant." In this manner, she hoped, the girls under her charge would take the "true missionary spirit" with them on their return to their people.

Having set the women's education program in motion, Pratt and his colleagues took time to reflect on just what result they anticipated from the training. In his 1881 report to Commissioner Hiram Price, Pratt charted out his expectations. Essentially he viewed the education of native girls as a supportive factor in the more important work of training boys. To enter American society, the Indian male needed a mate who would encourage his success and prevent any backsliding. "Of what avail is it," Pratt asked, "that the man be hard-working and industrious, providing by his labor, food and clothing for his household, if the wife, unskilled in cookery, unused to the needle, with no habits of order or neatness, makes what might be a cheerful, happy home only a wretched abode of filth and squalor?" Pratt charged Indian women with clinging to "heathen rites and superstitions" and passing them on to their children. They were, in effect, unfit as mothers and wives. Thus, a woman's education was supremely important, not so much for her own benefit as for that of her husband. Pratt did acknowledge that girls were required to learn more than boys. An Indian male needed only to learn a single trade; the woman, on the other hand, "must learn to sew and to cook, to wash and iron, she must learn lessons of neatness, order, and economy, for without a practical knowledge of all these she cannot make a home."

The size of the girls' program increased dramatically during the 1880s. The government was so taken with the apparent success of Carlisle and Hampton that it began to open similar schools in the West. As the industrial schools expanded, however, the women's program became institutionalized, causing a substantial deviation from the original concept. One reason for this change involved economic factors. The Indian schools, which for decades received $167 a year per student, suffered a chronic lack of funds; thus, to remain self-sufficient, they found themselves relying upon student labor whenever possible. Because they already believed in the educational value of manual labor, it was not a large step for school officials to begin relying upon student labor to keep the schools operating. By the mid-1880s, with hundreds of women attending the industrial schools, student labor had assumed a significant role in school operations. Thus, girls, originally expected to receive a useful education, found themselves becoming more important as an economic factor in the survival of the schools.

The girls' work program that developed at Hampton is typical of the increasing reliance on Indian labor. By 1883 the women's training section was divided into such departments as sewing, housekeeping, and laundry, each in the charge of a white matron or a black graduate. The forty-one girls as-signed to the sewing department made the school's bedding, wardrobe, and curtains. At Winona Lodge, the dormitory for Indian girls that also sup-ported the housework division, the matron described the work routine as follows: "All of the Indian girls, from eight to twenty-four years old, make their own clothes, wash and iron them, care for their rooms, and a great many of them take care of the teachers' rooms. Besides this they have extra work, such as sweeping, dusting, and scrubbing the corridors, stairs, hall, sewing-room, chapel, and cleaning other parts of the building." In addition, a large group of Indian girls worked in the school laundry doing the institu-tion's wash.

Conditions were even more rigorous at western schools where a lack of labor put additional demands on female students. At Genoa, Nebraska, the superintendent reported that the few girls enrolled in that school were kept busy doing housework. With the exception of the laundry, which was de-tailed to the boys, girls were responsible for the sewing and repair of gar-ments, including their own clothes, the small boys' wear, underwear for the large boys, and table linen. The kitchen, dining room, and dormitories were also maintained by women students. Similar circumstances prevailed at Al-buquerque, where Superintendent P. F. Burke complained of having to use boys for domestic chores. He was much relieved when enough girls en-rolled to allow "the making of the beds, sweeping, and cleaning both the boys' and girls' sleeping apartments." Because of inadequate facilities there were no girls enrolled when the Phoenix school opened in 1891; but as soon as a permanent building was constructed, Superintendent Wellington Rich requested twenty girls "to take the places now filled by boys in the several domestic departments of the school." Such uses of student labor were justi-fied as a method of preparing girls for the duties of home life.

Some employees of the Indian Service recognized that assembly line chores alone were not guaranteed to accomplish the goals of the program. Josephine Mayo, the girls' matron at Genoa, reported in 1886 that the work program was too "wholesale" to produce effective housewives. "Making a dozen beds and cleaning a dormitory does not teach them to make a room attractive and homelike," she remarked. Nor did cooking large quantifies of a single item "supply a family with a pleasant and healthy variety of food, nicely cooked." The matron believed that Indian girls needed to be taught in circumstances similar to those they were expected to occupy. She therefore suggested that small cottages be utilized in which girls could be instructed in the care of younger students and perform all the duties of a housewife. Although Mayo expressed a perceptive concern for the inherent problems of the system, her remarks had little impact on federal school officials. In the meantime, schools were expected to run effectively, and women continued to perform much of the required labor.

Not all the girls' programs, of course, were as routine or chore oriented as the ones cited above. Several of the larger institutions made sincere efforts to train young Indian women as efficient householders. Girls were taught to care for children, to set tables, prepare meals, and make domestic repairs. After 1896 Haskell Institute in Kansas provided women with basic commercial skills in stenography, typing, and bookkeeping. Nursing, too, received attention at some schools. A number of teachers, though conventional in their views of Indian women's role, succeeded in relaxing the rigid school atmosphere. Teachers at Hampton, for instance, regularly invited small groups of girls to their rooms for informal discussions. Here girls, freed from the restraints of the classroom, could express their feelings and receive some personal encouragement. Many institutions permitted their girls to have a dress "with at least some imitation of prevailing style" and urged them to take pride in their appearance.

The industrial schools reached their peak between 1890 and 1910. During this period as many as twenty-five nonreservation schools were in operation. The number of Indian women enrolled may have reached three thousand per annum during this period and females composed between 40 and 50 percent of the student body of most schools. The large number of young women can be attributed to several factors: girls were easier to recruit, they presented fewer disciplinary problems and could be more readily placed in the "outing" system, and after 1892 they could be sent to school without parental consent.

Women's education also became more efficient and standardized during the 1890s. This was due in large part to the activities of Thomas J. Morgan, who served as Indian commissioner from 1889 to 1893. Morgan advocated the education of Indian women as an important part of the acculturation process, believing that properly run schools could remove girls from the "degradation" of camp life and place them on a level with "their more favored white sisters." The commissioner hoped to accomplish this feat by completely systematizing the government's educational program. "So far as possible," he urged, "there should be a uniform course of study, similar methods of instruction, the same textbooks, and a carefully organized and well understood system of industrial training." His suggestions received considerable support, and by 1890, when he issued his "Rules for Indian Schools," the standardization of the Indian schools had begun. Morgan, like Pratt before him, fully expected his concept of education to rapidly produce American citizens. The results were not what the commissioner expected. While standardization proved more efficient, it also exacerbated some of the problems of the women's educational program.

Under the direction of Morgan and his successors, the Indian schools of the era became monuments to regimentation from which there was no escape. This development is obvious in the increasing emphasis on military organization. By the mid-nineties most girls were fully incorporated into

the soldierly routine. As one superintendent noted, all students were organized into companies on the first day of school. Like the boys, the girls wore
uniforms and were led by student officers who followed army drill regulations. Every aspect of student life was regulated. Anna Moore, a Pima girl
attending the Phoenix Indian School, remembered life in the girls' battalion
as one of marching "to a military tune" and having to drill at five in the
morning. Most school officials were united in their praise of military organization. Regimentation served to develop a work ethic; it broke the students'
sense of "Indian time" and ordered their life. The merits of military organization, drill, and routine in connection with discipline were explained by
one official who stated that "it teaches patriotism, obedience, courage, courtesy, promptness, and constancy."

Domestic science continued to dominate the women's program. Academic preparation for women never received much emphasis by industrial
school administrators despite Morgan's promise that "literary" training
would occupy half the students' time. . . . One reason for the lack of emphasis on academics was that by 1900 many school administrators had
come to feel that Indians were incapable of learning more. One school superintendent did not consider his "literary" graduates capable of accom-
plishing much in white society, while another educator described the
natives as a "child race."

The extent to which every feature of the girls' program was directed toward the making of proper middle-class housewives can be seen in the numerous directives handed down by the government. By the early twentieth
century every detail of school life was regulated. In 1904 Superintendent of
Indian Schools Estelle Reel issued a three-page circular on the proper
method of making a bed. Much of this training bore little relationship to
the reservation environment to which students would return. A few programs were entirely divorced from reality. The cooking course at Sherman
Institute in California, for instance, taught girls to prepare formal meals including the serving of raw oysters, shrimp cocktails, and croquettes. In another instance, Hampton teachers devoted some of their energies to
discussing attractive flower arrangements and the proper selection of deco-
rative pictures.

Another popular program was the "industrial" cottage. These originated in 1883 at Hampton when the school enrolled several married Indian
couples to serve as examples for the students. The couples were quartered
in small frame houses while learning to maintain attractive and happy
homes. Although the married students did not long remain at Hampton,
school officials began to use the cottages as model homes where squads of
Indian girls might practice living in white-style homes. By 1900 similar cottages were in use at western schools. The industrial cottage at Phoenix, for
example, operated a "well-regulated household" run by nine girls under a
matron's supervision. The "family" (with no males present) cleaned and

decorated the cottage, did the regular routine of cooking, washing, and sewing, and tended to the poultry and livestock in an effort "to train them to the practical and social enjoyment of the higher life of a real home."

The outing system also continued to be an integral part of the girls' program. As time went on, however, and the system was adopted at western locations, the original purposes of the outings faded. Initially designed as a vehicle for acculturation, the program at many locations became a means of providing servants to white householders. At Phoenix, for example, female pupils formed a pool of cheap labor available to perform domestic services for local families. From the opening of the school in 1891, demands for student labor always exceeded the pool's capacity. One superintendent estimated that he could easily put two hundred girls to work. Moreover, not all employers were interested in the welfare of the student. As the Phoenix superintendent stated in 1894, "The hiring of Indian youth is not looked upon by the people of this valley from a philanthropic standpoint. It is simply a matter of business." In theory, school authorities could return pupils to school at any time it appeared they were not receiving educational benefits; but as one newspaper reported, "What a howl would go up from residents of this valley if the superintendent would exercise this authority."

Even social and religious activities served an educational purpose. When Mrs. Merial Dorchester, wife of the superintendent of Indian schools, made a tour of western school facilities in the early 1890s, she recommended that school girls organize chapters of the King's Daughters, a Christian service organization. Several institutions implemented the program. At these locations girls were organized by age into "circles" to spend spare time producing handcrafted goods for charity. School officials supported such activity because the necessity of raising their own funds to pay dues instilled in the girls a spirit of Christian industry. The manufacture of goods for charity also enhanced their sense of service to others. Said one school superintendent, the organization is "effective in furnishing a spur to individual effort and makes the school routine more bearable by breaking the monotony of it." Although maintaining a nonsectarian stance, the schools encouraged all types of religious activity as an effective method of teaching Christian values and removing the girls from the home influence.

An important factor in understanding the women's program at the industrial schools is the reaction of the girls themselves. This presents some problems, however, since most school girls left no record of their experiences. Moreover, many of the observations that have survived were published in closely controlled school magazines that omitted any unfavorable remarks. Only a few reliable reminiscences have been produced, and even these are not very informative. Despite such limitations, however, several points are evident. The reaction of Indian girls to their education varied greatly. Some came willingly and with the approval of their parents. Once enrolled in school, many of these individuals took a keen interest in their education, accepted discipline as good for them, and worked hard to learn the ways of white society. An undetermined number may have come to school to escape intolerable conditions at home. Some evidence suggests that schools offered safe havens from overbearing parents who threatened to harm their children. For other girls the decision to attend a nonreservation school was made at considerable emotional expense, requiring a break with conservative parents, relatives, and tribesmen. In a few cases young women even lost their opportunity to marry men of their own tribe as they became dedicated to an outside lifestyle.

Many girls disliked school and longed to return home. The reasons are not hard to find. The hard work, discipline, and punishment were often oppressive. One Hopi girl recalled having to get down on her knees each Saturday and scrub the floor of the huge dining hall. "A patch of floor was scrubbed, then rinsed and wiped, and another section was attacked. The work was slow and hard on the knees," she remembered. Pima schoolgirl [Anna] Moore experienced similar conditions working in the dining hall at Phoenix: "My little helpers and I hadn't even reached our teen-aged years yet, and this work seemed so hard! If we were not finished when the 8:00 a.m. whistle sounded, the dining room matron would go around strapping us while we were still on our hands and knees. . . . We just dreaded the sore bottoms." In a number of instances, teachers and matrons added to the trauma by their dictatorial and unsympathetic attitudes. A few girls ran away from school. Those who were caught received humiliating punishment. Runaway girls might be put to work in the school yard cutting grass with scissors or doing some other meaningless drudgery. In a few cases recalcitrant young ladies had their hair cut off. Such experiences left many girls bitter and anxious to return to the old way of life.

The experiences of Indian girls when they returned home after years of schooling illustrate some of the problems in evaluating the success of the government program. For many years school officials reported great success for returned students. Accounts in articles and official documents maintained that numbers of girls had returned home, married, and established good homes. The Indian Bureau itself made occasional surveys purporting to show that returned students were doing well, keeping neat homes, and speaking English. These accounts contained a certain amount of truth. Some graduates adapted their education to the reservation environment and succeeded quite well. Many of these success stories were well publicized. There is considerable evidence to suggest, however, that the reports were overly optimistic and that most returning girls encountered problems.

A disturbingly large number of girls returned to traditional life upon returning home. The reasons are rather obvious. As early as 1882, the principal of Hampton's Indian Division reported that "there is absolutely no position of dignity to which an Indian girl after three years' training can look forward to with any reasonable confidence." Although conditions improved somewhat as time went on, work opportunities remained minimal. Girls were usually trained in only one specialty. As the superintendent of the Albuquerque school reported, girls usually returned home with no relevant skills. Some spent their entire school stay working in a laundry or sewing room, and though they became expert in one field, they had nothing to help them on the reservation. As the Meriam Report* later noted, some Indian girls spent so much time in school laundries that the institutions were in violation of state child labor laws. In another instance, one teacher noted how girls were taught to cook on gas ranges, while back on the reservation they had only campfires.

Moreover, the girls' educational achievements were not always appreciated at home. Elizabeth White tells the story of returning to her Hopi home an accomplished cook only to find that her family shunned the cakes and pies she made in place of traditional food, called her "as foolish as a white woman," and treated her as an outcast. As she later lamented, her school-taught domestic skills were inappropriate for the Hopis. Girls who refused to wear traditional dress at home were treated in like manner. Under these circumstances, many chose to cast off their learning, to marry, and return to traditional living. Those young women who dedicated themselves to living in the white man's style often found that reservations were intolerable, and unable to live in the manner to which they had become accustomed, they preferred to return to the cities. Once there the former students tended to become maids, although an undetermined number ended up as prostitutes and dance hall girls.

Employment opportunities for educated Indian women also pointed up some of the difficulties with the industrial schools. In fairness, it must be admitted that trained women probably had more opportunities than their male counterparts. Most of those who chose to work could do so; however, all positions were at the most menial level. If a girl elected to live within the white community, her employment choices were severely limited. About the only job available was that of domestic service, a carryover from the outing system. In this regard, the Indian schools did operate as employment agencies, finding jobs for their former students with local families. Despite the fact that some Indian women may have later come to feel that their work, despite its demeaning nature, provided some benefits for use in later life, many of their jobs proved unbearably hard. After being verbally abused, one former student wrote that "I never had any Lady say things like that to me." Another reported on her job, "I had been working so hard ever since I came here cleaning house and lots of ironing. I just got through

---

*The 1928 Meriam Report was an intense study of the conditions of American Indians and the operations of the Bureau of Indian Affairs, conducted by the Institute for Government Research under the auspices of the Department of the Interior. (Eds.)

ironing now I'm very tired my feet get so tired standing all morning." Unfortunately, few respectable jobs beyond domestic labor were available. Occasionally girls were trained as nurses or secretaries only to discover that they could find no work in Anglo society.

The largest employer of Indian girls proved to be the Indian Bureau. Many former students were able to secure positions at Indian agencies and schools; in fact, had it not been for the employment of former students by the paternalistic Indian service, few would have found any use for their training. The nature of the government positions available to Indian girls is revealing. Almost all jobs were menial in nature; only a few Indian girls were able to become teachers, and none worked as administrators. They were, rather, hired as laundresses, cooks, seamstresses, nurses' helpers, and assistant matrons. Often these employees received little more than room, board, and government rations, and even those who managed to be hired as teachers and nurses received less pay than their white counterparts. . . . Indian girls could find work, but only in the artificial environment of Indian agencies and schools located at remote western points and protected by a paternalistic government. Here they continued to perform tasks of domestic nature without promise of advancement. Nor were they assimilated into the dominant society as had been the original intent of their education.

School administrators were reluctant to admit the failings of the system. As early as the 1880s some criticism began to surface, but for the most part it was lost in the enthusiasm for training in a nonreservation environment. After 1900, however, critics became more vocal and persistent, arguing that the Indian community did not approve of this type of education, that most students gained little, and that employment opportunities were limited at best. More important, this type of education contributed little to the acculturation effort. As one opponent wrote, "To educate the Indian out of his [or her] home surroundings is to fill him with false ideas and to endow him with habits which are destructive to his peace of mind and usefulness to his community when the educational work is completed." Commissioner Leupp (1905–1909) was even more vocal. He generally accepted the increasingly prevalent theory that Indians were childlike in nature and incapable of assimilating into white society on an equal basis. Leupp suggested that the system failed to produce self-reliant Indians and, instead of giving Indian children a useful education, protected them in an artificial environment. Other school officials echoed the same sentiments. In this particular respect it was suggested that boarding school students were provided with all the comforts of civilization at no cost and thus failed to develop the proper attitude toward work. Upon returning to the reservations, therefore, they did not exert themselves and lapsed into traditionalism.

Despite increasing criticism, the women's educational program at the nonreservation schools operated without much change until after 1920. Girls were still taught skills of doubtful value, were hired out as maids

through the outing system, did most of the domestic l
and returned to the reservation either to assume tradi
some menial government job. By the late twenties, howe
to reform Indian education began to have some impact. Relying upon such
studies as the 1928 Meriam Report, reformers began to demand a complete
change in the Indian educational system. Among their suggestions were
that industrial boarding schools be phased out and the emphasis on work
training be reduced. Critics like [future Commissioner of Indian Affairs]
John Collier argued that the policy of removing girls from their homes to
educate them for a life among whites had failed. Instead, girls were discouraged from returning to the reservation and had received little to prepare
them for a home life. Collier's arguments eventually won out, especially
after he became Indian commissioner in 1933. Thus ended this particular attempt to convert Native American women into middle-class American
housewives. . . .

DOCUMENTS

Rules for Indian Schools, 1890

General Rules

39. The Sabbath must be properly observed. There shall be a Sabbath school
or some other suitable service every Sunday, which pupils shall be required
to attend. The superintendent may require employés to attend and participate in all the above exercises; but any employé declining as a matter of conscience shall be excused from attending and participating in any or all
religious exercises. . . .

41. All instruction must be in the English language. Pupils must be compelled to converse with each other in English, and should be properly re-
buked or punished for persistent violation of this rule. Every effort should
be made to encourage them to abandon their tribal language. To facilitate
this work it is essential that all school employés be able to speak English flu-
ently, and that they speak English exclusively to the pupils, and also to each
other in the presence of pupils.

42. Instruction in music must be given at all schools. Singing should be
a part of the exercises of each school session, and wherever practicable instruction in instrumental music should be given.

SOURCE: U.S. Bureau of Indian Affairs, "Rules for Indian Schools" *Annual Report of the Commissioner of Indian Affairs, 1890* (Washington, D.C., 1890), cxvi, cl–clii.

43. Except in cases of emergency, pupils shall not be removed from school either by their parents or others, nor shall they be transferred from a Government to a private school without special authority from the Indian Office.

44. The school buildings should be furnished throughout with plain, inexpensive, but substantial furniture. Dormitories or lavatories should be so supplied with necessary toilet articles, such as soap, towels, mirrors, combs, hair, shoe, nail, and tooth brushes, and wisp brooms, as to enable the pupils to form exact habits of personal neatness.

45. Good and healthful provisions must be supplied in abundance; and they must be well cooked and properly placed on the table. A regular bill of fare for each day of the week should be prepared and followed. Meals must be served regularly and neatly. Pains should be taken not only to have the food healthful and the table attractive, but to have the bill of fare varied. The school farm and dairy should furnish an ample supply of vegetables, fruits, milk, butter, cottage cheese, curds, eggs, and poultry. Coffee and tea should be furnished sparingly; milk is preferable to either, and children can be taught to use it. Pupils must be required to attend meals promptly after proper attention to toilet, and at least one employé must be in the dining room during each meal to supervise the table manners of the pupils and to see that all leave the table at the same time and in good order. . . .

47. So far as practicable, a uniform style of clothing for the school should be adopted. Two plain, substantial suits, with extra pair of trousers for each boy, and three neat, well-made dresses for each girl, if kept mended, ought to suffice for week-day wear for one year. For Sunday wear each pupil should be furnished a better suit. The pupils should also be supplied with underwear adapted to the climate, with night clothes, and with handkerchiefs, and, if the climate requires it, with overcoats and cloaks and with overshoes.

48. The buildings, outhouses, fences, and walks should at all times be kept in thorough repair. Where practicable, the grounds should be ornamented with trees, grass, and flowers.

49. There should be a flag staff at every school, and the American flag should be hoisted, in suitable weather, in the morning and lowered at sunset daily.

50. Special hours should be allotted for recreation. Provision should be made for outdoor sports, and the pupils should be encouraged in daily healthful exercise under the eye of a school employé; simple games should also be devised for indoor amusement. They should be taught the sports and games enjoyed by white youth, such as baseball, hopscotch, croquet, marbles, bean bags, dominoes, checkers, logomachy, and other word and letter games, and the use of dissected maps, etc. The girls should be instructed in simple fancy work, knitting, netting, crocheting, different kinds of embroidery, etc.

51. Separate play grounds, as well as sitting rooms, must be assigned the boys and the girls. In play and in work, as far as possible, and in all places except the school room and at meals, they must be kept entirely apart. It should be so arranged, however, that at stated times, under suitable supervision, they may enjoy each other's society; and such occasions should be used to teach them to show each other due respect and consideration, to behave without restraint, but without familiarity, and to acquire habits of politeness, refinement, and self-possession. . . .

53. Corporal punishment must be resorted to only in cases of grave violations of rules, and in no instances shall any person inflict it except under the direction of the superintendent to whom all serious questions of discipline must be referred.* Employés may correct pupils for slight misdemeanors only.

54. Any pupil twelve years of age or over, guilty of persistently using profane or obscene language; of lewd conduct; stubborn insubordination; lying; fighting; wanton destruction of property; theft; or similar misbehavior, may be punished by the superintendent either by inflicting corporal punishment or imprisonment in the guardhouse; but in no case shall any unusual or cruel or degrading punishment be permitted. . . .

Industrial Work

56. A regular and efficient system of industrial training must be a part of the work of each school. At least half of the time of each boy and girl should be devoted thereto—the work to be of such character that they may be able to apply the knowledge and experience gained, in the locality where they may be expected to reside after leaving school. In pushing forward the school-room training of these boys and girls, teachers, and especially superintendents, must not lose sight of the great necessity for fitting their charges for the every-day life of their after years.

57. A farm and garden, if practicable an orchard also, must be connected with each school, and especial attention must be given to instruction in farming, gardening, dairying, and fruit growing.

58. Every school should have horses, cattle, swine, and poultry, and when practicable, sheep and bees, which the pupils should be taught to care for properly. The boys should look after the stock and milk the cows, and the girls should see to the poultry and the milk.

---

*In some of the more advanced schools it will be practicable and advisable to have material offenses arbitrated by a school court composed of the advanced students, with school employés added to such court in very aggravated cases. After due investigation, the amount of guilt should be determined and the quantity of punishment fixed by the court, but the approval of the superintendent shall be necessary before the punishment is inflicted, and the superintendent may modify or remit but may not increase the sentence.

59. The farm, garden, stock, dairy, kitchen, and shops should be so managed as to make the school as nearly self-sustaining as practicable, not only because Government resources should be as wisely and carefully utilized as private resources would be, but also because thrift and economy are among the most valuable lessons which can be taught Indians. Waste in any department must not be tolerated.

60. The blacksmith, wheelwright, carpenter, shoemaker, and harness maker trades, being of the most general application, should be taught to a few pupils at every school. Where such mechanics are not provided for[,] the school pupils should, so far as practicable, receive instruction from the agency mechanics.

61. The girls must be systematically trained in every branch of housekeeping and in dairy work; be taught to cut, make, and mend garments for both men and women; and also be taught to nurse and care for the sick. They must be regularly detailed to assist the cook in preparing the food and the laundress in washing and ironing.

62. Special effort must be made to instruct Indian youth in the use and care of tools and implements. They must learn to keep them in order, protect them properly, and use them carefully.

A Government Official Describes Indian Race and Culture, 1905

We believe that the strength of our American life is due in no small part to the fact that various and different race elements have entered into the making of the American the citizen of the United States in the twentieth century. No one racial stock is exclusively in control in our land. The typical modern American is a fine "composite," with race elements drawn from many sources. We do not believe that the Government of the United States in dealing with its Indian wards would act righteously or wisely if it were to attempt to crush out from those who are of Indian descent all the racial traits which differentiate the North American Indian from the other race stocks of the world. Certain conceptions of physical courage, a certain heroic stoicism in enduring physical pain, an inherited tendency to respect one's self, even if that tendency shows itself at times in unwarrantable conceit, are race traits which have value, if the people who have them become civilized and subject themselves to the laws of social morality and to the obligation of industrial efficiency, which are essential if any race stock or any group of families is to hold its own in the modern civilized world.

SOURCE: U.S. Department of Interior, "Board of Indian Commissioners' Reports," in *Annual Reports* (June 30, 1905), H. Doc. 20: 59th Cong., 1st sess., 17–18.

But the facts seem to us to be that good results are to be hoped for not by keeping the North American Indians peculiar in dress or in customs. We think that the wisest friends of the Indian recognize with great delight and value highly the art impulse in certain Indian tribes, which has shown itself in Indian music, in Indian art forms—such as the birchbark canoe, in Indian basketry, and more rarely in Indian pottery. But we firmly believe that the way to preserve the best of what is distinctively characteristic in the North American Indians is to civilize and educate them, that they may be fit for the life of the twentieth century under our American system of self-government. Because we value the elements for good which may come into our American life through the stock of North American Indians, we wish to see children of Indian descent educated in the industrial and practical arts and trained to habits of personal cleanliness, social purity, and industrious family life. We do not believe that it is right to keep the Indians out of civilization in order that certain picturesque aspects of savagery and barbarism may continue to be within reach of the traveler and the curious, or even of the scientific observer. In the objectionable "Indian dances" which are breaking out afresh at many points we see not a desirable maintenance of racial traits, but a distinct reversion toward barbarism and superstition. We believe that while the effort should never be made to "make a white man out of an Indian," in the sense of seeking to do violence to respect to parents or a proper or intelligent regard for what is fine in the traits and the history of one's ancestors, it is still most desirable that all the Indians on our territory should come as speedily as possible to the white man's habits of home-making, industry, cleanliness, social purity, and family integrity.

Precisely as all intelligent American patriots have seen danger to our national life in the attempt, wherever it has been made, to perpetuate in the United States large groups of foreign-born immigrants who try to keep their children from learning English and seek to perpetuate upon our territory (at the cost of true Americanism for their children) what was characteristic in the life of their own people on other continents and in past generations, precisely as in such cases we feel that the hope of our American system lies in the public schools and such educational institutions as shall maintain standards of public living that inevitably bring the children of foreign-born immigrants into the great body of English-speaking, home-loving, industrious, and pure-minded Americans—precisely so does it seem to us that all the efforts of the Government, and far more of distinctive missionary effort on the part of the Christian people of this country than has ever yet been used with this end in view, should be steadily employed in the effort to make out of the Indian children of this country intelligent, English-speaking, industrious, law-abiding Americans. We believe that the breaking up of tribal funds as rapidly as practicable will help toward this end. Even if many of the Indians do for a time misuse money while they are learning how to use it properly, even if some of them squander it utterly, we believe that there is hope for the Indians in the future only as by education, faith in work, and obedience to Christian principles of morality and clean living, their children shall come to have the social standards and the social habits of our better American life throughout the land.

Our task is to hasten the slow work of race evolution. Inevitably, but often grimly and harshly by the outworking of natural forces, the national life of the stronger and more highly civilized race stock dominates in time the life of the less civilized, when races like the Anglo-Saxon and the Indian are brought into close contact. In our work for the Indians we want to discern clearly those influences and habits of life which are of the greatest advantage in leading races upward into Christian civilization; and these influences and habits we wish to make as strongly influential as possible, and as speedily as possible influential upon the life of all these American tribes. It is not unreasonable to hope that through governmental agencies and through the altruistic missionary spirit of one of the foremost Christian races and governments of the world much can be done to hasten that process of civilization which natural law, left to itself, works out too slowly and at too great a loss to the less-favored race. We want to make the conditions for our less-favored brethren of the red race so favorable that the social forces which have developed themselves slowly and at great expense of time and life in our American race and our American system of government shall be made to help in the uplifting of the Indians and to shorten that interval of time which of necessity must elapse between savagery and Christian civilization.

The Cutting of My Long Hair, c. 1885

The first day in the land of apples was a bitter-cold one; for the snow still covered the ground, and the trees were bare. A large bell rang for breakfast, its loud metallic voice crashing through the belfry overhead and into our sensitive ears. The annoying clatter of shoes on bare floors gave us no peace. The constant clash of harsh noises, with an undercurrent of many voices murmuring an unknown tongue, made a bedlam within which I was securely tied. And though my spirit tore itself in struggling for its lost freedom, all was useless.

A paleface woman, with white hair, came up after us. We were placed in a line of girls who were marching into the dining room. These were Indian girls, in stiff shoes and closely clinging dresses. The small girls wore sleeved aprons and shingled hair. As I walked noiselessly in my soft moccasins, I felt

SOURCE: Zitkala-Sa (Gertrude Simmons Bonnin), "The School Days of an Indian Girl," *Atlantic Monthly* (January–March, 1900), 45–47.

like sinking to the floor, for my blanket had been stripped from my shoulders. I looked hard at the Indian girls, who seemed not to care that they were even more immodestly dressed than I, in their tightly fitting clothes. While we marched in, the boys entered at an opposite door. I watched for the three young braves who came in our party. I spied them in the rear ranks, looking as uncomfortable as I felt.

A small bell was tapped, and each of the pupils drew a chair from under the table. Supposing this act meant they were to be seated, I pulled out mine and at once slipped into it from one side. But when I turned my head, I saw that I was the only one seated, and all the rest at our table remained standing. Just as I began to rise, looking shyly around to see how chairs were to be used, a second bell was sounded. All were seated at last, and I had to crawl back into my chair again. I heard a man's voice at one end of the hall, and I looked around to see him. But all the others hung their heads over their plates. As I glanced at the long chain of tables, I caught the eyes of a paleface woman upon me. Immediately I dropped my eyes, wondering why I was so keenly watched by the strange woman. The man ceased his mutterings, and then a third bell was tapped. Every one picked up his knife and fork and began eating. I began crying instead, for by this time I was afraid to venture anything more.

But this eating by formula was not the hardest trial in that first day. Late in the morning, my friend Judéwin gave me a terrible warning. Judéwin knew a few words of English; and she had overheard the paleface woman talk about cutting our long, heavy hair. Our mothers had taught us that only unskilled warriors who were captured had their hair shingled by the enemy. Among our people, short hair was worn by mourners, and shingled hair by cowards!

We discussed our fate some moments, and when Judéwin said, "We have to submit, because they are strong," I rebelled.

"No, I will not submit! I will struggle first!" I answered.

I watched my chance, and when no one noticed I disappeared. I crept up the stairs as quietly as I could in my squeaking shoes,—my moccasins had been exchanged for shoes. Along the hall I passed, without knowing whither I was going. Turning aside to an open door, I found a large room with three white beds in it. The windows were covered with dark green curtains, which made the room very dim. Thankful that no one was there, I directed my steps toward the corner farthest from the door. On my hands and knees I crawled under the bed, and cuddled myself in the dark corner.

From my hiding place I peered out, shuddering with fear whenever I heard footsteps near by. Though in the hall loud voices were calling my name, and I knew that even Judéwin was searching for me, I did not open my mouth to answer. Then the steps were quickened and the voices became excited. The sounds came nearer and nearer. Women and girls entered the room. I held my breath and watched them open closet doors and peep behind large trunks. Some one threw up the curtains, and the room was filled with sudden light. What caused them to stoop and look under the bed I do not know. I remember being dragged out, though I resisted by kicking and scratching wildly. In spite of myself, I was carried downstairs and tied fast in a chair.

I cried aloud, shaking my head all the while until I felt the cold blades of the scissors against my neck, and heard them gnaw off one of my thick braids. Then I lost my spirit. Since the day I was taken from my mother I had suffered extreme indignities. People had stared at me. I had been tossed about in the air like a wooden puppet. And now my long hair was shingled like a coward's! In my anguish I moaned for my mother, but no one came to comfort me. Not a soul reasoned quietly with me, as my own mother used to do; for now I was only one of many little animals driven by a herder.

Chapter 4

Woman's Sphere: Woman's Work

Women workers of the West.

During most of the nineteenth century the notion predominated that, when it came to work, men and women occupied separate spheres. Married women's work centered in the home; for unmarried women there were a few female occupations open. Elementary school teaching and nursing were deemed respectable for middle-class women. For the poor, domestic service and the in-home production of such items as clothing and artificial flowers were available.

During the final decades of the nineteenth century, America's urban growth and an expanding industrial economy opened innumerable jobs for men. For urban women there was some growth in opportunity, notably as factory workers in the garment industry, as secretaries and typists in business offices, and as sales clerks in department stores. However, adherence to the idea of a "separate sphere" and the belief that a woman's place was in the home persisted in most of America.

As you will see in Pamela Riney-Kehrberg's essay "Women in Wheat Country," it was in the agricultural regions of the Midwest and Great Plains that the old ideas about women and work broke down. Her essay focuses on Kansas, but conditions were similar in the rural regions of the neighboring states. What evidence is presented to demonstrate that on the farms of Kansas women's "sphere" was replaced by women's "spheres" and that her "place" expanded beyond the confines of the home? On the wheat farms of Kansas, "Women's work is never done" was indeed a truism.

Outside of the rural heartland, the popular belief in the notion of "women's work" demanded some justification for admitting females to certain jobs. Teaching was the first literacy-required occupation deemed suitable to a woman's nature. In the first document, Horace Mann, Secretary of the Massachusetts Board of Education and famous crusader for public schooling, applauds the entry of women as teachers in the primary grades, a position for which he believed they were particularly fit. Though this Annual Report was written in 1844, it expressed attitudes toward women that would remain common throughout the rest of the century. Note the reference to woman's special qualities with which "the Author of nature preadapted her." By the Civil War, the schoolmistress had almost completely replaced the schoolmaster in the nation's public elementary schools, a development that highlights the persuasiveness of Mann's argument. Of course, differences in salaries might also have exerted influence as communities hired teachers: in 1861, the average salary for male teachers in rural districts was $6.30 per week; for women, it was $4.05. In urban districts, men earned $18.00 per week; women, only $6.91.

Women attempting to enter prestigious, traditionally male occupations often met with considerable resistance and drew on huge stores of courage in their perseverance. The second document is a 1916 newspaper account of the recollections of Dr. Anna Manning Comfort, who graduated in the first class of the New York Medical College and Hospital for Women in 1865. How did the perception of a separate place for women within the medical profession shift between 1865 and 1916?

Although popular beliefs about women's natural capacities supported their entry into teaching, clerical jobs, nursing, factory work, librarianship, social work, and even medicine, they were also used to exclude women from positions of leadership in those fields, to deny them the right to vote, and to bar their entry into other professions. In 1872 the United States Supreme Court upheld a decision of the Illinois courts denying Myra Bradwell a license to practice law on the grounds of her sex. The third document presents Supreme Court Justice

Bradley's majority opinion in support of the Court's decision. Notice that his argument rested heavily on traditional perceptions of women's natures.

The Court's decision in Bradwell *v.* Illinois set back women's rights, yet the era saw victories as well. That same year (1872), the Illinois legislature removed all restrictions to women's entry into the professions. Similar actions were taken in other states. In 1869 Arabella Mansfield of Iowa had become the first woman licensed to practice law. By 1891 the nation boasted two hundred licensed women lawyers. (Of course, the figure represented less than 1 percent of all the nation's attorneys.) The struggle has continued well into our own century. How would you describe popular beliefs today concerning separate spheres for men and women in the home, in politics, and in the world of work?

ESSAY

Women in Wheat Country

Pamela Riney-Kehrborg

Dear cousin . . . I heard there was a lots a girls out there. Maybe there is one left for me, I wish you would find me a good girl out there. I am coming out there this fall or this winter. I don't care if she got money or not, just so that she is good. That is all I care for. If you find one please send me her picture and tell her to write. Now maybe you think I am making fun but I mean it. Please try your best and let me know as quick as you can. . . . Best regards to you and all and to the girl you find for me. Dear cousin write soon, soon, soon, soon, soon, soon.

Although almost comic in tone, this 1900 letter written by a young Reno County farmer to a cousin to the east reflected a grave reality in wheat country; a farm without a woman was at a serious disadvantage. Females, young and old, were an essential part of the economic fabric of wheat farming. They participated in a nearly lifelong cycle of work, attending to whatever tasks the farm and family demanded of them. From the moment that a girl was old enough to work, her mother trained her to labor in the family's agricultural enterprise. By the time she was a young woman, her work was vital to numerous aspects of the survival of her family's farm, from housekeeping to gardening and crop production. As a married woman on her own farm, she bore, reared, and trained the next generation of farmers; labored in her

SOURCE: Pamela Riney-Kehrborg, "Women in Wheat Country," *Kansas History* 23 (spring–summer, 2000), 56–68. Reprinted with permission of the author and the editor of *Kansas History*, a publication of the Kansas State Historical Society, Inc.

home, barnyard, and often fields; and cared for the needs of the larger community. As that somewhat desperate young man in Reno County knew, a farm without a woman was impoverished indeed.

Although earlier generations of historians often thought of farming as a male province, in the last twenty years scholars have increasingly acknowledged that women have played a vital role in the development of American agriculture. Throughout most of the nineteenth and early twentieth centuries, labor in the agricultural North was both scarce and expensive. Rather than attempt to hire the hands that they needed to farm their lands, families traditionally relied upon their own efforts to meet labor needs. This economic reality dictated that farm women bore and trained large numbers of children to work the family farm and participated actively themselves in agricultural labor, from dairying in the Northeast to corn and livestock production in the Midwest and wheat growing on the Great Plains.

How women have participated in their families' agricultural enterprises has varied from region to region and over time. A woman's activities also changed during the course of her own life cycle. The tasks expected from a teenaged girl, living on her parents' farm, might be quite different from those performed by a mature woman, either in or past her childbearing years. The writings of and about women on wheat farms reveal the complexity and variety of their tasks and the vital roles they played in developing their families' enterprises.

In the late nineteenth and early twentieth centuries growing up on a farm meant assuming an ever larger part of its work. In 1877 Ottilia Schulz was fourteen, and a worker. Her father's diary, which documented life on the Schulz family's farm in McPherson County, Kansas, describes the kind of work a daughter in her early teens might be expected to accomplish. Ottilia labored in the fields, pulling rye out of the wheat, shocking and stacking wheat, cutting sorghum, planting corn and potatoes, and herding cattle. She also ran errands for her busy parents. This did not exempt her from work inside the home, as Schulz noted: "Ottilie cleaning bedsteads and washing." Only three children remained in the Schulz home (Agnes, age twenty-one; Alexander Paul, nineteen; and Ottilia, fourteen), and Ottilia's parents expected her to be useful in whatever way was necessary, be it in the fields or in the home.

Bertha Benke of Barton County, Kansas, also was fourteen and one of three children when she wrote her diary. Her 1886–1887 writings detail her activities hunting eggs, picking peas, planting and harvesting corn, and cutting wheat with a scythe beside her father. Much of this work was a cooperative effort between Bertha, her nine year-old sister Ida, and her parents. When her brother Hermann was not away teaching school, he also worked in the fields. As Benke wrote on January 29, 1887: "Ida, myself, and P. [father] & M. [mother] went to work in the field all day. I and H. chop stalks and P. & M. pick them into large heaps, all the fore noon." Without the help of their daughters, the Benkes would have been hard pressed to accomplish the work of the farm. It should be noted, however, that Bertha Benke was not an overworked daughter. Her journal attests to the hours she spent hunting, swimming, drawing, and studying. Although Bertha was often "buisy,"she also had lazy days when she and Ida were free "to hunt some nise Flowers."

For a girl to work in the fields as well as in the home was not unusual. In 1916 Children's Bureau investigators studying a wheat farming community in western Kansas found that in their youth many Kansas-raised women had ventured beyond traditional female tasks. Of these women, a third had done only housework as girls, but nearly half had provided "some work in the fields. For girls raised in western Kansas this field work usually consisted of driving teams or herding cattle." Many girls, as well as boys, became familiar with crop and livestock production.

As their unmarried daughters matured, families set them to the tasks most needed by the family. The Capper family lived on a farm near Beverly in Lincoln County where they raised wheat, corn, kafir corn, and livestock. Four Capper children lived at home. Daughter Olive, age twenty-four, was the oldest, followed by Earl, fifteen; Rob, twelve; and Myrtle, seven. Olive generally participated in tasks that were stereotypically female. Aside from picking and shucking corn and occasionally working in the garden, Olive did not work outdoors. Instead, housekeeping was her contribution to the family economy. Washing and ironing filled many of her days as did sewing and mending. Olive described her work during one week in February: "I washed," "I ironed some," "I ironed in evening," "I washed and baked," "I finished ironing, baked bread & cut carpet rags today." Neighbors also hired Olive to do their housekeeping, although it is unclear if she kept her wages or contributed them to her family. Olive's mother was more likely to be in the fields working than Olive was, which may have reflected her mother's preferences or the best use of their individual abilities.

In 1879 Lottie Norton was twenty-two and her mother's full partner in housekeeping. Her tasks rarely took her into the fields, although she often did gardening chores such as planting potatoes and setting out cabbages. She did assist her father with corn and sorghum planting, as did many girls and young women, but she was more likely to be washing and sewing. Indeed, she took advantage of the family farm's close proximity to Fort Larned and took in soldiers' washing. Lottie contributed her earnings to the family coffers. As her mother wrote in the spring of 1880, "Lottie got a calico dress for a present for me and got none for herself. Also got some calico for the children. Spent all her wash money, poor child, and only got herself some cheap shoes and cheap gloves. I am ashamed to take the dress." Mary Norton worried about the weight of her eldest daughter's burdens. In the late spring of 1880 Mary wrote, "She has worked too hard this week—

helped plant the sorghum when it was very warm." Lottie Norton's life was a busy one, consumed with the needs of her parents, brothers, and sisters.

Mary and Lottie Norton spent the larger portion of their time working in the house and the garden, while others generally worked in the fields. This distribution of labor reflected the ages of the Norton children as well as their numbers. In 1879, when the Norton family diary began, Lottie was the oldest child in residence. Additionally, there were four Norton sons aged eleven to twenty, and five other children, nine years of age and younger. Lucy Ida was the youngest at one year old. With so many small children in the household and so many sons whom their parents considered old enough to do field work, it made great sense for the Norton women to focus their attentions on the household.

The adult women in the Schulz family divided their labors differently. Louisa Schulz and her daughter Agnes both worked inside and out, although Agnes spent more time in the fields than did her mother. Their apparent willingness to work in the fields may have been a reflection of the family's German heritage. German women, as well as women of Scandinavian and Eastern European descent, were more likely to work in the fields on a regular basis than native-born women, who sometimes considered field work undignified and unfeminine. Agnes, at twenty-one, moved regularly from the work in the fields to the work in the house. She shared the gardening with her mother. She weeded the wheat fields with her siblings and shocked with them as well. During harvest, the local men moved from farm to farm, cutting, binding, shocking, and threshing wheat. Agnes also followed the harvest, cooking for the men at various neighbors' houses and going into the fields when needed. As her father wrote in the midst of the wheat harvest, "harvesting upon Morrell's farm, Agnes prepairing dinner there & helping in the field, her nose bleeding several times, caused from the hot weather." When the crop no longer claimed her attention, she washed, sewed, scrubbed, made soap, and generally made herself useful to her family. Neither she nor her mother specialized in housekeeping to the exclusion of other farm tasks.

Agnes Schulz appeared to be helping her family in another way as well. As a twenty-one-year-old adult she was eligible to claim land under the Homestead Act. The act only required that a homesteader be a legal adult and the head of his or her own household to claim land; in that way, homesteading was open to both women and men. In 1887, although still resident on her parents' farm, Agnes Schulz made a land claim in her own right. The claim was contested, perhaps because she was not actually living on the land or working it herself, but the court dismissed the suit. Schulz's claim appeared to be a homestead acquired for family, rather than personal, purposes. Her land was very close to her parents' farm, and she continued to live and work at home, while her brother and a hired man did the plowing and planting. In the fall of 1877 Agnes might have been preparing to move to her land (she was purchasing dishes and other household items), but she had not done so by the summer of 1878. By making a land claim on neighboring acres, Agnes Schulz had effectively increased the size of her parents' farm by 160 acres, at least until such time as she might want to sell the land or marry. It is impossible to know how many daughters homesteaded for the purpose of increasing their families' holdings. Although questionable legally, their actions were enormously valuable to their parents.

In marriage farm women put their many years of experience to the test. To the housework, and sometimes field work, that they had performed as their parents' daughters, they added childbearing and child rearing. Families in farming communities tended to be large. In Kansas in 1900 the average family consisted of 4.57 persons. In heavily urban areas such as Johnson, Shawnee, and Sedgwick Counties, the average family was smaller. In more rural counties, such as those represented in this study, the average family was larger. Mothers on the Great Plains, and especially on new farms, often bore larger numbers of children than their counterparts farther to the east.

Circumstances forced women to integrate childbearing into the work of the farm to the best of their abilities. A 1916 study found that only about half of the farm women in a western Kansas county had hired help in the house when their babies were born, and fewer than one-fifth had any sort of help in the last months of pregnancy. This lack of help was not the result of poverty but of a shortage of female labor. As the researcher discovered, "pregnant mothers keep up their usual round of duties until labor begins, unless they are disabled by serious ill health." The story of Mrs. Green's pregnancy was typical. "Harvest occurred two and a half months before the baby was born, and Mrs. Green had six extra men to board for two weeks; but she had a hired girl for that time." A heavily pregnant Mrs. Green also had to tend to the threshers. "The thrashing crew came three weeks before the baby was born, just when the oldest boy was having the measles; but Mr. Green arranged so that none of the men boarded at the house." Mrs. Green integrated pregnancy and childbirth into her work, although she had the great good fortune of hired help and an accommodating husband. If Mrs. Green followed the patterns prevalent in her community, she would have nursed her baby throughout its first year of life, and perhaps into its second. Each new addition to the family complicated already busy schedules, and aside from the two weeks immediately following the birth of their babies, most mothers continued their usual round of work.

In 1890 Mary Logan of Decatur County experienced a threshing season much like Mrs. Green's. She found herself with no time to rest and recuperate immediately following childbirth. As she wrote many years later, "Before I was able to be up, the threshing machine came into the neighborhood, and if you did not get your threshing done when it came through the first time, there was no telling when it would come back. So Dan thought he must thresh." A fifteen-year-old girl came to help, but Mary Logan supervised.

"I gave them instructions from my bed and they killed and dressed four or five chickens, and kept the fire roaring in the stove all day. During the hot August days, this was almost too much for me, and I thought I was going to pass out." A thresher's wife came to her aid. "Mrs. Wintzen, came in and fanned me, and this and the fact that it cooled off at night was the only reason I was able to stand it." In retrospect, Logan believed that her husband had asked too much of her. "I should have put my foot down and said 'no threshers until I am up,' but Dan said it would save work to thresh out of shocks. We had a good crop that year and got money ahead." The successful harvest brought the Logans enough money to build a new house. This meant additional work for Mary Logan in the form of boarding the builders while they worked, and as she nursed a baby and cared for small children. Her experience was far from unusual.

Child care was at the center of any mother's life, but child care often meant child training. Once her daughters were old enough, one of the most essential jobs of any farm woman was to train them to assume the work of the household and farm. An 1874 essay in the *Kansas Farmer*, titled "What Shall We Teach our Daughters," captured the essence of a mother's task. In practical terms, mothers were to teach their daughters the fine art of homemaking:

> Give them a good, substantial, common education.
> Teach them how to cook a good meal of victuals.
> Teach them how to darn stockings and sew on buttons.
> Teach them how to make shirts.
> Teach them how to make bread.
> Teach them all of the mysteries of the kitchen, the dining room and
>   the parlor.

In addition to homemaking skills, the writer admonished mothers to teach their daughters common sense, morality, and "the essentials of life—truth, honesty, uprightness—then at a suitable time to marry." The author warned parents, "Rely upon it, that upon your teaching depends in a great measure the weal or woe of their after-life." Upon a mother's teaching also rested her own welfare and peace of mind. As the lives of young women such as Bertha Benke, Olive Capper, Lottie Norton, and the Schulz sisters demonstrate, a well-trained, willing daughter could do much to lighten the burdens of a hard-working mother. When such a daughter left home, a mother might grieve the loss of her company and assistance. When Lottie Norton married and moved to Illinois, her mother wrote, "Nobody knows how much I miss Lottie." She, like many other daughters, had eased her mother's burdens and carried much of the weight of the work in a very large household.

Child care and training had to be integrated into a large variety of housekeeping tasks. On the Norton family's Pawnee County farm, mother Mary raised ten children (an eleventh was by 1879 deceased), washed, scrubbed, baked, sewed, preserved food, and made a garden. When her husband and older sons left the family's cash-strapped farm to work in distant communities, she became the farm manager. On January 24, 1881, she described her household chores: "I've done nothing today but bake a little, make cranberry jelly, clean pantry shelves, cook, swept, etc. Every day, I think I'll have leisure to sew some. Guess I'm getting old and slow." She sometimes felt great ambivalence about her work: "I made a pair of pants for Charles today—an important event to note down, but that is about what my life amounts to." Mary Norton was not the only woman with less than charitable thoughts about housework. Nancy Cool of Cloud County must have captured the feelings of many women when she wrote on a hot July day, "Glad our folk, are all able and <u>willing</u> to eat: but it is very hot work for the women to cook." Women's work on the farm, like men's, was often repetitive, backbreaking, and uncomfortably warm.

These day-to-day tasks, which were more than enough to keep any woman busy, were eclipsed by harvest and threshing. As an observer wrote in 1916, "at wheat-harvest time, and often at thrashing, there comes an almost overwhelming rush of work because of the necessity of boarding crews. This is always a great burden." Mary Norton's experiences confirmed this assessment. On an August day she wrote, "I was taken ill last Saturday night with quite a severe attack of Bloody Flux. . . . We threshed last Saturday—had 327 bushes of wheat. It was a very hot day." For all concerned, harvest and threshing were the most arduous phases of crop production.

At the hottest time of the year, women went into the kitchen to cook for large numbers of men over wood and coal-fired stoves. One meal would hardly be concluded before preparations for the next began. The frenetic pace of harvest was the culmination of months of hard work. Women began planning for the event well in advance. As Elma Bamberg, who was raised on an Ellis County farm, reminisced, "The women were planning on the big groups they would have to feed. Most of them were sure there would be plenty of milk; the meat product was planned for since the previous cold months when it had been butchered and cured or stored in five or ten gallon crocks in lard." This advance planning included raising enough chickens for both meat and eggs and planting an early spring garden, "so they could have vegetables to set the table. Potatoes, though they were not fully matured could be dug and used, though it took a lot of hills to make a meal and a lot of scraping to prepare them." Bamberg asserted that "the woman's part was not so easy, but with foresight it was done year after year." This foresight was essential for the successful completion of both harvest and threshing.

Hot, home-cooked meals provided the fuel that kept laborers working. Women provided the ingenuity, planning, and sweat that brought those meals to the table. The panic in a husband's words is apparent when his wife decided to leave home four days before the threshers appeared.

> Mother took a bundle of clothes and Started for Alma's a foot, to work for her. I had asked her to Stay and help her family at home but She would not. I found her gone when I came home from the hay field for dinner. . . . It is hard for me to get the cows after dark and milk every night. I did not know Mother intended to leave home.

The day before the threshers arrived, a son went to try to retrieve his mother. "Lewis went C. C. King's found Mother there told her of the much work we had to do and asked her to come home to help but would not do it." While it is entirely unclear why "Mother" left prior to threshing and returned the following week, it is clear that her absence posed serious logistical problems for her family. Perhaps she had cooked and sweated through one harvest too many.

Women's participation in crop production was not confined to cooking and cleaning for the men who worked in the fields. Women often integrated field work into their already busy lives. The degree to which they did so depended upon a number of factors: need, ethnicity, inclination, number of children on the farm and their ages, and stage of a farm's development. Need was the most important factor determining a woman's actions. When need dictated, women worked in the fields. This was particularly true in busy times, such as harvesting and threshing. As previously stated, women from certain ethnic backgrounds were more likely to perform field work than others. German women did not necessarily see field work as men's work but as their work as well. Inclination, too, played an important role in determining a woman's actions. If a woman preferred to work outdoors, she might substitute a daughter's labors for her own inside the house. If she preferred to work indoors, she might send an older daughter out to work in her stead. As the case of the Norton family shows, a mother with a large number of children over twelve, and particularly boys, would have greater freedom to work in the house, rather than the fields. The large numbers of Norton children and their age and sex distribution allowed Mary Norton to devote her energies to the house and garden. Other families had different labor needs. By the 1880s the Cool household was shrinking. Only two daughters and one son made up the available work force. A third daughter lived at home, but she worked for wages off the farm. Nancy Cool worked outside of the house, helping her younger daughter Hattie with various chores. As Cool wrote, "Hattie and I took turns herding: Too hot for one to stand the sunshine very long at a time." Other women planted, harvested, and threshed as their circumstances dictated.

Farm women not only worked in their homes and fields but also found ways to earn sorely needed dollars. Many women sold milk, cream, butter, and eggs to supplement their families' incomes. Other women participated in the service economy. Lottie Norton, for example, took in soldiers' washing to aid her cash-poor family. Flora Heston, living on the frontier in Clark County, Kansas, found many ways to supplement her family's income from crop sales. She discovered that local bachelor farmers craved home baking. She wrote to her relatives in Indiana, "I sell bread to the fellows that batch around here; have sold $4.50 within less than two weeks. . . . I sell three small loaves for a quarter. . . . I can more than keep us in flour by selling bread." She also sold butter at twenty-five cents a pound. When she planted her garden, she planned to grow enough vegetables to sell to her neighbors. Heston made profitable use of her knitting skills as well. "Well, I must tell you what I am doing. I get yarn out of the store and knit it up into socks, make twenty-five cents on each pair as I get fifty cents a pair. I can knit a pair in three days." When the opportunity presented itself, she boarded the surveyor when he came to the county. The impact of Heston's money-making efforts, and those of many other farm women, could be described in a single phase: "every little bit helps."

It is important to remember that although many women in wheat country carried enormous family commitments, they also maintained a close relationship with the surrounding community, caring for the sick, injured, and dying. This generally happened later in life when their own children were grown. Such was the case of Nancy Cool. In 1879 her children were nearly grown, and all of them were thirteen years of age or older, giving her greater freedom to care for neighbors. She often was away from home "visiting the sick." Visiting the sick might mean nursing a local family recovering from "a desperate case of diptheria," delivering a baby, or visiting a neighbor such as Arthur Bishop, who had broken his leg. Occasionally, Cool received payment for her services, bringing needed cash into the family coffers. After delivering a baby at the Pilchard home, Cool wrote, "Mr. Pilchard "paid me 5,00 dollars in full of all accounts[.] They have another plough boy at their house arrived last night." Nancy Cool's world was bigger than home and farm; it also encompassed a community in need of her care and nurturing.

As agriculture in Kansas evolved during the late nineteenth and early twentieth centuries, women fulfilled many roles. From their childhoods onward they assumed an incredible variety of tasks. Like their brothers, they aided in planting, harvesting, herding, and dozens of other jobs related to crop and livestock production. Unlike their brothers, their parents expected them to become proficient in all of the tasks of household management as well. Marriage and motherhood meant the continuation of these chores, although generally with less emphasis on field work and more emphasis on the home. When need demanded, women found ways to supplement their families' incomes. When compassion required it, they attended to the needs of their neighbors, as well as their own. The farm that operated without the services of a woman operated at a decided handicap. . . .

71

DOCUMENTS

"Is Not Woman Destined to Conduct the Rising Generation?" 1844

One of the most extraordinary changes which have taken place in our schools, during the last seven years, consists in the great proportionate increase in the number of female teachers employed.

In 1837, the number of male teachers in all our public schools, including summer and winter terms, was,	2370
Of females.	3591
In the school year 1843–4, it was,–males	2529
Females	4581
Increase in the number of male teachers	159
Increase in the number of female teachers	990
During the same time, the number of schools, in the State, has increased only	418

This change in public sentiment, in regard to the employment of female teachers, I believe to be in accordance with the dictates of the soundest philosophy. Is not woman destined to conduct the rising generation, of both sexes, at least through all the primary stages of education? Has not the Author of nature preadapted her, by constitution, and faculty, and temperament, for this noble work? What station of beneficent labor can she aspire to, more honorable, or more congenial to every pure and generous impulse? In the great system of society, what other part can she act, so intimately connected with the refinement and purification of the race? How otherwise can she so well vindicate her right to an exalted station in the scale of being; and cause that shameful sentence of degradation by which she has so long been dishonored, to be repealed? Four-fifths of all the women who have ever lived, have been the slaves of man—the menials in his household, the drudges in his field, the instruments of his pleasure, or, at best, the gilded toys of his leisure days in court or palace. She has been outlawed from honorable service, and almost incapacitated, by her servile condition, for the highest aspirations after usefulness and renown. But a noble revenge awaits her. By a manifestation of the superiority of moral power, she can triumph over that physical power which has hitherto sub-

SOURCE: Horace Mann, *"Eighth Annual Report of the Secretary of the Board of Education (1844),"* in *Life and Words of Horace Mann*, vol. 3, ed. Mary Mann (Boston, 1891), 426–29.

jected her to bondage. She can bless those by whom she has been wronged. By refining the tastes and sentiments of man, she can change the objects of his ambition; and, with changed objects of ambition, the fields of honorable exertion can be divided between the sexes. By inspiring nobler desires for nobler objects, she can break down the ascendency of those selfish motives that have sought their gratification in her submission and inferiority. All this she can do, more rapidly, and more effectually than it can ever be done in any other way, unless through miracles, by training the young to juster notions of honor and duty, and to a higher appreciation of the true dignity and destiny of the race.

The more extensive employment of females for educating the young, will be the addition of a new and mighty power to the forces of civilization. It is a power, also, which, heretofore, to a very great extent, has been unappropriated; which has been allowed, in the administration of the affairs of men, to run to waste. Hence it will be an addition to one of the grandest spheres of human usefulness, without any subtraction from other departments—a gain without a loss. For all females—the great majority—who are destined, in the course of Providence, to sustain maternal relations, no occupation or apprenticeship can be so serviceable; but, in this connection, it is not unworthy of notice, that, according to the census of Massachusetts, there are almost eight thousand more females than males belonging to the State.

But if a female is to assume the performance of a teacher's duties, she must be endowed with high qualifications. If devoid of mental superiority, then she inevitably falls back into that barbarian relation, where physical strength measures itself against physical strength. In that contest, she can never hope to succeed; or, if she succeeds, it will be only as an Amazon, and not as a personification of moral power. Opportunities, therefore, should be everywhere opened for the fit qualification of female teachers; and all females possessing in an eminent degree, the appropriate natural endowments, should be encouraged to qualify themselves for this sacred work. Those who have worthily improved such opportunities, should be rewarded with social distinction and generous emoluments. Society cannot do less than this, on its own account, for those who are improving its condition; though for the actors themselves, in this beneficent work, the highest rewards must forever remain where God and nature have irrevocably placed them—in the consciousness of well-doing.

Could public opinion, on this one subject, be rectified, and brought into harmony with the great law of Christian duty and love, there are thousands of females amongst us, who now spend lives of frivolity, of unbroken wearisomeness and worthlessness, who would rejoice to exchange their days of painful idleness for such ennobling occupations; and who, in addition to the immediate rewards of well-doing, would see, in the distant prospect, the consolations of a life well spent, instead of the pangs of remorse for a frivolous and wasted existence.

Only Heroic Women Were
Doctors Then (1865), 1916

Changes in the position of women in the world in the last fifty years were emphasized by Dr. Anna Manning Comfort, graduate of the New York Medical College and Hospital for Women in its first class in 1865, at a luncheon in her honor, given by the Faculty and Trustees of the college at Delmonico's yesterday. Dr. Comfort was graduated at the age of 20, and she is only in the early seventies, alert and well preserved, though she has had a vigorous career, has been married, and is the mother of three children.

"Students of today have no idea of conditions as they were when I studied medicine," said Dr. Comfort. "It is difficult to realize the changes that have taken place. I attended the first meeting when this institution was proposed, and was graduated from the first class. We had to go to Bellevue Hospital for our practical work, and the indignities we were made to suffer are beyond belief. There were 500 young men students taking post-graduate courses, and we were jeered at and catcalled, and the 'old war horses,' the doctors, joined the younger men.

"We were considered aggressive. They said women did not have the same brains as men and were not trustworthy. All the work at the hospital was made as repulsively unpleasant for us as possible. There were originally six in the class, but all but two were unable to put up with the treatment to which we were subjected and dropped out. I trembled whenever I went to the hospital and I said once that I could not bear it. Finally the women went to the authorities, who said that if we were not respectfully treated they would take the charter from the hospital!

"As a physician there was nothing that I could do that satisfied people. If I wore square-toed shoes and swung my arms they said I was mannish, and if I carried a parasol and wore a ribbon in my hair they said I was too feminine. If I smiled they said I had too much levity, and if I sighed they said I had no sand.

"They tore down my sign when I began to practice, the drug stores did not like to fill my prescriptions, and the older doctors would not consult with me. But that little band of women made it possible for the other women who have come later into the field to do their work. When my first patients came and saw me they said I was too young, and they asked in horrified tones if I had studied dissecting just like the men. They were shocked at that, but they were more shocked when my bills were sent in to find that I charged as much as a man.

"I believe in women entering professions," said Dr. Comfort, "but I also believe in motherhood. For the normal woman it is no more of a tax to have

SOURCE: "Only Heroic Women Were Doctors Then," *New York Times*, April 9, 1916.

a profession as well as family life than it is for a man to carry on the multi-tudinous duties he has outside the family. I had three sons of my own and two adopted ones, and I am as proud of my motherhood as of my medical career. I gave as much of my personality to my children in an hour as some mothers do in ten. My children honored me and have been worth while in the world."

There were many expressions of esteem for Dr. Comfort and she was overcome when it was announced that money had been raised for an Anna Manning Comfort scholarship in the hospital.

Letters of regret were read from John Burroughs and Colonel Theodore Roosevelt among others.

"I believe in women in the medical profession, and in politics, and in all worthy pursuits," said John Burroughs.

"I am amazed to learn that this is the only institution in this State, and one of two in the United States, exclusively for the woman medical student," said Colonel Roosevelt. "There should be others and women of refinement would be drawn into the profession who will not study medicine in a co-educational college, and more women doctors are needed."

Dr. Walter G. Crump, who spoke of the need for medical colleges exclusively for women, said:

"We learn from the [1910] Flexner report that there is an overproduction of doctors, but nine out of ten of the women doctors practice. There are demands continually for women physicians which cannot be filled. They are needed in many places where women and girls are to be under a physician's care."

Dr. Mary A. Brinkman, who was one of the early graduates of the college, spoke. She said she could corroborate many of the things told by Dr. Comfort. . . .

Women's Separate Sphere, 1872

The claim of the plaintiff, who is a married woman, to be admitted to practice as an attorney and counsellor-at-law, is based upon the supposed right of every person, man or woman, to engage in any lawful employment for a livelihood. The Supreme Court of Illinois denied the application on the ground that, by the common law, which is the basis of the laws of Illinois, only men were admitted to the bar, and the legislature had not made any change in this respect, but had simply provided that no person should be admitted to practice as attorney or counsellor without having previously obtained a license for that purpose from two justices of the Supreme Court,

SOURCE: Justice Bradley's majority opinion in *Bradwell* v. *Illinois* (December 1872).

and that no person should receive a license without first obtaining a certificate from the court of some county of his good moral character. In other
respects it was left to the discretion of the court to establish the rules by
which admission to the profession should be determined. The court, however, regarded itself as bound by at least two limitations. One was that it
should establish such terms of admission as would promote the proper administration of justice, and the other that it should not admit any persons,
or class of persons, not intended by the legislature to be admitted, even
though not expressly excluded by statute. In view of this latter limitation
the court felt compelled to deny the application of females to be admitted as
members of the bar. Being contrary to the rules of the common law and the
usages of Westminster Hall* from time immemorial, it could not be supposed that the legislature had intended to adopt any different rule.

The claim that, under the fourteenth amendment of the Constitution,
which declares that no State shall make or enforce any law which shall
abridge the privileges and immunities of citizens of the United States, the
statute law of Illinois, or the common law prevailing in that State, can no
longer be set up as a barrier against the right of females to pursue any lawful employment for a livelihood (the practice of law included), assumes that
it is one of the privileges and immunities of women as citizens to engage in
any and every profession, occupation, or employment in civil life.

It certainly cannot be affirmed, as an historical fact, that this has ever
been established as one of the fundamental privileges and immunities of the
sex. On the contrary, the civil law, as well as nature herself, has always recognized a wide difference in the respective spheres and destinies of man
and woman. Man is, or should be, woman's protector and defender. The
natural and proper timidity and delicacy which belongs to the female sex
evidently unfits it for many of the occupations of civil life. The constitution
of the family organization, which is founded in the divine ordinance, as
well as in the nature of things, indicates the domestic sphere as that which
properly belongs to the domain and functions of womanhood. The harmony, not to say identity, of interests and views which belong, or should
belong, to the family institution is repugnant to the idea of a woman adopting a distinct and independent career from that of her husband. So firmly
fixed was this sentiment in the founders of the common law that it became a
maxim of that system of jurisprudence that a woman had no legal existence
separate from her husband, who was regarded as her head and representative in the social state; and, notwithstanding some recent modifications of
this civil status, many of the special rules of law flowing from and dependent upon this cardinal principle still exist in full force in most States. One
of these is, that a married woman is incapable, without her husband's con-

*Westminster Hall was the ancient seat of English law, established in the twelfth century.
(Eds.)

sent, of making contracts which shall be binding on her or him. This very incapacity was one circumstance which the Supreme Court of Illinois deemed important in rendering a married woman incompetent fully to perform the duties and trusts that belong to the office of an attorney and counsellor.

It is true that many women are unmarried and not affected by any of the duties, complications, and incapacities arising out of the married state, but these are exceptions to the general rule. The paramount destiny and mission of woman are to fulfil the noble and benign offices of wife and mother. This is the law of the Creator. And the rules of civil society must be adapted to the general constitution of things, and cannot be based upon exceptional cases.

The humane movements of modern society, which have for their object the multiplication of avenues for woman's advancement, and of occupations adapted to her condition and sex, have my heartiest concurrence. But I am not prepared to say that it is one of her fundamental rights and privileges to be admitted into every office and position, including those which require highly special qualifications and demanding special responsibilities. In the nature of things it is not every citizen of every age, sex, and condition that is qualified for every calling and position. It is the prerogative of the legislator to prescribe regulations founded on nature, reason, and experience for the due admission of qualified persons to professions and callings demanding special skill and confidence. This fairly belongs to the police power of the State; and, in my opinion, in view of the peculiar characteristics, destiny, and mission of woman, it is within the province of the legislature to ordain what offices, positions, and callings shall be filled and discharged by men, and shall receive the benefit of those energies and responsibilities, and that decision and firmness which are presumed to predominate in the sterner sex.

For these reasons I think that the laws of Illinois now complained of are not obnoxious to the charge of abridging any of the privileges and immunities of citizens of the United States.

Chapter 5

Life and Labor
in Industrial America

Child laborers in a Pennsylvania coal mine.

By the close of the nineteenth century, the benefits of industrialization had grown apparent. The United States had become a wealthy and powerful nation, a leader among the countries of the world. But it paid a price for this growth in terms of human suffering, a price that was only beginning to be realized. Working conditions were often abysmal; immigrant families engaged in cigar manufacturing, for example, both lived and labored in overcrowded, foul-smelling tenements. Factories and mines were designed with minimal concern for worker health and safety. Workers toiled long days at bare-subsistence wages, with virtually no compensation benefits or legal safeguards.

Bonnie Mitelman's article "Rose Schneiderman and the Triangle Fire" describes one of the most horrible examples of the consequences of such conditions. Although it focuses primarily on the tragedy of an industrial fire, the article also offers insights into working conditions in the garment industry, the attitudes of management toward their employees and workers toward their unions, and the circumstances that finally spurred public support and government action for workplace reform.

The first two documents illustrate that the hazards of the workplace were by no means restricted to the Greenwich Village garment district, but also included the tenement workshops of New York City and the coal mines of Pennsylvania.

What attitude is reflected in the miner's statement, "We are American citizens and we don't go to hospitals and poorhouses"?

If working conditions were so bad here, why did so many immigrants come to America from Europe? We might find one answer in the third document, the story of Rocco Corresca, a poor Italian immigrant. What does his description of his first days in the United States indicate about the hardships experienced by the newcomers? In the end, what was the consequence of Rocco's success in America?

ESSAY

Rose Schneiderman and the Triangle Fire

Bonnie Mitelman

On Saturday afternoon, March 25, 1911, in New York City's Greenwich Village, a small fire broke out in the Triangle Waist Company, just as the 500 shirtwaist employees were quitting for the day. People rushed about, trying to get out, but they found exits blocked and windows to the fire escape rusted shut. They panicked.

As the fire spread and more and more were trapped, some began to jump, their hair and clothing afire, from the eighth and ninth floor windows. Nets that firemen held for them tore apart at the impact of the falling bodies. By the time it was over, 146 workers had died, most of them young Jewish women.

A United Press reporter, William Shepherd, witnessed the tragedy and reported, "I looked upon the heap of dead bodies and I remembered these girls were the shirtwaist makers. I remembered their great strike of last year in which these same girls had demanded more sanitary conditions and more safety precautions in the shops. These dead bodies were the answer."

The horror of that fire touched the entire Lower East Side ghetto community, and there was a profuse outpouring of sympathy. But it was Rose Schneiderman, an immigrant worker with a spirit of social justice and a powerful way with words, who is largely credited with translating the ghetto's emotional reaction into meaningful, widespread action. Six weeks following the tragedy, and after years of solid groundwork, with one brilliant, well-timed speech, she was able to inspire the support of wealthy

SOURCE: Bonnie Mitelman, "Rose Schneiderman and the Triangle Fire," *American History Illustrated* 16 (July 1981): 38–47. Reprinted through courtesy of Cowles Magazines, publisher of *American History Illustrated*.

uptown New Yorkers and to swing public opinion to the side of the labor movement, enabling concerned civic, religious, and labor leaders to mobilize their efforts for desperately needed safety and industrial reforms.

The Triangle fire, and the deaths of so many helpless workers, seemed to trigger in Rose Schneiderman an intense realization that there was absolutely nothing or no one to help working women except a strong union movement. With fierce determination, and the dedication, influence, and funding of many other people as well, she battled to regulate hours, wages, and safety standards and to abolish the sweatshop system. In so doing, she brought dignity and human rights to all workers.

The dramatic "uprising of the 20,000" of 1909–10, in which thousands of immigrant girls and women in the shirtwaist industry had endured three long winter months of a general strike to protest deplorable working conditions, had produced some immediate gains for working women. There had been agreements for shorter working hours, increased wages, and even safety reforms, but there had not been formal recognition of their union. At Triangle, for example, the girls had gained a 52 hour week, a 12–15 percent wage increase, and promises to end the grueling subcontracting system. But they had not gained the only instrument on which they could depend for lasting change: a viable trade union. This was to have disastrous results, for in spite of the few gains that they seemed to have made, the workers won no rights or bargaining power at all. In fact, "The company dealt only with its contractors. It felt no responsibility for the girls."

There were groups as well as individuals who realized the workers' impotence, but their attempts to change the situation accomplished little despite long years of hard work. The Women's Trade Union League [WTUL] and the International Ladies' Garment Workers' Union, through the efforts of Mary Dreier, Helen Marot, Leonora O'Reilly, Pauline Newman, and Rose Schneiderman, had struggled unsuccessfully for improved conditions: the futility that the union organizers were feeling in late 1910 is reflected in the WTUL minutes of December 5 of that year.

A scant eight months after their historic waistmakers' strike, and three months before the deadly Triangle fire, a Mrs. Malkiel (no doubt Theresa Serber Malkiel, who wrote the legendary account of the strike, *The Diary of a Shirtwaist Striker: A Story of the Shirtwaist Makers' Strike in New York*) is reported to have come before the League to urge action after a devastating fire in Newark, New Jersey, killed twenty-five working women. Mrs. Malkiel attributed their loss to the greed and negligence of the owners and the proper authorities. The WTUL subsequently demanded an investigation of all factory buildings and it elected an investigation committee from the League to cooperate with similar committees from other organizations.

The files of the WTUL contain complaint after complaint about unsafe factory conditions; many were filled out by workers afraid to sign their names for fear of being fired had their employers seen the forms. They describe factories with locked doors, no fire escapes, and barred windows. *The New York Times* carried an article which reported that fourteen factories were found to have no fire escapes, twenty-three that had locked doors, and seventy-eight that had obstructed fire escapes. In all, according to the article, 99 percent of the factories investigated in New York were found to have serious fire hazards.

Yet no action was taken.

It was the Triangle fire that emphasized, spectacularly and tragically, the deplorable safety and sanitary conditions of the garment workers. The tragedy focused attention upon the ghastly factories in which most immigrants worked; there was no longer any question about what the strikers had meant when they talked about safety and sanitary reform, and about social and economic justice.

The grief and frustration of the shirtwaist strikers were expressed by one of them, Rose Safran, after the fire: "If the union had won we would have been safe. Two of our demands were for adequate fire escapes and for open doors from the factories to the street. But the bosses defeated us and we didn't get the open doors or the better fire escapes. So our friends are dead."

The families of the fire victims were heartbroken and hysterical, the ghetto's *Jewish Daily Forward* was understandably melodramatic, and the immigrant community was completely enraged. Their Jewish heritage had taught them an emphasis on individual human life and worth; their shared background in the *shtetl* [Jewish village in Eastern Europe] and common experiences in the ghetto had given them a sense of fellowship. They were, in a sense, a family—and some of the most helpless among them had died needlessly.

The senseless deaths of so many young Jewish women sparked within these Eastern Europeans a new determination and dedication. The fire had made reform absolutely essential. Workers' rights were no longer just socialist jargon: They were a matter of life and death.

The Triangle Waist Company was located on the three floors of the Asch Building, a 10-story, 135-foot-high structure at the corner of Greene Street and Washington Place in Greenwich Village. One of the largest shirtwaist manufacturers, Triangle employed up to 900 people at times, but on the day of the fire, only about 500 were working.

Leon Stein's brilliant and fascinating account of the fire, entitled simply *The Triangle Fire*, develops and documents the way in which the physical facilities, company procedures, and human behavior interacted to cause this great tragedy. Much of what occurred was ironic, some was cruel, some stupid, some pathetic. It is a dramatic portrayal of the eternal confrontation of the "haves" and the "have-nots," told in large part by those who survived.

Fire broke out at the Triangle Company at approximately 4:45 P.M. (because time clocks were reportedly set back to stretch the day, and because other records give differing times of the first fire alarm, it is uncertain exactly what time the fire started), just after pay envelopes had been distributed and employees were leaving their work posts. It was a small fire at first, and there was a calm, controlled effort to extinguish it. But the fire began to spread, jumping from one pile of debris to another, engulfing the combustible shirtwaist fabric. It became obvious that the fire could not be snuffed out, and workers tried to reach the elevators or stairway. Those who reached the one open stairway raced down eight flights of stairs to safety; those who managed to climb onto the available passenger elevators also got out. But not everyone could reach the available exits. Some tried to open the door to a stairway and found it locked. Others were trapped between long working tables or behind the hordes of people trying to get into the elevators or out through the one open door.

Under the work tables, rags were burning; the wooden floors, trim, and window frames were also afire. Frantically, workers fought their way to the elevators, to the fire escape, and to the windows—to any place that might lead to safety.

Fire whistles and bells sounded as the fire department raced to the building. But equipment proved inadequate, as the fire ladders reached only to the seventh floor. And by the time the firemen connected their hoses to douse the flames, the crowded eighth floor was completely ablaze.

For those who reached the windows, there seemed to be a chance for safety. The *New York World* describes people balancing on window sills, nine stories up, with flames scorching them from behind, until firemen arrived: "The nets were spread below with all promptness. Citizens were commandeered into service, as the firemen necessarily gave their attention to the one engine and hose of the force that first arrived. The catapult force that the bodies gathered in the long plunges made the nets utterly without avail. Screaming girls and men, as they fell, tore the nets from the grasp of the holders, and the bodies struck the sidewalks and lay just as they fell. Some of the bodies ripped big holes through the life nets."

One reporter who witnessed the fire remembered how,

> A young man helped a girl to the window sill on the ninth floor. Then he held her out deliberately, away from the building, and let her drop. He held out a second girl the same way and let her drop. He held out a third girl who did not resist. They were all as unresisting as if he were helping them into a street car instead of into eternity. He saw that a terrible death awaited them in the flames and his was only a terrible chivalry. He brought around another girl to the window. I saw her put her arms around him and kiss him. Then he held her into space—and dropped her. Quick as a flash, he was on the window sill himself. His coat fluttered upwards—the air filled his trouser legs as he came down. I could see he wore tan shoes.

Those who had rushed to the fire escape found the window openings rusted shut. Several precious minutes were lost in releasing them. The fire escape itself ended at the second floor, in an airshaft between the Asch Building and the building next door. But too frantic to notice where it ended, workers climbed onto the fire escape, one after another until, in one terrifying moment, it collapsed from the weight, pitching the workers to their death.

Those who had made their way to the elevators found crowds pushing to get into the cars. When it became obvious that the elevators could no longer run, workers jumped down the elevator shaft, landing on the top of the cars, or grabbing for cables to ease their descent. Several died, but incredibly, some did manage to save themselves in this way. One man was found, hours after the fire, beneath an elevator car in the basement of the building, nearly drowned by the rapidly rising water from the firemen's hoses.

Several people, among them Triangle's two owners, raced to the roof, and from there were led to safety. Others never had that chance. "When Fire Chief Croker could make his way into the [top] three floors," states one account of the fire, "he found sights that utterly staggered him. . . . He saw as the smoke drifted away bodies burned to bare bones. There were skeletons bending over sewing machines."

The day after the fire, *The New York Times* announced that "the building was fireproof. It shows hardly any signs of the disaster that overtook it. The walls are as good as ever, as are the floors: nothing is worse for the fire except the furniture and 141 [*sic*] of the 600 men and girls that were employed in its upper three stories."

The building *was* fireproof. But there had never been a fire drill in the factory, even though the management had been warned about the possible hazard of fire on the top three floors. Owners Max Blanck and Isaac Harris had chosen to ignore these warnings in spite of the fact that many of their employees were immigrants who could barely speak English, which would surely mean panic in the event of a crisis.

The New York Times also noted that Leonora O'Reilly of the League had reported Max Blanck's visit to the WTUL during the shirtwaist strike, and his plea that the girls return to work. He claimed a business reputation to maintain and told the Union leaders he would make the necessary improvements right away. Because he was the largest manufacturer in the business, the League reported, they trusted him and let the girls return.

But the improvements were never made. And there was nothing that anybody could or would do about it. Factory doors continued to open in instead of out, in violation of fire regulations. The doors remained bolted during working hours, apparently to prevent workers from getting past the inspectors with stolen merchandise. Triangle had only two staircases where there should have been three, and those two were very narrow. Despite the fact that the building was deemed fireproof, it had wooden window frames, floors, and trim. There was no sprinkler system. It was not legally required.

These were the same kinds of conditions which existed in factories throughout the garment industry; they had been cited repeatedly in the complaints filed with the WTUL. They were not unusual nor restricted to Triangle; in fact, Triangle was not as bad as many other factories.

But it was at Triangle that the fire took place.

The *Jewish Daily Forward* mourned the dead with sorrowful stories, and its headlines talked of "funerals instead of weddings" for the dead young girls. The entire Jewish immigrant community was affected, for it seemed there was scarcely a person who was not in some way touched by the fire. Nearly everyone had either been employed at Triangle themselves, or had a friend or relative who had worked there at some time or another. Most worked in factories with similar conditions, and so everyone identified with the victims and their families.

Many of the dead, burned beyond recognition, remained unidentified for days, as searching family members returned again and again to wait in long lines to look for their loved ones. Many survivors were unable to identify their mothers, sisters, or wives; the confusion of handling so many victims and so many survivors who did not understand what was happening to them and to their dead led to even more anguish for the community. Some of the victims were identified by the names on the pay envelopes handed to them at quitting time and stuffed deeply into pockets or stockings just before the fire. But many bodies remained unclaimed for days, with bewildered and bereaved survivors wandering among them, trying to find some identifying mark.

Charges of first- and second-degree manslaughter were brought against the two men who owned Triangle, and Leon Stein's book artfully depicts the subtle psychological and sociological implications of the powerful against the oppressed, and of the Westernized, German-Jewish immigrants against those still living their old-world, Eastern European heritage. Ultimately, Triangle owners Blanck and Harris were acquitted of the charges against them, and in due time they collected their rather sizable insurance.

The shirtwaist, popularized by Gibson girls, had come to represent the new-found freedom of females in America. After the fire, it symbolized death. The reaction of the grief-stricken Lower East Side was articulated by socialist lawyer Morris Hillquit:

> The girls who went on strike last year were trying to readjust the conditions under which they were obliged to work. I wonder if there is not some connection between the fire and that strike. I wonder if the magistrates who sent to jail the girls who did picket duty in front of the Triangle shop realized last Sunday that some of the responsibility may be theirs. Had the strike been successful, these

girls might have been alive today and the citizenry of New York would have less of a burden upon its conscience.

For the first time in the history of New York's garment industry there were indications that the public was beginning to accept responsibility for the exploitation of the immigrants. For the first time, the establishment seemed to understand that these were human beings asking for their rights, not merely troublemaking anarchists.

The day after the Triangle fire a protest meeting was held at the Women's Trade Union League, with representatives from twenty leading labor and civic organizations. They formed "a relief committee to cooperate with the Red Cross in its work among the families of the victims, and another committee . . . to broaden the investigation and research on fire hazards in New York factories which was already being carried on by the League."

The minutes of the League recount the deep indignation that members felt at the indifference of a public which had ignored their pleas for safety after the Newark fire. In an attempt to translate their anger into constructive action, the League drew up a list of forceful resolutions that included a plan to gather delegates from all of the city's unions to make a concerted effort to force safety changes in factories. In addition, the League called upon all workers to inspect factories and then report any violations to the proper city authorities and to the WTUL. They called upon the city to immediately appoint organized workers as unofficial inspectors. They resolved to submit the following fire regulations suggestions: compulsory fire drills, fireproof exits, unlocked doors, fire alarms, automatic sprinklers, and regular inspections. The League called upon the legislature to create the Bureau of Fire Protection and finally, the League underscored the absolute need for all workers to organize themselves at once into trade unions so that they would never again be powerless.

The League also voted to participate in the funeral procession for the unidentified dead of the Triangle fire.

The city held a funeral for the dead who were unclaimed. "More than 120,000 of us were in the funeral procession that miserable rainy April day," remembered Rose Schneiderman. "From ten in the morning until four in the afternoon we of the Women's Trade Union League marched in the procession with other trade-union men and women, all of us filled with anguish and regret that we had never been able to organize the Triangle workers."

Schneiderman, along with many others, was absolutely determined that this kind of tragedy would never happen again. With single-minded dedication, they devoted themselves to unionizing the workers. The searing example of the Triangle fire provided them with the impetus they needed to gain public support for their efforts.

They dramatized and emphasized and capitalized on the scandalous working conditions of the immigrants. From all segments of the community came cries for labor reform. Stephen S. Wise, the prestigious reform rabbi, called for the formation of a citizens' committee. Jacob H. Schiff, Bishop David H. Greer, Governor John A. Dix, Anne Morgan (of *the* Morgans) and other leading civic and religious leaders collaborated in a mass meeting at the Metropolitan Opera House on May 2 to protest factory conditions and to show support for the workers.

Several people spoke at that meeting on May 2, and many in the audience began to grow restless and antagonistic. Finally, 29-year-old Rose Schneiderman stepped up to the podium.

In a whisper barely audible, she began to address the crowd.

> I would be a traitor to these poor burned bodies, if I came here to talk good fellowship. We have tried you good people of the public and we have found you wanting. The old Inquisition had its rack and its thumbscrews and its instruments of torture with iron teeth. We know what these things are today: the iron teeth are our necessities, the thumbscrews the high-powered and swift machinery close to which we must work, and the rack is here in the fire-proof structures that will destroy us the minute they catch on fire.
>
> This is not the first time girls have burned alive in the city. Every week I must learn of the untimely death of one of my sister workers. Every year thousands of us are maimed. The life of men and women is so cheap and property is so sacred. There are so many of us for one job it matters little if 140-odd are burned to death.
>
> We have tried you, citizens; we are trying you now, and you have a couple of dollars for the sorrowing mothers and daughters and sisters by way of a charity gift. But every time the workers come out in the only way they know to protest against conditions which are unbearable, the strong hand of the law is allowed to press down heavily upon us.
>
> Public officials have only words of warning to us—warning that we must be intensely orderly and must be intensely peaceable, and they have the workhouse just back of all their warnings. The strong hand of the law beats us back when we rise into the conditions that make life bearable.
>
> I can't talk fellowship to you who are gathered here. Too much blood has been spilled. I know from my experience it is up to the working people to save themselves. The only way they can save themselves is by a strong working-class movement.

Her speech has become a classic. It is more than just an emotional picture of persecution; it reflects the pervasive sadness and profound understanding that comes from knowing, finally, the cruel realities of life, the perspective of history, and the nature of human beings.

The devastation of that fire and the futility of the seemingly successful strike that had preceded it seemed to impart an undeniable truth to Rose Schneiderman: They could not fail again. The events of 1911 seemed to have made her, and many others, more keenly aware than they had ever been that the workers' fight for reform was absolutely essential. If they did not do it, it would not be done.

In a sense, the fire touched off in Schneiderman an awareness of her own responsibility in the battle for industrial reform. This fiery socialist worker had been transformed into a highly effective labor leader.

The influential speech she gave did help swing public opinion to the side of the trade unions, and the fire itself had made the workers more aware of the crucial need to unionize. Widespread support for labor reform and unionization emerged. Pressure from individuals, such as Rose Schneiderman, as well as from groups like the Women's Trade Union League and the International Ladies' Garment Workers' Union, helped form the New York State Factory Investigating Commission, the New York Citizens' Committee on Safety, and other regulatory and investigatory bodies. The League and Local 25 (the Shirtwaist Makers' Union of the ILGWU) were especially instrumental in attaining a new Industrial Code for New York State, which became "the most outstanding instrument for safeguarding the lives, health, and welfare of the millions of wage earners in New York State and . . . in the nation at large."

It took years for these changes to occur, and labor reform did not rise majestically, Phoenix-like, from the ashes of the Triangle fire. But that fire, and Rose Schneiderman's whispered plea for a strong working-class movement, had indeed become the loud clear call for action.

DOCUMENTS

Tenement Cigarmakers, c. 1890

Take a row of houses in East Tenth Street. . . . They contained thirty-five families of cigarmakers, with probably not half a dozen persons in the whole lot of them, outside of the children, who could speak a word of English, though many had been in the country half a lifetime. This room with two windows giving on the street, and a rear attachment without windows, called a bedroom by courtesy, is rented at $12.25 a month. In the front room[,] man and wife work at the bench from six in the morning till nine at night. They make a team, stripping the tobacco leaves together; then he

SOURCE: Jacob Riis, *How the Other Half Lives* (New York: Scribner's, 1903), 103–108.

makes the filler, and she rolls the wrapper on and finishes the cigar. For a thousand they receive $3.75, and can turn out together three thousand cigars a week. The point has been reached where the rebellion comes in, and the workers in these tenements are just now on a strike, demanding $5.00 and $5.50 for their work. The manufacturer having refused, they are expecting hourly to be served with notice to quit their homes, and the going of a stranger among them excites their resentment, until his errand is explained. While we are in the house, the ultimatum of the "boss" is received. He will give $3.75 a thousand, not another cent. Our host is a man of seeming intelligence, yet he has been nine years in New York and knows neither English nor German. Three bright little children play about the floor.

His neighbor on the same floor has been here fifteen years, but shakes his head when asked if he can speak English. He answers in a few broken syllables when addressed in German. With $11.75 rent to pay for like accommodation, he has the advantage of his oldest boy's work besides his wife's at the bench. Three properly make a team, and these three can turn out four thousand cigars a week, at $3.75. This Bohemian has a large family; there are four children, too small to work, to be cared for. . . . [T]his Bohemian's butcher's bill for the week, with meat at twelve cents a pound . . . is from two dollars and a half to three dollars. . . . Here is a suite of three rooms, two dark, three flights up. The ceiling is partly down in one of the rooms. "It is three months since we asked the landlord to fix it," says the oldest son, a very intelligent lad who has learned English in the evening school. His father has not had that advantage, and has sat at his bench, deaf and dumb to the world about him except his own, for six years. He has improved his time and become an expert at his trade. Father, mother, and son together, a full team, make from fifteen to sixteen dollars a week. . . .

Probably more than half of all the Bohemians in this city are cigarmakers, and it is the herding of these in great numbers in the so-called tenement factories, where the cheapest grade of work is done at the lowest wages, that constitutes at once their greatest hardship and the chief grudge of other workmen against them. . . .

Men, women and children work together seven days in the week in these cheerless tenements to make a living for the family, from the break of day till far into the night. Often the wife is the original cigarmaker from the old home, the husband having adopted her trade here as a matter of necessity, because, knowing no word of English, he could get no other work. As they state the cause of the bitter hostility of the trades unions, she was the primary bone of contention in the day of the early Bohemian immigration. The unions refused to admit the women, and, as the support of the family depended upon her to a large extent, such terms as were offered had to be accepted. The manufacturer has ever since industriously fanned the antagonism between the unions and his hands, for his own advantage. The victory rests with him, since the Court of Appeals decided that the law, passed a few years ago, to prohibit cigarmaking in tenements was unconstitutional, and thus put an end to the struggle. While it lasted, all sorts of frightful stories were told of the shocking conditions under which people lived and worked in these tenements, from a sanitary point of view especially, and a general impression survives to this day that they are particularly desperate. The Board of Health, after a careful canvass, did not find them so then. I am satisfied from personal inspection, at a much later day, guided in a number of instances by the union cigarmakers themselves to the tenements which they considered the worst, that the accounts were greatly exaggerated. Doubtless the people are poor, in many cases very poor; but they are not uncleanly, rather the reverse; they live much better than the clothing-makers in the Tenth Ward, . . .

"Our Daily Life Is Not a Pleasant One," 1902

I am thirty-five years old, married, the father of four children, and have lived in the coal region all my life. Twenty-three of these years have been spent working in and around the mines. My father was a miner. He died ten years ago from "miners' asthma [black lung disease]."

Three of my brothers are miners; none of us had any opportunities to acquire an education. We were sent to school (such a school as there was in those days) until we were about twelve years of age, and then we were put into the screen room of a breaker to pick slate. From there we went inside the mines as driver boys. As we grew stronger we were taken on as laborers, where we served until able to call ourselves miners. We were given work in the breasts and gangways. There were five of us boys. One lies in the cemetery—fifty tons of top rock dropped on him. He was killed three weeks after he got his job as a miner—a month before he was to be married.

In the fifteen years I have worked as a miner I have earned the average rate of wages any of us coal heavers get. To-day I am little better off than when I started to do for myself. I have $100 on hand; I am not in debt; I hope to be able to weather the strike without going hungry.

I am only one of the hundreds you see on the street every day. The muscles on my arms are no harder, the callous on my palms no deeper than my neighbor's whose entire life has been spent in the coal region. By years I am only thirty-five. But look at the marks on my body; look at the lines of worriment on my forehead; see the gray hairs on my head and in my mustache; take my general appearance, and you'll think I'm ten years older.

SOURCE: *Independent* 54 (June 12, 1902): 1407–10.

You need not wonder why. Day in and day out, from Monday morning to Saturday evening, between the rising and the setting of the sun, I am in the underground workings of the coal mines. From the seams water trickles into the ditches along the gangways; if not water, it is the gas which hurls us to eternity and the props and timbers to a chaos.

Our daily life is not a pleasant one. When we put on our oil soaked suit in the morning we can't guess all the dangers which threaten our lives. We walk sometimes miles to the place—to the main way or traveling way, or to the mouth of the shaft on top of the slope. And then we enter the darkened chambers of the mines. On our right and on our left we see the logs that keep up the top and support the sides which may crush us into shapeless masses, as they have done to many of our comrades.

We get old quickly. Powder, smoke, after-damp, bad air—all combine to bring furrows to our faces and asthma to our lungs.

I did not strike because I wanted to; I struck because I had to. A miner—the same as any other workman—must earn fair living wages, or he can't live. And it is not how much you get that counts. It is how much what you get will buy. I have gone through it all, and I think my case is a good sample.

I was married in 1890, when I was 23 years old—quite a bit above the age when we miner boys get into double harness [married]. The woman I married is like myself. She was born beneath the shadow of a dirt bank; her chances for school weren't any better than mine; but she did have to learn how to keep house on a certain amount of money. After we paid the preacher for tying the knot we had just $185 in cash, good health and the good wishes of many friends to start us off.

Our cash was exhausted in buying furniture for housekeeping. In 1890 work was not so plentiful, and by the time our first baby came there was room for much doubt as to how we would pull out. Low wages, and not much over half time in those years, made us hustle. In 1890–91, from June to May, I earned $368.72. That represented eleven months' work, or an average of $33.52 per month. Our rent was $10 per month; store not less than $20. And then I had my oil suits and gum boots to pay for. The result was that after the first year and a half of our married life we were in debt. Not much, of course, and not as much as many of my neighbors, men of larger families, and some who made less money, or in whose case there had been sickness or accident or death. These are all things which a miner must provide for.

I have had fairly good work since I was married. I made the average of what we contract miners are paid; but, as I said before, I am not much better off than when I started.

In 1896 my wife was sick eleven weeks. The doctor came to my house almost every day. He charged me $20 for his services. There was medicine to buy. I paid the drug store $18 in that time. Her mother nursed her, and we kept a girl in the kitchen at $1.50 a week, which cost me $15 for ten weeks, besides the additional living expenses.

In 1897, just a year afterward, I had a severer trial. And mind, in those years, we were only working about half time. But in the fall of that year one of my brothers struck a gas feeder. There was a terrible explosion. He was hurled downward in the breast and covered with the rush of coal and rock. I was working only three breasts away from him and for a moment was unable to realize what had occurred. Myself and a hundred others were soon at work, however, and in a short while we found him, horribly burned over his whole body, his laborer dead alongside of him.

He was my brother. He was single and had been boarding. He had no home of his own. I didn't want him taken to the hospital, so I directed the driver of the ambulance to take him to my house. Besides being burned, his right arm and left leg were broken, and he was hurt internally. The doctors—there were two at the house when we got there—said he would die. But he didn't. He is living and a miner today. But he lay in bed just fourteen weeks, and was unable to work for seven weeks after he got out of bed. He had no money when he was hurt except the amount represented by his pay. All of the expenses for doctors, medicine, extra help and his living were borne by me, except $25, which another brother gave me. The last one had none to give. Poor work, low wages and a sickly woman for a wife had kept him scratching for his own family.

It is nonsense to say I was not compelled to keep him, that I could have sent him to a hospital or the almshouse. We are American citizens and we don't go to hospitals and poorhouses. . . .

An Italian Bootblack's Story, 1902

We came to Brooklyn to a wooden house in Adams Street that was full of Italians from Naples. [A man named] Bartolo had a room on the third floor and there were fifteen men in the room, all boarding with Bartolo. He did the cooking on a stove in the middle of the room and there were beds all around the sides, one bed above another. It was very hot in the room, but we were soon asleep, for we were very tired.

The next morning, early, Bartolo told us to go out and pick rags and get bottles. He gave us bags and hooks and showed us the ash barrels. On the streets where the fine houses are the people are very careless and put out good things, like mattresses and umbrellas, clothes, hats and boots. We brought all these to Bartolo and he made them new again and sold them on the sidewalk; but mostly we brought rags and bones. The rags we had to wash in the backyard and then we hung them to dry on lines under the

SOURCE: *Independent* 54 (December 4, 1902): 2865–67.

ceiling in our room. The bones we kept under the beds till Bartolo could find a man to buy them.

Most of the men in our room worked at digging the sewer. Bartolo got them the work and they paid him about one quarter of their wages. Then he charged them for board and he bought the clothes for them, too. So they got little money after all.

Bartolo was always saying that the rent of the room was so high that he could not make anything, but he was really making plenty. He was what they call a padrone* and is now a very rich man. The men that were living with him had just come to the country and could not speak English. They had all been sent by the young man we met in Italy. Bartolo told us all that we must work for him and that if we did not the police would come and put us in prison.

He gave us very little money, and our clothes were some of those that were found on the street. Still we had enough to eat and we had meat quite often, which we never had in Italy. Bartolo got it from the butcher—the meat that he could not sell to other people—but it was quite good meat. Bartolo cooked it in the pan while we all sat on our beds in the evening. Then he cut it into small bits and passed the pan around, saying:

"See what I do for you and yet you are not glad. I am too kind a man, that is why I am so poor."

We were with Bartolo nearly a year, but some of our countrymen who had been in the place a long time said that Bartolo had no right to us and we could get work for a dollar and a half a day, which, when you make it *lire* (reckoned in the Italian currency) is very much. So we went away one day to Newark and got work on the street. Bartolo came after us and made a great noise, but the boss said that if he did not go away soon the police would have him. Then he went, saying that there was no justice in this country.

We paid a man five dollars each for getting us the work and we were with that boss for six months. He was Irish, but a good man and he gave us our money every Saturday night. We lived much better than with Bartolo, and when the work was done we each had nearly $200 saved. Plenty of the men spoke English and they taught us, and we taught them to read and write. That was at night, for we had a lamp in our room, and there were only five other men who lived in that room with us.

We got up at half-past five o'clock every morning and made coffee on the stove and had a breakfast of bread and cheese, onions, garlic and red herrings. We went to work at seven o'clock and in the middle of the day we had soup and bread in a place where we got it for two cents a plate. In the evenings we had a good dinner with meat of some kind and potatoes. We

*A padrone is a labor boss who secured employment for immigrants. (Eds.)

got from the butcher the meat that other people would not buy because they said it was old, but they don't know what is good. We paid four or five cents a pound for it and it was the best, tho I have heard of people paying sixteen cents a pound.

When the Newark boss told us that there was no more work Francisco and I talked about what we would do and we went back to Brooklyn to a saloon near Hamilton Ferry, where we got a job cleaning it out and slept in a little room upstairs. There was a bootblack named Michael on the corner and when I had time I helped him and learned the business. Francisco cooked the lunch in the saloon and he, too, worked for the bootblack and we were soon able to make the best polish.

Then we thought we would go into business and we got a basement on Hamilton Avenue, near the Ferry, and put four chairs in it. We paid $75 for the chairs and all the other things. We had tables and looking glasses there and curtains. We took the papers that have the pictures in and made the place high toned. Outside we had a big sign that said:

THE BEST SHINE FOR TEN CENTS

Men that did not want to pay ten cents could get a good shine for five cents, but it was not an oil shine. We had two boys helping us and paid each of them fifty cents a day. The rent of the place was $20 a month, so the expenses were very great, but we made money from the beginning. We slept in the basement, but got our meals in the saloon till we could put a stove in our place, and then Francisco cooked for us all. That would not do, tho, because some of our customers said that they did not like to smell garlic and onions and red herrings. I thought that was strange, but we had to do what the customers said. So we got the woman who lived upstairs to give us our meals and paid her $1.50 a week each. She gave the boys soup in the middle of the day—five cents for two plates. . . .

We had said that when we saved $1,000 each we would go back to Italy and buy a farm, but now that the time is coming we are so busy and making so much money that we think we will stay. We have opened another parlor near South Ferry, in New York. We have to pay $30 a month rent, but the business is very good. The boys in the place charge sixty cents a day because there is so much work.

Chapter 6

The Triumph of Racism

New Orleans street scene, circa 1895.

In the decades following the Civil War, while the northern and western states turned to industrialization with the aid of immigrant laborers, the South remained largely agricultural. Some white Southerners, like Henry Grady of the *Atlanta Constitution,* urged the former Confederate states to follow the example of the rest of the nation and build cities, factories, and railroads. Indeed, the South did experience a modicum of industrial and urban growth before World War I. But the region still lagged behind the rapid pace of change elsewhere in the United States.

In another way, too, the white South continued to look to the past. Once Congress admitted the ex-Confederate states back into the union and federal troops had withdrawn from the South, white Southerners were free to pursue a system of race relations more to their taste than that imposed by Radical Republicans during the Reconstruction era (1865–1876). This system stipulated that blacks be segregated in most areas of public life, be denied the right to vote, and generally be limited to working as landless farmers.

In his essay on the Supreme Court's *Plessy* v. *Ferguson* decision (1896), Keith Weldon Medley points out that among the Southern states, postwar Louisiana offered the brightest hope for easing racial inequality. African Americans participated in politics and benefited from the integration of many public facilities for a number of years after the removal of federal troops. But soon the rising tide of white racism destroyed their dreams; as in other states around the turn of the century, Louisiana ultimately established a rigid system of white supremacy.

It was one thing for white legislators to enact measures to disfranchise and segregate African Americans; it was another for these laws to receive the sanction of the United States Supreme Court. After all, the Fourteenth and Fifteenth Amendments to the Constitution seem to preclude such legislation. Medley's essay centers on the case of Homer Plessy's challenge to Louisiana's separate coach law. How did the Supreme Court manage to conclude that segregation did not violate the Fourteenth Amendment, which supposedly guarantees equal protection of the law? What implications did the Plessy decision hold for racial segregation in other areas of southern life?

Segregation was only one of the injustices suffered by African Americans in the age of Jim Crow. From the 1880s until World War I, there were approximately 100 lynchings yearly, mostly of blacks and mostly in the South. Not all mob executions were lynchings; some blacks were burned to death—this witnessed by hundreds of spectators who were known to fight over bones to take home as souvenirs. Only a small number of these acts of violence involved allegations of black men raping white women. In most cases, the mere accusation of rape was sufficient to trigger the gathering of a mob. The first document presents Senator Benjamin Tillman's defense of such acts of terror in an address on the floor of the United States Congress. On what grounds did he argue that lynching was justified?

Faced with the triumph of racism at the turn of the century, blacks protested through organizations such as the National Association for the Advancement of Colored People (NAACP). In the second document, W.E.B. Du Bois, a founder of the NAACP, issues a call for equality. In view of the conditions portrayed in the essay and Senator Tillman's racial outbursts, do you think that there was any real possibility for the realization of Du Bois's program in the first decade of the twentieth century?

While black leaders and intellectuals debated future programs and strategies, many Southern blacks took matters into their own hands and headed north. The third document is a letter from a black Mississippi mechanic to the *Chicago Defender,* an influential black newspaper. The letter reflects the determination of African Americans to find a better life in the North, the reluctance of Southern whites to let them leave, and the key role that the Defender played in encouraging northward migration.

ESSAY

The Birth of "Separate but Equal"

Keith Weldon Medley

> On Tuesday evening, a Negro named [Homer] Plessy was
> arrested by Private Detective Cain on the East Louisiana
> train and locked up for violating Section 2 of Act 111 of
> 1890, relative to separate coaches. . . . He waived examina-
> tion yesterday before Recorder Monlin and was sent before
> the criminal court under $500 bond.

This modest announcement appeared in the New Orleans *Daily Picayune* on
June 9, 1892. Little noticed at the time, it recorded a moment of tragic significance for the people of America. For it marked not only the end of an era
that had begun with Reconstruction, but the start of a half-century in which
the rights and hopes of black people in the South, briefly raised up by Reconstruction, were all but extinguished.

In time it would make famous the names of a New Orleans shoemaker
and a judge from Massachusetts, as the joint label on the landmark Supreme
Court decision *Plessy* v. *Ferguson.* The issue was apparently resolved by the
Court in 1896. But the running racial and judicial struggle involved did not
have its most dramatic climax until a half-century later, with the decision
known as *Brown* v. *Board of Education.*

Confrontation over a place in a public conveyance suggests a parallel
with Rosa Parks. But her refusal to give up her bus seat to a white passenger
in Montgomery, Alabama, was partly triggered by happenstance. Plessy's
action on that warm New Orleans afternoon a century ago was an act of
civil disobedience carefully planned and orchestrated by a group of black
Republicans, lawyers and journalists known in the French-speaking areas of
New Orleans as the Comité des Citoyens.

The story of their case and of their calculated yet desperate judicial fight
is rooted not merely in the history of what happened in the South after the
Civil War, but in the texture of life in New Orleans itself. Even before the
Civil War, New Orleans had been a rich, cosmopolitan trading port and a
place where people of color had accomplished a great deal.

Originally French, then Spanish, then French again before being bought
by Thomas Jefferson in 1803 (along with what would become half of the
United States), it was a city with a remarkable mix of colors and cultures, as
well as a penchant for violence and vice. On the eve of the war in 1860, the

population was pushing 170,000, including 25,000 Irish and 20,000 German immigrants, and 15,000 African-American slaves about to be freed. But New Orleans also had a greater concentration of free people of color than any other city in the Deep South, some 10,000 people who had gained their freedom well before the Civil War began.

Homer Plessy was born free in March 1862, only a month before Yankee gunboats overran the city's Mississippi River defenses, taking control of the port while the war lasted. Like Plessy's family, many black New Orleanians were French-speaking and Roman Catholic. Some had come from Haiti to escape the bloody revolution at the beginning of the 19th century, when Haitians won their independence from France. Some had fought in 1815 with Andrew Jackson against the British in the Battle of New Orleans. The majority were working class, but many were landowners, businessmen, skilled artisans.

Full Inheritances and Paternal Surnames

Though interracial marriage had been officially banned and streetcars segregated, the city had fewer social restrictions about intermingling between whites and blacks than other areas in the South. Many de facto marriages between the races lasted a lifetime; the children produced often received full inheritances and paternal surnames. Some were sent to Europe for their education. Some became rich and prominent citizens.

So hopes ran high on June 11, 1864, as thousands joyfully gathered in Congo Square, the site of weekend slave gatherings, to celebrate a great event: on May 9 of that year, Louisiana had approved an emancipation ordinance. Ratification of the 13th Amendment to the Constitution would come in 1865, followed by the 14th in 1868, which said that if you were born in the United States you were a citizen, and that no state could deprive you of your rights, liberty or property without due process of law. By 1870 the 15th Amendment made clear that no citizen could be deprived of the right to vote on the basis of race, color or previous condition of servitude.

In 1867 New Orleans removed the black stars previously used to designate the city's segregated streetcars. That was the year of the Reconstruction Act, passed by still-powerful Radical Republicans in Washington, which sent U.S. armies of occupation into the South and gave military commanders in five areas there the right to protect life and property with federal force. They set up a procedure to register voters and see that lately freed slaves were allowed to vote, held elections, established black schools, and created machinery whereby Southern states were to ratify the 14th Amendment. In New Orleans and all over the South, Army commanders had the power to appoint and dismiss local officials.

By 1869 when Homer Plessy was 7, New Orleans began experimenting with integrated public schools—the only Southern city to do so. Blacks served with whites on juries and public boards. New Orleans had an integrated police department with a color-blind municipal pay scale. Thanks to Reconstruction, too, Plessy grew to manhood while blacks, who made up most of the Republican Party in the South, voted enthusiastically in large numbers and served in high office. Between the years 1868 and 1896, racial intermarriage was made legal, and Louisiana elected 32 black state senators and 95 state representatives. It had the only black governor in U.S. history before the late 1980s. (In the same period the South as a whole voted 600 black state representatives into office and sent 16 black congressmen to Washington.)

Apparently Plessy left no papers. City records, however, tell a good deal about him and about the racially mixed, middle-class faubourg, or suburb, where he lived. He began making shoes in 1879, married Louise Bordenave in 1888 and attended Mass at St. Augustine's Catholic Church on St. Claude Street. The church had been established by whites and free people of color before the war; services were conducted in French and Latin. The newlyweds could afford to rent a house near the corner of Ursulines Street on North Claiborne Avenue in the Faubourg Tremé.

Outside the Plessys' bedroom window was Congregation Hall, home of Saturday night "grand dancing festivals" where, for 15 cents, New Orleanians swayed to the sounds of Professor Moret's String Band. By the 1890s, Tremé had become an integrated enclave of several races, numbering among its residents many musicians and artists, who tended to be radical and egalitarian. There were also a number of dramatic clubs and benevolent religious societies that would contribute heavily to the Comité des Citoyens, among them the Société des Francs Amis (Homer Plessy became its vice president), which provided medical and funeral expenses for dues-paying members.

Following the Civil War, the full-scale occupation of the South as a defeated nation, along with Reconstruction programs, cost the American taxpayers considerable money, not including the pay and maintenance of the 6,000-odd federal soldiers. Yet for years the Republican Party, dominated by former abolitionists, maintained the political power and the will necessary to try remaking the former Confederate States.

There was no swift and easy way, however, for four million ex-slaves, just freed and without education, to be integrated into a racist, bitterly defeated and economically collapsing South. Race hatred, intimidation and riots flared. The Ku Klux Klan spread pamphlets and terror, which eventually included the murder of influential Reconstruction figures both black and white. It also embarked on the systematic intimidation of newly enfranchised black voters. The power of the Republican Party in Southern states, overwhelmingly based on those same black voters, began to wane, and Southern Democrats started to take back the South. The power of Republicans in Washington, especially after the Recession of 1873, was vulnerable to Democrats who could claim that Reconstruction cost money and had no hope of success.

In the North there had been optimistic expectations for economic recovery in a free-labor South and for the immediate effects of black suffrage. "We need no vast expenditures. We need no standing army," Senator Richard Yates, a Radical Republican, had once declared. "The ballot will finish the Negro question." By the early 1870s that was clearly not so, and just as clear was the fact that many states in the North and West, which as late as 1868 did not permit black suffrage or integration, would not long concern themselves with the rights of blacks in the South. After the ratification of the 15th Amendment, an Illinois newspaper expressed a prevalent Northern view: "The Negro is now a voter and a citizen. Let him hereafter take his chances in the battle of life."

The specific political event that brought an end to Reconstruction and the withdrawal of occupation troops from the South was the Presidential election of 1876. Republicans had dominated national politics since Lincoln. But in 1876 neither Republican Rutherford B. Hayes nor Democrat Samuel J. Tilden got enough undisputed electoral votes to win. A deal was made, known as the Hayes-Tilden Compromise. Hayes would become President by being ceded the electoral votes of a number of Southern states in return for recalling the armies of occupation (they departed in 1877) and yielding to Democrats the control of the last three Southern states—including Louisiana—still run by the Republican Party. For their part, Southern Democratic leaders in those states agreed to maintain civil rights policies.

Among them was Louisiana's Democratic gubernatorial candidate Francis T. Nicholls, an ex-Confederate general who lost an arm and a leg in the Civil War. Nicholls swore to uphold "equal rights and common interests" and to "obliterate the color line in politics." For a while he kept his word. But without the Reconstruction programs and the bayonets of the armies to support them, lately freed blacks were at a hopeless disadvantage. All over the South, the advances made in the 1870s began to be undone. The pace accelerated in 1883 when the Supreme Court, which was also changing its makeup, declared the civil rights enforcement act of 1875 unconstitutional. This meant that the federal government, lacking the means and will, pretty well got out of the business of making sure that the new civil rights laws were applied in the South.

The erosion of civil rights went more slowly in New Orleans than elsewhere. But the city began reestablishing segregated schools, and in 1890 Nicholls approved the Louisiana Legislature's passage of the Separate Car Act.

The act decreed "equal but separate accommodations for the white and colored races" on Louisiana railway cars. Under its terms any railway company that did not provide separate coaches for blacks and whites could be fined $500. Except for "nurses attending children of the other race," individual whites and blacks would be forbidden to ride together, or risk a $25 fine or 20 days in jail. It was the passage of this bill that finally launched Homer

Plessy into history. The fight involved a black newspaper, *The Crusader*, the six remaining black state senators and ultimately the Comité des Citoyens, which coalesced around *The Crusader*.

At the State Capitol, Senator Henry Demas thundered at his fellow legislators: "Like the Jews, we have been driven from our houses and firesides, from our churches and schoolhouses . . . and from the elevated avenues of livelihood, and now, in order to reach the lowest depth of infamy . . . you are willing to forget that you are men and vote for the passage of this bill." But the Separate Car Act passed the Louisiana Senate by a vote of 23 to 6.

The Crusader was a formidable enemy. A weekly founded in 1889 by attorney Louis Martinet to combat the increasingly virulent racism of other New Orleans papers, it called itself "spicy, progressive, liberal, stalwart, fearless," and stood for "A Free Vote and Fair Count, Free Schools, Fair Wages, Justice and Equal Rights." It cost a nickel and carried classified ads for everything from pianos, sails, cotton scales and first communion wreaths to ointments that claimed to "relax"—straighten—the hair. *The Crusader's* star contributor was Rodolphe Desdunes. The son of a Cuban mother and a Haitian father, Desdunes worked as a customs agent by day and, with smoking pen, scribbled polemical columns by night. Hundreds of his articles, still preserved in the archives of Xavier University in New Orleans, offer a window into the desperate fight to keep civil rights from slipping away.

"Colored people have largely patronized the railroads heretofore," Desdunes wrote on July 19, 1890. "They can withdraw the patronage from these corporations and travel only by necessity." He proposed a boycott not unlike the one launched in Montgomery, Alabama, 70 years later.

The 1890s were not a good time to exercise civil disobedience in the American South, or to get on the wrong side of a mob, whether you were black or not. The year 1892 alone produced 226 mob murders, mostly of black men, the highest number in the recorded history of lynchings. In New Orleans, on March 14, 1891, a newspaper editor and a prominent attorney led a crowd of several thousand to Parish Prison. Angry over the acquittal of Italian immigrants accused of the killing of police chief David Hennessy, they broke in, hunted down a group of 11 Italians, shot them, then hanged some from streetlamps and shot them again. Mournfully reflecting on the mood in New Orleans, a black woman told a reporter: "Thank God it wasn't a nigger who killed the Chief."

To combat what became known as the "Jim Crow car law," *The Crusader* and the Comité des Citoyens acquired a small but influential membership. It involved C. C. Antoine, a former officer in the Union Army, who had served four years (1873–77) as Louisiana's lieutenant governor, and wealthy philanthropist Aristide Mary, who had financed lawsuits against other re-segregated establishments.

The Comité also included sail manufacturer Arthur Estéves, who became its president. To fight the Jim Crow car law, it was prepared to solicit funds not only from benevolent, social and religious societies in town but from former abolitionists in such faraway cities as Washington, D.C., Chicago and San Francisco. About $3,000 was quickly raised to launch two test cases: one to challenge legal segregation of trains on interstate routes and one to challenge segregation on conveyances within the state. The aim: to "seek redemption" from the Supreme Court of the United States. "We find this the only means left us," a Comité statement concluded. "We must have recourse to it, or sink into a state of helpless inferiority."

It was a forlorn hope, but not as forlorn as it would become in the slow process of going through the legal system. For one thing, on the face of it, if you gave any thought to the intent of the men who wrote the 14th Amendment, the Separate Car Act seemed a clear violation of the constitutional rights of the black citizens of Louisiana. But public opinion in the North had changed rapidly, and so, in the years after 1877, had the makeup of the Supreme Court, which lost its reasonable mix of justices sympathetic to the subject of civil rights.

Some railroad companies initially had been against the bill. It was going to cost money to build and run extra cars—for the bill implied that if a half empty "white" car was waiting, and even if only one black passenger showed up, he or she would have to have a whole separate-but-equal vehicle made available. In a city that had for so long seen so much racial mixing, railway conductors would now have to decide who was white and who was black—a touchy business, especially since some wives and husbands would not be allowed to ride together.

One of the reasons that Homer Plessy was picked for the job was that he had fair skin. Had it been left to chance, he probably could have ridden the train in the "whites only" section unnoticed. But by prearrangement between the Comité and the East Louisiana Railroad, everything was ready for him when he came.

On June 7, 1892, Plessy strolled to the Press Street depot, which included a restaurant and a combination waiting room and ticket office (both still open to him), bought a first-class ticket and, ignoring the new "Colored Only" sign, sat down in the coach reserved for whites. It was to depart at 4:15 P.M., cross a bridge spanning Lake Pontchartrain and pass through Abita Springs for a two-hour run to Covington.

Hardly had the train started moving when conductor J. J. Dowling approached Plessy. "Are you a colored man?" he asked. "Yes," answered Plessy. "Then you will have to retire to the colored car," said Dowling. Plessy stated that he had paid for his ticket and intended to ride to Covington. Dowling signaled the engineer to stop. A private detective, Captain Chris Cain, hired by the Comité, came aboard and warned Plessy: "If you are colored you should go into the car set apart for your race. The law is plain and must be obeyed."

When Plessy again refused, he was taken a half-mile down to Elysian Fields Avenue for booking at the Fifth Precinct Station. Members of the Comité met him, and a judge released him on temporary bail. The next day a story in a New Orleans daily described Plessy as a "snuff-colored descendant of Ham." After a hearing, Comité member Paul Bonseigneur plunked down a $500 bond (raised by putting his own house in hock) to guarantee Plessy's appearance for trial. Plessy was 30 years old. The future of constitutional rights for blacks in America would ride on his day in court.

Enter John Howard Ferguson, 54, the judge whose name would forever be linked to Plessy's in American history. The lawyer son of a shipowner on the island of Martha's Vineyard, Massachusetts, Ferguson had come South after hearing of opportunities there from returning Civil War soldiers. He was what Southerners called a carpetbagger—meaning anybody who came South after the fighting to administer the remade South or to look for profit in the South's adversity. He married the daughter of a prominent local attorney, a Louisiana Unionist noted for his condemnations of slavery, and began practicing law. Ferguson served in Governor Nicholls' 1876 Legislature. Eventually he campaigned for Murphy Foster, the man who replaced Nicholls as governor and engineered passage of the Separate Car Act. Ferguson was made a judge and assigned the Plessy case a month after Plessy's arrest.

But only a short time after becoming a judge, in another Comité-generated case, he ruled that the Separate Car Act was unconstitutional on trains that traveled through several states—because of the federal government's predominant interest in interstate commerce. The Comité celebrated the decision, and Louis Martinet chortled in print: "Jim Crow is dead as a doornail."

He was wrong. At Plessy's arraignment, *Homer Adolph Plessy* v. *The State of Louisiana*, one of Plessy's lawyers, James Walker, argued that neither the state nor any railroad conductor representing it had the right to deny Plessy's liberty on the basis of race, since Plessy was a citizen, and the 14th Amendment clearly said that "no state shall make or enforce any law which shall abridge the privileges or immunities of any citizen of the United States." Judge Ferguson did not agree. The state, he claimed, had a legal right to regulate railroad companies operating solely within the state. Plessy had not been deprived of his liberty. "He was simply deprived of the liberty of doing as he pleased, and of violating a penal statute with impunity."

A swift appeal was presented to the State Supreme Court, which instantly agreed with Ferguson's decision. The 14th Amendment guaranteed black individuals "equality" but did not guarantee "identity or community" with white society. The glum Comité now could look only northward to the

Supreme Court of the United States in Washington. As time passed, Plessy's prospects grew worse.

In the decade leading up to 1896, when the case at last was argued before the Court, seven Justices had been replaced—mostly by men who shared the increasingly prevalent belief that Reconstruction had largely failed and that blacks must fend for themselves. The only holdovers from Reconstruction times were John Marshall Harlan of Kentucky, a Hayes appointee, and the aging Stephen J. Field, who had been appointed in 1863 by Lincoln.

Attorney Albion Tourgée, who eventually argued the case for the Comité, estimated that only one Justice would firmly lean to Plessy's side, three would be uncertain and five, frankly opposed. In a letter to Louis Martinet he added a foreboding postscript: "It is of the utmost importance that we should not have a decision *against* us as the court has *never* reversed itself on a constitutional question."

Tourgée was not the only one to notice the changing temper of the Supreme Court. In 1894 Louisiana again placed racial restrictions on marriage and prohibited citizens of opposite races from using the same railroad depot waiting rooms.

The Comité's chances dwindled as the climate of opinion changed, even among people of color. Voices in some quarters argued that resisting white supremacy always evoked harsher responses, and that the struggle for decent conditions was what mattered most, not integration. In 1895 Booker T. Washington, head of Tuskegee Institute, publicly called for accommodation with segregation. Washington argued that in the face of white hatred, integration simply stirred up opposition. The main thing was to concentrate on making segregated schools work, on learning trades and on getting ahead in life.

But the Comité had pledged to see the case to the end. By late fall 1895 everything was in place. Albion Tourgée, with lawyers S. F. Phillips and F. D. McKenny, had filed final papers for the October 1895 term in *Homer A. Plessy* v. *J. H. Ferguson.* Tourgée went before the Supreme Court in April 1896. State arguments were made by Louisiana's Attorney General M. J. Cunningham and lawyers Lionel Adams and Alexander Porter Morse.

On May 18 the Court issued a ruling. With only one dissent it granted states the right to forcibly segregate people of different races. Writing for the majority, Justice Henry Billings Brown, appointed by Benjamin Harrison, dismissed Plessy's 14th Amendment claims and, as precedent, pointed to the existence of separate schools in the District of Columbia and the long-standing bans on interracial marriage. The only test of such segregation, he said, would be whether or not the regulations were reasonable. The Court also stated that "legislation is powerless to eradicate racial instincts or to abolish distinctions based upon physical differences." As for determining who was black or white, that was left to the discretion of each state.

The lone dissenter was Justice John Marshall Harlan. "The destinies of two races in this country," Harlan wrote, "are indissolubly linked together, and the interests of both require that the common government of all shall not permit the seeds of race hate to be planted under the sanction of law. . . . The thin disguise of 'equal' accommodations for passengers in railroad coaches will not mislead anyone, nor atone for the wrong this day done."

The decision was remanded to the Supreme Court of Louisiana on September 28, 1896. The Comité issued a final statement: "In passing laws which discriminate between its citizens," it declared, "the State was wrong. . . . Notwithstanding this decision . . . we, as freemen, still believe that we were right, and our cause is sacred."

On January 11, 1897, Homer Plessy returned to court for sentencing. By then, times had changed dramatically. The Comité had disbanded; *The Crusader* had ceased publication. All over the South, white supremacists were firmly in control of the Legislatures. Judge Ferguson had stepped down in 1896, and Judge Joshua Baker was presiding. Plessy changed his plea to guilty, paid a $25 fine and walked out into the brave new world of a segregated Louisiana.

Those in the black community who thought racial separation would bring peace were in for a rude awakening. Emboldened by the Supreme Court's Plessy decision, in February 1898 Louisiana called a constitutional convention in New Orleans to lay down a blueprint for white supremacy. Endorsed by Governor Foster, the delegates made it illegal to run an integrated school, allocated state money as a "pension fund" for the relatives of Confederate soldiers, declared the Louisiana Democratic Party a "whites only" organization and used various devices, such as the "grandfather clause," to keep blacks and immigrants from voting. "Our mission was to establish the supremacy of the white race," the chairman of the judiciary committee bluntly declared. In the four years from 1896 to 1900, more than 120,000 black voters were removed from the rolls, their numbers dropping from 45 percent to 4 percent of eligible voters. By 1900 Louisiana did not have a single black representative in its Legislature. There would be none until 1967.

While legislation made things "separate," the "equal" treatment of the Supreme Court ruling seldom materialized. The greatest disaster would come in education. The South spent very little money on black schools. In New Orleans, the city school board did not open a public high school for blacks until 1917. Even then, black teachers were paid less than their white counterparts, and their pupils received second-hand books and supplies.

One by one the civil rights gains of Reconstruction vanished. So too did the principals in the *Plessy* v. *Ferguson* case. Judge Ferguson died in 1915 at age 77. In a front-page story, the *Times-Picayune* lauded him as one who "allied himself with the Democratic reform element" and "took part in the struggle for white supremacy." He was buried in the Lafayette Cemetery on Washington Avenue. In August 1925, some 50,000 white-robed members of the Ku Klux Klan marched in Washington, D.C.

Homer Plessy had died a few months earlier that year. His obituary in the *Times-Picayune* was simple: "PLESSY—on Sunday, March 1, 1925, at 5:10 A.M., Homer A. Plessy, 63 years, beloved husband of Louise Bordenave." On the front page of the same paper was the headline "Supreme Court Puts Approval on Segregation," referring to a Louisiana Supreme Court ruling that upheld a segregated housing ordinance in New Orleans. Plessy lies with his mother's family in St. Louis Cemetery No. 1, a 200-year-old integrated Catholic graveyard in the Tremé area. Fifteen years after his death there were only 886 registered black voters in the state of Louisiana.

Nearly 15 more years would pass before NAACP attorney Thurgood Marshall obtained a rehearing of Plessy's cause in another landmark case, *Brown* v. *Board of Education*. In that instance, the Court overturned the 1896 ruling and declared "separate but equal" to be unconstitutional. That time, Homer Plessy won.

DOCUMENTS

A United States Senator Defends Lynching, 1907

Mr. President, the Senator from Wisconsin speaks of "lynching bees." As far as lynching for rape is concerned, the word is a misnomer. When stern and sad-faced white men put to death a creature in human form who has deflowered a white woman, there is nothing of the "bee" about it. There is more of the feeling of participating as mourner at a funeral. They have avenged the greatest wrong, the blackest crime in all the category of crimes, and they have done it, not so much as an act of retribution in behalf of the victim as a duty and as a warning as to what any man may expect who shall repeat the offense. They are looking to the protection of their own loved ones. . . .

Now let me suppose a case. Let us take any Senator on this floor—I will not particularize—take him from some great and well-ordered State in the North, where there are possibly twenty thousand negroes, as there

SOURCE: *The Congressional Record*, Senate, 59th Cong., 2nd sess., 1907. Document from Bibliobase®, edited by Michael Bellesiles. Copyright © Houghton Mifflin Company. Reprinted by permission.

are in Wisconsin, with over two million whites. Let us carry this Senator to the backwoods in South Carolina, put him on a farm miles from a town or railroad, and environed with negroes. We will suppose he has a fair young daughter just budding into womanhood: and recollect this, the white women of the South are in a state of siege; the greatest care is exercised that they shall at all times where it is possible not be left alone or unprotected, but that can not always and in every instance be the case. That Senator's daughter undertakes to visit a neighbor or is left home alone for a brief while. Some lurking demon who has watched for the opportunity seizes her: she is choked or beaten into insensibility and ravished, her body prostituted, her purity destroyed, her chastity taken from her, and a memory branded on her brain as with a red-hot iron to haunt her night and day as long as she lives. Moore has drawn us the picture in most graphic language:

> One fatal remembrance, one sorrow that throws
> Its bleak shade alike o'er our joys and our woes,
> To which life nothing darker or brighter can bring,
> For which joy hath no balm and affliction no sting.

In other words, a death in life. This young girl thus blighted and brutalized drags herself to her father and tells him what has happened. Is there a man here with red blood in his veins who doubts what impulses the father would feel? Is it any wonder that the whole countryside rises as one man and with set, stern faces seek the brute who has wrought this infamy? Brute, did I say? Why, Mr. President, this crime is a slander on the brutes. No beast of the field forces his female. He waits invitation. It has been left for something in the shape of a man to do this terrible thing. And shall such a creature, because he has the semblance of a man, appeal to the law? Shall men coldbloodedly stand up and demand for him the right to have a fair trial and be punished in the regular course of justice? So far as I am concerned he has put himself outside the pale of the law, human and divine. He has sinned against the Holy Ghost. He has invaded the holy of holies. He has struck civilization a blow, the most deadly and cruel that the imagination can conceive. It is idle to reason about it; it is idle to preach about it. Our brains reel under the staggering blow and hot blood surges to the heart. Civilization peels off us, any and all of us who are men, and we revert to the original savage type whose impulses under any and all such circumstances has always been to "kill! kill! kill!"

I do not know what the Senator from Wisconsin would do under these circumstances; neither do I care. I have three daughters, but, so help me God, I had rather find either one of them killed by a tiger or a bear and gather up her bones and bury them, conscious that she had died in the purity of her maidenhood, than have her crawl to me and tell me the horrid story that she had been robbed of the jewel of her womanhood by a black fiend.

106

A Call for Equality, 1905

. . . We believe that [Negro] American citizens should protest emphatically and continually against the curtailment of their political rights. We believe in manhood suffrage: we believe that no man is so good, intelligent or wealthy as to be entrusted wholly with the welfare of his neighbor.

We believe also in protest against the curtailment of our civil rights. All American citizens have the right to equal treatment in places of public entertainment according to their behavior and deserts.

We especially complain against the denial of equal opportunities to us in economic life; in the rural districts of the south this amounts to peonage and virtual slavery; all over the south it tends to crush labor and small business enterprises: and everywhere American prejudice, helped often by iniquitous laws is making it more difficult for Negro-Americans to earn a decent living.

Common school education should be free to all American children and compulsory. High school training should be adequately provided for all, and college training should be the monopoly of no class or race in any section of our common country. We believe that in defense of its own institutions, the United States should aid common school education, particularly in the south, and we especially recommend concerted agitation to this end. We urge an increase in public high school facilities in the south, where the Negro-Americans are almost wholly without such provisions. We favor well-equipped trade and technical schools for the training of artisans, and the need of adequate and liberal endowment for a few institutions of higher education must be patent to sincere well-wishers of the race.

We demand upright judges in courts, juries selected without discrimination on account of color and the same measure of punishment, and the same efforts at reformation for black as for white offenders. We need orphanages and farm schools for dependent children, juvenile reformatories for delinquents, and the abolition of the dehumanizing convict-lease system. . . .

We hold up for public execration the conduct of two opposite classes of men; the practice among employers of importing ignorant Negro-American laborers in emergencies, and then affording them neither protection nor permanent employment; and the practice of labor unions of proscribing and boycotting and oppressing thousands of their fellow-toilers, simply because they are black. These methods have accentuated and will accentuate the war of labor and capital, and they are disgraceful to both sides. . . .

We regret that this nation has never seen fit adequately to reward the black soldiers who in its five wars, have defended their country with their

SOURCE: W.E.B. Du Bois, *Cleveland Gazette,* July 22, 1905.

blood, and yet have been systematically denied the promotions which their abilities deserve. And we regard as unjust, the exclusion of black boys from the military and navy training schools. . . .

The Negro race in America, stolen, ravished and degraded, struggling up through difficulties and oppression, needs sympathy and receives criticism; needs help and is given hindrance, needs protection and is given mob violence, needs justice and is given charity, needs leadership and is given cowardice and apology, needs bread and is given a stone. This nation will never stand justified before God until these things are changed.

Especially are we surprised and astonished at the recent attitude of the church of Christ—on the increase of a desire to bow to racial prejudice, to narrow the bounds of human brotherhood, and to segregate black men in some outer sanctuary. This is wrong, unchristian and disgraceful to twentieth century civilization. . . .

And while we are demanding, and ought to demand, and will continue to demand the rights enumerated above, God forbid that we should ever forget to urge corresponding duties upon our people.

> The duty to vote.
> The duty to respect the rights of others.
> The duty to work.
> The duty to obey the laws.
> The duty to be clean and orderly.
> The duty to send our children to school,
> The duty to respect ourselves, even as we respect others. . . .

"I Want to Come North," 1917

GRANVILLE, MISSISSIPPI, MAY 16, 1917

Dear Sir [editor of the *Defender*]: This letter is a letter of information of which you will find stamp envelop for reply. I want to come north some time soon but I do not want to leve here looking for a job where I would be in dorse all winter. Now the work I am doing here is running a guage edger in a saw mill. I know all about the grading of lumber. I have been working in lumber about 25 or 27 years. My wedges here is $3.00 a day 11 hours a day. I want to come North where I can educate my 3 little children also my wife. Now if you cannot fit me up at what I am doing down here I can learn anything any one els can. also there is a great deal of good women cooks here would leave any time all they want is to know where to go and some

SOURCE: Emmett J. Scott, "Letters of Negro Migrants of 1916–1918," *Journal of Negro History* 4 (July 1919): 435.

way to go. please write me at once just how I can get my people where they can get something for their work. There are women here cookeing for $1.50 and $2.00 a week. I would like to live in Chicago or Ohio or Philadelphia. Tell Mr. Abbott [owner of the *Defender*] that our pepel are tole that they can not get anything to do up there and they are being snatched off the trains here in Greenville and a rested but in spite of all this, they are leaving every day and every night 100 or more is expecting to leave this week. Let me here from you at once.

Chapter 7

America Goes to War

An American doughboy awaits the attack order.

In April 1917, after months of debate and disagreement on whether to join the war in Europe, the United States declared war on Germany. Unlike the major European powers embroiled in the conflict since 1914, America's participation in the war was brief—only about a year and a half. Nevertheless, the war exerted a tremendous impact on Americans, soldiers and civilians alike. For the first time, Americans went off to fight on European soil, and they felt certain that their participation would play a crucial role in defeating the Germans and their allies.

The United States had to mobilize its economy in order to support its allies and build an army to fight in Europe. After some confusion, the nation's industrial and agricultural might was effectively organized and financed. The building of an army also required great effort. The immense problems encountered in creating a fighting force capable of assisting our allies on the battlefields are vividly described in an essay by Meirion and Susie Harries. Based on your reading of this piece, what appear to have been the most difficult challenges facing the civilian and military leaders in their efforts to create this force? How effectively, in your opinion, did they meet the challenges? Finally, what does the essay indicate were the most serious obstacles a new recruit had to overcome in making the transition from civilian to military life?

Throughout the war, the federal government used propaganda to convince the public that the cause was noble, a clash between the forces of good and evil. Victory required the absolute loyalty and support of all citizens; any hint of questionable patriotism prompted great concern. For German Americans particularly, the patriotic near-hysteria of these times proved a terrible burden. In restaurants sauerkraut was renamed "liberty cabbage," and hamburger emerged as "liberty steak." Cincinnati's German Street was renamed English Street, and Pittsburgh banned the playing of Ludwig van Beethoven's music. German Americans were harassed and threatened with physical harm if they failed to demonstrate their commitment to the American war effort. The pressure on German Americans to declare their loyalty is vividly reflected in the first document, a statement by a German American distributed by the Committee on Public Information, an agency created by the federal government to generate public support for the war. How did the author's assessment of the war enable him to embrace the American cause without cutting his emotional ties to his native land?

Although a large segment of the population opposed entry into the war right up until 1917, support for the war effort flourished once the United States joined the conflict. Nevertheless, not all Americans supported the war; those who did not and refused to serve in the armed forces on the grounds of religion or conscience suffered condemnation. The second document reveals the experiences and convictions of Mennonites, who, despite their profound religious objections to the war, were drafted into the army. What relationship, if any, can you discern between the patriotic fervor of wartime society and intensified intolerance?

As the essay reveals, conscientious objectors were not the only ones to suffer prejudice during the war. The final document is a directive issued by a French liaison office to French officers at the insistence of the American army. What does it reveal about white America's attitudes toward black troops and African Americans generally?

ESSAY

Building a National Army

Meirion and Susie Harries

In the early fall of 1917, watchers by the rail tracks would have seen a remarkable display of young Americans riding to their appointed camps and cantonments, an unrehearsed pageant of America's ethnic diversity: Chocktaws and Cochin Chinese, "Hebrews" (the Army's classification) from everywhere in the Diaspora, Greeks, Italians, English, Irish, Scots, Slavs, Swedes, Germans, Austrians, Albanians, Poles, Armenians, Syrians, Finns, Hispanics, and Japanese. (In Hawaii, the National Guard gained its first Japanese company.) Blacks went on separate trains.

To this army of Babel came men of all shapes and sizes: lanky recruits of Scots blood from the mountains of North Carolina, short and stocky Mediterraneans from the Northeast, where recent immigration had been heaviest. The minimum size was five feet, one inch and 128 pounds; any smaller, and the man would have been unable to carry the regulation army pack (though occasionally lighter men were accepted if they had special skills). The maximum was six feet, six inches; any taller, and the man was likely to have poor circulation. The weight limits were 190 pounds for infantry, engineers, and artillery and 165 pounds for the cavalry.

The average recruit measured five feet, seven and a half inches and weighed 141½ pounds, a meaningless statistic in this miscellany of manhood—except at the unit level, where the average was crucial in determining the sizes of uniforms to be supplied and quantity of rations allocated. Divisions with a high proportion of immigrants from eastern Europe received a smaller average ration and smaller uniforms than midwestern divisions formed of strapping Scandinavians and Germans. Few were racially as mixed as New York's 77th Division, whose theme song ran: "The Jews and the Wops,/The Dutch and the Irish cops,/They're all in the Army now" and which boasted forty-two different languages or dialects spoken in its ranks.

During the war, some 400,000 first-generation immigrants were drafted, including some who were alien enemies and ineligible. This influx was too much for Major General George Bell of the 33rd Division, whose contingent of around 15,000 National Guard volunteers had been fleshed out with conscripts. He complained to the Adjutant General that "the local boards in

SOURCE: *The Last Days of Innocence: America at War, 1917–1918*, by Meirion and Susie Harries, 127–41. Copyright © 1997 by Meirion and Susie Harries; maps copyright © 1997 by Anita Karl and Jim Kemp. Reprinted by permission of Random House, Inc.

Illinois had very evidently spared men of the draft age of American birth or stock at the expense of those of foreign birth or patronage."

Many who had known only the ghettos of the East Coast cities could not speak English or understand commands. Bombarded with unintelligible instructions and forced to eat such unfamiliar substances as boiled potatoes and stewed apricots, they created serious morale problems in their units. Recent German or Austrian immigrants had the additional anxiety, so military intelligence reported, of having been warned that "if it were known in their home countries that they were in the American army, their families would be hunted out and killed." This rumor was recognized as one of many deliberate propaganda attempts to disrupt recruitment and ruin morale in the camps. Army authorities believed the Lutheran Church Board to be one of Germany's instruments, noting "its efforts to place its pastors in as many camps, forts and other military establishments as possible."

The plight of these first-generation immigrants was compounded by prejudice. Anti-Semitism inevitably surfaced. One night, six weeks after his induction from the Bronx, Private Otto Gottschalk found himself dragged from his tent, stripped, and thrown into a ditch of black muck. He was forced to drink the filthy water and was then badly beaten.

In the early days of the draft, a high proportion of "unsuitable" immigrants appears to have been sent straight back to the ghetto. Later, attempts were made to fit them for service. Where there were enough of them, immigrants were branded together into "development battalions" under officers of their own. At one point, Camp Gordon, in Georgia, had two Slav companies and two Italian and one Russian-Jewish battalion. They quickly became well disciplined and proficient in drill, and when asked how many of them were ready and willing to go abroad immediately, 92 percent stepped forward.

This jumble of colors, cultures, and languages, European, Asian, and Latin, mercilessly underlined the isolation of the black Americans who formed a large section of the intake—larger, perhaps, than was just. No blacks were appointed to the draft boards, and local boards often used their powers to conscript a far higher proportion of blacks than whites relative to population. In part, this was to compensate for the higher number of whites enlisting voluntarily. (Blacks, after all, had very few units to volunteer for.) But draft boards also had a tendency to use selective service as a means of "cleaning up" the neighborhood. A General Staff report noted, "The physical condition of a large part of the colored draft is very poor. Many must be entirely eliminated and a large proportion of those left are not fit for combat duty. The Surgeon General reports that 50% are infected with venereal disease." There was no organized conspiracy to fill the Army with the poorest and "least socially desirable" blacks, but, judging from the results, that is often what happened.

Whatever damage the draft boards had inflicted by their "selection" techniques the Army compounded by its treatment of its black draftees. Few received more than six weeks' training, and their living conditions were often appalling. In October 1917, black stevedore and labor battalions were formed at Camp Hill, Virginia. Six thousand men arrived at the camp to find "no barracks, no mess halls, no clothing, no sanitary arrangements of any kind." In the coldest winter in Virginia for twenty-five years, those who could find room packed themselves into small, dirty tents pitched on the bare earth, while the less fortunate were obliged to stand in front of fires all night. Those who inevitably fell sick were taken to the crowded large tent that served as a hospital, where they lay on the frozen ground with neither cots nor thick blankets.

Camp Hill was an extreme case, but a War Department inspector criticized the white officers of all these black noncombatant units for their indifference to their men. The NCOs, he continued, had often been promoted to their positions "because of previous knowledge of negroes, usually gotten on plantations, public works, turpentine farms and the like." At Camp Hill, an NCO was often selected from the ranks "because he is a 'husky' and will beat and abuse the men. Two such sergeants are in the guard house now for killing other soldiers under their command." The seeds of hatred, inefficiency, and even mutiny were being sown.

The inevitable consequence was low morale and indifference among black labor units when they got to Europe. "We have experienced considerable difficulty in getting the proper amount of work out of the negro stevedores at the various ports," W. W. Atterbury, Pershing's Director General of Transportation, was later to complain. "Fining them and putting them in the guard-house is very little punishment for them and to be dishonorably discharged and sent home is just what they desire." From Liverpool, one of England's major ports, the commanding officer of a detachment of stevedores reported that police and local citizens had begged for them to be withdrawn. "They are without exception the most worthless aggregation of humanity that was ever collected in one unit."

As for the black combat troops, who had originally been intended to share facilities with white troops, they were eventually consigned to segregated units; worse, they were at no point allowed to assemble and train as complete divisions in the United States. While white divisions could seek to develop esprit and identity from the beginning of their training, the fragmented black divisions barely knew what their senior officers looked like, so infrequently could these officers visit the various units scattered among the cantonments in which the National Army was training.

Arriving at the railheads, the new recruits were marshaled into columns by newly commissioned lieutenants trying to summon up the principles of command. The officers at least had the advantage of being in uniform; the recruits were still in civilian clothes, many wearing their best suits as if they were going to a wedding and clutching a few belongings or the remains of the food they had been given for the journey by the send-off committees in their hometowns.

After a brisk march, they got their first sight of the camp or cantonment that was to be home for months to come: "a far-spreading city of wooden buildings," one remembered, "whose flat roofs extended one after another in exact order like the biscuits in a baker's pan." (He was describing one of the sixteen hutted cantonments built for the National Army; members of the National Guard, who were used to living in tents, were housed in sixteen canvas cities farther south.)

If the recruits still cherished any spark of chivalry or romance about their induction, the medical orderlies waiting inside the gates soon introduced a note of gritty realism. Inspections for vermin and venereal disease and a vicious schedule of inoculations against smallpox, typhoid, and other contagious diseases left the new arrivals with barely the strength to crawl to their barracks.

And what they found there was rarely inspiriting. The basic design of the company barracks was sound. Each was to be a two-storied wooden building, the second floor a vast dormitory lined with iron cots, the first floor equipped with kitchen, storerooms, mess hall, and captain's office. Unfortunately, few of the buildings were ready. The delay in deciding on the precise size and structure of the infantry division had entailed constant alterations to the cantonment blueprint. Infirmary buildings, for example, were planned at a time when the Table of Organization prescribed thirty-three men for the medical detachment of an infantry regiment. This number was increased to forty-eight, and the building was too small before it was ever used.

The quality of the work that had been done left much to be desired. Far to the south, near a Houston still in shock after the summer massacre,* the officers and men of the Illinois National Guard—now designated the 33rd Division—found Camp Logan "in a decidedly unfinished state." The hospital had been built without heating or running water—the construction quartermaster had put in two faucets on his own initiative—and the engineers pronounced the storehouses to be so faulty that it was only a matter of time before they collapsed. At Camp MacArthur, Texas, the builders laid water mains made of wood that had been lying around for months, and when the water was turned on, typhoid ran through the camp.

All these camps were huge, and the numbers rose as the war progressed. Camp Dix, near Trenton, New Jersey, was built for 38,000 men but at one point housed 54,500. The sanitation demands of such concentrations of human life were immense, yet little thought had been given to them.

*Several black soldiers were killed in a race riot in 1917. (Eds.)

Camp Sherman, Ohio, produced without effort 982,500 pounds of garbage a month and its horses 120 tons of manure a day. The men of Camp Custer, Michigan, filled 1,200 garbage cans a day. None of the camps had water-proof surfaces where the trash cans could be kept, so the earth around the cans became a morass of mashed and rotting waste, magnificent breeding grounds for flies—but nothing compared to the lakes of sewage that loitered in the vicinity of most camps.

At Camp Lee, Virginia, home to the 80th Division, a single creek carried the daily consignment of effluent into a marsh nearby, where it settled. The division's engineers decided to clear the marsh by dredging a channel, but in damming the creek to permit dredging to begin, they created, in the words of a visiting entomologist, a "semi-solid mass of sewage 600 feet long and alive with fly larvae." The comfort levels of latrines matched their sanitary standards; the seats in most had a square hole—an easier shape to cut than an oval.

Among the new arrivals at the camps and cantonments were the conscientious objectors. The Selective Service Act had forced the draft boards to induct them for combatant or noncombatant duty, depending on the nature of their objection, but several months passed before the War Department laid down a policy as to their treatment.

Newton Baker's* intention was that the government's attitude to those who had "personal scruples" about the war should be reasonably liberal, especially in the case of those whose objections were religious: Mennonites (who had come from Russia specifically to avoid war), Quakers, Dukhobors, Seventy-Day Adventists, Plymouth Brethren, Christadelphians, and so on. He specifically ordered that Mennonites and the members of certain other sects should not be compelled to wear uniforms, as their raiment was a tenet of their faith. It was his express wish that conscientious objectors should be segregated from serving soldiers, given noncombatant duty if they had been deemed eligible for it, and treated with "tact and consideration."

The military authorities had far less sympathy. Going "soft on slackers," they felt, was unfair to ordinary conscripts. Many objectors, now that they had been inducted, flatly refused to perform even noncombatant duties, since these still served the purpose of the war, and declined to obey army discipline, wear uniforms, march, drill, or even, in extreme cases, keep clean. Most of the division commanders, like Leonard Wood at Camp Funston, Kansas, felt it their duty to convert them to the ways of war. The pressure they applied took various forms—verbal abuse, humiliation, courts-martial and exaggerated legal penalties, beating, and, in extreme cases, what amounted to torture.

---

*Newton Baker was Secretary of War from 1916 to 1921. (Eds.)

Hutterites, whose faith forbade them to cut their hair, had their beards shaved off by force. Dukhobors were forced into military dress or tormented if they refused. One who was ducked under a faucet on a freezing day subsequently died of pneumonia; his widow, upon receiving his body for burial, was appalled to find it in full uniform, a desecration of his faith.

The most brutal treatment was generally reserved for those whose scruples were ideological rather than religious—and this included not only socialists and others with political objections to the war but those whose objections were made in the name of humanity rather than that of any recognized creed. A great many were eventually "persuaded" to accept military discipline or noncombatant duties, but almost four thousand held out.

Sheldon W. Smith refused to sign the Army's clothing slip. "They put a pen in my hand and held it there to make a mark. . . . Next I was stripped in a violent manner and taken inside and dressed [in uniform] amidst arm twisting, thumping etc." Then he was taken to the bathhouse, where he was stripped again, held under the shower, and scrubbed with a broom. His captors whipped him with their belts, put a rope around his neck, and lashed it to a pipe, hauling on it until he could not breathe and all the while shouting at him to give in. "The bathing was continued until I was chilled and shook all over; part of the time they had me on my back with face under a faucet and held my mouth open. They got a little flag ordering me to kiss it and kneel down to it."

When the severity of the treatment being handed out in some camps was brought to Baker's attention at the end of 1917, he was horrified and ordered that, from the start of 1918, all "personal scruples," including nonreligious ones, should be classed as objections of conscience and his previous strictures observed. Baker would ultimately review all courtmartial sentences, disapproving a tenth of them altogether and mitigating a further 185 out of a total of 540. None of the seventeen death sentences was carried out.

But in the interim neither he nor the President would intervene any more closely to protect individual rights. The force of public opinion—from the press, the parents of serving soldiers, even the clergy—was against the objectors, and it was a factor neither Wilson nor Baker was prepared to ignore.

Far more worrisome to the Army than either immigrants or conscientious objectors were the draft boards' peculiar ideas as to what constituted physical suitability for service on the Western Front. Of the conscripts inducted during the war, an estimated 196,000 had venereal disease on arrival at camp. Of the 22,000 men examined at Camp Lewis, Washington, 5,000 had thyroid enlargement. Orthopedic problems, particularly foot defects, were commonplace; in one camp, 18 percent of the men had foot trouble, which drill soon revealed. The dentists at Camp Lee examined 38,963 draftees and found 10,596 suffering from infected root canals.

Problems varied with the conscripts' ethnic stock. According to Army Medical Department statistics, French Canadians had the poorest overall health in general: a high incidence of stunted growth, tuberculosis, and nervous and mental defects. Germans and Austrians were prone to alcoholism, varicose veins, and flat feet. "Sections of the black belt of the South," medical officers reported, showed higher-than-average arthritis, manic-depressive psychoses, and heart valve disease, lower-than-average obesity.

From an intake of 6,600 at one camp—and these were men who had passed through the mill of the draft boards—1,600 were immediately discharged as unfit and/or "unsuited, worthless, non-English-speaking, illiterate and venereally diseased." Where there was some hope of remedying the defects, the men were assigned to holding units. Camp Devens, Massachusetts, for example, had a battalion including 134 venereal, 151 neuropsychiatric, 368 cardiovascular, and 1,271 orthopedic cases.

Whatever their vital statistics or their moral standards, the raw levies all had one thing in common; they were in the camps and cantonments to be trained individually in the skills of the soldier and collectively, with their officers, molded into efficient units ready for war. The War Department's strategy had no frills. Besides instructors sent over from Europe by the English and French, they produced company-grade officers—captains and lieutenants—to train the men and then depended on the regular army (and, to a lesser extent, National Guard) officers—majors, colonels, and above—to weld the companies into battalions, regiments, and brigades. The objective was a division that was militarily efficient, a responsive organism of great power.

Many of the professional officers had theoretical knowledge of how to handle large units, but none had any practical experience of anything resembling a 28,000-man division; nevertheless, they rose to their task. The newly commissioned company-grade officers, in the Army for less than half a year, were even further at sea, each finding himself suddenly responsible for the welfare, discipline, and instruction of 250 men, with no protective shield of seasoned drill sergeants to cow the insubordinate.

Black company-grade officers of the 92nd Division struggled to create cohesion and maintain morale. Not only was the division never assembled in one place, but hanging over it was General Ballou's warning that "white men made the Division, and they can break it just as easily if it becomes a trouble-maker." The officers hardly advanced their own cause. "The vast majority of colored officers," remembered the regimental surgeon of the 349th Field Artillery, "held themselves distinctly aloof from the colored enlisted men . . . [who] used to nickname their colored officers 'Monkey Chasers.'"

At first, not surprisingly, the key figures in the National Army cantonments were the eight hundred or so British and French instructors. They were all veterans, often with wound stripes on their sleeves, and they brought the callousness of the front with them. "We made an attack one day," one told his pupils.

> As our first wave carried the enemy trench, they heard shouts from a dugout: "Kamerad!" The Germans surrendered. The first wave rushed on, leaving it to the second wave to take the prisoners. As soon as the first wave had passed, the Germans emerged from their dugout with a hidden machine gun and broke it out on the backs of the men who had been white enough not to give them the cold steel. So now, men, when we hear "Kamerad" coming from the depths of a dugout in a captured trench we call down: "How many?" If the answer comes back "Six," we decide that one hand grenade ought to be enough to take care of six and toss it in.

It was impossible in these home camps for either men or units to be made fully ready for combat. Communications being what they were, the knowledge and experience accumulating daily in France was simply not crossing the Atlantic. After six months of war, the General Staff in Washington recognized that it was receiving information that was at best three weeks old. In France, Pershing created an elaborate system of schools to provide instruction for every branch and level of the service: staff officers, unit commanders, candidates for commissions, specialists from every staff and supply department, artillerymen, intelligence officers, pilots. Ideally, all the incomers should have achieved a basic level of competence before crossing to France, but the AEF* schools were equipped to improve on the training of any unit in any branch, with the benefit of having more immediate knowledge of field conditions.

At Langres, forty miles south of Chaumont, Pershing established the critically important Staff College, which, in a frenetic three-month course, attempted to turn out war managers. In addition, his Training Branch developed a three-month training cycle for divisions in France, covering small-unit training, staff work, and combined arms practice and ending with a period in the trenches brigaded with Allied units.

Infantry training was only one of the specializations that together created the complex mechanisms of a division. A man's occupation in civilian life would often dictate his role in the Army: typists were assigned to headquarters staff, garment workers to the quartermaster, construction workers to engineer battalions, pharmacists to medical units, cooks to the kitchens, backwoodsmen to sniper units. In theory, motorized transportation units should have been especially hard to staff. There were usually men who knew how to handle horses, but in 1917 truck and tractor drivers were few and far between. Nevertheless, the appeal of driving was irresistible and

---

*American Expeditionary Force (Eds.)

men often lied about their experience with motor vehicles in order to get behind the wheel.

Native Americans made some of the U.S. Army's most awe-inspiring soldiers. Though Americanization was accelerating, and as many Indians were lawyers, doctors, and engineers by 1914 as were employed in hunting, trapping, or guiding, many still brought skills that adapted remarkably well to conditions on the Western Front. Possibly because of Chief of Staff Hugh Scott's deep interest in their culture, they were not discriminated against, provided there was "no colored admixture." In all, 6,509 were inducted and the same number volunteered, a total of almost 30 percent of all adult Indian males. The percentages varied from tribe to tribe: roughly 40 percent of the Oklahoma Osage and Quapaw served, while less than 1 percent of the Navajo did so. In the federal Indian schools where Americanization had free rein, almost 100 percent of males enlisted, many lying about their age. "I felt no American could or should be better than the first American," explained one Siletz volunteer.

In 1917–1918, young Indian males were still in touch with traditional hunting and fighting skills. In the cantonments, they provided an object lesson to the urban conscripts in techniques of concealment and stealth by slipping across "no-man's-land" to snatch a "German" from the trenches opposite. Their languages were regarded as excellent substitutes for code, though a new vocabulary had to be evolved to deal with the terminology of modern war: machine guns became "little guns shoot fast" and battalions were indicated by "one, two and three grains of corn."

Zane Grey,* touring Wild West shows, and other more authentic by-products of a culture so recently vibrant had all imprinted the Germans with stereotypical images of "Red Indians." They were terrified of the specter of the "red man" and drafted extra snipers into sectors where Indians were spotted, "specially to pick off these dangerous men." Recognizing an opportunity for psychological warfare, the War Department gave serious thought to "attempting a limited number of night raids with men camouflaged as Indians in full regalia."

In the early days of sorting and allocating men, the Army relied a good deal on personal impressions and the direct question "What can you do?" But this was the second decade of the twentieth century, when the psychologist had begun to make an impression, and when Pershing complained that "too many mental incompetents were being shipped abroad," it seemed time to try newer methods. Psychologist Robert M. Yerkes was able to persuade the War Department "to adopt a scientific basis for assessing the quality of the new recruits."

*A well-known author of the American West (Eds.)

During the war, 3 million soldiers were given intelligence tests—one test for the literate, another for those considered illiterate. (The literacy test itself provided perhaps the biggest shock: throughout the Army, 24.9 percent of men could neither read the paper nor write a letter home—in English, at least—and this was the criterion employed.) Men who were rated "feebleminded" because they scored so low on the intelligence test were immediately discharged from the Army without review by a disability board—until the authorities realized that many college graduates were using this as an ingenious escape route from the Army.

By today's standards, the tests were obviously flawed, geared remorselessly to the middle-class native English speaker with questions on literature, tennis, and the like. Even so, a grading of "A" to "E" offered a simple, convenient reference tool to personnel officers struggling to allocate thousands of new recruits in a hurry. Once the men with relevant experience had been assigned, each company would receive a mixture of grades. Men who had scored lower than "C" would not be permitted to apply for commissions.

Life in the Army offered the clearest demonstration that the grip of the federal government was closing ever more tightly around the individual. It was a protective as well as coercive clasp. In the late 1890s, William Gibbs McAdoo (then a dealer in railway bonds) had helped the "penniless and starving" wives and families of servicemen in the Spanish-American War. Now, as Secretary of the Treasury, he urged that "the basis of the family's support . . . should be an allotment of a fixed proportion of the soldier's pay." Enlisted married men were obliged to make over half their $33 monthly pay to their families, which the government then supplemented.

The allotment could not fully compensate for the induction of a husband or son. Draft boards seem to have applied the "genuine dependency" exemption very narrowly, and across the country division headquarters were inundated with applications for the release of enlisted men or for more money in lieu. Desperate letters told of starving children, sick and bedridden relatives. In their bemused incoherence and their combination of greed and optimism with genuine hardship, these were a constant source of amusement to headquarters staff, who circulated a list of the choicest pleas. "My boy has been put in charge of a spittoon. Will I get more money now?" "I didn't know my husband had a middle name, and if he did, I do not think it was 'None.'" "You ask for my allotment number: I have four boys and two girls." "I am writing to ask you why I have not received my elopement." "I have not received my husband's pay and will be forced to lead an immortal life." "Please return my marriage certificate. Baby has not eaten in three days."

Material support was only one aspect of the government's paternalism. McAdoo and Cabinet colleagues such as Daniels, Baker, and Wilson made the soldier's moral welfare in camp their concern as well. Baker, a reformer by inclination, remembered the public outrage in 1916 at the plague of brothels spreading along the Mexican border with the soldiers. He knew people were afraid of the effects of these huge new concentrations of troops, and he threw his weight behind a morality campaign; by the end of 1917, some 110 red-light districts near camps had been closed. At the level of private enterprise, the concerned citizens of the National Allied Relief Committee raised funds to bus vulnerable American servicemen through "the London danger zone" and save them "from the distressing and terrible dangers of the streets."

For help in finding something to take the place of the customary army pleasures, Baker turned to a friend, Raymond Fosdick, a thirty-three-year-old moralist and social reformer and the brother of the well-known clergyman Harry Emerson Fosdick. Baker asked him to provide the men with "wholesome recreation and enjoyment." This he was to achieve by coordinating the various voluntary organizations operating in the camps—bodies such as the YMCA, the Jewish Welfare Board, and the Knights of Columbus, up to thirty-six of them in some camps. Under Fosdick's Committee on Training Camp Activities, the men came to enjoy community songs, Liberty Theaters (occasionally graced by the singing of the President's daughter Margaret), YMCA huts (blacks usually excluded) where they could read magazines and write letters, Hostess Houses (separately provided for blacks) where they could meet female visitors in civilized surroundings, athletics, football and baseball, and educational programs aimed particularly at illiterates and the foreign-born. A small pamphlet published by the YMCA in 1917 offered the man about to go overseas a remarkable selection of handy French expressions: "I should like very much to see the periscope of a submarine"; "I have pawned my watch"; "A piece of shell hit me in the arm"; "Do not stick your head above the trench"; "Here I am, here I stay."

The young American male in those days was deemed by the War Department to be remarkably ignorant about sex; Fosdick's committee set out to put him straight. He was taught the facts of life and the risks of low life. "A German bullet is cleaner than a whore," announced one poster, showing a surprising lack of tact. "You wouldn't use another man's toothbrush. Why use his whore?" The potentially horrific results of normal intercourse seem so to have traumatized the youths of America that some of the young men moved swiftly from a state of ignorance to a widespread preference for alternatives, or so the Paris prostitutes claimed.

The motive of the military authorities for combating vice was military efficiency, not spiritual improvement. Where Fosdick's civilians concentrated on deterrence and moral suasion, the Army blandly provided prophylaxis at any hour of the day and night, somewhat undermining the credibility of the righteous. Contracting a venereal disease was a punishable offense, but this was because it was careless and unnecessary and detracted from the soldier's usefulness, not because it was wicked.

Neither military personnel nor civilians were entirely successful in combating venereal disease. At some camps the scale of the problem verged on the unmanageable. So many conscripts on leave from the camps in Kansas and Missouri headed for the prostitutes on Kansas City's Twelfth Avenue that it had been nicknamed "Woodrow Wilson Avenue—a piece at any price." Local authorities often refused to cooperate in the campaign against the local red-light district, which might be a useful factor of a community's economy. Seattle had to be declared off limits, New Orleans failed to see the point of the campaign, and Galveston, Texas, remained an open city. Where prostitutes were pushed out, they often took up residence in the black districts of town, beyond the reach of the authorities' interest, and into the vacuum stepped the amateurs, hero-worshiping girls, some as young as twelve, who were determined to give themselves to the uniform.

In France, Pershing was very much more draconian, certainly more so than the natives. The French provided licensed brothels for their troops, and in 1918 Premier Georges Clemenceau offered similar services to the AEF. When Baker saw the letter, he exclaimed to Fosdick, "For God's sake, Raymond, don't show this to the President or he'll stop the war." Pershing personally inspected the VD returns every day. He declared red-light districts off limits and had them patrolled; MPs were then found to have the highest incidence of VD in the AEF. Men returning to camp drunk were automatically assumed to be infected and were treated, by force if necessary.

The Army also fought a constant, if losing, battle at home against the temptations of alcohol. In the "dry" states, soldiers helped bootleggers make a killing; in "wet" ones, the authorities created "dry" zones around the camps, but the regulations proved nearly impossible to enforce. Men found lemon or ginger "extracts" with a 9 percent alcohol content perfectly satisfactory. The punishment for selling liquor to men in uniform was a year's imprisonment, so the soldiers took off their tunics or paid the proprietor in advance, whereupon the barman "treated" them to drinks.

In Pershing's domain, beyond the reach of the moral crusaders, military efficiency was again the only criterion. Spirits were forbidden, but the men were allowed to buy beer and wine, and "Major Van Rooge" and "Captain Van Blank" became constant companions. Pershing did curb the intake by supporting the move to retain half the pay even of men without dependants. The soldiers' spending power worried him because of the impact it was having on the morale of French and British soldiers, who were paid far less. "$10 a month," he remarked, "is more spending money than a man in the trenches ought to have."

Drugs, which were widely used in society, duly made their appearance in the Army. Military intelligence gave warning of the sale to troops in southern cantonments of "the Chihuahua or Marihuana weed. This is a plant smoked by Mexicans of the lower classes; its use produces insanity and homicidal mania." The death-dealing weed proved popular, and by the summer of 1918 it had spread as far as Seattle. At Camp Devens, Special

Agent Kelleher surprised a narcotics dealer in barracks at six one evening "with a complete outfit of hypodermic syringes, a spoon for heating the concoction, and quite a lot of morphine." Waiting in line were three conscripts with their sleeves rolled up.

DOCUMENTS

German-American Loyalty, 1917

My emotions tell me one thing at this awful time, but my reason tells me another. As a German by birth it is a horrible calamity that I may have to fight Germans. That is natural, is it not? But as an American by preference, I can see no other course open. . . .

For 25 years Germany has shown dislike for the United States—the Samoan affair, the Hongkong contretemps, the Manila Bay incident, the unguarded words of the Kaiser himself, and, lastly, the Haitian controversy in 1914. . . . And it has not been from mere commercial or diplomatic friction. It is because their ideals of government are absolutely opposite. One or the other must go down. It is for us to say now which it shall be.

Because of my birth and feelings beyond my control I have no particular love for the French and less for the British. But by a strange irony of fate I see those nations giving their blood for principles which I hold dear, against the wrong principles of people I individually love. It is a very unhappy paradox, but one I can not escape. I do not want to see the allies triumph over the land of my birth. But I very much want to see the triumph of the ideas they fight for.

It sickens my soul to think of this Nation going forth to help destroy people many of whom are bound to me by ties of blood and friendship. But it must be so. It is like a dreadful surgical operation. The militaristic, undemocratic demon which rules Germany must be cast out. It is for us to do it—now. I have tried to tell myself that it is not our affair, that we should have contented ourselves with measures of defense and armed neutrality. But I know that is not so. The mailed fist has been shaken under our nose before. If Prussianism triumphs in this war the fist will continue to shake. We shall be in real peril, and those ideas for which so much of the world's best blood has been spilled through the centuries will be in danger of extinction. It seems to me common sense that we begin our defense by immediate attack when the demon is occupied and when we can command assistance.

SOURCE: C. Kotzenabe, "German-American Loyalty," in Committee on Public Information, War Information Series, *American Loyalty* (Washington, D.C.: Government Printing Office, 1917), 5–6.

There is much talk of what people like me will do, and fear of the hyphen. No such thing exists. The German-American is as staunch as the American of adoption of any other land and perhaps more so. Let us make war upon Germany, not from revenge, not to uphold hairsplitting quibbles of international law, but let us make war with our whole heart and with all our strength, because Germany worships one god and we another and because the lion and the lamb can not lie down together. One or the other must perish.

Let us make war upon the Germany of the Junkerthum,* the Germany of frightfulness, the Germany of arrogance and selfishness, and let us swear not to make peace until the Imperial German Government is the sovereign German people.

Letters from Mennonite Draftees, 1918

DEAR BROTHER————:

I went to Camp Cody, N. Mex., June 25, 1918. At first I drilled without a rifle, but later was asked to take one, explaining that the President's orders concerning the C. O.'s [conscientious objectors] required it, and I would get into noncombatant service in due time. I accepted it, and in two weeks was transferred to the infantry where, of course, I was asked again to take the rifle, and I saw that I had been deceived. I refused and explained why. Several nights after this, while I was in bed, some privates threw water into my bed, put a rope around my neck and jerked me out on the floor.

The next day two sergeants came to my tent and took me out, tied a gun on my shoulder and marched me down the street, one on each side of me, kicking me all the way. I was asked again whether I would take the rifle and drill. I refused and was taken to the bath-house, put under the shower bath where they turned on the water, alternating hot and cold, until I was so numb that I could scarcely rise. Just then one of the higher officers came in and asked what they were about. They explained that they were giving me a bath. The officer told me to dress and go to my tent, that he wanted to interview me himself. He asked if I would take a rifle and drill. I told him that I could not. He ordered my sergeant to put me on company street work until they got my transfer, and in three weeks I was given noncombatant service.

VERY TRULY YOURS,————

SOURCE: J. S. Hartzler, *Mennonites in the World War or Nonresistance Under Test* (Scottdale, Pa.: Mennonite Publishing House, 1922), 124–27.
Junkerthum refers to the Prussian military aristocracy. (Eds.)

DEAR BROTHER:

I came home Wednesday evening, Feb. 5. To get home, receive a hearty welcome and many expressions of joy for the effort made to maintain the faith, was alone worth the hardships which we endured.

I had been gone a few days more than ten months, of which I spent twenty-four days in our company, ten days in detention camp, seventy-eight days in the guard-house, one night in the Kansas City Police "lock-up," one hundred ninety-seven days in the disciplinary barracks (Fort Leavenworth, Kans.) and two days on the way home. . . .

I do not approve of such practices as the world was engaged in, and will give them neither moral nor material support though it may mean imprisonment or even death for not doing so. If the army would never kill a man, I can not see how a person could become a part of it, giving moral and material support to its maintenance and still retain a Christian character. The standards it upholds and the injustices it practices are unbelievable to a man who never saw them. . . . The only part that I can have in the army is suffering its punishments. Its purposes and those of Christianity are as different as night and day. The aims of the army are coercion, terrorism, carnal force; the ideals of Christianity are love, meekness, gentleness, obedience to the will of God, etc. When these ideals are maintained to the best of our ability, by God's grace He will provide care and protection in ways not imagined by man.

As to noncombatant service: all branches of service have one purpose; viz., to make the whole system a stronger organization of terrorism, destruction, and death. While I would not have been directly killing any one, I would have been doing a man's part in helping another do the act, and lending encouragement to the same. To support a thing and refuse to do the thing supported is either ignorance or cowardice. To refuse to go to the trenches and still give individual assistance to another doing so, is either an improper knowledge of the issues at stake or downright fear to face the bullets. I have a greater conscientious objection against noncombatant than against combatant service. I feel that the principle is the same, and that both are equally wrong. I would feel guilty toward the other man to accept service where the danger was not so great. . . .

To an observer it may have seemed ridiculous to refuse to even plant flowers at the base hospital. In the first place, that was the duty of the working gang under the quartermaster's department. Technically I would not have been doing military duty for I had not "signed up"; virtually I would have been rendering service because I was at work. . . . The farther one went with the military officers the farther they demanded him to go. I felt that the farther I went the less reason I could give for stopping, so I concluded that the best place to stop was in the beginning. It was on the charge

126

of refusing to plant flowers that I received my court-martial sentence of ten years of hard labor in the disciplinary barracks at Fort Leavenworth, Kans.

FRATERNALLY YOURS,———

Racism and the Army, 1918

French Military Mission

STATIONED WITH THE AMERICAN ARMY

AUGUST 7, 1918

*Secret Information Concerning Black
American Troops*

1. It is important for French officers who have been called upon to exercise command over black American troops, or to live in close contact with them, to have an exact idea of the position occupied by Negroes in the United States. The information set forth in the following communication ought to be given to these officers and it is to their interest to have these matters known and widely disseminated. It will devolve likewise on the French Military Authorities, through the medium of the Civil Authorities, to give information on this subject to the French population residing in the cantonments occupied by American colored troops.

2. The American attitude upon the Negro question may seem a matter for discussion to many French minds. But we French are not in our province if we undertake to discuss what some call "prejudice." American opinion is unanimous on the "color question" and does not admit of any discussion.

The increasing number of Negroes in the United States (about 15,000,000) would create for the white race in the Republic a menace of degeneracy were it not that an impassable gulf has been made between them.

As this danger does not exist for the French race, the French public has become accustomed to treating the Negro with familiarity and indulgence.

This indulgence and this familiarity are matters of grievous concern to the Americans. They consider them an affront to their national policy. They are afraid that contact with the French will inspire in black Americans aspirations which to them [the whites] appear intolerable. It is of the utmost importance that every effort be made to avoid profoundly estranging American opinion.

SOURCE: W.E.B. DuBois, ed., "Documents of the War," *The Crisis* 28 (May 1919): 16–18. Document from Bibliobase®, edited by Michael Bellesiles. Copyright © by Houghton Mifflin Company. Reprinted by permission.

Although a citizen of the United States, the black man is regarded by the white American as an inferior being with whom relations of business or service only are possible. The black is constantly being censured for his want of intelligence and discretion, his lack of civic and professional conscience and for his tendency toward undue familiarity.

The vices of the Negro are a constant menace to the American who has to repress them sternly. For instance, the black American troops in France have, by themselves, given rise to as many complaints for attempted rape as all the rest of the army. And yet the [black American] soldiers sent us have been the choicest with respect to physique and morals, for the number disqualified at the time of mobilization was enormous.

Conclusion

1. We must prevent the rise of any pronounced degree of intimacy between French officers and black officers. We may be courteous and amiable with these last, but we cannot deal with them on the same plane as with the white American officers without deeply wounding the latter. We must not eat with them, must not shake hands or seek to talk or meet with them outside of the requirements of military service.

2. We must not commend too highly the black American troops, particularly in the presence of [white] Americans. It is all right to recognize their good qualities and their services, but only in moderate terms, strictly in keeping with the truth.

3. Make a point of keeping the native cantonment population from "spoiling" the Negroes. [White] Americans become greatly incensed at any public expression of intimacy between white women with black men. They have recently uttered violent protests against a picture in the "Vie Parisienne" entitled "The Child of the Desert" which shows a [white] woman in a "cabinet particulier" with a Negro. Familiarity on the part of white women with black men is furthermore a source of profound regret to our experienced colonials who see in it an over-weening menace to the prestige of the white race.

Military authority cannot intervene directly in this question, but it can through the civil authorities exercise some influence on the population.

PART I

Suggestions for Further Reading

On Southern black Americans after the Civil War, consult two works by Eric Foner: *Nothing but Freedom: Emancipation and Its Legacy* (1983) and his impressive *Reconstruction: America's Unfinished Revolution, 1863–1967* (1988). See also John Hope Franklin, *Reconstruction After the Civil War* (1961); Leon Litwack, *Been in the Storm So Long: The Aftermath of Slavery* (1979); and Howard Rabinowitz, *Race Relations in the Urban South, 1865–1890* (1980). On black poverty, see Jay R. Mandle, *The Roots of Black Poverty* (1978). C. Vann Woodward, *The Strange Career of Jim Crow* (1966), remains an important work. See also Edward Ayers, *The Promise of the New South: Life After Reconstruction* (1992), and Jacqueline Jones, *The Disposed: America's Underclass from the Civil War to the Present* (1992). Neil McMillen, *Dark Journey: Black Mississippi in the Age of Jim Crow* (1989), is especially good. Very comprehensive is Leon F. Litwack, *Trouble in Mind: Black Southerners in the Age of Jim Crow* (1998). For the culture of segregation in the South, see Grace Elizabeth Hall, *Making Whiteness: The Culture of Segregation in the South, 1890–1940* (1998). A book dealing with memory of the Civil War after Reconstruction is David W. Dwight, *Race and Reunion: The Civil War in American Memory* (2001).

For settlement of the frontier, general works are Donald Worster, *Under Western Skies: Nature and History in the American West* (1992); Richard White *"It's Your Misfortune and None of My Own": A History of the American West* (1991); and Richard Bartell, *The New Country: Social History of the American Frontier, 1776–1890* (1974). An older book of value is Everett Dick, *Sod House Frontier: 1854–1890* (1937). See also W. Eugene Hollon, *The Great American Desert* (1966), and Joe B. Frantz and Julian E. Choate, Jr., *The American Cowboy: The Myth and the Reality* (1955). A comprehensive view of the West is presented in Rodman Paul, *The Far West and the Great Plains in Transition, 1859–1900* (1988), while a more controversial view is found in Patricia Nelson Limerick, *The Legacy of Conquest: The Unbroken Past of the American West* (1987). See also Walter Nugent, *Into the West: The Story of Its People* (1999).

On American Indians, consult Francis Paul Prucha, *The Great White Father: The United States Government and the American Indians* (1984); Angie Debo, *A History of the Indians of the United States* (1970); and Vine Deloria, Jr., *Custer Died for Your Sins: An Indian Manifesto* (1969). On reform and assimilation, see Robert W. Mardock, *Reformers and the American Indians* (1971), and Frederick E. Hoxie, *A Final Promise: The Campaign to Assimilate the Indians, 1880–1920* (1984). On the New Deal and the Indians, see Philip Kenneth, *John Collier's Crusade for Indian Reform, 1920–1954* (1977). On education, see Margaret Szasz, *Education and the American Indian: the Road to Self-Determination, 1928–1973* (1974). Rex Smith, *Moon of the Popping Trees:*

The Tragedy at Wounded Knee and the End of the Indian Wars (1975), is a good book on cultural conflict. On boarding schools, see Clyde Ellis, *To Change Them Forever: Indian Education at the Rainy Mountain Boarding School, 1893–1920* (1996), and David Wallace Adams, *Education for Extinction: American Indians and the Boarding School Experience, 1875–1928* (1995). For urbanization of American Indians, see Donald L. Fixico, *The Urban Indian Experience in America* (2000).

For women after the Civil War, there are a number of useful works. General books are Peter Filene, *Him/Her Self: Sex Roles in Modern America* (1975), and Sheila M. Rothman, *Woman's Proper Place: A History of Changing Ideals and Practices, 1870 to the Present* (1978). On women and education, see Barbara Solomon, *In the Company of Educated Women* (1985). On women and reform, see Theda Skocpol, *Protecting Soldiers and Mothers: The Political Origins of Social Policy in the United States* (1992). On women and work, consult David Katzman, *Seven Days a Week: Women and Domestic Service in Industrializing America* (1978); Leslie Tentler, *Wage-Earning Women: Industrial Work and Family in the United States, 1900–1930* (1979); Dee Garrison, *Apostles of Culture: The Public Libraries and American Society, 1876–1920* (1979); Barbara Harris, *Beyond Her Sphere: Women and the Professions in American History* (1978); and Nancy Dye, *As Equals and Sisters: The Labor Movement and the Women's Trade Union League of New York* (1980). On changing attitudes and practices about birth control, see Linda Gordon, *Woman's Body, Woman's Right: A Social History of Birth Control in America* (1979), and James Reed, *From Private Vice to Public Virtue: The Birth Control Movement and American Society Since 1830* (1977). On feminism, the standard work is Eleanor Flexner, *Century of Struggle: The Women's Rights Movement in the United States* (1959). Also helpful are William O'Neill, *Everyone Was Brave: A History of Feminism in America* (1971), and William Leach, *True Love and Perfect Union: The Feminist Reform of Sex and Society* (1980). For feminism in the early twentieth century, Nancy Cott, *The Grounding of Modern Feminism* (1987), is also stimulating. See also Suzanne M. Sinke, *Dutch Immigrant Women in the United States, 1880–1920* (2002), as an example of the new immigration history focusing on women. Alice Kessler-Harris, *In Pursuit of Equity: Women, Men, and the Quest for Economic Citizenship in Twentieth-Century America* (2001), deals with the century after 1900. Linda Gordon, *The Great Arizona Orphan Abduction* (1999), covers women and ethnic conflict. A book focusing on one profession is Ellen S. More, *Restoring the Balance: Women Physicians and the Profession of Medicine, 1850–1995* (1999). Sarah Deutsch, *Women and the City: Gender, Space, and Power in Boston, 1870–1940* (2000), is an excellent study.

On immigration, Stephan Thernstrom, ed., *The Harvard Encyclopedia of American Ethnic Groups* (1980), is outstanding. Two general works are Leonard Dinnerstein and David Reimers, *Ethnic Americans: A History of Immigration and Assimilation* (1999), and John Bodnar, *The Transplanted: A History of Immigrants in Urban America* (1985). On the Italians, see Virginia

Yans-McLaughlin, *Family and Community: Italian Immigrants in Buffalo, 1880–1930* (1977), and Humbert Nelli, *Italians in Chicago, 1880–1930: A Study in Ethnic Mobility* (1970). On Jews, see Moses Rischin, *The Promised City: New York's Jews, 1870–1914* (1962), and Irving Howe, *World of Our Fathers: The Journey of the East European Jews to America and the Life They Found and Made* (1976). Useful comparative studies are Thomas Kessner, *The Golden Door: Italian and Jewish Mobility in New York City, 1880–1915* (1977), and John Bodnar et al., *Lives of Their Own: Blacks, Italians and Poles in Pittsburgh, 1900–1960* (1982). On New York City, consult Nathan Glazer and Daniel Patrick Moynihan, *Beyond the Melting Pot: The Negroes, Puerto Ricans, Jews, Italians and Irish of New York City* (1963). See also Frederick M. Binder and David M. Reimers, *All the Nations Under Heaven: An Ethnic and Racial History of New York City* (1995), and Nancy Foner, *From Ellis to JFK: New York's Two Great Waves of Immigration* (2001). For immigration restriction, John Higham, *Strangers in the Land: Patterns of American Nativism, 1860–1925* (1968), is the standard work, but see also Mathew Fry Jacobson, *Whiteness of a Different Color: European Immigrants and the Academy of Race* (1998); Desmond King, *Making Americans: Immigration, Race and the Origins of the Diverse Democracy* (2000); Gary Gerstle, *American Crucible: Race and Nation in the Twentieth Century* (2001); and Alan Kraut, *The Huddled Masses: The Immigrant in American Society, 1880–1921* (2001).

For Jewish women, see Sydney Stahl Weinberg, *The World of Our Mothers: The Lives of Jewish Immigrant Women* (1988). Jewish women also are covered in Susan Glenn, *Daughters of the Shtetl* (1989), while Kathy Peis, *Cheap Amusements: Leisure in Turn-of-the-Century New York* (1985), explores the lives of working-class immigrant women in New York City. For Irish women, see Hasia Diner, *Erin's Daughters in America: Irish Immigrant Women in the Nineteenth Century* (1983). For Chinese women, see Judy Yung, *Unbound Feet: A Social History of Chinese Women in San Francisco* (1995). See also Sucheng Chan, *Asian Americans: An Interpretive History* (1991).

For industrialization and American workers, see Herbert Gutman, *Work, Culture and Society in Industrializing America* (1976); Stephan Thernstrom, *The Other Bostonians* (1973); and Melvyn Dubofsky, *Industrialism and the American Worker, 1865–1920* (1975). David Brody, *Steelworkers in America: The Non-Union Era* (1976), is an excellent book. On workers in the Southern cotton mills, see Jacqueline Dowd Hall et al., *Like a Family: The Making of a Southern Cotton Mill World* (1987).

For the migration of blacks to the North, Forette Henri, *Black Migration: Movement North, 1900–1920* (1976), provides a general overview. For particular cities, see Gilbert Osofsky, *Harlem: The Making of a Ghetto, 1890–1930* (1968); David Katzman, *Before the Ghetto: Black Detroit in the Nineteenth Century* (1973); Allan Spear, *Black Chicago: The Making of a Ghetto, 1890–1920* (1967); and Thomas Lee Philpott, *The Slum and the Ghetto: Neighborhood Deterioration and Middle Class Reform, Chicago, 1880–1930* (1976). Two excellent studies of white racism are George Frederickson, *The Black Image in the White Mind: The Debate on Afro-American Character and Destiny, 1817–1914* (1971), and Joel Williamson, *The Crucible of Race* (1984). An outstanding study of black culture is Lawrence Levine, *Black Culture and Black Consciousness: Afro-American Folk Thought from Slavery to Freedom* (1977). For a new view of the migration north, see James R. Grossman, *Land of Hope: Chicago, Black Southerners and the Great Migration* (1989).

On World War I, Frederick Luebke, *Bonds of Loyalty: German Americans and World War I* (1974), is informative. For the home front, see David Kennedy, *Over Here: The First World War and American Society* (1980). On women during the war, see Maurie W. Greenwald, *Women, War and Work: The Impact of World War I on Women Workers in the United States* (1980). For military aspects of the war, the standard treatment is Edward Coffman, *The War to End All Wars: The American Military Experience in World War I* (1968). On the economy, see Ronald Schofer, *America in the Great War* (1991).

PART II

Modern American Society
1920–Present

Chapter 8

Intolerance: A Bitter Legacy of Social Change

A Ku Klux Klan ritual.

At the turn of the century, few issues sparked so much debate and concern as the large-scale immigration to the United States from southern and eastern Europe. To many native-born Americans, whose roots lay in northern and western Europe, these millions of newcomers came to symbolize the disappearance of an older, simpler American society. Native-born Americans feared that the new immigrants would not adapt to established ways and values, and that they would lower the standard of living by taking jobs from American citizens and by working for low wages. During World War I, several prominent leaders also expressed apprehension about the potential for divided loyalties on the part of immigrants. Such leaders as Theodore Roosevelt believed that immigrants, especially German Americans, might retain allegiance to Germany, the nation's wartime enemy. Roosevelt wanted absolute patriotism—what he called "100 percent Americanism."

Fear and dread of foreigners intensified in the postwar years, with eastern European Jews and Roman Catholics being blamed for many of the nation's social problems. As one result of this mood, the Ku Klux Klan revived. This post–Civil War vigilante group had first directed its hatred toward blacks, and later toward immigrants, whom it feared and despised. Within a few years of its reemergence in the early 1920s, the Klan spread its message of bigotry not only in the South, where it originated, but throughout the rest of the country as well. The Klan's growth and influence was imposing but brief. David Chalmers's essay "The Hooded Knights Revive Rule by Terror in the Twenties" examines the revival and eventual decline of the Klan during that decade. According to the essay, what attractions did the Klan hold for the thousands who joined it?

The first document comes from a 1926 article, "The Klan's Fight for Americanism," by Klan leader Hiram Evans. Notice how Evans's message combines bigotry and an alleged adherence to traditional American values. How does the document help to explain the Klan's appeal in sections of the country as different from each other in racial and ethnic makeup as Oregon, Georgia, and Massachusetts?

Although Evans's rantings seem outrageous to modern sensibilities, many people during this period, even in the highest levels of government, echoed the Klan philosophy. Evidence of this is found in the second document, an excerpt from congressional testimony in 1921 concerning U.S. immigration policy. Although those testifying do not refer to any specific countries of origin in their condemnation of immigrants, federal legislation passed in 1924 (the National Origins Act) makes it clear that legislators believed immigrants from some countries to be less desirable than those from others. The new approach, generally referred to as the national-origins system, gave preference to immigrants from northern and western Europe; it severely limited immigration from the rest of the continent, and virtually barred Asians.

In 1952 Congress passed the McCarran-Walter Act, which was also based on the national-origins system. The final document reveals how the Senate subcommittee introducing the bill continued to defend this prejudicial system; both the Senate and the House demonstrated their concurrence through passage of the Act. In 1965 Congress finally replaced this law with a nondiscriminatory one.

ESSAY

---·•··---

The Hooded Knights Revive
Rule by Terror in the Twenties

David Chalmers

D. W. Griffith's 1915 melodrama, *The Birth of a Nation*, was a blockbuster of a motion picture, and it helped revive the Ku Klux Klan. The Kentucky-born Griffith created his pioneering film from a novel written by a North Carolinian named Thomas Dixon. Dixon's life was built on eloquence and passion. A fellow-student and friend of Woodrow Wilson at Johns Hopkins graduate school, Dixon had been a legislator, Baptist preacher, lecturer, novelist, playwright, and actor, always reaching out to a larger audience. Griffith gave him his biggest one.

Dixon's 1905 book, *The Clansman: An Historical Romance of the Ku Klux Klan*, was one of three that he wrote on the Invisible Empire which his uncle had helped lead in the Carolina piedmont. The story revolved around two star-crossed families, the Camerons and the Stonemans, one from the South and the other from the North. Their sons and daughters fell in love, but the War Between the States separated them and Reconstruction brought them disaster. Congressman Stoneman, copied from life after Radical Republican leader Thaddeus Stephens, was presented as a crippled, hate-filled villain, urged on by his mulatto mistress to degrade the captured South. With the murder of "The Great Soul," Abraham Lincoln, there was nothing to stop him. Black tyranny ruled the South, black corruption stained its legislative halls, and brutish black lust stalked its womanhood. However, at this darkest moment, the hooded knights of the Ku Klux Klan, led by young Ben Cameron, Civil War hero and beloved of Stoneman's daughter, rode forth to save the South and its downtrodden people.

D. W. Griffith took Dixon's story and made it into the movies' first colossal spectacular. In place of the usual fifteen-minute flicker, Griffith created a three-hour epic, dramatically restaging the war's battles, Sherman's March to the Sea, and Lincoln's assassination at Ford's Theater. Congressman Stoneman comes to the Southern town of Piedmont to oversee his schemes for melding the races. Cameron's "Little Sister," as he called her, and her mother, Mrs. Lenoir, leap from a cliff to their deaths after ravishment by a black renegade soldier. Cameron is arrested and sentenced to death for murder; Stoneman's son, in love with Cameron's sister, takes his

SOURCE: David Chalmers, "The Hooded Knights Revive Rule by Terror in the Twenties," *American History Illustrated* 14 (February 1980): 28–37. Reprinted through courtesy of Cowles Magazines, publisher of *American History Illustrated*.

place. Just in time, the Klan arrives to save the living, avenge the fallen, and reunite the lovers.

Breaking the former static role of the camera, using angles, movement, and changing focus, expanding irises, reaching in and out of close-ups, juxtaposing, and paralleling, Griffith created his masterpiece. As the bugle call rang out and the Klan rode to the rescue, theater orchestras pounded out themes from Wagner and "The Hall of the Mountain King." Audiences rose cheering in the South, and crowds demonstrated in protest in the North. The picture was seen by President Woodrow Wilson, members of Congress and the Supreme Court, and millions of spectators at $2 apiece, while William J. Simmons, a fraternal organizer, colonel in the Woodmen of the World, and failed Methodist minister, dreamed of a revival of the Klan itself.

"Colonel" Simmons's plan for the Klan was revealed in the words of the advertisement which he inserted in the December 7, 1915, Atlanta *Journal.* The "Knights of the Ku Klux Klan" was "A High Class Order for Men of Intelligence and Character." It was to be "The World's Greatest *Secret,* Social, Patriotic, Fraternal, Beneficiary Order." In other words, it was to be a lodge, a fraternity. The fact that it was to exclude all who were not white, native-born, or Protestant did not make it substantially different from other such organizations and most college fraternities. It was the chance factor of its Southern origin that provided the dynamic element—the name and legend of the Ku Klux Klan. In *The Birth of a Nation,* whose Atlanta advertisement shared the page with Simmons's hand-drawn announcement of the Klan, Thomas Dixon and D. W. Griffith had engraved an image of flowing robes and mystic, masked, night-riding, patriotic violence on the national imagination. While most fraternities guarded their lodge hall secrets against outsiders and aliens, the vigilante heritage of the Klan took it out into the cow-pastures and city streets to protect its version of American values.

Simmons's initial plans had been less extravagant. His specialty was lodge ritual. He had hoped for a mildly successful organization in the Southeast to which he could sell memberships, regalia, and insurance. World War I enabled the Klan to do a little public marching and patriotic snooping. After the war the Klan, with a small membership in Georgia and Alabama, emerged into a time of opportunity. The heightened emotions and restlessness that were not immediately stilled by an end to the fighting, the manly camaraderie of the war and the habit of violence, people going home and not going home, black men who had served in the Army or who had left the farms for the cities and Northern factories—all were unsettling elements.

There were race riots in Chicago, Omaha, and Knoxville, in Duluth, Springfield, and Tulsa, in Texas, Arkansas, Kansas, and Florida. Large numbers of immigrants were arriving from the Southern and Eastern European dwelling places of the Roman Catholic, Jew, Slav, and Bolshevik. Life in the cities was confusing; the war to end war had turned sour, and the attempt to make society better by prohibition was either being flouted or downright corrupted. As with the original Ku Klux Klan, the unsettled times and the mysterious name (now potent with the legacy of its vigilante role during Reconstruction) undoubtedly shaped the direction the Klan would take for years to come.

Simmons engaged a pair of fund raisers, Edward Young Clarke and Mrs. Elizabeth Tyler, who were the Southern Publicity Association, to handle recruitment. Simmons was to receive $2 of the $10 initiation fee paid by each new member. The rest was to go to Clarke, Tyler, and their salesmen. The results were phenomenal. The Klan made good copy and the press rushed to spread reports of its doings. Within a year membership was nationwide and soared to almost 100,000.

The basic Southern emphasis on patriotism and white supremacy was expanded into the protection of basic morality and 100 percent Americanism. The American way of life and moral values were to be guarded not only against the Negroes, but from Roman Catholics, Jews, and Orientals, from aliens and immigrants, from bootleggers and road houses, from crime and corrupt politicians, from marital infidelity and sexual immorality, and from scoffers and unbelievers. Salesmen, or "kleagles," were selected from the Masonic and other lodges, touring lecturers from the evangelical ministry, and the country was divided and subdivided into sales districts. Local groups brought the Klan into town to combat bootlegging or corrupt city government, and Atlanta's usual advice to new chapters was to "clean up the town." Crosses burned on nearby hillsides, sheeted horsemen paraded down Main Street on Saturday night and the next morning marched down church aisles to make donations while choirs sang "The Old Rugged Cross" or "Onward Christian Soldiers."

Georgia . . . was the cradle for the reborn Klan. Colonel Simmons's blazing cross on Stone Mountain had been its first annunciation and Peachtree Street in Atlanta brought the robed faithful to its Imperial Palace. For fifty years Georgians would march in its parades and elect its candidates, as well as fight against its violence and intolerance. Nathan Bedford Forest Klan No. 1 was the Imperial Empire's mother lodge, and in 1920 when Simmons triumphantly attended the annual reunion of the United Confederate Veterans in Houston, its Exalted Cyclops Nathan Bedford Forrest III rode beside him.

The Klan spread through the cities and small towns of Georgia. The mighty Robert E. Lee No. 1 of Birmingham was the heart of its strength in Alabama and Sam Houston No. 1 led the way in Texas, although probably outstripped in size and violence by Dallas's No. 66 and Beaumont's No. 7. Klan organizers did well in northern Louisiana and throughout Arkansas, but the Imperial Empire's earliest bastion of terror was in Texas and Oklahoma. Klan salesmen jumped across the continent to California, selling patriotism, fraternity, and moral enforcement. They spread out from Los Angeles, and moved northward across the border to power in Oregon, offering anti-Catholicism to the descendants of the New England and Midwestern Puritans. Its legions grew in Missouri and Kansas, and its salesmen worked their way up the Mississippi Valley, across the Great Plains, and into the mountain states. In 1924 Colorado became even a greater success story than Oregon, as the Klan helped elect the mayor of Denver, the governor, and both senators.

But in no realm did Klan political power become greater than in Indiana. Its ambitious Grand Dragon D. C. Stephenson built his organization on a bloc by bloc basis throughout the state, carrying in tow the governor and both senators, negotiating for the purchase of Valparaiso University, and working his own way toward the White House. The Klan's fraternal appeal to what its Ohio Grand Dragon described as "the submerged majority of Protestants" swelled the tide of its membership in Cincinnati, Columbus, Toledo, Akron, and the steel centers of the Mahoning Valley. The Klan did well in the small towns and industrial cities of central Michigan and among the anti-Catholic socialists of Wisconsin. It signed up its thousands in Chicago and the suburbs, battling against an anti-Klan city administration. In "Bloody Herrin" County down in fundamentalist southern Illinois, where the mountain people from Kentucky and Tennessee shared their country uneasily with French and Italian immigrant coal miners, labor conflict turned into a murderous Klan and anti-Klan war that brought in the National Guard some eight times in four years.

Nor was the East immune from the recruitments of the Invisible Empire. Torn from its past as an instrument by which the post–Civil War Reconstruction was undone, the Klan, which was mainly Democratic in the South, was Republican in the North. In both sections it represented the old moral values against the newcomers and social change. There was the same concern about foreigners, the Roman Catholic "threat" to the public schools, and the enforcement of prohibition. Klan marchers brought in by chartered trains "to give the micks something to think about" were attacked by mobs in the western Pennsylvania mill towns of Carnegie, Lilly, and Scottdale, but in the Philadelphia suburbs and down in Lancaster County, once the Klan got organized, it stayed organized.

While New York City was generally enemy territory, Klan weddings, christenings, church visits, volunteer fire departments, parades, rallies, county fair days, and local political victories marked the Klan as a leading organization in Long Island's Suffolk and Nassau counties. Upstate, Klan domain stretched from its Binghamton headquarters to Buffalo. It entered New Jersey from New York and Pennsylvania and despite denunciation at church conferences, it found a home among Methodist prohibitionists and along the seacoast from Atlantic City to Cape May. Portions of the Klan-infiltrated National Guard were disarmed in Rhode Island. Boston's Mayor [James] Michael Curley cracked down on Klan meetings with the same sternness he had shown to the birth control crusader Margaret Sanger (despite American Civil Liberties Union protest in both cases), and Klansmen and Irishmen fought on summer nights in central Massachusetts. On the other side of the ethnic line, the prominent Boston blue-blood author Lothrop Stoddard found no conflict between his Americanism and that of the Klan, which also helped elect *Mayflower* descendant William Owen Brewster governor of Maine.

Simmons's talents lay in the area of lodge ritual and florid oratory, and many of his rising territorial leaders felt that he was not fully capitalizing on the Klan's potential. Led by the Dallas dentist Hiram Wesley Evans, whom Simmons had brought to Atlanta to help run things at the Imperial Palace, they staged a coup on the eve of the first national Klonvokation in 1922. When Simmons realized that he had been pushed upstairs out of control of the Klan, he was furious. Evans only laughed and replied, "Let's get the money, colonel."

There has never been a reliable tally of the number who belonged to the Klan. Between its veil of secrecy and its public boastings, the estimates run from two to four million members. During its peak years in the early twenties, members were streaming in and out in such numbers that the Klan itself probably never knew its own size. The consensus of historians is that Indiana took the lead with perhaps several hundred thousand Klansmen, Klanswomen, Tri-K's, and Junior Klansmen, with Texas, Oklahoma, Illinois, Ohio, and Pennsylvania probably close to 100,000 each. At one time or another in the 1920s, perhaps at least one out of every ten white, native-born, Protestant adult males belonged to the Invisible Empire. While sheer size did not necessarily mean political domination or long life for a Klan realm, in communities all across the country its strength gave a sense of power and immunity from the law. The mayor of Enid, Oklahoma, explained to the American Civil Liberties Union that since the Klan had 1,500 members and he had ten policemen, there was no point in investigating a reported Klan flogging.

A part of the fraternal excitement of the Klan was violence, a heritage from its Reconstruction days and not out of keeping with the Klan's vigilante role as a fighter against crime and immorality. The Klan was secret, masked, decentralized, and righteous, often operating with community approval and police participation. Although some Northern realms such as Ohio and Pennsylvania had their "Night Riders" and "Triple S" ("Super-Secret-Society") squads, the Southwest particularly liked "a little rough stuff." In the early twenties there were regular whippings and tar-and-feather parties in the meadows along Dallas's Trinity River bottoms. The

Mer Rouge murders* brought a portion of Louisiana close to civil war, and Governor Jack Walton got himself impeached when he called out the National Guard and imposed martial law on much of Klan-ridden Oklahoma. Texas and Oklahoma led the way, but Klan floggers were also active in Georgia, Alabama, Florida, North Carolina, and Kern County, California, with scattered incidents elsewhere. In those areas where the Klan dominated, however, it was the fellow white, native-born Anglo-Saxon, Protestant rather than the Negro, Roman Catholic, Jew, or alien who was on the receiving end—which may be a commentary on the extent of the alien danger against which the Klan warned.

What drew its scores of thousands to the Klan? Later generations have looked upon the hooded knights as sour, defensive, bigoted, and something of a joke. To their contemporaries, they were serious business. Famed juvenile court judge, Ben Lindsey, who fought the Klan in Denver, commented, "They paid ten dollars to hate somebody and they were determined to get their money's worth." Julian Harris, son of the creator of the Uncle Remus tales, won a Pulitzer Prize for the anti-Klan campaign of his Columbus, Georgia, *Enquirer-Sun*. Taking the popular booster slogan "It's Great To Be a Georgian," he asked, "Is it great to be a citizen of a state whose governor is a member of and subservient to that vicious masked gang?" New Jersey Methodist Bishop E. H. Hughes found it necessary to remind his fellow ministers that "It is not Anglo-Saxon blood but the blood of Jesus Christ that has made us what we are."

However, to the Klansmen, their purpose was a positive expression of good fellowship and what America was all about. The Klan was a reform movement, even as prohibition was. It was a means to protect society, to keep things good "the way they had been," to get rid of criminals and corrupt politicians, dangerous radicals and those who scoffed at or violated church and home, bought illegal alcohol, or threatened racial purity and the Anglo-Saxon heritage of America.

People prefer simple explanations and scapegoats. Presidents Warren Harding and Calvin Coolidge, the Congress, and the Supreme Court hardly seemed dangerous forces for change. The Klansman found a symbol that he enjoyed blaming: the outsider-alien, personified in the Roman Catholic Church and personalized in the Roman Pope. Ex-priests and "escaped" nuns were popular on the Klan lecture circuit where stories of papal intrigue, convent sin, guns hidden in church basements, and the menace of the Knights of Columbus were staples. From Maine to California, the Klan girded its emotional loins against the Roman menace. While no Episcopal,

---

*On August 24, 1922, in Mer Rouge, Louisiana, two white critics of the Ku Klux Klan were brutally tortured and then hanged by Klan members. (Eds.)

Methodist, or Baptist convention approved of the Klan and many church leaders denounced it, the Klan appeared to be taking a noisy leadership in protecting community morality. In short, it was doing what the churches talked about: the Klan spoke their language, made donations, and filled their benches. So it was very difficult for many ministers and parishioners to turn it down.

In addition to fraternalism, nativism, and the protection of basic moral Americanism, the Invisible Empire offered fellowship, excitement, and a sense of power—and advantage. The ritual and life of the Klan were those of the lodge, and the Ku Klux Klan was the fastest growing fraternity of the 1920s, far outdistancing the newly formed American Legion. Through the early years, Klansmen gathered at monster initiations, cross burnings and rallies, at Klan Day at the state fair in Dallas or the inauguration of Grand Dragon D. C. Stephenson at Kokomo. From the lodge halls of Birmingham's Robert E. Lee No. 1 to Phoenix's Kamelback Klan No. 6, from Shreveport and Grand Island, Portland, New Haven, Beaumont, Bangor, Billings, Binghamton, and Bakersfield, Klansmen felt that they were part of a fullthroated, rising, powerful force in the nation.

Of course there was always the possibility of more than the psychological advantage of being in on it. Merchants put "TWK" (Trade With a Klansman) and "SYMWA" (Spend Your Money With Americans) stickers in their shop windows. Rising young politicians such as lawyer Hugo Black in Alabama joined, and county judge hopeful Harry Truman of Independence, Missouri, went through the first steps before he withdrew. With its soaring membership, the Klan seemed to have the votes.

Earle Mayfield in Texas was its first genuine U.S. Senator, and in Arkansas the Klan had its own primary first to decide which brother to support in the regular Democratic party one. Success whetted the appetites of the imperial potentates in Atlanta, and other eager hopefuls, from Maine to California. Altogether, the Klan substantially helped elect both senators from Colorado, Indiana, Oklahoma, and Alabama, and one each from Iowa, Oregon, Texas, Georgia, Tennessee, and Kentucky, as well as governors in Maine, Kansas, California, Wisconsin, Colorado, Indiana, Ohio, Tennessee, Alabama, Georgia, and Oregon. While some only accepted Klan support, at least five of the senators and four of the governors were Klan members.

In 1924, the Klan played a major role in presidential politics. The two candidates battling it out at the Democratic Convention Madison Square Garden were the "wet," Catholic, New York governor, Al Smith, and the Georgia-born senator from California, William Gibbs McAdoo. McAdoo was not a bigot, but he had important support from Klan regions. The Platform Committee presented a plank opposing racial or religious discrimination, but the Smith supporters, and others, wanted the Klan denounced by name. As the Convention fought over the three crucial syllables, the supporters in the galleries chanted "Ku, Ku, McAdoo!" and "Booze! Booze! Booze!" at each other. The party's elder statesman and three times nominee, William Jennings Bryan, was hissed and booed when he asked for party unity and compassion, not condemnation, for those who belonged to the Klan. By an embittered 542 3/20 to 541 3/20 vote, the angry, shouting delegates failed to name the Klan. It was the climax of the Convention. Afterward it took nine days and 103 ballots to eventually send out John W. Davis as the compromise candidate to lose the election to Calvin Coolidge, who kept silent about it all.

In many communities, as the mayor of Enid, Oklahoma, had told the American Civil Liberties Union, the Klan held unchallenged power. That power, however, was unimaginative and soon squandered. The Klan was conservative, not revolutionary, and had little program other than to enjoy the spoils of office. Its members were a mixed bag of town and city blue- and white-collar workers, shopkeepers, and professional men. Although a potent force in politics, the Klan probably knew as little about economics as Warren G. Harding. Where it became involved, the Klan was pro-business and manipulated. Its leaders were friends to the electrical utilities in Oregon, and to the oil companies in Texas. In Kansas its top attorney also represented the anti-labor Associated Industries, and the Klan opposed street car regulation in Denver, public power ownership in Minneapolis, and the United Mine Workers in Kentucky. In the zones of emergence of the Northern cities, instead of organizing exclusionist neighborhood improvement associations, Klansmen spent their time at parades, church socials, fried chicken dinners, and lectures by Klan clergymen from Atlanta. The Klan's prime concern was fellowship and morality, not economics and urban dynamics.

On the national scene, the Klan supported immigration restriction, Federal aid to public education (as a counter to parochial schools), and non-participation in such "foreign" organizations as the League of Nations and the World Court. In state legislatures, Klansmen concentrated on protecting the flag, the Bible, racial purity, and the little red schoolhouse. This meant patriotic observances and readings from the King James Bible in the schools, and the exclusion of Roman Catholic teachers, or at least their wearing of religious garb. In Oregon the Klan combined with other fraternal lodges to pass a compulsory public school law, which the U.S. Supreme Court soon overruled.

But politics helped to undo the Klan's imperium. Leadership from Atlanta and in the state realms was remarkably inept. Conflict over which Klan candidate was going to be endorsed in Texas, Arkansas, and Oregon left bitter feelings. A jump to the Republican party did help produce a Klan senator from Oklahoma and a shift the other way elected a Democratic governor in Oregon, but the internal costs were high. State realms did not like being dictated to from Atlanta, and local Klansmen were no happier with the divisive, manipulative politics and authoritarian candidate-picking of their own Grand Dragons, who, in turn, had been imposed on the membership. Generally, the Klan was not successful in replacing other political associations and loyalties, and the men Klansmen elected, as well as those who told the Klansmen whom to elect, turned out to be of equally poor quality.

Although the Klan numbers and power often grew impressively, there was almost always someone to fight it, an editor such as Julian Harris or the Emporia, Kansas, *Gazette's* William Allen White to expose it, or a district attorney such as future Texas Governor Dan Moody, Denver's Philip Van Cise, or Alabama Attorney General Charles McCall to investigate and indict it. The New York *World;* Memphis *Commercial Appeal;* Columbus, Georgia, *Enquirer-Sun;* Montgomery, Alabama, *Advertiser;* and Indianapolis *Times* received Pulitzer Prizes for their anti-Klan campaigns.

Initially, all press coverage helped spread the Klan, and violence gave the Klan a "hell-of-a-fellow" sense of power. By the mid-1920s, almost everything the Klan did or that was reported about it revealed its ineptitude, immorality, corruption, and community destructiveness. When Indiana Grand Dragon D. C. Stephenson, the most powerful leader of the Northern Klan, went to prison for a sex murder, the Klan's reputation was further badly damaged. The more the Klan's linen was hung out in public, the dirtier it appeared for all to see, and the Invisible Empire was almost continually in court to settle internal disputes. Colonel Simmons and "Doc" Evans fought over who would be Imperial Wizard; Grand Dragons struggled against Imperial headquarters, and local klaverns against their state realms. The leadership on most levels ruled dictatorially and was out for the money. This struggle for the spoils and the exploitation of the membership wrecked the Klan in practically every state where it existed. By the latter half of the 1920s, membership was melting away. In 1926, when the Klan staged its second national parade down Pennsylvania Avenue in Washington, D.C., only half as many Klansmen and women came, and they marched in columns of four instead of sixteen and twenty abreast as they had done the year before.

During its years of glory, the Klan produced no statesmanlike leaders or social programs, but rather violence, local turmoil, and scandal. By the latter 1920s the country had settled down—even if the Klan had not—to enjoy Republican prosperity. The dangers of Rome or Russia seemed more distant and less real. The Klan's role in the American fraternal world had been irreparably damaged by its mismanagement and extremism. The self-confidence of the great early days had become a sour defensiveness laboring under a damaged reputation, which contrasted badly with a more dominant American optimism.

Even in 1928 when the Democrats picked the Irish Catholic Al Smith as [their] presidential candidate, Klan leaders could not produce a revival. With the crash and Great Depression of the 1930s, the Klan ranks thinned to even fewer thousands. Shrunken to the Southeastern United States, the Klan sometimes had friends in power and engaged in occasional night riding and anti-union violence. It denounced the New Deal as communistic, but offered no alternatives.

At the end of the 1930s, Imperial Wizard Hiram Evans sold the Klan's Peachtree Street Palace to the Roman Catholic Church and the Klan itself to a veterinarian, Jimmy Colescott, from Terre Haute in the once potent realm of Indiana. A joint meeting with the German-American bund, in New Jersey, drew bad publicity. World War II, gas rationing, and a lien from the Internal Revenue Service for back taxes temporarily put the Imperial Empire out of business.

It was brought back to life after the end of the greater war in Europe, and maintains a fragmented existence mainly in the Southeast today, unmasked by state and local laws and watched by the F.B.I. It failed as a resistance movement during the civil rights days of the 1950s and 1960s in the South. Despite the annual compulsion of the press, wire services, and television to rediscover the Klan and announce its "revival," the Klan endures but has not regained any of the unity, numbers, or influence it once had in the 1920s. It was still capable of violence, but at the end of the 1970s, the most serious Klan watcher, the Anti-Defamation League, computed the strength of the various contending Klans at no more than 10,000.

DOCUMENTS

The Klan's Fight for Americanism, 1926

The real indictment against the Roman Church is that it is, fundamentally and irredeemably, in its leadership, in politics, in thought, and largely in membership, actually and actively alien, un-American and usually anti-American. The old stock Americans, with the exception of the few such of Catholic faith—who are in a class by themselves, standing tragically torn between their faith and their racial and national patriotism—see in the Roman Church today the chief leader of alienism, and the most dangerous alien power with a foothold inside our boundaries. It is this and nothing

SOURCE: Hiram Evans, "Klan's Fight for Americanism," *North American Review* 123 (March–May 1926): 33–63. Reprinted by permission of the University of Northern Iowa.

else that has revived hostility to Catholicism. By no stretch of the imagination can it fairly be called religious prejudice, though, now that the hostility has become active, it does derive some strength from the religious schism.

We Americans see many evidences of Catholic alienism. We believe that its official position and its dogma, its theocratic autocracy and its claim to full authority in temporal as well as spiritual matters, all make it impossible for it as a church, or for its members if they obey it, to cooperate in a free democracy in which Church and State have been separated. It is true that in this country the Roman Church speaks very softly on these points, so that many Catholics do not know them. It is also true that the Roman priests preach Americanism, subject to their own conception of Americanism, of course. But the Roman Church itself makes a point of the divine and unalterable character of its dogma, it has never seen fit to abandon officially any of these un-American attitudes, and it still teaches them in other countries. Until it does renounce them, we cannot believe anything except that they all remain in force, ready to be called into action whenever feasible, and temporarily hushed up only for expediency.

The hierarchical government of the Roman Church is equally at odds with Americanism. The Pope and the whole hierarchy have been for centuries almost wholly Italian. It is nonsense to suppose that a man, by entering a church, loses his race or national loyalties. The Roman Church today, therefore, is just what its name says—Roman; and it is impossible for its hierarchy or the policies they dictate to be in real sympathy with Americanism. Worse, the Italians have proven to be one of the least assimilable of people. The autocratic nature of the Catholic Church organization, and its suppression of free conscience or free decision, need not be discussed; they are unquestioned. Thus it is fundamental to the Roman Church to demand a supreme loyalty, overshadowing national or race loyalty, to a power that is inevitably alien, and which at the best must inevitably inculcate ideals un-American if not actively anti-American. . . .

The facts are that almost everywhere, and especially in the great industrial centers where the Catholics are strongest, they vote almost as a unit, under control of leaders of their own faith, always in support of the interests of the Catholic Church and of Catholic candidates without regard to other interests, and always also in support of alienism whenever there is an issue raised. They vote, in short, not as American citizens, but as aliens and Catholics! They form the biggest, strongest, most cohesive of all the alien *blocs*. On many occasions they form alliances with other alien *blocs* against American interests, as with the Jews in New York today, and with others in the case of the recent opposition to immigrant restriction. . . .

There are three of these great racial instincts, vital elements in both the historic and the present attempts to build an America which shall fulfill the aspirations and justify the heroism of the men who made the nation. These are the instincts of loyalty to the white race, to the traditions of America, and to the spirit of Protestantism, which has been an essential part of Americanism ever since the days of Roanoke and Plymouth Rock. They are condensed into the Klan slogan: "Native, white, Protestant supremacy."

First in the Klansman's mind is patriotism—America for Americans. He believes religiously that a betrayal of Americanism or the American race is treason to the most sacred of trusts, a trust from his fathers and a trust from God. He believes, too, that Americanism can only be achieved if the pioneer stock is kept pure. . . .

Americanism, to the Klansman, is a thing of the spirit, a purpose and a point of view, that can only come through instinctive racial understanding. It has, to be sure, certain defined principles, but he does not believe that many aliens understand those principles, even when they use our words in talking about them. Democracy is one, fairdealing, impartial justice, equal opportunity, religious liberty, independence, self-reliance, courage, endurance, acceptance of individual responsibility as well as individual rewards for effort, willingness to sacrifice for the good of his family, his nation and his race before anything else but God, dependence on enlightened conscience for guidance, the right to unhampered development—these are fundamental. But within the bounds they fix there must be the utmost freedom, tolerance, liberalism. In short, the Klansman believes in the greatest possible diversity and individualism within the limits of the American spirit. But he believes also that few aliens can understand that spirit, that fewer try to, and that there must be resistance, intolerance even, toward anything that threatens it, or the fundamental national unity based upon it.

The second word in the Klansman's trilogy is "white." The white race must be supreme, not only in America but in the world. This is equally undebatable, except on the ground that the races might live together, each with full regard for the rights and interests of others, and that those rights and interests would never conflict. Such an idea, of course, is absurd; the colored races today, such as Japan, are clamoring not for equality but for their supremacy. The whole history of the world, on its broader lines, has been one of race conflicts, wars, subjugation or extinction. This is not pretty, and certainly disagrees with the maudlin theories of cosmopolitanism, but it is truth. The world has been so made that each race must fight for its life, must conquer, accept slavery or die. The Klansman believes that the whites will not become slaves, and he does not intend to die before his time.

Moreover, the future of progress and civilization depends on the continued supremacy of the white race. The forward movement of the world for centuries has come entirely from it. Other races each had its chance and either failed or stuck fast, while white civilization shows no sign of having reached its limit. Until the whites falter, or some colored civilization has a miracle of awakening, there is not a single colored stock that can claim even equality with the white; much less supremacy.

The third of the Klan principles is that Protestantism must be supreme; that Rome shall not rule America. The Klansman believes this is not merely because he is a Protestant, nor even because the Colonies that are now our nation were settled for the purpose of wresting America from the control of Rome and establishing a land of free conscience. He believes it also because Protestantism is an essential part of Americanism; without it America could never have been created and without it she cannot go forward. Roman rule would kill it.

Congress Debates Immigration Restriction, 1921

HOUSE OF REPRESENTATIVES

Mr. [Lucian Walton] PARISH [D.-Tex.]. We should stop immigration entirely until such a time as we can amend our immigration laws and so write them that hereafter no one shall be admitted except he be in full sympathy with our Constitution and laws, willing to declare himself obedient to our flag, and willing to release himself from any obligations he may owe to the flag of the country from which he came.

It is time that we act now, because within a few short years the damage will have been done. The endless tide of immigration will have filled our country with a foreign and unsympathetic element. Those who are out of sympathy with our Constitution and the spirit of our Government will be here in large numbers, and the true spirit of Americanism left us by our fathers will gradually become poisoned by this uncertain element.

The time once was when we welcomed to our shores the oppressed and downtrodden people from all the world, but they came to us because of oppression at home and with the sincere purpose of making true and loyal American citizens, and in truth and in fact they did adapt themselves to our ways of thinking and contributed in a substantial sense to the progress and development that our civilization has made. But that time has passed now; new and strange conditions have arisen in the countries over there; new and strange doctrines are being taught. The Governments of the Orient are being overturned and destroyed, and anarchy and bolshevism are threatening the very foundation of many of them, and no one can foretell what the future will bring to many of those countries of the Old World now struggling with these problems.

Our country is a self-sustaining country. It has taught the principles of real democracy to all the nations of the earth; its flag has been the synonym

SOURCE: *Congressional Record*, April 20, 1921, 450, December 10, 1921, 177.

of progress, prosperity, and the preservation of the rights of the individual, and there can be nothing so dangerous as for us to allow the undesirable foreign element to poison our civilization and thereby threaten the safety of the institutions that our forefathers have established for us.

Now is the time to throw about this country the most stringent immigration laws and keep from our shores forever those who are not in sympathy with the American ideals. It is the time now for us to act and act quickly, because every month's delay increases the difficulty in which we find ourselves and renders the problems of government more difficult of solution. We must protect ourselves from the poisonous influences that are threatening the very foundation of the Governments of Europe; we must see to it that those who come here are loyal and true to our Nation and impress upon them that it means something to have the privileges of American citizenship. We must hold this country true to the American thought and the American ideals. . . .

Mr. [James V.] McClintic [D.-Okla.]. Some time ago it was my privilege to visit Ellis Island, not as a member of the committee but as a private citizen interested in obtaining information relative to the situation which exists at that place. I stood at the end of a hall with three physicians, and I saw them examine each immigrant as they came down the line, rolling back the upper eyelid in order to gain some information as to the individual's physical condition. I saw them place the chalk marks on their clothing which indicated that they were in a diseased condition, so that they could be separated when they reached the place where they were to undergo certain examinations. Afterwards I went to a large assembly hall where immigrants came before the examiners to take the literacy test, and the one fact that impressed me more than anything else was that practically every single immigrant examined that day had less than $50 to his credit. . . .

Practically all of them were weak, small of stature, poorly clad, emaciated, and in a condition which showed that the environment surrounding them in their European homes was indeed very bad.

It is for this reason that I say the class of immigrants coming to the shores of the United States at this time are not the kind of people we want as citizens in this country. It is a well-known fact that the majority of immigrants coming to this country at the present time are going into the large industrial centers instead of the agricultural centers of the United States, and when it is taken into consideration that the large centers are already crowded to the extent that there was hardly sufficient living quarters to take care of the people, it can be readily seen that this class of people, instead of becoming of service to the communities where they go, they will become charges to be taken care of by charitable institutions. The week I visited Ellis Island I was told that 25,000 immigrants had been unloaded at that port. From their personal appearance they seemed to be the offcasts of the countries from which they came. . . .

National-Origins Formula Reaffirmed, 1951

The subcommittee [on immigration and naturalization] is cognizant of the facts existing at the time of the adoption of the national-origins formula and the bitter charges of discrimination hurled at the incorporation of the principle in our immigration laws. The formula is still subjected to such charges but they seem to have lost some of their force over the intervening period of years. Experience has demonstrated that the national-origins formula has been more of a numerically restrictive measure than a means of automatically selecting immigrants from the various nationalities in desired proportions.

Without giving credence to any theory of Nordic superiority, the subcommittee believes that the adoption of the national-origins formula was a rational and logical method of numerically restricting immigration in such a manner as to best preserve the sociological and cultural balance in the population of the United States. There is no doubt that it favored the peoples of the countries of northern and western Europe over those of southern and eastern Europe, but the subcommittee holds that the peoples who had made the greatest contribution to the development of this country were fully justified in determining that the country was no longer a field for further colonization, and henceforth, further immigration would not only be restricted but directed to admit immigrants considered to be more readily assimilable because of the similarity of their cultural background to those of the principal components of our population. . . .

SOURCE: U.S. Congress, Senate Committee on the Judiciary, *U.S. Immigration and Naturalization,* S. Rept. 1515, 82d Cong., 1st sess., 1951, 455.

Chapter 9

Morals and Manners in the 1920s

Bathing beauties and the automobile, two symbols of the Roaring Twenties.

Following World War I, many Americans eagerly embraced what President Warren G. Harding called "a return to normalcy." The term conveyed a nostalgic vision of an America dotted with small towns and farms, with men and women
pursuing traditional roles, oblivious to events in other parts of the world. But the
clock could not be turned back. Indeed, this image of the "good old days" was
not an accurate view of the nation even before the war. The sweeping urban-
industrial revolution of post–Civil War America had stretched the social fabric
and would continue to do so.

The 1920 census provided dramatic evidence of the changes, revealing that
for the first time a majority of Americans lived in urban areas. More Americans
than ever before, including many women, now worked in factories and offices
and saw their style of living affected by the automobile, the movies, a vast array
of new consumer goods, and better housing. For much of the younger generation, the good days were not to be found in some distant past; they were to be
enjoyed right now.

The essay by John D'Emilio and Estelle Friedman centers on the sexual revolution of the 1920s, particularly among American youth. How extensive were the post–World War I changes that the authors describe? How do D'Emilio and Friedman account for the revolution in sexual mores during the 1920s?

No one, as D'Emilio and Friedman indicate, was more prominently identified with the new morality than Margaret Sanger. In the first document, she strongly advocates family planning. What reasons does she give for families to control their size and the spacing of children? Does her argument have a contemporary quality in light of today's debates on abortion?

Many Americans were shocked by the ideas put forth by Sanger and alarmed by many of the societal changes that marked the decade. Some offered plans for countering these developments. In the second document, Senator Henry Myers of Montana singles out for criticism the movies (and the messages that they conveyed), to which millions—especially the young—flocked weekly. Could the movies have wielded as much influence as the senator claimed? What do you think his proposal of censorship would have accomplished?

Criticism of the social climate in the United States did not originate in the 1920s; neither did attempts at reform. Nonetheless, in 1920 reformers had great hopes for a new age about to dawn. In that year the century-old battle against the consumption of alcoholic beverages appeared to have been won with the passage of the Eighteenth Amendment to the Constitution (Prohibition). However, the third document—an excerpt from a statement issued in 1931 by a government commission established to investigate the effectiveness of the amendment and its accompanying legislation—provides findings to the contrary. Can you give any examples of illegal behavior widely practiced today? What are the difficulties in outlawing an activity that a large segment of the public deems acceptable?

ESSAY

The Sexual Revolution

John D'Emilio and Estelle Friedman

In the winter of 1924, the sociologists Robert and Helen Lynd arrived in Muncie, Indiana, to embark upon an intensive investigation of life in a small American city. The study that resulted, *Middletown*, became an American classic. Casting their net widely, the Lynds examined work, home, youth,

SOURCE: John D'Emilio and Estelle Friedman, *Intimate Matters: A History of Sexuality in America*, 239–42, 256–65. Copyright © 1988 by John D'Emilio and Estelle Friedman. Reprinted by permission of HarperCollins Publishers, Inc.

leisure, religious beliefs, and civic institutions in an effort to draw a complex picture of life in the modern age. In the process, *Middletown* had much to say about the social context that was shaping sexuality in the 1920s and that would continue to affect American mores.

In order to emphasize the rapidly changing nature of social life in an industrial era, the Lynds offered 1890 as a counterpoint to the 1920s. Reflecting the small-town values that still survived at the turn of the century in parts of the country, males and females moved in different spheres; daughters remained at home with their mothers, and adolescent boys entered the public world of work which their fathers inhabited. Young men and women rarely mingled without the careful chaperonage of adults. Socializing continued to take place in public settings that brought families and community residents together. Once a couple had embarked upon a serious courtship, they gained the permission to be alone together, but most often in the family parlor or on the front porch, not far from parental supervision. A heavy taboo hung over sexual relations outside of marriage. Sex was an intensely private matter that came into public view only occasionally, when Muncie's small red-light district overstepped its boundaries, angering the citizenry.

Even as the Lynds described it, contemporary readers would have recognized this as the portrait of a world irrevocably lost. Indeed, the youth of Muncie, for whom change had been most dramatic, would not even have remembered what that earlier world was like. Instead, by the 1920s, adolescents moved in a youth-centered world, based in the high schools that most now attended. School had become, according to the Lynds, "a place from which they go home to eat and sleep." Males and females met in classes, at after-school activities and evening socials. Cars provided privacy, and marked the end of the "gentleman caller" who sat in the parlor. A majority of the students went out with friends four or more evenings a week. Youth patronized movies together, drove to nearby towns for weekend dances, and parked in lovers' lanes on the way home. Almost half of Muncie's male high school students, and a third of its female students, had participated in the recent vogue of the "petting" party; girls who did not were decidedly less popular. After graduation, boys and girls alike left home to work. Increasing economic independence led to less parental supervision over premarital behavior, at the same time that work allowed the young to continue to meet away from home.

This new autonomy and mobility of youth came at a time when Muncie society, through many of the items and activities of a consumer economy, was focused more and more on sexuality. The newspaper advice columns of Dorothy Dix and other syndicated writers instructed female readers in how to catch a man, the thrill and magic of love, and the nature of modern marriage at the same time that relationships were being redefined in romantic, erotic terms. Popular songs of the decade, such as "It Had to Be You," taught that love was a mysterious experience that occurred in a flash when the "chemistry" was right. Sex adventure magazines had become big sellers with stories titled "The Primitive Lover" ("She wanted a caveman husband") and "Indolent Kisses." Muncie's nine movie theaters, open daily and offering twenty-two programs a week, filled their houses by offering such fare as *Married Flirts, Rouged Lips,* and *Alimony.* One popular film of the decade, *Flaming Youth,* attracted audiences by promising images of "neckers, petters, white kisses, red kisses, pleasure-mad daughters, sensation-craving mothers."

The world that the Lynds described, of autonomous youth coming of age in a social environment where erotic images beckoned, has remained fixed in the popular view of the 1920s as a time of new sexual freedoms. Frederick Lewis Allen, in his best-selling account of the decade, *Only Yesterday,* looked at the cultural landscape and detected a "revolution in manners and morals." Images from the 1920s abound to sustain his assessment—flappers and jazz babies; rumble seats and raccoon coats; F. Scott Fitzgerald novels and speakeasies; petting parties and Hollywood sex symbols. And, in fact, despite the evidence of change in sexual mores in the years before World War I, the 1920s do stand out as a time when something in the sexual landscape decisively altered and new patterns clearly emerged. The decade was recognizably modern in a way that previous ones were not. The values, attitudes, and activities of the pre-Depression years unmistakably point to the future rather than the past.

One reason, perhaps, why the twenties have loomed so large as a critical turning point is that patterns of behavior and sexual norms formerly associated with other groups in the population had, by then, spread to the white middle class. The more lavish cabaret appropriated the music and dancing of black and white working-class youth. Movie palaces replaced storefront theaters, and Hollywood directors churned out feature-length films that attracted youths and adults of every class. Bohemian radicals relinquished their proprietorship over the work of modern sexual theorists such as Ellis and Freud, whose ideas received wide currency. Purity crusaders lost the momentum of the prewar years and found themselves rapidly left behind by a culture that scoffed at the sexual prudery of its ancestors. Although each of these developments had roots in the prewar era, not until the 1920s did they experience a full flowering.

The sexual issues that preoccupied the 1920s—the freedom of middle-class youth, the continuing agitation over birth control, debates about the future of marriage, the commercial manipulation of the erotic—suggest the direction in which American values were heading. Sexual expression was moving beyond the confines of marriage, not as the deviant behavior of prostitutes and their customers, but as the normative behavior of many Americans. The heterosocial world in which youth matured encouraged the trend, and the growing availability of contraceptives removed some of the danger attached to nonmarital heterosexuality. New ideas about the essential healthfulness of sexual expression reshaped marriage, too, as couples approached conjugal life with the expectation that erotic enjoyment, and not simply spiritual union, was an integral part of a successful marital relationship. To be sure, resistance to these modern norms surfaced. Some supporters of a new "companionate" marriage advocated it as a way of containing the excesses of youthful libido, while the new visibility of the erotic in popular culture antagonized some and spawned opposition. But, in general, American society was moving by the 1920s toward a view of erotic expression that can be defined as sexual liberalism—an overlapping set of beliefs that detached sexual activity from the instrumental goal of procreation, affirmed heterosexual pleasure as a value in itself, defined sexual satisfaction as a critical component of personal happiness and successful marriage, and weakened the connections between sexual expression and marriage by providing youth with room for some experimentation as preparation for adult status.

At times during the succeeding generation, the crises that punctuated mid-twentieth-century American life seemed to obscure this trend. Under the pressure of the Depression of the 1930s, for instance, the consumerism and commercialized amusements that gave play to sexual adventure temporarily withered. Sobriety and gloom replaced the buoyant exuberance of the previous decade. Dating became a simpler affair, while the anxieties of unemployment and hard times created sexual tensions in many marriages. Birth control became less an issue of freedom for women, and more a method of regulating the poor. After World War II, the impulse to conform and settle down after years of depression, war, and cold war encouraged a rush to early marriage and saw the birth rate zoom upward. Sexual experimentation appeared lost in a maze on suburban housing developments as a new generation took on family responsibilities and raised more children than their parents had. The erotic seemed to disappear under a wave of innocent domesticity, captured in television shows like *Father Knows Best* or the Hollywood comedies of Rock Hudson and Doris Day. A resurgent purity impulse attacked symbols of sexual permissiveness such as pornography and imposed penalties on those who deviated too sharply from family values.

Despite these appearances, however, the forces that fed sexual liberalism developed apace. The availability and accessibility of reliable contraceptives highlighted the divorce of sexual activity from the procreative consequences that inhibited erotic enthusiasm. Sexual imagery gradually became an integral feature of the public realm, legitimate and aboveground. A youth culture that encouraged heterosexual expressiveness became ubiquitous. Couples looked to marriage as a source of continuing erotic pleasures. By the mid-1960s, sexual liberalism had become the dominant ethic, as powerful in its way as was the civilized morality of the late nineteenth century. . . .

Birth control offers perhaps the most dramatic example of the change that occurred in American sexual mores during the middle of the twentieth century. At the start of the 1920s, it still bore the mark of radicalism, and the birth control movement appeared to many as a threat to moral order. The federal Comstock law, with its prohibition on the importation, mailing, and interstate shipment of contraceptive information and devices, remained in effect, and almost half of the states, including most of the populous ones of the Northeast and Midwest, had their own anti-contraceptive statutes. To agitate for birth control placed one outside the law. By the late 1960s, however, virtually all legal impediments to access had collapsed, and the federal government was actively promoting it. Advances in technology and shifts in values made reliable contraceptives an integral feature of married life as well as widely available to the unmarried.

For most of the 1920s and 1930s Margaret Sanger remained the key figure in the birth control movement and the individual most responsible for the changes that occurred. Though her leadership and visibility provided continuity with the pre–World War I agitation, the politics of the movement was undergoing an important shift. Government repression of radicalism and the decline of organized feminism after suffrage altered the context in which the fight for birth control was occurring. Sanger adapted to the new circumstances by detaching the question of contraception from larger social issues and movements. Throughout the twenties and thirties, she campaigned solely to make contraception freely available to women.

Even with a narrowed focus, however, Sanger remained a militant fighter, willing to use any means necessary to achieve her goals. She continued to risk arrest, believing as she did that "agitation through violation of the law was the key to the public." She also propagandized widely, through the pages of her journal (the *Birth Control Review*), through the books that she authored, and through her extensive speaking tours and public conferences. With the backing of her organization, the American Birth Control League, Sanger lobbied for legislative change and embarked once again on a venture in clinical services when she established the Clinical Research Bureau in 1923.

Sanger's lobbying efforts and the clinic that she supported point to an important way in which her strategy was evolving. In New York State in the 1920s, she campaigned for a "doctors only" bill, designed to allow physicians to provide contraceptives, but restricting that right to licensed practitioners. The Clinical Research Bureau, though it provided female clients with contraceptive devices, existed mainly to gather data that would persuade a science-conscious profession that safe, reliable methods of fertility control were available. Both initiatives aimed at enlisting the medical profession as allies in her cause, since its hostility to contraception constituted a major obstacle to success. In the process, however, the politics of birth control tilted in a more conservative direction. From a key issue in the struggle for female emancipation, contraception was gradually becoming a matter of professional health care. . . .

As one might expect, the contraceptive revolution moved hand in hand with changes in both sexual behavior and attitudes. Historians of twentieth-century mores have tended to underplay this shift, by emphasizing instead the stability of one important index of sexual behavior, the female premarital coital rate. For women coming of age in the 1920s, the incidence of premarital intercourse jumped sharply, to roughly fifty percent of the cohort, and thereafter remained relatively constant until the late 1960s. Yet hidden behind the stability of these figures lay a whole world of sexual change. Activity that provoked guilt in the 1920s had become integrated by the 1960s into a new code of sexual ethics that made it morally acceptable. What was daring and nonconformist in the earlier period appeared commonplace a generation later. And, as attitudes and ideals altered, so too did aspects of sexual activity. Dating, necking, and petting among peers became part and parcel of the experience of American youth, providing an initiatory stage, uncommon for their elders, leading to the coital experience of adulthood and marriage. To marriage itself, couples brought new expectations of pleasure, satisfaction, and mutual enjoyment, encouraged by a more explicit advice literature that emphasized the sexual component of conjugal life. The integration of contraception into middle-class married life also meant that the reproductive requirement for marital intimacy had receded far into the background. Though experience might not always live up to these new standards, men and women in the mid-twentieth century were approaching marriage with heightened anticipation of physical pleasure.

Evidence abounds of shifts in both standards and patterns of behavior among American youth in the decades after World War I. During the 1920s, white college youth captured the lion's share of attention of contemporaries seeking to chart the society's changing values. Although less than thirteen percent of the eighteen- to twenty-one-year-old population were enrolled in colleges at the end of the 1920s, the numbers had more than tripled since 1890. For the first time, a distinctive subculture took shape among the middle-class young, with values and activities that set them apart from their parents' generation.

College — Sexual innovation played a key role in this new world of youth. Particularly in coeducational institutions, heterosocial mixing became the norm. Young men and women mixed casually in classes, extracurricular activities, and social spaces, with a great deal of freedom from adult supervision. Dating in pairs, unlike the informal group socializing of the nineteenth century, permitted sexual liberties that formerly were sanctioned only for couples who were courting. College youth flaunted their new freedoms. As one male editor of a campus paper provocatively expressed it, "there are only two kinds of co-eds, those who have been kissed, and those who are sorry they haven't been kissed." Magazines debated the implications of "petting parties," an increasingly common feature of college life. One study of college youth during the 1920s found that ninety-two percent of coeds had engaged in petting, and that those "rejecting all sex play feel that they are on the defensive."

What a relatively small percentage of middle-class youth were experiencing in college, much larger numbers tasted in high school. By the 1920s, high school had become a mass experience, with almost three-quarters of the young enrolled. Here, too, adolescent boys and girls encountered one another daily, with casual interaction throughout the day that often continued into evening social activities. One observer of youthful mores estimated that a large majority of high school youth engaged in hugging and kissing and that a significant minority "do not restrict themselves to that, but go further, and indulge in other sex liberties which, by all the conventions, are outrageously improper." Automobiles allowed young people still living at home greater freedom of movement than ever before. Groups of teenagers might drive to the next town for a Saturday-night dance; on weeknights, too, it became easier to escape parental supervision. So quickly and widely did cars become an essential part of this heterosocial world of youth that one commentator labeled the auto "a house of prostitution on wheels." Assessing these changes, Ben Lindsey, a Colorado juvenile court judge who had dealt with the young for a generation, considered them to be reflective of a historic transformation in American life. "Not only is this revolt from the old standards of conduct taking place," he wrote, "but it is unlike any revolt that has ever taken place before. Youth has always been rebellious. . . . But this is different. It has the whole weight and momentum of a new scientific and economic order behind it."

Although the innovations in sexual behavior among middle-class youth were real, they nonetheless operated within certain peer-defined limits. Young men took liberties with women of their own class that their parents would have considered improper, but the sexual freedom of the 1920s was hardly a promiscuous one. The kissing and petting that occurred among couples who dated casually did not often progress beyond that. Surveys of sexual behavior among white middle-class women revealed that the generation coming of age in the 1920s had a significantly higher incidence of premarital intercourse than women born in the preceding decades. But the evidence also suggests that, for the most part, young women generally restricted coitus to a single partner, the man they expected to marry. "Going all the way" was permissible, but only in the context of love and commitment. For men, the changes in female sexual behavior had important implications. Beginning in the 1920s, the frequency of recourse to prostitution began to decline. As Lindsey noted, "with the breaking up of those districts, [boys] turned to girls of their own class, a thing they had seldom done in the past."

As young people adopted the novel practice of dating, they shaped, learned, and refashioned its rules. Newspaper advice columns in the years after World War I printed letters from confused youth who wondered whether a good-night kiss was an appropriate ending for an evening date, and who searched for words to define the feelings aroused by the dating relationship. By the 1930s, the elaboration of this teenage ritual had produced words other than "love" to describe the emotions, and had differentiated "courting" and "keeping company" from the more casual, and common, practices of "going out" and "going steady." When the Lynds returned to Muncie in the 1930s, one young man reported to them that "the fellows regard necking as a taken-for-granted part of a date. We fellows used occasionally to get slapped for doing things, but the girls don't do that much any more. . . . Our high school students of both sexes . . . know everything and do everything—openly." Although he likely exaggerated in his claims about "everything," numerous surveys of American youth confirm the widening boundaries of permissible sexual activity. The rapid acceptance of this peer-directed system of dating, as well as the quick demise of its predecessor, can be inferred from changes in that reliable arbiter of social behavior, Emily Post's *Etiquette.* A chapter which, in the 1923 edition, was titled "Chaperons and Other Conventions" became "The Vanishing Chaperon and Other New Conventions" four years later; the passing of another decade brought the wistful heading "The Vanished Chaperon and Other Lost Conventions." One study of high school students in St. Louis on the eve of World War II found dating to be ubiquitous, with most couples returning home after one in the morning. Freed from parental supervision for long hours, boys and girls alike exhibited "a fairly general acceptance of the naturalness" of kisses and light petting as part of a date. Indeed, St. Louis's high school students proved far more tolerant about sexual matters than about other kinds of behavior such as smoking and drinking.

The system of dating, at least as it evolved between the two world wars, did not extend to all youth. Its adoption depended upon surplus income for clothes and entertainment, access to automobiles outside major cities, school attendance to enforce peer-based norms, and sufficient population density to sustain a range of commercialized amusements. Its contours thus mark it as a ritual of white middle-class youth in the cities and suburbs.

Among poor blacks in the rural South, for instance, older patterns of sociability persisted as young people experienced both traditional freedoms and constraints. With few sanctions against premarital intercourse, "sex play," according to one observer, "becomes matter-of-fact behavior for youth." As one young girl explained it, "I ain't never thought of there being anything wrong about it." Denied access because of segregation, poverty, and rural isolation from most of the places where formal dating took place, young rural blacks met at church, harvest festivals, picnics, and while working in the fields, much as they had in the past. Yet, an awareness of the world beyond the small rural community also generated a "longing for pleasures like those of the city." One young man expressed his discontent by telling an interviewer, "there ain't no decent place to take a girl. . . . If you ain't got a car, you just ain't nowhere." Meanwhile, black parents of moderate wealth and status, in an effort to differentiate themselves from the rural masses and to provide education and mobility for the next generation, socialized their children into strict moral codes. In his study of youth in the Black Belt before World War II, Charles Johnson found that among the elite, even young men accepted rigid standards of chastity. Parents kept close rein on their daughters, as the testimony of one North Carolina girl made clear: "Yes, I have a boy friend. He calls on me and takes me to socials. Sometimes mama lets me go to movies with him in the afternoon, but if he goes with me at night papa and mama go too."

For white youth as well, rural and small-town residence affected patterns of sexual interaction. In rural communities many young people lacked mobility. "I had no car," explained one youth who bemoaned his inability to date. "We lived 20 miles from town and to get to town I had to ride with my father or some other adult." Then, too, in smaller communities adults were able to watch the behavior of the young more closely. "I'll tell you, it's really tough getting it in a small town," one young man complained. "Everyone has their eyes on you and especially on the girl. You can hardly get away with anything." A young man who moved to the city when he was seventeen noted the difference it made. He had never felt much sexual desire during his years in the country, he commented, but city life with its abundant opportunities suddenly seemed to generate "much more interest in it."

Although urban working-class youth did not share in the sexual culture of the middle class, this by no means implied a sentence of chastity. In some cases it could translate into freedom from the constraints of peer-enforced norms. In cities and towns, white and black youth who dropped out of high school or who did not immediately marry after graduation found themselves earning wages, yet without the expense of maintaining a household. Removed from the web of daily gossip that shaped the behavior of high school and college students, they were more likely to move beyond petting in their sexual relationships. Dance halls, bowling alleys, skating rinks, and, after prohibition, bars provided settings for young men and women to meet; automobiles, bought with hard-earned wages, offered privacy. One high school dropout embarked upon her first sexual affair with a dance-hall partner. "I made up my mind at the dance Oscar could have it," she recalled. "Oh, it was wonderful. That night, I thought, 'I don't care if I have a baby.'" Several more relationships ensued before she married in her late teens. The thriving business in condoms that Malcolm X operated at a Boston dance hall suggests the ease with which sexual favors could be exchanged among working-class youth in the city. So, too, does evidence of prenuptial conceptions and illegitimacy among the poor and the working

161

class. In one Illinois town, over half of the girls who did not graduate from high school gave birth within eight months of their wedding. And almost a quarter of the births in the lowest social class of whites occurred outside of marriage.

By accelerating the shift to city living, and by providing youth with more economic autonomy and freedom from adult supervision, World War II brought unprecedented opportunities for premarital experience. The war released millions of youth from the social environments that inhibited erotic expression, and threw them into circumstances that opened up new sexual possibilities. Millions of young men left home to join the military, while many young women migrated in search of employment. The demands of wartime drew teenagers into the paid labor force while weakening the influence that family and community held over their behavior.

Ample testimony from the war years confirms the sexual expressiveness of youth. For many young women, men in uniform held erotic appeal. "When I was 16," one college student recalled,

> I let a sailor pick me up and go all the way with me. I had intercourse with him partly because he had a strong personal appeal for me, but mainly because I had a feeling of high adventure and because I wanted to please a member of the armed forces.

Another, rebuffed by a sailor boyfriend who felt she was too young, went on to have affairs with fifteen others by war's end. Civilian men, too, partook of the sexual freedom of the war years. One teenager described his life then as "a real sex paradise. The plant and the town were just full of working girls who were on the make. Where I was, a male war worker became the center of loose morality. It was a sex paradise." A high school student lost his virginity with a woman of thirty whose husband was overseas. "We weren't in love," he recalled, "although we were very fond of each other. The times were conducive for this sort of thing. Otherwise, nothing would ever have happened between us."

The response of moral reformers points to the changes that had occurred since the previous generation. Whereas those of the First World War focused on the dangers of prostitution, by the 1940s it was the behavior of "amateur girls"—popularly known as khaki-wackies, victory girls, and good-time Charlottes—that concerned moralists. "The old time prostitute in a house or formal prostitute on the street is sinking into second place," wrote one venereal-disease expert. "The new type is the young girl in her late teens and early twenties, the young woman in every field of life who is determined to have one fling or better." Efforts to scare GIs into continence by emphasizing the danger of disease had little impact on men who, according to one officer, "think as little of a gonorrheal infection as they do of the ordinary common cold." Or, as another phrased it, "the sex act cannot be made unpopular." Local law-enforcement officials worked overtime to contain the sexual behavior of young women, yet their efforts only seemed to confirm the perception that prostitution was not the issue. Arrests for selling sexual favors rose less than twenty percent during the war years, but charges of disorderly conduct increased almost two hundred percent, and those for other morals offenses, such as promiscuous behavior or patronizing bars too frequently, increased nearly as much. . . .

DOCUMENTS

Happiness in Marriage, 1926

We must recognize that the whole position of womanhood has changed today. Not so many years ago it was assumed to be a just and natural state of affairs that marriage was considered as nothing but a preliminary to motherhood. A girl passed from the guardianship of her father or nearest male relative to that of her husband. She had no will, no wishes of her own. Hers not to question why, but merely to fulfill duties imposed upon her by the man into whose care she was given.

Marriage was synonymous with maternity. But the pain, the suffering, the wrecked lives of women and children that such a system caused, show us that it did not work successfully. Like all other professions, motherhood must serve its period of apprenticeship.

Today women are on the whole much more individual. They possess as strong likes and dislikes as men. They live more and more on the plane of social equality with men. They are better companions. We should be glad that there is more enjoyable companionship and real friendship between men and women.

This very fact, it is true, complicates the marriage relation, and at the same time ennobles it. Marriage no longer means the slavish subservience of the woman to the will of the man. It means, instead, the union of two strong and highly individualized natures. Their first problem is to find out just what the terms of this partnership are to be. Understanding full and complete cannot come all at once, in one revealing flash. It takes time to arrive at a full and sympathetic understanding of each other, and mutually to arrange lives to increase this understanding. Out of the mutual adjustments, harmony must grow and discords gradually disappear.

These results cannot be obtained if the problem of parenthood is thrust upon the young husband and wife before they are spiritually and economically prepared to meet it. For naturally the coming of the first baby means

SOURCE: Margaret Sanger, *Happiness in Marriage* (New York: Blue Ribbon Books, 1926), 83–97.

that all other problems must be thrust aside. That baby is a great fact, a reality that must be met. Preparations must be made for its coming. The layette must be prepared. The doctor must be consulted. The health of the wife may need consideration. The young mother will probably prefer to go to the hospital. All of these preparations are small compared to the regime after the coming of the infant.

Now there is a proper moment for every human activity, a proper season for every step in self-development. The period for cementing the bond of love is no exception to this great truth. For only by the full and glorious living through these years of early marriage are the foundations of an enduring and happy married life rendered possible. By this period the woman attains a spiritual freedom. Her womanhood has a chance to bloom. She wins a mastery over her destiny; she acquires self-reliance, poise, strength, a youthful maturity. She abolishes fear. Incidentally, few of us realize, since the world keeps no record of this fact, how many human beings are conceived in fear and even in repugnance by young mothers who are the victims of undesired maternity. Nor has science yet determined the possibilities of a generation conceived and born of conscious desire.

In the wife who has lived through a happy marriage, for whom the bonds of passionate love have been fully cemented, maternal desire is intensified and matured. Motherhood becomes for such a woman not a penalty or a punishment, but the road by which she travels onward toward completely rounded self-development. Motherhood thus helps her toward the unfolding and realization of her higher nature.

Her children are not mere accidents, the outcome of chance. When motherhood is a mere accident, as so often it is in the early years of careless or reckless marriages, a constant fear of pregnancy may poison the days and nights of the young mother. Her marriage is thus converted into a tragedy. Motherhood becomes for her a horror instead of a joyfully fulfilled function.

Millions of marriages have been blighted, not because of any lack of love between the young husband and wife, but because children have come too soon. Often these brides become mothers before they have reached even physical maturity, before they have completed the period of adolescence. This period in our race is as a rule complete around the age of twenty-three. Motherhood is possible after the first menstruation. But what is physically possible is very often from every other point of view inadvisable. A young woman should be fully matured from every point of view—physically, mentally and psychically—before maternity is thrust upon her. . . .

The problem of premature parenthood is intensified and aggravated when a second infant follows too rapidly the advent of the first, and inevitably husband and wife are made the slaves of this undreamed of situation, bravely trying to stave off poverty, whipped to desperation by the heavy hand of chance and involuntary parenthood. How can they then recapture their early love? It is not surprising that more often they do not even trouble themselves to conceal the contempt which is the bitter fruit of that young and romantic passion. . . .

Instead of being a self-determined and self-directing love, everything is henceforward determined by the sweet tyranny of the child. I have known of several young mothers, despite a great love for the child, to rebel against this intolerable situation. Vaguely feeling that this new maternity has rendered them unattractive to their husbands, slaves to a deadly routine of bottles, baths and washing, they have revolted. I know of innumerable marriages which have been wrecked by premature parenthood.

Love has ever been blighted by the coming of children before the real foundations of marriage have been established. Quite aside from the injustice done to the child who has been brought accidentally into the world, this lamentable fact sinks into insignificance when compared to the injustice inflicted by chance upon the young couple, and the irreparable blow to their love occasioned by premature or involuntary parenthood.

For these reasons, in order that harmonious and happy marriage may be established as the foundation for happy homes and the advent of healthy and desired children, premature parenthood must be avoided. Birth Control is the instrument by which this universal problem may be solved.

Moving Pictures Evoke Concern, 1922

Moving pictures, their educational influence for good or for bad, their growing importance as a factor in our civilization, the announced determination of those controlling the industry boldly to enter politics, and the desirability of regulation by law through censorship constitute a subject of acknowledged importance to the American people. . . .

The motion picture is a great invention, and it has become a powerful factor for good or bad in our civilization. It has great educational power for good or bad. It may educate young people in the ways of good citizenship or in ways of dissoluteness, extravagance, wickedness, and crime. It furnishes recreation, diversion, and amusement at a cheap price to many millions of our people—largely the young. It is the only form of amusement within the means of millions. It possesses great potential possibilities for good. It may furnish not only amusement but education of a high order.

Through motion pictures the young and the old may see depicted every good motive, laudable ambition, commendable characteristic, ennobling trait of humanity. They may be taught that honesty is the best policy; that virtue and worth are rewarded; that industry leads to success. Those who live in the country or in small interior towns, and who never visit large

SOURCE: A speech by Senator Henry Myers, *Congressional Record*, June 29, 1922, 9655–57.

cities, may see pictured the skyscrapers, the crowded streets, the rush and jam of metropolitan cities. Those who live in the interior, and never see the seacoast, may see on the screen the great docks and wharves of seaports and see the loading and unloading of giant ocean steamers. Those who live in crowded cities, and never see the country or get a glimpse of country life, may have depicted to them all the beauties of rural life and scenery. All may see scenes of the luxuriant Tropics, the grandeur of Alpine Mountains, polar conditions, life in the Orient. The cities, palaces, cathedrals, ports, rural life, daily routine, scenic attractions, mode of living of every country on the globe, may be brought to our doors and eyes for a small price. The industry may be made an education to the young.

However, from all accounts, the business has been conducted, generally speaking, upon a low plane and in a decidedly sordid manner. Those who own and control the industry seem to have been of the opinion that the sensual, the sordid, the prurient, the phases of fast life, the ways of extravagance, the risqué, the paths of shady life, drew the greatest attendance and coined for them the most money, and apparently they have been out to get the coin, no matter what the effect upon the public, young or old; and when thoughtful people have suggested or advocated official censorship, in the interest of good citizenship and wholesome morals, the owners of the industry have resented it and, in effect, declared that it was nobody's business other than theirs and concerned nobody other than them what kind of shows they produced; that if people did not like their shows they could stay away from them; that it was their business, and they would conduct it as they might please. At least they have vigorously fought all attempts at censorship and resented them. . . .

I have no doubt young criminals got their ideas of the romance of crime from moving pictures. I believe moving pictures are doing as much harm today as saloons did in the days of the open saloon—especially to the young. They are running day and night, Sunday and every other day, the year round, and in most jurisdictions without any regulation by censorship. I would not abolish them. They can be made a great force for good. I would close them on Sunday and regulate them week days by judicious censorship. Already some dozen or more States have censorship laws, with the right of appeal to the courts, and the movement is on in many other States.

When we look to the source of the moving pictures, the material for them, the personnel of those who pose for them, we need not wonder that many of the pictures are pernicious.

The pictures are largely furnished by such characters as Fatty Arbuckle, of unsavory fame, notorious for his scandalous debauchery and drunken orgies, one of which, attended by many "stars," resulted in the death of Virginia Rappe, a star artist; William Desmond Taylor, deceased, murdered for some mysterious cause; one Valentino, now figuring as the star character in rape and divorce sensations. Many others of like character might be mentioned.

At Hollywood, Calif., is a colony of these people, where debauchery, riotous living, drunkenness, ribaldry, dissipation, free love, seem to be conspicuous. Many of these "stars," it is reported, were formerly bartenders, butcher boys, sopers, swampers, variety actors and actresses, who may have earned $10 or $20 a week, and some of whom are now paid, it is said, salaries of something like $5,000 a month or more, and they do not know what to do with their wealth, extracted from poor people, in large part, in 25 or 50 cent admission fees, except to spend it in riotous living, dissipation, and "high rolling."

These are some of the characters from whom the young people of today are deriving a large part of their education, views of life, and character-forming habits. From these sources our young people gain much of their views of life, inspiration, and education. Rather a poor source is it not? Looks like there is some need for censorship, does it not? There could be some improvement, could there not? . . .

Prohibition Nonobserved, 1931

There is a mass of information before us as to a general prevalence of drinking in homes, in clubs, and in hotels; of drinking parties given and attended by persons of high standing and respectability; of drinking by tourists at winter and summer resorts; and of drinking in connection with public dinners and at conventions. In the nature of the case it is not easy to get at the exact facts in such a connection, and conditions differ somewhat in different parts of the country and even to some extent from year to year. This is true likewise with respect to drinking by women and drinking by youth, as to which also there is a great mass of evidence. In weighing this evidence much allowance must be made for the effect of new standards and independence and individual self-assertion, changed ideas as to conduct generally, and the greater emphasis on freedom and the quest for excitement since the war. As to drinking among youth, the evidence is conflicting. Votes in colleges show an attitude of hostility to or contempt for the law on the part of those who are not unlikely to be leaders in the next generation. It is safe to say that a significant change has taken place in the social attitude toward drinking. This may be seen in the views and conduct of social leaders, business and professional men in the average community. It may be seen in the tolerance of conduct at social gatherings which would not have been possible a generation ago. It is

SOURCE: U.S. Congress, House, U.S. National Commission on Law Enforcement, *Enforcement of the Prohibition Laws of the United States*, H. Doc. 722, 71st Cong., 3d sess., 1931, 21.

reflected in a different way of regarding drunken youth, in a change in the class of excessive drinkers, and in the increased use of distilled liquor in places and connections where formerly it was banned. It is evident that, taking the country as a whole, people of wealth, business men and professional men, and their families, and, perhaps, the higher paid workingmen and their families, are drinking in large numbers in quite frank disregard of the declared policy of the National Prohibition Act. . . .

Chapter 10

The Depression Years

A family of the Great Depression.

The crusades against changing morals and manners during the 1920s seem trivial when compared to the challenges of the Great Depression of the 1930s. Although the United States had suffered economic declines before, the Great Depression was the worst ever: nearly a quarter of the work force was unemployed by 1933, banks failed, the stock market crashed, businesses declared bankruptcy, and families lost their homes and farms.

In the "The Ordeal of the American People," David M. Kennedy provides a vivid description of American suffering during the 1930s as reported by Lorena Hickok. A veteran reporter and close friend of Eleanor Roosevelt, Hickok had been sent by Harry Hopkins, head of relief programs under the Roosevelt administration, to travel the country in order to determine and describe what Kennedy terms "the human reality of the Depression." The essay describes how differences "in gender, age, race, occupation, and region mediated the Depression's impact on particular individuals." How might the life and plans for the future of a person with a background and status similar to your own have been affected by the onset of the Depression? What did Hickok discover about the so-called prosperity of the pre-Depression 1920s?

When urban families ran out of funds, they survived as best they could. The first document consists of excerpts from the testimony of Jacob Billikopf, executive director of the Federation of Jewish Charities in Philadelphia, before a Senate subcommittee studying the issue. What light does the document shed on the reasons why millions of Americans responded so positively to President Franklin Roosevelt's message of hope and to his New Deal programs of relief and public employment?

Today we think of California as a land of sunshine and wealth. Indeed, and after World War II millions of Americans, as well as many immigrants, set out for California in pursuit of the good life. Still, the second document points out that many of those heading for the Golden State during the depression years were Okies—farmers from Texas, Oklahoma, and elsewhere on the southern plains— who were driven from their homes by poverty and great clouds of dust. John Steinbeck's novel *The Grapes of Wrath* brought the plight of these dust bowl refugees to the attention of the public, as did the writings of political activist Carey McWilliams. The second document, a statement by McWilliams before a Congressional committee, describes the conditions facing the Okies in California. That the Okies continued to flock to and remain in California reveals the desperate situation from which they fled. Why did they choose California as the place to rebuild their lives?

The final document tells about the miseries of black families—especially women—in Depression-era New York City. How does the reading support claims that African Americans were the poorest and the most disadvantaged Americans during the 1930s? What does the document suggest about racism?

The New Deal programs, particularly those directed toward relief and reform, helped many businesses, farmers, and workers survive the worst ravages of the 1930s, but economic woes persisted until the boom of World War II finally vanquished the Great Depression.

ESSAY

The Ordeal of the American People
David M. Kennedy

I saw old friends of mine—men I had been to school with—digging ditches and laying sewer pipe. They were wearing their regular business suits as they worked because they couldn't afford overalls and rubber boots. If I ever thought, "There, but for the grace of God—" it was right then.

—Frank Walker, president of the
National Emergency Council, 1934

"What I want you to do," said Harry Hopkins to Lorena Hickok in July 1933, "is to go out around the country and look this thing over. I don't want statistics from you. I don't want the social-worker angle. I just want your own reaction, as an ordinary citizen.

"Go talk with preachers and teachers, businessmen, workers, farmers. Go talk with the unemployed, those who are on relief and those who aren't. And when you talk with them don't ever forget that but for the grace of God you, I, any of our friends might be in their shoes. Tell me what you see and hear. All of it. Don't ever pull your punches."

The Depression was now in its fourth year. In the neighborhoods and hamlets of a stricken nation millions of men and women languished in sullen gloom and looked to Washington with guarded hope. Still they struggled to comprehend the nature of the calamity that had engulfed them. Across Hopkins's desk at the newly created Federal Emergency Relief Administration flowed rivers of data that measured the Depression's impact in cool numbers. But Hopkins wanted more—to touch the human face of the catastrophe, taste in his own mouth the metallic smack of the fear and hunger of the unemployed, as he had when he worked among the immigrant poor at New York's Christadora settlement house in 1912. Tied to his desk in Washington, he dispatched Lorena Hickok in his stead. In her he chose a uniquely gutsy and perceptive observer who could be counted on to see without illusion and to report with candor, insight, and moxie. . . .

Hickok resigned from the Associated Press in June 1933, took a month-long motoring holiday through New England and eastern Canada with Eleanor [Roosevelt], and started off on her new assignment from Hopkins. She set out to interview plain folk and local big shots, housewives and working stiffs, cotton lords and miners, waitresses and mill hands, tenant

Source: David M. Kennedy, *Freedom from Fear: The American People in Depression and War,* 160–70 (New York: Oxford University Press, 1999). Copyright © 1999 by David M. Kennedy. Used by permission of Oxford University Press, Inc.

farmers and relief administrators. At night she holed up in spare hotel rooms and pecked out her impressions on a portable typewriter. Soon her reports started arriving in Hopkins's Washington office, from the sooty coal districts of Pennsylvania and West Virginia and Kentucky in August, from stoically suffering New England villages in September, from the wheat-fields of North Dakota in October. They continued to come for nearly two more years, from the cotton belt of Georgia, the Carolinas, Alabama, and Texas, and from the ranches, mining camps, fruit orchards, and raw cities of the Far West. She saw with a seasoned reporter's eye and wrote in an earthy, no-foolin' style that managed to be at once unsentimentally cool and warmly sympathetic. "Mr. Hopkins said today," an admiring Eleanor wrote her in December 1933, "that your reports would be the best history of the Depression in future years."

From the charts and tables accumulating on his desk even before Hickok's letters began to arrive, Hopkins could already sketch the grim out-lines of that history. Stockholders, his figures confirmed, had watched as three-quarters of the value of their assets had simply evaporated since 1929, a colossal financial meltdown that blighted not only the notoriously idle rich but struggling neighborhood banks, hard-earned retirement nest eggs, and college and university endowments as well. The more than five thou-sand bank failures between the Crash and the New Deal's rescue operation in March 1933 wiped out some $7 billion in depositors' money. Accelerating foreclosures on defaulted home mortgages—150,000 homeowners lost their property in 1930, 200,000 in 1931, 250,000 in 1932—stripped millions of peo-ple of both shelter and life savings at a single stroke and menaced the bal-ance sheets of thousands of surviving banks. Several states and some thirteen hundred municipalities, crushed by sinking real estate prices and consequently shrinking tax revenues, defaulted on their obligations to cred-itors, pinched their already scant social services, cut payrolls, and slashed paychecks. Chicago was reduced to paying its teachers in tax warrants and then, in the winter of 1932–33, to paying them nothing at all.

Gross national product had fallen by 1933 to half its 1929 level. Spend-ing for new plants and equipment had ground to a virtual standstill. Busi-nesses invested only $3 billion in 1933, compared with $24 billion in 1929. Some industries, to be sure, were effectively Depression-proof; shoe and cigarette manufacturers, for example, experienced only minor slumps. Other industries, however, dependent on discretionary spending, had all but gone out of business. Only one-third as many automobiles rolled off the assembly lines in 1933 as in 1929, a slowdown that induced commensurate shrinkage in other heavy industries. Iron and steel production declined by 60 percent from pre-Crash levels. Machine-tool makers cut their output by nearly two-thirds. Residential and industrial construction shriveled to less than one-fifth of its pre-Depression volume, a wrenching contraction that spread through lumber camps, steel mills, and appliance factories, disemploying thousands of loggers, mill hands, sheet-metal workers, engineers, architects, carpenters, plumbers, roofers, plasterers, painters, and electricians. Mute shoals of jobless men drifted through the streets of every American city in 1933.

Nowhere did the Depression strike more savagely than in the American countryside. On America's farms, income had plummeted from $6 billion in what for farmers was the already lean year of 1929 to $2 billion in 1932. The net receipts from the wheat harvest in one Oklahoma county went from $1.2 million in 1931 to just $7,000 in 1933. Mississippi's pathetic $239 per capita income in 1929 sank to $117 in 1933.

Unemployment and its close companion, reduced wages, were the most obvious and the most wounding of all the Depression's effects. The government's data showed that 25 percent of the work force, some thirteen million workers, including nearly four hundred thousand women, stood idle in 1933. The great majority of the men and many of the women were heads of households, the sole breadwinners for their families. Yet if misery was widespread, its burdens were not uniformly distributed. Differences in gender, age, race, occupation, and region powerfully mediated the Depression's impact on particular individuals. To borrow from Tolstoy, every unhappy family was unhappy in its own way. Different people suffered and coped, and occasionally prevailed, according to their own peculiar circumstances.

Working women at first lost their jobs at a faster rate than men—then reentered the work force more rapidly. In the early years of the Depression, many employers, including the federal government, tried to spread what employment they had to heads of households. That meant firing any married woman identified as a family's "secondary" wage-earner. But the gender segregation in employment patterns that was already well established before the Depression also worked to women's advantage. Heavy industry suffered the worst unemployment, but relatively few women stoked blast furnaces in the steel mills or drilled rivets on assembly lines or swung hammers in the building trades. The teaching profession, however, in which women were highly concentrated and indeed constituted a hefty majority of employees, suffered pay cuts but only minimal job losses. And the underlying trends of the economy meant that what new jobs did become available in the 1930s, such as telephone switchboard operation and clerical work, were peculiarly suited to women.

Unemployment fell most heavily on the most predictably vulnerable: the very young, the elderly, the least educated, the unskilled, and especially, as Hickok was about to discover, on rural Americans. It fell with compound force on blacks, immigrants, and Mexican-Americans. Workers under twenty or over sixty were almost twice as likely as others to be out of a job. Hopkins's studies showed that one-fifth of all the people on the federal relief rolls were black, a proportion roughly double the African-American presence in the population. Most of them were in the rural South.

Some of the jobless never appeared on the relief rolls at all because they simply left the country. Thousands of immigrants forsook the fabled American land of promise and returned to their old countries. Some one hundred thousand American workers in 1931 applied for jobs in what appeared to be a newly promising land, Soviet Russia. More than four hundred thousand Mexican-Americans, many of them U.S. citizens, returned to Mexico in the 1930s, some voluntarily but many against their will. Immigration officials in Santa Barbara, California, herded Mexican farm workers into the Southern Pacific depot, packed them into sealed boxcars, and unceremoniously shipped them southward.

The typical unemployed urban worker on relief, Hopkins found, "was a white man, thirty-eight years of age and the head of a household. . . . [H]e had been more often than not an unskilled or semi-skilled worker in the manufacturing or mechanical industries. He had had some ten years' experience at what he considered to be his usual occupation. He had not finished elementary school. He had been out of any kind of job lasting one month or more for two years, and had not been working at his usual occupation for over two and a half years." Hopkins stressed particularly the problems of the elderly, who, he concluded, "through hardship, discouragement and sickness as well as advancing years, [have] gone into an occupational oblivion from which they will never be rescued by private industry." That line of thinking, driven by the specter of permanent, structural unemployment as a result of accelerating technological change, and looking toward removing supposedly obsolescent elderly workers from the wage-labor markets altogether, would in time lead to the landmark Social Security Act of 1935.

Hopkins's statistical data revealed still other aspects of the Depression's impact. Facing an uncertain future, young people were postponing or canceling plans to marry; the marriage rate had fallen since 1929 by 22 percent. The Depression's gloom seeped even into the nation's bedrooms, as married couples had fewer children—15 percent fewer in 1933 than in 1929. Even the divorce rate declined by 25 percent, as the contracting economy sealed the exits from unhappy marriages. Unemployment could also powerfully rearrange the psychological geometry of families. "Before the depression," one jobless father told an interviewer, "I wore the pants in this family, and rightly so. During the depression, I lost something. Maybe you call it self-respect, but in losing it I also lost the respect of my children, and I am afraid that I am losing my wife." "There certainly was a change in our family," said another victim of unemployment, "and I can define it in just one word—I relinquished power in the family. I think the man should be boss in the family. . . . But now I don't even try to be the boss. She controls all the money. . . . The boarders pay her, the children turn in their money to her, and the relief check is cashed by her or the boy. I toned down a good deal as a result of it." Said another: "It's only natural. When a father cannot support his family, supply them with clothing and good food, the children are bound to lose respect. . . . When they see me hanging around the house all the time and know that I can't find work, it has its effect all right."

When Hickok sallied forth to reconnoiter the Depression's human toll in 1933, the country was, to be sure, wallowing in the deepest trough of the unemployment crisis. But despite the New Deal's exertions and innovations, and contrary to much later mythology, in no subsequent year in the 1930s would the unemployment rate fall below 14 percent. The average for the decade as a whole was 17.1 percent. The Depression and the New Deal, in short, were Siamese twins, enduring together in a painful but symbiotic relationship that stretched to the end of the decade. The dilemmas and duration of that relationship helped to account for both the failures and the triumphs of the New Deal.

In Pennsylvania, Hickok's first destination, Governor Gifford Pinchot had reported in the summer of 1932 that some 1,150,000 persons were "totally unemployed." Many others were on "short hours." Only two-fifths of Pennsylvania's normal working population, Pinchot concluded, had full-time work. Elsewhere, the Ford Motor Company in Detroit had laid off more than two-thirds of its workers. Other giant industries followed suit. Westinghouse and General Electric in 1933 employed fewer than half as many workers as in 1929. In Birmingham, Alabama, another of Hickok's destinations, Congressman George Huddleston reported that only 8,000 of some 108,000 workers still had full-time employment in 1932; 25,000 had no work at all, and the remaining 75,000 counted themselves lucky to toil a few days per week. "Practically all," said Huddleston, "have had serious cuts in their wages and many of them do not average over $1.50 a day."

Later investigators calculated that nationwide the combined effects of unemployment and involuntary part-time employment left half of America's usual work force unutilized throughout the Depression decade—a loss of some 104 million person-years of labor, the most perishable and irreplaceable of all commodities. Similar calculations suggest that the "lost output" in the American economy of the 1930s, measured against what would have been produced if 1920s rates of employment had held, amounted to some $360 billion dollars—enough at 1929 prices to have built 35 million homes, 179 million automobiles, or 716,000 schools.

Like Hopkins, observers then and later have struggled to make human sense out of these numbingly abstract numbers. One thinking exercise goes as follows: imagine that on New Year's Day 1931, when the depression was not yet "Great," one hundred thousand people, all of them gainfully employed, most of them the sole means of livelihood for their families, sat beneath the beaming California sun in the Rose Bowl, filling the eight-year-old Pasadena stadium to capacity to watch Alabama's Crimson Tide play the Washington State Cougars in the sixteenth annual Rose Bowl Game. When the game ended, the loudspeakers announced that every person in attendance that day had just lost his or her job. On exiting, the stunned fans were handed further notices. Sixty-two thousand were informed that they would not be employed for at least a year to follow; forty-four thousand of those were given two-year layoffs; twenty-four thousand, three years; eleven thousand received the grim news that they would be unemployed for four years or more (an approximation of the patterns in the unemployment statistics for the decade of the 1930s). Then imagine that this spectacle was repeated at the Rose Bowl, without even the consolation of a football game, the following week—and the week after that, and again after that, for 130 weeks. At the rate of a hundred thousand persons summarily laid off in successive weeks it would take two and one-half years, until July 1933, the date of Hickok's departure on her assignment for Hopkins, to reach the sum of thirteen million unemployed.

But even such mental exercises as that run up against what Hopkins called "the natural limit of personal imagination and sympathy. You can pity six men," Hopkins sagely noted, "but you can't keep stirred up over six million." It was to compensate for those natural deficiencies of the imagination that he was sending Lorena Hickok on her mission. From her reportage he hoped to vivify real faces and voices out of the statistical dust. She did not disappoint him.

Hickok set out in quest of the human reality of the Depression. She found that and much more besides. In dingy working-class neighborhoods in Philadelphia and New York, in unpainted clapboard farmhouses in North Dakota, on the ravaged cotton farms of Georgia, on the dusty mesas of Colorado, Hickok uncovered not just the effects of the economic crisis that had begun in 1929. She found herself face to face as well with the human wreckage of a century of pell-mell, buccaneering, no-holds-barred, free-market industrial and agricultural capitalism. As her travels progressed, she gradually came to acknowledge the sobering reality that for many Americans the Great Depression brought times only a little harder than usual. She discovered, in short, what historian James Patterson has called the "old poverty" that was endemic in America well before the Depression hit. By his estimate, even in the midst of the storied prosperity of the 1920s some forty million Americans, including virtually all nonwhites, most of the elderly, and much of the rural population, were eking out unrelievedly precarious lives that were scarcely visible and practically unimaginable to their more financially secure countrymen. "The researches we have made into standards of living of the American family," Hopkins wrote, "have uncovered for the public gaze a volume of chronic poverty, unsuspected except by a few students and by those who have always experienced it." From this perspective, the Depression was not just a passing crisis but an episode that revealed deeply rooted structural inequities in American society.

The "old poor" were among the Depression's most ravaged victims, but it was not the Depression that had impoverished them. They were the "one-third of a nation" that Franklin Roosevelt would describe in 1937 as chronically "ill-housed, ill-clad, ill-nourished." By suddenly threatening to push millions of other Americans into their wretched condition, the Depression pried open a narrow window of political opportunity to do something at last on behalf of that long-suffering one-third, and in the process to redefine the very character of America.

Departing from Washington in a car acquired with Eleanor's help and nicknamed "Bluette," Hickok headed first for the hills and ravines of the Appalachian soft-coal district, a dismally hardscrabble region stretching through western Pennsylvania, West Virginia, and Kentucky. She was starting at the bottom. "In the whole range of Depression," said Gifford Pinchot, "there is nothing worse than the condition of the soft coal miners." Soft, or bituminous, coal had been for nearly two centuries the basic fuel that powered the global industrial revolution, but even before World War I the coal-burning era was everywhere on the wane. Diesel engines had replaced coal-fired boilers in steamships and locomotives. Coalbins were disappearing from basements as Americans abandoned smudgy coal furnaces for clean-burning gas or oil or smokeless electric heating systems. Plagued by competition from these new energy sources, especially the recently tapped oil fields in southern California, Oklahoma, and the vast Permian Basin in West Texas, coal displayed through the 1920s all the classical symptoms of a sick industry: shrinking demand, excess supply, chaotic disorganization, cutthroat competition, and hellish punishment for workers.

The Depression exacerbated this already calamitous cycle. Operators fought more savagely than ever to stay alive by cutting prices and paychecks. At one point some of them even begged the government to buy the mines "at any price. . . . Anything so we can get out of it." Coal that had fetched up to $4 a ton in the mid-1920s sold for $1.31 a ton in 1932. Miners who had earned seven dollars a day before the Crash now begged the pit-boss for the chance to squirm into thirty-inch coal seams for as little as one dollar. Men who had once loaded tons of coal per day grubbed around the base of the tipple for a few lumps of fuel to heat a meager supper—often nothing more than "bulldog gravy" made of flour, water, and lard. The miner's diet, said United Mine Workers president John L. Lewis, "is actually below domestic animal standards."

Stranded without work in isolated company towns, living on the owners' sufferance in company housing, in debt to the company store, cowed by insecurity and occasional strong-arm tactics into a subdued, passive frame of mind, the miners struck Hickok as a singularly pathetic lot. "Some of them have been starving for eight years," she reported to Hopkins. "I was told there are children in West Virginia who never tasted milk! I visited one group of 45 blacklisted miners and their families, who had been living in tents two years. . . . Most of the women you see in the camps are going without shoes or stockings. . . . It's fairly common to see children entirely naked." The ravages of tuberculosis, "black lung" disease, and asthma, as well as typhoid, diphtheria, pellagra, and severe malnutrition, were everywhere apparent. Some miners' families, said Hickok, "had been living for days on green corn and string beans—and precious little of that. And some had nothing at all, actually hadn't eaten for a couple of days. At the Continental Hotel in Pineville [Kentucky] I was told that five babies up one of those creeks had died of starvation in the last ten days. . . . Dysentery is so common that nobody says much about it. 'We begin losing our babies with dysentery in September,'" one of Hickok's informants casually remarked.

Patriotic, religious, gentle, of "pure Anglo-Saxon stock," these mountain folk impressed Hickok as "curiously appealing." Yet she found both their stark destitution and their stoic resignation appalling. Here began her real education—and through her, Hopkins's and Roosevelt's—about the awful dimensions of the human damage the Depression had laid bare and about the curious apathy with which many Americans continued to submit to their fates. Sixty-two percent of the people in ten eastern Kentucky mining counties looked to federal relief for their very survival in the summer of 1933, Hickok learned. Twenty-eight thousand families, more than 150,000 souls, depended on local relief offices for grocery orders that they could present to the company store. Then, on August 12, owing to delays in the Kentucky state government's provision of funds to match the federal government's appropriations, even that minimal assistance stopped. Little groups of people, many of them illiterate, straggled to closed relief agencies, stared helplessly at written notices announcing the end of aid, and silently shuffled away. Given their desperate plight, "I cannot for the life of me understand," Hickok mused, "why they don't go down and raid the Blue Grass country." . . .

DOCUMENTS

The Great Depression in Philadelphia, 1933

Relief stopped in Philadelphia on June 25 [1932]. For months previously 52,000 destitute families had been receiving modest grocery orders and a little milk.

SOURCE: Jacob Billikopf, testimony from U.S. Congress, Senate Subcommittee of the Committee on Manufacturers, Hearings, *Federal Aid for Unemployment Relief,* 72d Cong., 2d sess., 1933, 8–11.

The average allowance to a family at that time was about $4.35 per week, no provision being made for fuel, clothing, rent or any of the minimum accessories that go to make up the family budget.

Their rent was unpaid, their credit and their borrowing power exhausted. Most of them were absolutely dependent for existence on the food orders supplied through State funds administered by the Committee for Unemployment Relief. Then there were no more funds, and relief—except for a little milk for half-sick children, and a little Red Cross flour—was suddenly discontinued. And Philadelphia asked itself what was happening to these 52,000 families. There were no reports of people starving in the streets, and yet from what possible source were 52,000 families getting enough food to live on?

It was a fair question and the Community Council under the direction of Mr. Ewan Clague, a competent economist and in charge of its Research Bureau, set out to find the answer by a special study of 400 families who had been without relief for a period varying from 10 to 25 days. The families were not picked out as the worst cases, but as stated before were fairly typical of the 52,000.

According to Mr. Clague, and I am quoting him quite liberally, the count of the 400 families showed a total of 2,464 persons. The great majority ranged from five to eight persons per family.

In their effort to discover how these 2,464 human beings were keeping themselves alive the investigators inquired into the customary sources of family maintenance, earnings, savings, regular help from relatives, credit and, last but not least, the neighbors.

Some current income in the form of wages was reported by 128 families, though the amounts were generally small and irregular, two or three dollars a week perhaps, earned on odd jobs, by selling knickknacks on the street or by youngsters delivering papers or working nights. For the whole 128 the average wage income was $4.16 a week and 272 families of the 400 had no earnings whatsoever.

Savings were an even more slender resource. Only 54 families reported savings and most of these were nothing more than small industrial insurance policies with little or no cash surrender value, technically an asset, actually an item of expense. This does not mean that these families had not had savings—take for instance, the Baker family—father, mother, and four children. They had had $1,000 in a building and loan association which failed. They had had more than $2,000 in a savings bank, but the last cent had been withdrawn in January, 1931. They had had three insurance policies, which had been surrendered one by one. Both the father and the oldest son were tubercular, the former at the moment being an applicant for sanitarium care. This family—intelligent, clean, thrifty, and likable—one of thousands at the end of their rope—had had savings as a resource even a year ago, but not now.

The same situation, it was found, prevailed in regard to regular help from relatives. In the early stages of the depression a large proportion of relief families could count on this help in some form. But of our 400 families only 33 reported assistance from kinsfolk that could be counted on, and this assistance was slender indeed: A brother paid the rent to save eviction, a brother-in-law guaranteed the gas and electric bills, a grandmother, working as a scrubwoman, put in a small sum each week. Most of the relatives it was found were so hard pressed that it was all they could do to save themselves. As a matter of fact many relatives had moved in with the families and were recorded as members of the household.

In the absence of assets or income the next line of defense is credit. But most of the 400 families were bogged down in debt and retained only a vestige of credit. Take the item of rent or building and loan payments: Three hundred and forty-nine of the families were behind—some only a month or two, some for a year, a few for two or three years, with six months as the average for the group. . . .

Thus, then, the picture of the 400 families shaped itself. Gradually no income, such as there was slight, irregular and undependable; shelter still available so long as landlords remained lenient; savings gone, credit exhausted.

But what of food, the never ending, ever pressing necessity for food? In this emergency the outstanding contribution has been made by neighbors. The poor are looking after the poor. In considerably more than a third of the 400 families the chief source of actual subsistence when grocery orders stopped was the neighbors. The supply was by no means regular or adequate but in the last analysis, when all other resources failed the neighbors rallied to tide the family over a few days. Usually it was leftovers, stale bread, meat bones for soup, a bowl of gravy. Sometimes the children are asked in for a meal. One neighbor sent two eggs a day regularly to a sick man threatened with tuberculosis. This help was the more striking since the neighbors themselves were often close to the line of destitution and could illy spare the food they shared. The primitive communism existing among these people was a constant surprise to the visitors. More than once a family lucky enough to get a good supply of food called in the entire block to share the feast. There is absolutely no doubt that entire neighborhoods were just living from day to day sharing what slight resources any one family chanced to have. Without this mutual help the situation of many of the families would have been desperate.

As a result of all these efforts, what did these families have? What meals did they get and of what did these meals consist? About 8 per cent of the total number were subsisting on one meal a day. Many more were getting only two meals a day, and still others were irregular, sometimes one meal, sometimes two, occasionally by great good fortune, three. Thirty-seven per cent of all families were not getting the normal three meals a day.

When the content of these meals is taken into consideration the facts are still more alarming. Four families had absolutely no solid food whatever— nothing but a drink, usually tea or coffee. Seventy-three others had only one food and one drink for all meals, the food in many cases being bread made from Red Cross flour. Even in the remaining cases, where there were two or three articles of food, the diets day after day and week after week consisted usually of bread, macaroni, spaghetti, potatoes, with milk for the children. Many families were getting no meat and very few vegetables. Fresh fruits were never mentioned, although it is possible that the family might pick these up in the streets occasionally.

These diets were exceedingly harmful in their immediate effects on some of the families where health problems are present. In a number of cases the children are definitely reported on a hospital diagnosis as anemic. Occasionally the adults are likewise affected. The MacIntyre family for instance: These two older people have an adopted child 8 years of age. The husband is a bricklayer by trade and the wife can do outside housework. They have had occasional odd jobs over the past year but have been very hard pressed. For the three meals immediately preceding the visit they reported the menus as follows: Dinner, previous day, bread and coffee; breakfast, bread and coffee; lunch, corn, fish, bread, and coffee; one quart of milk for the little girl for the entire three meals.

Also their health problems were serious. The wife has had several operations, the husband is a possible tuberculosis case, and the child is underweight. All three have also been receiving medical attention from a hospital for the past three years. The little girl has been nervous, has fainted at times, and is slightly deformed from rickets. Being undernourished, she needs cod-liver oil, milk, oranges, and the food which was possible only when the family was on relief. She went to camp for two weeks and returned up to weight and in good spirits. But relief was cut off while she was away, and she came back to meals of milk, coffee, and bread. In the short time at home she had become fretful and listless, refusing to take anything but milk. This whole family promised to be in serious health difficulties if their situation were long continued.

The Okies in California, 1939

The most characteristic of all housing in California in which migrants reside at the moment is the shacktown or cheap subdivision. Most of these settlements have come into existence since 1933 and the pattern which obtains is

SOURCE: Carey McWilliams, testimony from U.S. Congress, House Select Committee to Investigate the Interstate Migration of Destitute Citizens, *Hearings*, 76th Cong., 3d sess., 1941, 2543–44.

somewhat similar throughout the State. Finding it impossible to rent housing in incorporated communities on their meager incomes, migrants have created a market for a very cheap type of subdivision of which the following may be taken as being representative:

In Monterey County, according to a report of Dr. D. M. Bissell, county health officer, under date of November 28, 1939, there are approximately three well-established migrant settlements. One of these, the development around the environs of Salinas, is perhaps the oldest migrant settlement of its type in California. In connection with this development I quote a paragraph of the report of Dr. Bissell:

"This area is composed of all manners and forms of housing without a public sewer system. Roughly, 10,000 persons are renting or have established homes there. A chief element in this area is that of refugees from the Dust Bowl who inhabit a part of Alisal called Little Oklahoma. Work in lettuce harvesting and packing and sugar beet processing have attracted these people who, seeking homes in Salinas without success because they aren't available, have resorted to makeshift adobes outside the city limits. Complicating the picture is the impermeable substrata which makes septic tanks with leaching fields impractical. Sewer wells have resulted with the corresponding danger to adjacent water wells and to the water wells serving the Salinas public. Certain districts, for example, the Airport Tract and parts of Alisal, have grown into communities with quite satisfactory housing, but others as exemplified by the Graves district are characterized by shacks and lean-tos which are unfit for human habitation." . . .

Typical of the shacktown problem are two such areas near the city limits of Sacramento, one on the east side of B Street, extending from Twelfth Street to the Sacramento city dump and incinerator; and the other so-called Hoovertown, adjacent to the Sacramento River and the city filtration plant. In these two areas there were on September 17, 1939, approximately 650 inhabitants living in structures that, with scarcely a single exception, were rated by the inspectors of this division as "unfit for human occupancy." The majority of the inhabitants were white Americans, with the exception of 50 or 60 Mexican families, a few single Mexican men, and a sprinkling of Negroes. For the most part they are seasonally employed in the canneries, the fruit ranches, and the hop fields of Sacramento County. Most of the occupants are at one time or another upon relief, and there are a large number of occupants in these shacktowns from the Dust Bowl area. Describing the housing, an inspector of this division reports:

"The dwellings are built of brush, rags, sacks, boxboard, odd bits of tin and galvanized iron, pieces of canvas and whatever other material was at hand at the time of construction."

Wood floors, where they exist, are placed directly upon the ground, which because of the location of the camps with respect to the Sacramento River, is damp most of the time. To quote again from the report:

"Entire families, men, women, and children, are crowded into hovels, cooking and eating in the same room. The majority of the shacks have no sinks or cesspools for the disposal of kitchen drainage, and this, together with garbage and other refuse, is thrown on the surface of the ground."

Because of the high-water table, cesspools, where they exist, do not function properly; there is a large overflow of drainage and sewage to the surface of the ground. Many filthy shack latrines are located within a few feet of living quarters. Rents for the houses in these shacktowns range from $3 to $20 a month. In one instance a landlord rents ground space for $1.50 to $5 a month, on which tenants are permitted to erect their own dugouts. The Hooverville section is composed primarily of tents and trailers, there being approximately 125 tent structures in this area on September 17, 1939. Both areas are located in unincorporated territory. They are not subject at the present time to any State or county building regulation. In Hooverville, at the date of the inspection, many families were found that did not have even a semblance of tents or shelters. They were cooking and sleeping on the ground in the open and one water tap at an adjoining industrial plant was found to be the source of the domestic water supply for the camp. . . .

The Bronx Slave Market, 1935

The Bronx Slave Market! What is it? Who are its dealers? Who are its victims? What are its causes? How far does its stench spread? What forces are at work to counteract it?

Any corner in the congested sections of New York City's Bronx is fertile soil for mushroom "slave marts." The two where the traffic is heaviest and the bidding is highest are located at 167th street and Jerome avenue and at Simpson and Westchester avenues. . . .

. . . Not only is human labor bartered and sold for slave wage, but human love also is a marketable commodity. But whether it is labor or love that is sold, economic necessity compels the sale. As early as 8 A.M. they come; as late as 1 P.M. they remain.

Rain or shine, cold or hot, you will find them there—Negro women, old and young—sometimes bedraggled, sometimes neatly dressed—but with the invariable paper bundle, waiting expectantly for Bronx housewives to buy their strength and energy for an hour, two hours, or even for a day at the munificent rate of fifteen, twenty, twenty-five, or, if luck be with them, thirty cents an hour. If not the wives themselves, maybe their husbands, their sons, or their brothers, under the subterfuge of work, offer worldly-wise girls higher bids for their time.

SOURCE: Ella Baker and Marvel Cooke in *The Crisis* 42 (November 1935): 331.

Who are these women? What brings them here? Why do they stay? In the boom days before the onslaught of the depression in 1929, many of these women who are now forced to bargain for day's work on street corners, were employed in grand homes in the rich Eighties, or in wealthier homes in Long Island and Westchester, at more than adequate wages. Some are former marginal industrial workers, forced by the slack in industry to seek other means of sustenance. In many instances there had been no necessity for work at all. But whatever their standing prior to the depression, none sought employment where they now seek it. They come to the Bronx, not because of what it promises, but largely in desperation.

Paradoxically, the crash of 1929 brought to the domestic labor market a new employer class. The lower middle-class housewife, who, having dreamed of the luxury of a maid, found opportunity staring her in the face in the form of Negro women pressed to the wall by poverty, starvation and discrimination.

Where once color was the "gilt edged" security for obtaining domestic and personal service jobs, here, even Negro women found themselves being displaced by whites. Hours of futile waiting in employment agencies, the fee that must be paid despite the lack of income, fraudulent agencies that sprung up during the depression, all forced the day worker to fend for herself or try the dubious and circuitous road to public relief.

As inadequate as emergency relief has been, it has proved somewhat of a boon to many of these women, for with its advent, actual starvation is no longer their ever-present slave driver and they have been able to demand twenty-five and even thirty cents an hour as against the old fifteen and twenty cent rate. In an effort to supplement the inadequate relief received, many seek this open market.

And what a market! She who is fortunate (?) enough to please Mrs. Simon Legree's* scrutinizing eye is led away to perform hours of multifarious household drudgeries. Under a rigid watch, she is permitted to scrub floors on her bended knees, to hang precariously from window sills, cleaning window after window, or to strain and sweat over steaming tubs of heavy blankets, spreads and furniture covers.

Fortunate, indeed, is she who gets the full hourly rate promised. Often, her day's slavery is rewarded with a single dollar bill or whatever her unscrupulous employer pleases to pay. More often, the clock is set back for an hour or more. Too often she is sent away without any pay at all.

*Mrs. Simon Legree is a reference to the wife of the villain of *Uncle Tom's Cabin.* (Eds.)

Chapter 11

World War II: The Home Front

Homefront workers, both men and women, contribute to the war effort.

The New Deal exerted an enormous impact on American society. For the embattled farmers and workers and their families described in the previous chapter, the federal government offered relief, mortgage aid, crop payments, and even employment—programs that helped to restore the nation's flagging morale and maintain the people's faith in their government and economic system.

Yet as dramatic and innovative as the New Deal was, World War II brought even more upheavals in the lives of Americans. Nearly 15 million men and women found themselves serving in the armed forces, and the government intervened in an unprecedented way in the economy. Rationing of such products as butter, meat, sugar, and gasoline was introduced, and war contracts, initiated as early as 1939, stimulated the manufacture of millions of uniforms and the production of hundreds of thousands of ships, airplanes, tanks, and pieces of military equipment. While millions served in the army, navy, air corps, and marines, many civilians flocked to urban centers to work in the booming military economy.

William O'Neill's essay "The People Are Willing" describes numerous changes unfolding during this period, changes that enabled the United States to outproduce its enemies and win the war. But as O'Neill notes, innovations did not always come easily. What does he identify as the major challenges in uniting the American people and its economic system behind the war effort? How does he account for the many difficulties and government "bungling," especially in the early days of the war? Finally, how did the nation eventually achieve both full production and unity of purpose?

O'Neill's essay also discusses the impact of the war on particular groups. The first document is by a young man who joined the navy in 1939, nearly two years before America entered the conflict. Why did this young man leave his farm for the navy, and what does his choice indicate about the connection between the coming war and the eventual end of the Great Depression?

The essay also points to major changes in the lives of American women, among them the appearance of Rosie the Riveter, symbol of those who took wartime jobs formerly reserved strictly for men. One Rosie is represented by the second document, taken from Augusta H. Clawson's *Shipyard Diary of a Woman Welder*. How would you describe her reactions to her new job?

In spite of dislocations on the homefront, most Americans found that their standard of living improved during the war years. For Japanese Americans on the West Coast, however, this was not the case. Native-born American citizens of Japanese ancestry as well as Japanese immigrants were interned in virtual concentration camps, an imprisonment ordered by President Franklin Roosevelt and sanctioned by the United States Supreme Court on the ground of national security. The last document, a government report issued in 1984 about the wartime internment of civilians, describes some of the conditions encountered by these unfortunate Americans. In 1942, Earl Warren, then attorney general of California, responded to questions regarding the civil rights of Japanese Americans by stating, "I believe, sir, that in time of war every citizen must give up some of his normal rights." Even accepting this premise, does it justify the treatment Japanese Americans received, as described in the document?

ESSAY

The People Are Willing
William O'Neill

After Pearl Harbor a flood of volunteers overwhelmed recruiting offices, especially in the South. When the entire Lepanto, Arkansas, football team joined the Navy, one member attempted suicide after failing to pass his physical. "I was afraid folks would think I was yellow because I didn't get into the service," he explained. Millions who were ineligible to serve wished to know what civilians could do to further the war effort. . . .

Most Americans believed that government did not need to be overly effective because the people themselves could manage. While they overstated its benefits, voluntarism was a fact of life, and Americans were capable—within limits—of doing what elsewhere were functions of government. This attribute manifested itself immediately after Pearl Harbor. Agencies like the Red Cross and local civilian defense offices were overwhelmed with offers to help. Because many commodities would soon be scarce, scrap drives were organized that collected not only rubber items but paper, fats, bones, a wide variety of metal goods, and other essential materials.

Towns convened meetings to discuss ways of aiding the war effort. Citizens' committees sprang up. Neighborhoods organized. When a Milwaukee air-raid warden could not afford a telephone, the other families on his block agreed to donate 10 cents a month apiece so he could subscribe to the service. In Chicago 23,000 block captains were sworn in at a mass ceremony by the head of the Office of Civilian Defense. West Coast hospitals reeled before waves of enthusiastic blood donors. The hottest literary property of 1942 was the Red Cross first aid manual, which, though not considered a book and therefore omitted from best seller lists, sold 8 million copies. Farmers began plowing at night in order to put their spring crops in early. Shipyard employees in San Francisco offered to work Sundays for free. That summer an event called The National Salvage Fair was held in New York as part of a campaign to establish Salvage Sewing Workrooms in which volunteers could use mill ends and scraps of cloth to make garments for the needy and establish a clothing reserve.

Though very much in the American grain, efforts such as these suffered from the limitations intrinsic to thousands of uncoordinated local schemes, often inspired by an excess of willing hands rather than any clear sense of purpose. By summer *Life* was overflowing with complaints. Congress was

SOURCE: Abridged and reprinted with the permission of The Free Press, a division of Simon & Schuster Adult Publishing Group from *A Democracy at War: America's Fight at Home and Abroad in World War II*, by William L. O'Neill. Copyright © 1993 by William L. O'Neill.

not doing a good job. Neither were the people. All the powerful interest groups continued to pursue their own agendas. Every scrap campaign had failed, the rubber drive most of all. People were still motoring frivolously. Washington was asking too little, and getting what it asked for. Everyone was living their dream of a "Hollywood war," instead of facing up to the real one in which sacrifices would have to be made.

These complaints were well founded. In 1941 when aluminum was in short supply, the call went out for housewives to turn in their pots and pans. Ten thousand tons of aluminum would build 4,000 fighter planes was what they were told. Obedient to duty's call, women stripped their kitchens and donated 70,000 tons of aluminum, apparently solving the problem. It transpired that only virgin aluminum was suitable for aircraft, so the donated cookware gathered dust until it was finally sold to scrap dealers. Then the stuff was turned into new pots and pans, women buying back what they had previously given.

More serious than bungling was government's reluctance to take full advantage of civilian support for the war effort, especially that of women. The public was encouraged to buy war bonds and practice conservation. Otherwise, it often seemed as if Washington did not want public participation in national defense, which had been the case before Pearl Harbor. In January 1941 one of Dr. Gallup's polls had revealed that 67 percent of those questioned were willing "to spend one hour each day training for home guard, nursing, first aid work, ambulance driving," and similar activities.

Though officials frequently remarked on the gravity of the world situation and the need to prepare for hardships, they seldom took their own advice. When asked what people could do, Frank Bane, Chief of the National Defense Advisory Commission's Division on State and Local Cooperation, suggested that it might be nice if women living near Army posts would help entertain the troops. They could also work as volunteers in the overburdened health and welfare programs of "war boom" towns, laudable suggestions, to be sure, but hardly a call to action.

In August the president of the General Federation of Women's Clubs—an old, large, and conservative body—complained that women were being discriminated against "intolerably" in the civil-defense program. The Office of Civilian Defense did not even have a women's division. There were only seven women in the entire federal government at the policymaking level. Women were excluded from serving in Civil Aeronautics Authority programs for training student pilots. The female Assistant National Civilian Defense Director had just resigned because Director Fiorello La Guardia disapproved of her effort to have the WPA survey and catalogue volunteer associations around the country, many of them women's groups, as possible contributors to civil defense.

Women were joining the Red Cross and other emergency related bodies in large numbers, but not because government was encouraging them to, or promising that if war came it would utilize their services. This lack of interest would not change very much after Pearl Harbor. In the age of total war the United States would make a semitotal effort, a limitation that was prefigured by government's earlier policy on civilian defense. This prejudice against women would seriously weaken the war effort.

It was obvious that vast numbers of men in uniform would be performing clerical tasks and other duties that were not gender-specific. Yet military leaders were slow to admit that women could do these jobs as well, if not better than, men, thereby freeing able-bodied males for combat. Early in 1942 the Army agreed to accept 10,000 volunteers for a Women's Army Auxiliary Corps only because a bill introduced in Congress by Representative Edith Nourse Rogers (R, MA) forced its hand. The Navy went on refusing to accept women in any capacity. There were plenty of men as yet undrafted, the military's reasoning went—which was true at the time, but this surplus did not last, forcing a change of heart. . . .

Lacking official outlets, women formed numerous paramilitary groups of their own, including the Powder Puff Platoon of Joplin, Missouri, the Green Guards of Washington, and the Women's Defense School of Boston, which taught a course in field cooking modeled on that of the Army. Some 25,000 women volunteered for the Women's Ambulance and Defense Corps of America, whose slogan was "The Hell We Can't." Its more than 50 chapters trained women to serve as air-raid wardens, security guards, and couriers for the armed forces. However, most who wished to contribute joined the Red Cross, which, with 3.5 million female volunteers, was by far the most important outlet for patriotic womanhood.

Some government agencies actually recognized opportunity when they saw it. The Office of Civilian Defense employed a number of female volunteers. The Office of Price Administration used 50,000 women in five states to conduct a three-day canvas in July 1942, during which they briefed 450,000 retailers on the new price regulations. For the most part, though, except for defense contractors who gradually warmed to the idea of hiring women workers, volunteer organizations remained the main outlets.

Of these latter groups, the most controversial was the American Women's Voluntary Services, founded by a group of Anglophile socialites in 1940 to prepare women for emergency work in a London-style blitz. It soon enrolled 350,000 members in almost every state. To refute mockers who accused them of being social butterflies out on a lark, AWVS cast a remarkably broad net for the times, organizing several units in Harlem, at least one Chinese chapter, a number of Hispanic units, and one affiliate consisting entirely of Taos tribeswomen. Defying local taboos, the New Orleans chapter bravely included Negro women. When it became evident that America was not going to be attacked by German bombers, the AWVS took on new assignments. In New York members sold $5 million worth of war bonds. In California there were AWVS "chuckwagons" that delivered food, including late-night snacks, to Coast Guard stations and remote military sites. In San Francisco AWVS women taught Braille to blinded veterans. Others organized agricultural work camps in California and Colorado. Some New York suburbs had ambulances staffed entirely by AWVS members.

Though it was the biggest, AWVS was by no means the only volunteer women's organization that made a place for itself in the war effort. At least three other women's groups provided land and air ambulance services. There were also volunteer groups of working women, such as WIRES (Women in Radio and Electric Service), WAMS (Women Aircraft Mechanics), and WOWS (Women Ordnance Workers)—the latter of whom by 1943 had a membership of 33,000 in dozens of munitions plants. As part of an elaborate recruiting campaign, Oldsmobile created WINGS (also known as the "Keep 'Em Winning Girls"), workers who were given uniforms with a torch-and-wing insignia on the front pocket. So that housewives should not feel excluded, the *Ladies Home Journal* organized WINS (Women in National Service), saying that housewives were "the largest army in the nation fighting on the home front." The outpouring of female volunteers in a host of organizations enabled women to accomplish much, and suggested how much more they might have done had there been a system in place to take full advantage of their enthusiasm. Even as it was, when in April 1942 ten thousand women volunteers marched down Fifth Avenue in New York there were so many different uniforms that no one could identify them all. . . .

While the numerous complaints about government's incompetence and neglect were fully justified, it was important to keep in mind that the mills of American democracy were supposed to grind slowly. Though this was not apparent at first, the mess in Washington would improve. Private initiatives too would become more fruitful. Scrap drives got better, the rule seeming to be that behind every successful local drive there was one especially determined person. In Seattle, which had a very big one, that man was a local jeweler by the name of Leo Weisfield.

A landmark effort was the great Nebraska scrap drive of 1942, inspired by Henry Doorly, publisher of the state's biggest newspaper, the Omaha *World-Herald*. A unique feature of his plan was that prizes worth up to $2,000 in war bonds would be given to individuals and organizations who collected the most scrap, regardless of whether it was sold to dealers or donated gratis. This was a significant feature, not just because it meant that donors could mingle patriotism with profit, but because scrap dealers had the heavy equipment required to salvage large metal structures.

The drive collected 135 million tons of scrap, the equivalent of 103 pounds for every person in Nebraska. By comparison, the previous national scrap campaign collected only 213 million tons in its first two weeks, an average of barely more than a pound and a half for each American. Many

Nebraska companies donated trucks, 40 a day on average, which were employed to transport scrap. The *World-Herald* itself contributed nine tons of old press parts which a frugal foreman had been stockpiling for 30 years. In the town of Oldrege a local department-store owner and a farm-implement dealer set up a nonprofit corporation that paid $10 a ton for salvage, a dollar and a half above the going rate. To finance it they borrowed money from the local bank, and with the aid of hundreds of volunteers ended up breaking even—a feat they accomplished by sorting the scrap, which enabled them to resell it to dealers for a premium that covered their overpayments.

Rural salvage was the most rewarding because of its scale. While townspeople were turning in old appliances, the countryside yielded up treasures in the form of disused iron bridges, farm machinery, and 537 tons of abandoned track donated by the Burlington Railroad. When the prizes were given out, the individual winner was a section hand for the Burlington who brought in 97,000 pounds of scrap. The winning business was a dinette in Norfolk whose owner hired two women to run the place while he collected 81,000 pounds of salvage. The junior prize went to the Omaha Future Farmers of America, who took time out from agricultural pursuits to amass a staggering 445,000 pounds.

The most successful state drive yet, the Nebraska model was widely copied, demonstrating that the will was there and could be mobilized with inventive planning. If the weakness of democracy was inefficient government, the strength was volunteerism, especially when it exploited the national love of competition.

An example of what could be done with official support was gasoline rationing, which went into effect on December 1, 1942—tardily, of course, but as so often happened, delay was needed to convince people that the rubber crisis really existed. Americans who hated rationing, complied with the rules as a whole, despite the inevitable chiseling and the rise of black marketeers and forgers of gas-ration permits. It helped that most people walked to work (40 percent) or took public transportation (23 percent). Even the 36 percent who commuted by car ultimately accepted gasoline rationing. Though only 49 percent of all Americans saw a need for it when first proposed, by the end of 1942 the great majority of motorists (73 percent) supported gasoline rationing. The 35 mph speed limit won almost universal approval, 89 percent of car owners backing it. Fortunately, though the black market in gasoline eventually became a big business, it never grew so large as to jeopardize the war effort.

Rationing, an inconvenience to some, meant real sacrifice for others—such as small businesses that depended on the drive-in trade. Nine hundred restaurants in Los Angeles alone closed within the first two weeks after rationing took effect. Labor and other kinds of shortages would also devastate small businessmen and farmers. In Arkansas, 6,000 small businesses would fail by 1943 for lack of workers, while the state's farm population declined from 667,000 in 1940 to 292,000 by the spring of 1944.

In January 1943 pleasure driving was banned completely on the East Coast, where a genuine gasoline shortage existed, virtually emptying the streets of major cities. Compliance was encouraged by police officers, who confiscated the gas-ration books of offending drivers. If after a court hearing the accused were found guilty of frivolous motoring, the fine was in gasoline coupons rather than cash—a powerful and effective deterrent. More important than stiff fines was patriotism, since experience would demonstrate that programs with which most Americans did not agree were ultimately unenforceable.

Conversely, programs that Americans believed in could not be stopped. Victory gardens were a case in point. Food production and conservation had been strongly encouraged in the First World War, and many families that did not ordinarily grow their own produce established kitchen gardens in response. People took it for granted that food would be short this time as well. They began planting vegetables in the spring, despite the Department of Agriculture, which initially dragged its feet. By April 1942, at least 6 million gardens were being cultivated, inspiring Secretary of Agriculture Claude Wickard to call for 18 million victory gardens—a goal that was easily reached. In 1943, more than 8 million tons of produce was grown on 20 million individual plots, many of them very small. In cities with populations above 100,000, victory gardens averaged only 500 square feet in size—that is, about 20 by 25 feet—but nevertheless amounted collectively to 7 million acres, an area the size of Rhode Island.

Victory gardens appeared everywhere, not only on private lots but in parks, before the San Francisco City Hall, in the yards of schools and prisons, wherever there was arable soil, and hands to do the tilling. The Agriculture Department reported that the amount of vegetables grown in victory gardens exceeded "the total commercial production for fresh sale for civilian and non-civilian use." This was all the more impressive because, after being grown, much of this produce had to be canned—hence the slogan, "Eat what you can and can what you can't," no small thing, as a mistake could result in glass canisters exploding, or even bacterial growths that were potentially lethal.

Most of the conservation burden fell on women—and children, too, who were good collectors of scrap. In the fully mobilized household there were separate holders for tins, rags, bottles, paper, and bones. Tin cans were washed and flattened. Tinfoil and rubber bands were collected in balls. Bottle caps, chewing gum wrappers, and flashlight batteries were saved for later recycling. Because it was used to make munitions, schools had "Fat Parades," enabling children to make ceremonial deposits of accumulated kitchen grease. In rural areas they collected milkweeds, whose silken fibers would be stuffed into life jackets. . . .

Secretary of the Treasury Henry Morgenthau . . . wanted bonds sold widely and in such a way as to make Americans "war-minded." He believed this was even more important than helping finance defense purchases. To sell bonds was to sell the war, so bond drives were aimed at the average American rather than at wealthy investors—which meant, in turn, drawing heavily on the popular culture. Movie stars played important parts, with Hollywood organizing seven tours that played in 300 communities. Dorothy Lamour alone, the star of a series of "Road" pictures with Bob Hope and Bing Crosby, was credited with selling $350 million worth of bonds. Carole Lombard, a popular movie actress, gave her life to the cause, dying in a plane crash on her way home from a bond tour. In addition to bonds, "war stamps" costing only pennies were sold—mainly to children, though sometimes to adults, as when scantily-clad showgirls covered their flesh with 10¢ savings stamps for happy businessmen to peel off and purchase. Every form of hucksterism was employed in this cause, few managing to escape it. . . .

Despite occasional lapses, [President] Roosevelt did not truly believe in propaganda. In 1917, precisely because opinion was divided on the merits of intervention, Washington had cranked up a vast publicity machine to bolster the war effort. A Committee on Public Information was created to that end, which distributed 75 million pamphlets, issued 6,000 press releases, placed ads in leading magazines, enlisted a corps of "Four-Minute Men" who gave short, canned talks emphasizing German atrocities, and in other ways sought to promote war fever. The intellectual content of most of this is suggested by some of the war films endorsed by CPI, such as "The Prussian Cur" and "The Kaiser, the Beast of Berlin." . . .

After World War I many felt that the mixture of propaganda and intimidation had encouraged the violation of basic American rights, inflamed passions, contributed to vigilante action, stimulated xenophobia, oversimplified the issues, and aroused unrealistic expectations. FDR was not going to repeat the mistake. Public relations was one thing, a ministry of domestic propaganda another. Congress seconded his motion, conservatives fearing that government propaganda campaigns would glorify Roosevelt, the New Deal, and liberal internationalism—what Congresswoman Clare Boothe Luce referred to as "globaloney." . . .

Given Washington's lack of interest in propaganda, writers eager to aid the war effort were inspired to create their own. West Coast patriots formed the Hollywood Writer's Mobilization. Its counterpart on the East Coast was organized by Rex Stout, author of the popular Nero Wolfe detective novels, who launched the Writer's War Board two days after Pearl Harbor. Initially it helped sell war bonds, but soon grew "into a liaison office between writers and government departments, a kind of unpaid extension of the Office of War Information." Looking back, a former member described its purpose thusly. "The government was slow; we were fast. They were timid; we were bold. They used official gobbledygook; we had some wit. World War II was strangely unemotional and needed a WWB to stir things up." As this suggests, the mobilized wordsmiths put a high premium on ardor.

Members not only wrote advertising copy for war bonds, but used every known outlet to reach the public. The WWB itself might instigate a campaign; other times it responded to official requests. An example of the latter case occurred when the Air Force wanted to promote the enlistment of flight crew other than pilots. WWB's contribution included 12 short stories, 24 syndicated columns, three radio broadcasts, one novel, one handbook, and two popular songs—one of them entitled "I Wanna Marry a Bombardier." The campaign had to be terminated after it produced a surplus of volunteers. . . .

These were America's strengths, a lack of regimentation, the refusal to indoctrinate; and most of all the initiative of ordinary people organizing, conserving, collecting, recycling, buying war bonds—or if, like writers and entertainers, they had special skills, devoting them to public service. That government never found a way of fully exploiting their eagerness to help was its biggest wartime failure, and a curious one in light of the opinion polls showing a willingness to give beyond what was ever asked of civilians. . . .

Civilians contributed more to the winning of World War II than to any previous American conflict—on the homefront, but directly too in the battle against the U-boats. In this campaign the front lines were manned not just by sailors and fliers, but by civilian seamen of the U.S. merchant fleet, thousands of whom lost their lives to keep Britain and Russia going. Many more would have died had it not been for a handful of men in government and business who played key roles at critical points that were to make a tremendous difference. . . .

The war changed everything except human needs and desires. Many once ordinary tasks became fiendishly difficult to perform. Numerous goods previously taken for granted all but disappeared, were replaced by inferior substitutes, or disappeared altogether. People got by as best they could and some discovered in the war a welcome degree of excitement. Most found it possible, despite shortages and censorship, to amuse themselves, taking their pleasure in ways that tell us much about the American people and what they considered important.

It seems fair to say that life on the homefront was most difficult for married women. A 48-hour week and long commutes were the rule for all workers, regardless of gender. Because so many goods and services—including household appliances and supplies, certain foodstuffs, domestic help, and medical care—were in short supply, wives and mothers, whether employed or not, had to devote more time to such activities as housework and getting their children to doctors. Shopping was further complicated by ration books and the need to go from store to store looking for scarce products.

Like their husbands, service wives could "take it" and did not let fear for their absent loved ones keep them from shouldering what often were heavy burdens. One Illinois mother was left to care for three small boys when her husband went overseas. She worked eight hours a day in a local canning factory, yet managed to run a Cub Scout troop, keep a victory garden, and put a hot meal on the table every night—if only tunafish casserole. When the fare prompted complaints she serenely replied, as every mother did in those years, "Think of the poor, starving children in Europe."

Consumers had to return used toothpaste tubes in order to buy new ones, while tinfoil and cellophane simply disappeared—as did bobby pins, which were replaced by wooden toothpicks and thread. Mostly a drain, shopping could be adventuresome if you had the right kind of luck. In April 1945, Audrey Davis triumphantly wrote to her husband at sea:

> Honey, I'm a success. I got sheets! Such a time—went to four of the biggest stores first and was turned down cold. Finally ended up in the basement of J. C. Penney's . . . and saw some bedding so on the off-chance, I asked. The girl said, shhh, and sneaked into a back room and brought out some carefully wrapped—didn't even know what I had bought, until I got home. I felt like someone buying hooch during Prohibition.

New clothes were devoid of elastic thread and webbing, metal buttons, zippers, hooks and eyes, silk, nylon, canvas, duck, and sometimes leather. Coats could not have pleats, gussets, bellows, yokes. A "victory suit," which carried economy to the point of eliminating lapels, was ruled out. To save wool, double-breasted suits could not be vested, and no suit could come with more than one pair of pants. Cloth could not go over cloth, eliminating trouser cuffs and patch pockets. Women's skirts were limited in length and circumference and certain dyes, especially greens and browns, were sometimes unavailable. Girdles, still everyday wear for women, had to be made of bone or piano wire instead of rubber. Shoes, when you could get them, came in six colors only, three of them shades of brown. Almost anything from coffee to canned goods, half the 1943 production went overseas, could run out without notice, cigarette shortages being a particular trial for a nation of smokers.

Irritation over rationing was continuous and so sharp that in 1943 Leon Henderson, one of the most brilliant New Dealers, had to resign as head of the Office of Price Administration even though he was, according to economist Kenneth Galbraith (who worked for him), one of the "unsung heroes of World War II". . . . Urban Americans grew used to queuing up. Not only were food and clothing rationed, but the number of ration "points" required for specific items fluctuated, obliging every housewife to update her calculations on a weekly, or even daily, basis. Black-marketeering, especially in meat, aggravated shortages. For some, getting meat was a major preoccupation. One mother seems never to have written her son abroad without addressing the problem, although in the mandatory positive voice, as when she told him of her discovery that "Spam fried in butter makes a very tasty Easter dinner."

* * *

A striking feature of the war effort, and a source of many problems, was the enormous increase in physical mobility. Including service personnel, 27.3 million people moved from their original county of residence. In the period 1935–40, an unusually active one, total civilian mobility had amounted to 2.8 million persons a year, but during each of the peak war years it averaged 4.7 million. With automobile use restricted, most long-distance travel was by train, putting enormous stress on the rail system and also the passengers—jammed into overcrowded and poorly maintained cars which were slow and often late due to breakdowns or from having been side-tracked for high-priority troop trains.

Difficult as travel became, starting over in strange places was worse. Adolescents were particularly affected, not only because relocation is emotionally most difficult at that age, but also because so many were going to work full-time or entering the services. In 1940 the number of employed persons between the ages of 14 and 17 was 1.7 million, whereas in 1944 it came to 4.61 million, of whom 1.43 million were part-time students. During World War II the decline in child labor was temporarily reversed, as also the trend toward longer periods of education. Total school attendance for the 14–19 age group in 1940 came to 9.159 million persons, whereas by 1944 it had fallen to 7.93 million. The number of boys and girls aged 14 to 18 who were employed rose from 1 million in 1940 to 2.9 million—the number of mill girls alone rising from 271,000 to 950,000.

By May 1943 some 1.8 million boys and girls under the age of 18 were employed by farms and factories. One Lockheed plant had 1,500 boys laboring as riveters and electricians and in metal fabrication and assembly work. According to the firm, two boys in four hours could accomplish more than an adult worker during a regular eight-hour shift. For those children who remained in school full-time, life was harder, too, as teacher quality declined and class sizes went up. In Arkansas by the 1945–46 school year half the prewar teachers were gone and 72 percent of their replacements had completed less than a semester of college. During 1942–43, out of 170,000 Arkansas youngsters between the ages of 13 and 18 about 100,000 failed to attend school, some taking jobs but many because teachers were not available.

As might be expected, crime rates were strongly influenced by the physical and social changes affecting such a large number of people. Since so many young males, the principal crime-committing group, were in uniform, most crimes declined—except possibly rapes, though as they were seldom reported, the statistics are not very useful. But the number of murders, a more reliable figure, fell from 8,329 in 1940 to a low of 6,675 in 1944. Auto thefts went up in 1942 when new cars became unavailable, but the total number of reported crimes followed the same curve as murders, falling after 1940 and rising again only in 1945 when veterans began reentering civilian life. Suicides declined by a third, from about 19,000 in 1940 to some 13,000 four years later. It is an all too human irony that life seemed more worth living in wartime, the suicide rate showing this even more than the rising birthrate.

All these figures are evidence that—not to make light of its hardships— the war was more interesting than the peace had been. The war put an end to Depression America and gave meaning to ordinary lives, since all citizens were to some degree participants in the national effort. Everything changed, not always for the better, to be sure, but change of itself was often welcome after the monotonous years of austerity that followed the stock market crash of 1929. Many people were given jobs they never expected to get, saw places they would otherwise not have known, and lived richer lives. . . .

DOCUMENTS

Joining the Navy (1939), c. 1991

Well, growing up on the farm in the thirties wasn't very pleasant. I remember the banks going broke, the Depression, and then there were the dry years. I just didn't have a very good experience with living on a farm, and there weren't any jobs when I graduated out of high school, so I decided to join the navy. Part of their propaganda was "Join the navy, see the world, and learn a trade." The pay was $21.00 a month which sounded pretty good at that time. So I figured that would be a good opportunity to get off the farm.

John Zimola, Wahoo
U.S. Navy firecontrolman,
cruiser USS *Louisville*, Pacific Theater
(enlisted in 1939)

SOURCE: *Nebraska History* 72, no. 4 (winter 1991): 169. Testimony taken 1988–91.

Shipyard Diary of a Woman Welder (1940s), 1944

Sunday

I am back from my first day on the Ways [staging on which ships are built], and I feel as if I had seen some giant phenomenon. It's incredible! It's inhuman! It's horrible! And it's marvelous! I don't believe a blitz could be noisier—I didn't dream that there could be so much noise, anywhere. My ears are still ringing like high-tension wires, and my head buzzes. When you first see it, when you look down Way after Way, when you see the thousands each going about his own business and seeming to know what to do, you're so bewildered you can't see anything or make sense out of it.

First came the bus ride to the Yard. Crowded as usual. I was intrigued by knowing that this time I was going to Mart's Marsh. The name has always fascinated me. I gather that it refers to bottom or marshy land once owned by a family named Mart. From the [welding] school our road led along the water where I could see several of the ships already launched and now lying at the outfitting dock to receive the finishing touches. It was easy to spot the various stages of completion; each ship gets moved up one when a new ship arrives for outfitting.

When the bus came to a stop, I followed the crowd across a pontoon bridge between rails at which stood guards checking for badges. The far side of the bridge brought us to the part of the Yard where the prefabricated parts are stored, right in the open, pile upon pile. I saw a huge building marked "Assembly Shop," another "Marine Shop," and still another "Pipe Assembly." There were lots of little houses marked with numbers. Most of them seemed to be in the sixties. And I was looking for check-in station No. 1.

I hunted and hunted without success, and finally asked someone where "new hires" check in. He immediately directed me. I showed my badge, told my number, and was given another badge to be picked up and turned in daily as we did at school. It was marked "New Hire." About then who should come along but Red-headed Marie and the Big Swede! We went together to the Welders' Office where our off days were assigned to us. I was given "C" day and told that it was the only day available. This means that I get Tuesday off this week, Wednesday next, and so on. The Big Swede said she had to have "D" day to get a ride to work and to have the same day as her husband. Although "C" day was "the only one available," strangely enough she was given "D" day. One has to learn to insist on what one wants even when told it is impossible.

SOURCE: From *Shipyard Diary of a Woman Welder,* by Augusta H. Clawson, illustrated by Boris Givotovsky. Copyright © 1944 by Penguin Books, Inc. Used by permission of Viking Penguin, a division of Penguin Group (USA).

The Big Swede is a real pal. She had not forgotten the patch for my overall trouser leg. She had cut a piece from an old pair of her husband's, scrubbed it to get the oil out, and brought it to me with a needle stuck in the center and a coil of black thread ready for action. "Here," she said, "I knew you wouldn't have things handy in a hotel room. Now you mend that hole before you catch your foot in it and fall." . . .

Today my book on welding came from the Washington office. I read that a welder's qualifications are "physical fitness which insures a reasonable degree of endurance during a full day of work; steady nerves and considerable muscular strength." For a shipyard welder I'd amend that to read: "An unreasonable degree of endurance during a full day of strain, plus muscular strength, plus no nerves." If you haven't the muscular strength before you start, you will have it afterward. If you haven't the nerves before, you may have them afterward, though I doubt it. By tomorrow I shall be "reasonably" acclimated, but tonight I quite frankly "ain't."

I, who hate heights, climbed stair after stair after stair till I thought I must be close to the sun. I stopped on the top deck. I, who hate confined spaces, went through narrow corridors, stumbling my way over rubber-coats leads—dozens of them, scores of them, even hundreds of them. I went into a room about four feet by ten where two shipfitters, a shipfitter's helper, a chipper, and I all worked. I welded in the poop deck lying on the floor while another welder spattered sparks from the ceiling and chippers like giant woodpeckers shattered our eardrums. I, who've taken welding, and have sat at a bench welding flat and vertical plates, was told to weld braces along a baseboard below a door opening. On these a heavy steel door was braced while it was hung to a fine degree of accuracy. I welded more braces along the side, and along the top. I did overhead welding, horizontal, flat, vertical. I welded around curved hinges which were placed so close to the side wall that I had to bend my rod in a curve to get it in. I made some good welds and some frightful ones. But now a door in the poop deck of an oil tanker is hanging, four feet by six of solid steel, by my welds. Pretty exciting!

The men in the poop deck were nice to me. The shipfitter was toothless. The grinder had palsy, I guess, for his hands shook pitifully and yet he managed to handle that thirty-pound grinder. The welder was doing "pick-up" work, which meant touching up spots that had been missed. An inspector came through and marked places to chip, and the ship's superintendent stopped and woke the shipfitter's helper. . . .

As a result of all this, I feel very strongly that we'd go to the Yard better prepared if in the school we did more welding in varied positions. Even a fillet weld of two plates could be placed on the floor, and one could get down and do it there and so learn something of what will later be required in the Yard. I don't see why, too, the butterflies, the clips, and even the bolts couldn't be welded at various angles in school. We could practice some one-handed welding instead of always using two hands while sitting at a bench with plates conveniently placed. There are times when you have to use one hand to cling to a ladder or a beam while you weld with the other. I notice that the most experienced welders I have watched seldom use two hands. One large, fine-looking woman (Norwegian, I think) who has been there three months told me: "They don't teach us enough at school. Why don't they let us weld there the same things we'll do here?" I countered with, "Oh, they do teach a lot or we'd be no good here at all; but what you say would certainly help." I think she "has something," however. We do need more experience in setting our machines and recognizing when they are too hot or too cold. Struggling with an inaccurate setting and the wrong amount of heat makes a harder day than doing a lot of actual work. Yet it's hardly the fault of the training that we lack adequate experience. More and more I marvel at training that in eight days can give enough to make us worth anything on the job. And we are worth something. We're building ships.

Conditions in the Camps
(1942–1945), 1948

A visiting reporter from *The San Francisco Chronicle* described quarters at Tule Lake:

> Room size—about 15 by 25, considered too big for two reporters.
> Condition—dirty.
> Contents—two Army cots, each with two Army blankets, one pillow, some sheets and pillow cases (these came as a courtesy from the management), and a coal-burning stove (no coal). There were no dishes, rugs, curtains, or housekeeping equipment of any kind. (We had in addition one sawhorse and three pieces of wood, which the management did not explain.)

The furnishings at other camps were similar. At Minidoka, arriving evacuees found two stacked canvas cots, a pot-bellied stove and a light bulb hanging from the ceiling; at Topaz, cots, two blankets, a pot-bellied stove and some cotton mattresses. Rooms had no running water, which had to be carried from community facilities. Running back and forth from the laundry room to rinse and launder soiled diapers was a particular inconvenience. . . .

SOURCE: Commission on Wartime Relocation and Internment of Civilians, *Personal Justice Denied* (Washington, D.C.: Government Printing Office, 1984), pp. 159–161.

Others, however, found not even the minimal comforts that had been planned for them. An unrealistic schedule combined with wartime short-ages of labor and materials meant that the WRA* had difficulty meeting its construction schedule. In most cases, the barracks were completed, but at some centers evacuees lived without electric light, adequate toilets or laun-dry facilities. . . .

Mess Halls planned for about 300 people had to handle 600 or 900 for short periods. Three months after the project opened, Manzanar still lacked equipment for 16 of 36 messhalls. At Gila:

> There were 7,700 people crowded into space designed for 5,000.
> They were housed in messhalls, recreation halls, and even latrines.
> As many as 25 persons lived in a space intended for four.

As at the assembly centers, one result was that evacuees were often de-nied privacy in even the most intimate aspects of their lives. . . . Even when families had separate quarters, the partitions between rooms failed to give much privacy. Gladys Bell described the situation at Topaz:

> [T]he evacuees . . . had only one room, unless there were around ten in the family. Their rooms had a pot-bellied stove, a single elec-tric light hanging from the ceiling, an Army cot for each person and a blanket for the bed. Each barrack had six rooms with only three flues. This meant that a hole had to be cut through the wall of one room for the stovepipe to join the chimney of the next room. The hole was large so that the wall would not burn. As a result, every-thing said and some things whispered were easily heard by people living in the next room. Sometimes the family would be a couple with four children living next to an older couple, perhaps of a dif-ferent religion, older ideas and with a difference in all ways of life— such as music.

Despite these wretched conditions the evacuees again began to rebuild their lives. Several evacuees recall "foraging for bits of wallboard and wood" and dodging guards to get materials from the scrap lumber piles to build shelves and furniture. . . . Eventually, rooms were partitioned and shelves, tables, chairs and other furniture appeared. Paint and cloth for cur-tains and spreads came from mail order houses at evacuee expense. Flowers bloomed and rock gardens emerged; trees and shrubs were planted. Many evacuees grew victory gardens. One described the change:

> [W]hen we entered camp, it was a barren desert. When we left camp, it was a garden that had been built up without tools, it was green around the camp with vegetation, flowers, and also with arti-ficial lakes, and that's how we left it.

*Wartime Relocation Administration (Eds.)

The success of evacuees' efforts to improve their surroundings, however, was always tempered by the harsh climate. In the western camps, particularly Heart Mountain, Poston, Topaz and Minidoka, dust was a principal problem. Monica Sone described her first day at Minidoka:

> [W]e were given a rousing welcome by a dust storm. . . . We felt as if we were standing in a gigantic sand-mixing machine as the sixty-mile gale lifted the loose earth up into the sky, obliterating everything. Sand filled our mouths and nostrils and stung our faces and hands like a thousand darting needles. Henry and Father pushed on ahead while Mother, Sumi and I followed, hanging onto their jackets, banging suitcases into each other. At last we staggered into our room, gasping and blinded. We sat on our suitcases to rest, peeling off our jackets and scarves. The window panels rattled madly, and the dust poured through the cracks like smoke. Now and then when the wind subsided, I saw other evacuees, hanging on to their suitcases, heads bent against the stinging dust. The wind whipped their scarves and towels from their heads and zipped them out of sight.

In desert camps, the evacuees met severe extremes of temperature as well. In winter it reached 35 degrees below zero and summers brought temperature as high as 115°. Because the desert did not cool off at night, evacuees would splash water on their cots to be cool enough to sleep. Rattlesnakes and desert wildlife added danger to discomfort.

The Arkansas camps had equally unpleasant weather. Winters were cold and snowy while summers were unbearably hot and humid, heavy with chiggers and clouds of mosquitos. . . .

The WRA walked a fine line in providing for evacuees' basic needs. On the one hand was their genuine sympathy for the excluded people. On the other was a well-founded apprehension that the press and the politicians would seek out and denounce any evidence that evacuees were being treated generously. WRA's compromise was to strive for a system that would provide a healthy but Spartan environment. They did not always succeed, and it was usually the evacuees who suffered when they failed.

Chapter 12

Moving to Suburbia: Dreams and Discontents

A postwar family views its dream house.

World War II set off an economic boom marked by the steady growth of family and individual incomes that lasted, with few interruptions, until 1973. Never before had the nation experienced such prosperity. Never before had material products that Americans associated with "the good life"—automobiles, dishwashers, stereos, televisions, and more—become so readily available to large segments of the population.

The keystone of the middle-class dream was home ownership. During the 1930s and 1940s, the lyrics of popular ballads like "My Blue Heaven" had expressed the desire for a bungalow in the suburbs, in which husband, wife, and children would live an idyllic life. But wartime demands for the construction of military bases and for defense industries had brought private home building, already slowed by the Depression, to a virtual halt. Within a few years of the war's end, however, the building boom was under way. Kenneth Jackson's essay "The Baby Boom and the Age of the Subdivision" describes how the postwar demand for suburban housing, fueled by veterans and their growing families, was served by government assistance and enterprising builders. Among the latter, William

Levitt was possibly the most ingenious; the housing tracts that he built, called Levittowns, came to symbolize post–World War II construction. Which innovations in home construction and community planning were most likely responsible for establishing Levitt's reputation?

Jackson describes not only the birth of postwar suburbs but also the lifestyles that characterized those communities. Although large numbers of people voted their approval of suburban life by deciding to relocate their families, the movement was not without critics. The homogeneity and conformity of housing developments were frequent targets, as illustrated by the first document, Malvina Reynolds's popular song of the early 1960s, "Little Boxes." Do the lyrics give a fair picture of the suburbs?

If the houses looked alike, what of the people living in them? White families at least had a choice, if they had the means, to live where they chose. For black Americans, suburban housing patterns were limited. The second document, a 1994 summary of residential housing patterns, points to a factor to which Kenneth Jackson alluded, racial segregation. What does this report tell us about race relations in suburban America?

In the years since the above report appeared, growing numbers of African Americans have been moving to the suburbs, resulting in an increase in towns where housing patterns are racially mixed. The third document, an examination of Massachusetts suburbs, points to another recent phenomenon, the settlement by large numbers of immigrants in the nation's suburban communities. Considering the depictions of the suburbs found in the essay and three documents, how would you describe the major changes in the population and other aspects of America's suburbs from the post–World War II years to the present?

ESSAY

The Baby Boom and the Age of the Subdivision
Kenneth Jackson

> What the Blandings wanted . . . was simple enough: a two-story house in quiet, modern good taste, . . . a good-sized living room with a fire place, a dining room, pantry, and kitchen, a small lavatory, four bedrooms and accompanying baths, . . . a roomy cellar . . . plenty of closets.
> —Eric Hodgins,
> *Mr. Blandings Builds His Dream House* (1939)

SOURCE: From *Crabgrass Frontier: The Suburbanization of the United States,* by Kenneth T. Jackson. Copyright © 1985 by Oxford University Press, Inc. Used by permission of Oxford University Press, Inc.

> No man who owns his own house and lot can be a
> Communist. He has too much to do.
>
> —*William J. Levitt, 1948*

At 7 P.M. (Eastern time) on August 14, 1945, radio stations across the nation interrupted normal programming for President Harry S Truman's announcement of the surrender of Japan. It was a moment in time that those who experienced it will never forget. World War II was over. Across the nation, Americans gathered to celebrate their victory. In New York City two million people converged on Times Square as though it were New Year's Eve. In smaller cities and towns, the response was no less tumultuous, as spontaneous cheers, horns, sirens, and church bells telegraphed the news to every household and hamlet, convincing even small children that it was a very special day. To the average person, the most important consequence of victory was not the end of shortages, not the restructuring of international boundaries or reparations payments or big power politics, but the survival of husbands and sons. Some women regretted that their first decent-paying, responsible jobs would be taken away by returning veterans. Most, however, felt a collective sigh of relief. Normal family life could resume. The long vigil was over. Their men would be coming home.

In truth, the United States was no better prepared for peace than it had been for war when the German *Wehrmacht* crossed the Polish frontier in the predawn hours of September 1, 1939. For more than five years military necessity had taken priority over consumer goods, and by 1945 almost everyone had a long list of unfilled material wants.

Housing was the area of most pressing need. Through sixteen years of depression and war, the residential construction industry had been dormant, with new home starts averaging less than 100,000 per year. Almost one million people had migrated to defense areas in the early 1940s, but new housing for them was designated as "temporary," in part as an economy move and in part because the real-estate lobby did not want emergency housing converted to permanent use after the war. Meanwhile, the marriage rate, after a decade of decline, had begun a steep rise in 1940, as war became increasingly likely and the possibility of separation added a spur to decision making. In addition, married servicemen received an additional fifty dollars per month allotment, which went directly to the wives. Soon thereafter, the birth rate began to climb, reaching 22 per 1,000 in 1943, the highest in two decades. Many of the newcomers were "good-bye babies," conceived just before the husbands shipped out, partly because of an absence of birth control, partly because the wife's allotment check would be increased with each child, and partly as a tangible reminder of a father who could not know when, or if, he would return. During the war, government and industry both played up the suburban house to the families of absent servicemen, and between 1941 and 1946 some of the nation's most promising architects published their "dream houses" in a series in the *Ladies' Home Journal.*

After the war, both the marriage and the birth rates continued at a high level. In individual terms, this rise in family formation coupled with the decline in housing starts meant that there were virtually no homes for sale or apartments for rent at war's end. Continuing a trend begun during the Great Depression, six million families were doubling up with relatives or friends by 1947, and another 500,000 were occupying quonset huts or temporary quarters. Neither figure included families living in substandard dwellings or those in desperate need of more room. In Chicago, 250 former trolley cars were sold as homes. In New York City a newly wed couple set up housekeeping for two days in a department store window in hopes that the publicity would help them find an apartment. In Omaha a newspaper advertisement proposed: "Big Ice Box, 7 × 17 feet, could be fixed up to live in." In Atlanta the city bought 100 trailers for veterans. In North Dakota surplus grain bins were turned into apartments. In brief, the demand for housing was unprecedented.

The federal government responded to an immediate need for five million new homes by underwriting a vast new construction program. In the decade after the war, Congress regularly approved billions of dollars worth of additional mortgage insurance for the Federal Housing Administration. Even more important was the Servicemen's Readjustment Act of 1944, which created a Veterans Administration mortgage program similar to that of FHA. This law gave official endorsement and support to the view that the 16 million GI's of World War II should return to civilian life with a home of their own. Also, it accepted the builders' contention that they needed an end to government controls but not to government insurance on their investments in residential construction. According to novelist John Keats, "The real estate boys read the Bill, looked at one another in happy amazement, and the dry, rasping noise they made rubbing their hands together could have been heard as far away as Tawi Tawi."

It is not recorded how far the noise carried, but anyone in the residential construction business had ample reason to rub their hands. The assurance of federal mortgage guarantees—at whatever price the builder set—stimulated an unprecedented building boom. Single-family housing starts spurted from only 114,000 in 1944, to 937,000 in 1946, to 1,183,000 in 1948, and to 1,692,000 in 1950, an all-time high. However, . . . what distinguished the period was an increase in the number, importance, and size of large builders. Residential construction in the United States had always been highly fragmented in comparison with other industries, and dominated by small and poorly organized house builders who had to subcontract much of the work because their low volume did not justify the hiring of all the craftsmen needed to put up a dwelling. In housing, as in other areas of the economy, World War II was beneficial to large businesses. Whereas before 1945, the typical contractor had put up fewer than five houses per year, by 1959, the median single-family builder put up twenty-two structures. As early as 1949, fully 70 percent of new homes were constructed by only 10 percent of the firms (a percentage that would remain roughly stable for the next three decades), and by 1955 subdivisions accounted for more than three-quarters of all new housing in metropolitan areas.

Viewed from an international perspective, however, the building of homes in the United States remained a small-scale enterprise. In 1969, for example, the percentage of all new units built by builders of more than 500 units per year was only 8.1 percent in the United States, compared with 24 percent in Great Britain and 33 percent in France. World War II, therefore, did not transform the American housing industry as radically as it did that of Europe.

The family that had the greatest impact on postwar housing in the United States was Abraham Levitt and his sons, William and Alfred, who ultimately built more than 140,000 houses and turned a cottage industry into a major manufacturing process. They began on a small scale on Long Island in 1929 and concentrated for years on substantial houses in Rockville Center. Increasing their pace in 1934 with a 200-unit subdivision called "Strathmore" in Manhasset, the Levitts continued to focus on the upper-middle class and marketed their tudor-style houses at between $9,100 and $18,500. Private commissions and smaller subdivisions carried the firm through the remainder of the prewar period.

In 1941 Levitt and Sons received a government contract for 1,600 (later increased to 2,350) war workers' homes in Norfolk, Virginia. The effort was a nightmare, but the brothers learned how to lay dozens of concrete foundations in a single day and to preassemble uniform walls and roofs. Additional contracts for more federal housing in Portsmouth, Virginia, and for barracks for shipyard workers at Pearl Harbor provided supplemental experience, as did William's service with the Navy Seabees from 1943 to 1945. Thus, the Levitts were among the nation's largest home builders even before construction of the first Levittown.

Returning to Long Island after the war, the Levitts built 2,250 houses in Roslyn in 1946 in the $17,500 to $23,500 price range, well beyond the means of the average veteran. In that same year, however, they began the acquisition of 4,000 acres of potato farms in the Town of Hempstead, where they planned the biggest private housing project in American history.

The formula for Island Trees, soon renamed Levittown, was simple. After bulldozing the land and removing the trees, trucks carefully dropped off building materials at precise 60-foot intervals. Each house was built on a concrete slab (no cellar); the floors were of asphalt and the walls of composition rock-board. Plywood replaced ¾-inch strip lap, ¾-inch double lap was changed to ⅜-inch for roofing, and the horse and scoop were replaced by the bulldozer. New power hand tools like saws, routers, and nailers helped increase worker productivity. Freight cars loaded with lumber went directly into a cutting yard where one man cut parts for ten houses in one day.

The construction process itself was divided into twenty-seven distinct steps—beginning with laying the foundation and ending with a clean sweep of the new home. Crews were trained to do one job—one day the white-paint men, then the red-paint men, then the tile layers. Every possible part, and especially the most difficult ones, were preassembled in central shops, whereas most builders did it on site. Thus, the Levitts reduced the skilled component to 20–40 percent. The five-day work week was standard, but they were the five days during which building was possible; Saturday and Sunday were considered to be the days when it rained. In the process, the Levitts defied unions and union work rules (against spray painting, for example) and insisted that subcontractors work only for them. Vertical integration also meant that the firm made its own concrete, grew its own timber, and cut its own lumber. It also bought all appliances from wholly owned subsidiaries. More than thirty houses went up each day at the peak of production.

Initially limited to veterans, this first "Levittown" was twenty-five miles east of Manhattan and particularly attractive to new families that had been formed during and just after the war. Squashed in with their in-laws or in tiny apartments where landlords frowned on children, the GI's looked upon Levittown as the answer to their most pressing need. Months before the first three hundred Levitt houses were occupied in October 1947, customers stood in line for the four-room Cape Cod box renting at sixty dollars per month. The first eighteen hundred houses were initially available only for rental, with an option to buy after a year's residence. Because the total for mortgage, interest, principal, and taxes was *less* than the rent, almost everyone bought; after 1949 all units were for sale only. So many of the purchasers were young families that the first issue of *Island Trees*, the community newspaper, opined that "our lives are held closely together because most of us are within the same age bracket, in similar income groups, live in almost identical houses and have common problems." And so many babies were born to them that the suburb came to be known as "Fertility Valley" and "The Rabbit Hutch."

Ultimately encompassing more than 17,400 separate houses and 82,000 residents, Levittown was the largest housing development ever put up by a single builder, and it served the American dream-house market at close to the lowest prices the industry could attain. The typical Cape Cod was down-to-earth and unpretentious; the intention was not to stir the imagination, but to provide the best shelter at the least price. Each dwelling included a twelve-by-sixteen-foot living-room with a fireplace, one bath, and two bedrooms (about 750 square feet), with easy expansion possibilities upstairs in the unfinished attic or outward into the yard. Most importantly, the floor plan was practical and well-designed, with the kitchen moved to the front of the house near the entrance so that mothers could watch their children from kitchen windows and do their washing and cooking with a minimum of movement. Similarly, the living room was placed in the rear and given a picture window overlooking the back yard. This early Levitt house was as basic to post–World War II suburban development as the Model T had been to the automobile. In each case, the actual design features were less important than the fact that they were mass-produced and thus priced within the reach of the middle class.

William Jaird Levitt, who assumed primary operating responsibility for the firm soon after the war, disposed of houses as quickly as other men disposed of cars. Pricing his Cape Cods at $7,990 (the earliest models went for $6,990) and his ranches at $9,500, he promised no down payment, no closing costs, and "no hidden extras." With FHA and VA "production advances," Levitt boasted the largest line of credit ever offered a private home builder. He simplified the paperwork required for purchase and reduced the entire financing and titling transaction to two half-hour steps. His full-page advertisements offered a sweetener to eliminate lingering resistance—a Bendix washer was included in the purchase price. Other inducements included an eight-inch television set (for which the family would pay for the next thirty years). So efficient was the operation that *Harper's Magazine* reported in 1948 that Levitt undersold his nearest competition by $1,500 and still made a $1,000 profit on each house. As *New York Times* architecture critic Paul Goldberger has noted, "Levittown houses were social creations more than architectural ones—they turned the detached, single-family house from a distant dream to a real possibility for thousands of middle-class American families."

Buyers received more than shelter for their money. When the initial families arrived with their baby strollers and play pens, there were no trees, schools, churches, or private telephones. Grocery shopping was a planned adventure, and picking up the mail required sloshing through the mud to Hicksville. The Levitts planted apple, cherry, and evergreen trees on each plot, however, and the development ultimately assumed a more parklike appearance. To facilitate development as a garden community, streets were curvilinear (and invariably called "roads" or "lanes"), and through traffic was shunted to peripheral thoroughfares. Nine swimming pools, sixty playgrounds, ten baseball diamonds, and seven "village greens" provided open space and recreational opportunities. The Levitts forbade fences (a practice later ignored) and permitted outdoor clothes drying only on specially designed, collapsible racks. They even supervised lawn-cutting for the first few years—doing the jobs themselves if necessary and sending the laggard families the bill.

Architectural critics, many of whom were unaccustomed to the tastes or resources of moderate-income people, were generally unimpressed by the repetitious houses on 60-by-100-foot "cookie cutter lots" and referred to Levittown as "degraded in conception and impoverished in form." From the Wantagh Parkway, the town stretched away to the east as far as the eye could see, house after identical house, a horizon broken only by telephone poles. Paul Goldberger, who admired the individual designs, thought that the whole was "an urban planning disaster," while [social critic] Lewis Mumford complained that Levittown's narrow range of house type and income range resulted in a one-class community and a backward design. He noted that the Levitts used "new-fashioned methods to compound old-fashioned mistakes."

But Levittown was a huge popular success where it counted—in the marketplace. On a single day in March 1949, fourteen hundred contracts were drawn, some with families that had been in line for four days. "I truly loved it," recalled one early resident. "When they built the Village Green, our big event was walking down there for ice cream."

In the 1950s the Levitts shifted their attention from Long Island to an equally large project near Philadelphia. Located on former broccoli and spinach farms in lower Bucks County, Pennsylvania, this new Levittown was built within a few miles of the new Fairless Works of the United States Steel Corporation, where the largest percentage of the community's residents were employed. It was composed on eight master blocks, each of about one square mile and focusing on its own recreational facilities. Totaling about 16,000 homes when completed late in the decade, the town included light industry and a big, 55-acre shopping center. According to Levitt, "We planned every foot of it—every store, filling station, school, house, apartment, church, color, tree, and shrub."

In the 1960s, the Levitt forces shifted once again, this time to Willingboro, New Jersey, where a third Levittown was constructed within distant commuting range of Philadelphia. This last town was the focus of Herbert Gans's well-known account of *The Levittowners*. The Cape Cod remained the basic style, but Levitt improved the older models to resemble more closely the pseudo-colonial design that was so popular in the Northeast.

If imitation is the sincerest form of flattery, then William Levitt has been much honored in the past forty years. His replacement of basement foundations with the radiantly heated concrete slab was being widely copied as early as 1950. Levitt did not actually pioneer many of the mass-production techniques—the use of plywood, particle board, and gypsum board, as well as power hand tools like saws, routers, and nailers, for example—but his developments were so widely publicized that in every large metropolitan area, large builders appeared who adopted similar methods. . . .

FHA and VA programs made possible the financing of their immense developments. Title VI of the National Housing Act of 1934 allowed a builder to insure 90 percent of the mortgage of a house costing up to nine thousand dollars. Most importantly, an ambitious entrepreneur could get an FHA "commitment" to insure the mortgage, and then use that "commitment" to sign himself up as a temporary mortgagor. The mortgage lender (a bank or savings and loan institution) would then make "production advances" to the contractor as the work progressed, so that the builder needed to invest very little of his own hard cash. Previously, even the largest builders could not bring together the capital to undertake thousand-house developments. FHA alone insured three thousand houses in Henry J. Kaiser's Panorama City, California; five thousand in Frank Sharp's Oak Forest; and eight thousand in Klutznick's Park Forest project.

However financed and by whomever built, the new subdivisions that were typical of American urban development between 1945 and 1973 tended to share five common characteristics. The first was peripheral location. A Bureau of Labor Statistics survey of home building in 1946–1947 in six metropolitan regions determined that the suburbs accounted for at least 62 percent of construction. By 1950 the national suburban growth rate was ten times that of central cities, and in 1954 the editors of *Fortune* estimated that 9 million people had moved to the suburbs in the previous decade. The inner cities did have some empty lots—serviced by sewers, electrical connections, gas lines, and streets—available for development. But the filling-in process was not amenable to mass production techniques, and it satisfied neither the economic nor the psychological temper of the times.

The few new neighborhoods that were located within the boundaries of major cities tended also to be on the open land at the edges of the built-up sections. In New York City, the only area in the 1946–1947 study where city construction was greater than that of the suburbs, the big growth was on the outer edges of Queens, a borough that had been largely undeveloped in 1945. In Memphis new development moved east out Summer, Poplar, Walnut Grove, and Park Avenues, where FHA and VA subdivisions advertised "No Down Payment" or "One Dollar Down" on giant billboards. In Los Angeles, the fastest-growing American city in the immediate postwar period, the area of rapid building focused on the San Fernando Valley, a vast space that had remained largely vacant since its annexation to the city in 1915. In Philadelphia thousands of new houses were put up in farming areas that had legally been part of the city since 1854, but which in fact had functioned as agricultural settlements for generations.

The second major characteristic of the postwar suburbs was their relatively low density. In all except the most isolated instances, the row house completely lost favor; between 1946 and 1956, about 97 percent of all new single-family dwellings were completely detached, surrounded on every side by their own plots. Typical lot sizes were relatively uniform around the country, averaging between 1/5 (80 by 100 feet) and 1/10 (40 by 100 feet) of an acre and varying more with distance from the center than by region. Moreover, the new subdivisions allotted a higher proportion of their land area to streets and open spaces. Levittown, Long Island, for example, was settled at a density of 10,500 per square mile, which was about average for postwar suburbs but less than half as dense as the streetcar suburbs of a half-century earlier. This design of new neighborhoods on the assumption that residents would have automobiles meant that those without cars faced severe handicaps in access to jobs and shopping facilities.

This low-density pattern was in marked contrast with Europe. In war-ravaged countries east of the Rhine River, the concentration upon apartment buildings can be explained by the overriding necessity to provide shelter quickly for masses of displaced and homeless people. But in comparatively unscathed France, Denmark, and Spain, the single-family house was also a rarity. In Sweden, Stockholm committed itself to a suburban pattern along subway lines, a decision that implied a high-density residential pattern. Nowhere in Europe was there the land, the money, or the tradition for single-family home construction.

The third major characteristic of the postwar suburbs was their architectural similarity. A few custom homes were built for the rich, and mobile homes gained popularity with the poor and the transient, but for most American families in search of a new place to live some form of tract house was the most likely option. In order to simplify their production methods and reduce design fees, most of the larger developers offered no more than a half-dozen basic house plans, and some offered half that number. The result was a monotony and repetition that was especially stark in the early years of the subdivision, before the individual owners had transformed their homes and yards according to personal taste.

But the architectural similarity extended beyond the particular tract to the nation as a whole. Historically, each region of the country had developed an indigenous residential style—the colonial-style homes of New England, the row houses of Atlantic coastal cities, the famous Charleston town houses with their ends to the street, the raised plantation homes of the damp bayou country of Louisiana, and the encircled patios and massive walls of the Southwest. This regionalism of design extended to relatively small areas; early in the twentieth century a house on the South Carolina coast looked quite different from a house in the Piedmont a few hundred miles away.

This tradition began eroding after World War I, when the American dream house became . . . the Cape Cod cottage, a quaint one-and-a-half-story dwelling. This design remained popular into the post–World War II years, when Levittown featured it as a bargain for veterans. In subsequent years, one fad after another became the rage. First, it was the split-level, then the ranch, then the modified colonial. In each case, the style tended to find support throughout the continent, so that by the 1960s the casual suburban visitor would have a difficult time deciphering whether she was in the environs of Boston or Dallas.

The ranch style, in particular, was evocative of the expansive mood of the post–World War II suburbs and of the disappearing regionality of style. It was almost as popular in Westchester County as in Los Angeles County. Remotely derived from the adobe dwellings of the Spanish colonial tradition and more directly derived from the famed prairie houses of [architect]

212

Frank Lloyd Wright, with their low-pitched roofs, deep eaves, and pronounced horizontal lines, the typical ranch style houses of the 1950s were no larger than the average home a generation earlier. But the one-level ranch house suggested spacious living and an easy relationship with the outdoors. Mothers with small children did not have to contend with stairs. Most importantly, the postwar ranch home represented newness. In 1945 the publisher of the *Saturday Evening Post* reported that only 14 percent of the population wanted to live in an apartment or a "used" house. Whatever the style, the post–World War II house, in contrast to its turn-of-the-century predecessor, had no hall, no parlor, no stairs, and no porch. And the portion of the structure that projected farthest toward the street was the garage.

The fourth characteristic of post–World War II housing was its easy availability and thus its reduced suggestion of wealth. To be sure, upper-income suburbs and developments sprouted across the land, and some set high standards of style and design. Typically, they offered expansive lots, spacious and individualized designs, and affluent neighbors. But the most important income development of the period was the lowering of the threshold of purchase. At every previous time in American history, and indeed for the 1980s as well, the successful acquisition of a family home required savings and effort of a major order. After World War II, however, because of mass-production techniques, government financing, high wages, and low interest rates, it was quite simply cheaper to buy new housing in the suburbs than it was to reinvest in central city properties or to rent at the market price.

The fifth and perhaps most important characteristic of the postwar suburb was economic and racial homogeneity. The sorting out of families by income and color began even before the Civil War and was stimulated by the growth of the factory system. This pattern was noticeable in both the exclusive Main Line suburbs of Philadelphia and New York and in the more bourgeois streetcar developments which were part of every city. The automobile accentuated this discriminatory "Jim Crow" pattern. In Atlanta, where large numbers of whites flocked to the fast-growing and wealthy suburbs north of the city in the 1920s, [it was] reported that: "By 1930, if racism could be measured in miles and minutes, blacks and whites were more segregated in the city of Atlanta than ever before." But many pre-1930 suburbs—places like Greenwich, Connecticut; Englewood, New Jersey; Evanston, Illinois; and Chestnut Hill, Massachusetts—maintained an exclusive image despite the presence of low-income or minority groups living in slums near or within the community.

The post-1945 developments took place against a background of the decline of factory-dominated cities. What was unusual in the new circumstances was not the presence of discrimination—Jews and Catholics as well as blacks had been excluded from certain neighborhoods for generations—but the thoroughness of the physical separation which it entailed. The Levitt organization, which was no more culpable in this regard than any other urban or suburban firm, publicly and officially refused to sell to blacks for two decades after the war. Nor did resellers deal with minorities. As William Levitt explained, "We can solve a housing problem, or we can try to solve a racial problem. But we cannot combine the two." Not surprisingly, in 1960 not a single one of the Long Island Levittown's 82,000 residents was black.

The economic and age homogeneity of large subdivisions and sometimes entire suburbs was almost as complete as the racial distinction. Although this tendency had been present even in the nineteenth century, the introduction of zoning—beginning with a New York City ordinance in 1916—served the general purpose of preserving residential class segregation and property values. In theory zoning was designed to protect the interests of all citizens by limiting land speculation and congestion. And it was popular. Although it represented an extraordinary growth of municipal power, nearly everyone supported zoning. By 1926 seventy-six cities had adopted ordinances similar to that of New York. By 1936, 1,322 cities (85 percent of the total) had them, and zoning laws were affecting more property than all national laws relating to business.

In actuality zoning was a device to keep poor people and obnoxious industries out of affluent areas. And in time, it also became a cudgel used by suburban areas to whack the central city. Advocates of land-use restrictions in overwhelming proportion were residents of the fringe. They sought through minimum lot and set-back requirements to insure that only members of acceptable social classes could settle in their privileged sanctuaries. Southern cities even used zoning to enforce racial segregation. And in suburbs everywhere, North and South, zoning was used by the people who already lived within the arbitrary boundaries of a community as a method of keeping everyone else out. Apartments, factories, and "blight," euphemisms for blacks and people of limited means, were rigidly excluded.

While zoning provided a way for suburban areas to become secure enclaves for the well-to-do, it forced the city to provide economic facilities for the whole area and homes for people the suburbs refused to admit. Simply put, land-use restrictions tended to protect residential interests in the suburbs and commercial interests in the cities because the residents of the core usually lived on land owned by absentee landlords who were more interested in financial returns than neighborhood preferences. For the man who owned land but did not live on it, the ideal situation was to have his parcel of earth zoned for commercial or industrial use. With more options, the property often gained in value. In Chicago, for example, three times as much land was zoned for commercial use as could ever have been profitably employed for such purposes. This overzoning prevented inner-city residents from receiving the same protection from commercial incursions as was afforded suburbanites. Instead of becoming a useful tool for the rational ordering of land in metropolitan areas, zoning became a way for suburbs to pirate from the city only its desirable functions and residents. Suburban governments became like so many residential hotels, fighting for the upper-income trade while trying to force the deadbeats to go elsewhere.

Because zoning restrictions typically excluded all apartments and houses and lots of less than a certain number of square feet, new home purchasers were often from a similar income and social group. In this regard, the postwar suburbs were no different from many nineteenth-century neighborhoods when they were first built. Moreover, Levittown was originally a mix of young professionals and lower-middle-class blue-collar workers.

As the aspiring professionals moved out, however, Levittown became a community of the most class-stratifying sort possible. This phenomenon was the subject of one of the most important books of the 1950s. Focusing on a 2,400-acre project put up by the former Public Housing Administrator Phillip Klutznick, William H. Whyte's *The Organization Man* sent shudders through armchair sociologists. Although Whyte found that Park Forest, Illinois, offered its residents "leadership training" and an "ability to chew on real problems," the basic portrait was unflattering. Reporting excessive conformity and a mindless conservatism, he showed Park Foresters to be almost interchangeable as they fought their way up the corporate ladder, and his "organization man" stereotype unfortunately became the norm for judging similar communities throughout the nation.

By 1961, when President John F. Kennedy proclaimed his New Frontier and challenged Americans to send a man to the moon within the decade, his countrymen had already remade the nation's metropolitan areas in the short space of sixteen years. From Boston to Los Angeles, vast new subdivisions and virtually new towns sprawled where a generation earlier nature had held sway. In an era of low inflation, plentiful energy, federal subsidies, and expansive optimism, Americans showed the way to a more abundant and more perfect lifestyle. Almost every contractor-built, post–World War II home had central heating, indoor plumbing, telephones, automatic stoves, refrigerators, and washing machines.

There was a darker side to the outward movement. By making it possible for young couples to have separate households of their own, abundance further weakened the extended family in America and ordained that most children would grow up in intimate contact only with their parents and siblings. The housing arrangements of the new prosperity were evident as early as 1950. In that year there were 45,983,000 dwelling units to accommodate the 38,310,000 families in the United States and 84 percent of American households reported less than one person per room.

Critics regarded the peripheral environment as devastating particularly to women and children. The suburban world was a female world, especially during the day. Betty Friedan's 1963 classic *The Feminine Mystique* challenged the notion that the American dream home was emotionally fulfilling for women. As Gwendolyn Wright has observed, their isolation from work opportunities and from contact with employed adults led to stifled frustration and deep psychological problems. Similarly, Sidonie M. Gruenberg warned in the *New York Times Magazine* that "Mass produced, standardized housing breeds standardized individuals, too—especially among youngsters." Offering neither the urbanity and sophistication of the city nor the tranquility and repose of the farm, the suburb came to be regarded less as an intelligent compromise than a cultural, economic, and emotional wasteland. No observer was more critical than Lewis Mumford, however. In his 1961 analysis of *The City in History*, which covered the entire sweep of civilization, the famed author reiterated sentiments he had first expressed more than four decades earlier and scorned the new developments which were surrounding every American city:

> In the mass movement into suburban areas a new kind of community was produced, which caricatured both the historic city and the archetypal suburban refuge: a multitude of uniform, unidentifiable houses, lined up inflexibly, at uniform distances, on uniform roads, in a treeless communal waste, inhabited by people of the same class, the same income, the same age group, witnessing the same television performances, eating the same tasteless prefabricated foods, from the same freezers, conforming in every outward and inward respect to a common mold, manufactured in the central metropolis. Thus, the ultimate effect of the suburban escape in our own time is, ironically, a low-grade uniform environment from which escape is impossible.

Secondly, because the federally supported home-building boom was of such enormous proportions, the new houses of the suburbs were a major cause of the decline of central cities. Because FHA and VA terms for new construction were so favorable as to make the suburbs accessible to almost all white, middle-income families, the inner-city housing market was deprived of the purchasers who could perhaps have supplied an appropriate demand for the evacuated neighborhoods.

The young families who joyously moved into the new homes of the suburbs were not terribly concerned about the problems of the inner-city housing market or the snobbish views of Lewis Mumford and other social critics. They were concerned about their hopes and their dreams. They were looking for good schools, private space, and personal safety, and places like Levittown could provide those amenities on a scale and at a price that crowded city neighborhoods, both in the Old World and in the New, could not match. The single-family tract house—post–World War II style—whatever its aesthetic failings, offered growing families a private haven in a heartless world. If the dream did not include minorities or the elderly, if it was accompanied by the isolation of nuclear families, by the decline of public transportation, and by the deterioration of urban neighborhoods, the creation of good, inexpensive suburban housing on an unprecedented scale was a unique achievement in the world.

DOCUMENTS

"Little Boxes," 1962

Little boxes on the hillside, little boxes made of ticky tacky,
Little boxes on the hillside, little boxes all the same.
There's a green one and a pink one and a blue one and a yellow
    one,
And they're all made out of ticky tacky and they all look just the
    same.

And the people in the houses all went to the university
Where they were put in boxes and they came out all the same;
And there's doctors, and there's lawyers and there's business
    executives
And they're all made out of ticky tacky and they all look just the
    same.

And they all play on the golf course and drink their martini dry
And they all have pretty children and the children go to school
And the children go to summer camp and then to the university
Where they are all put in boxes and they come out all the same.

Coda (retard like a music box running down)

Segregation in the Suburbs, *1994*

Roosevelt, L.I.—When Marshella Atkinson's parents decided to leave Brooklyn for Long Island, the enthusiasm of friends and teachers made her smile with anticipation.

Perhaps they pictured the swimming pools of nearby Levittown, or the shopping centers of Garden City, or the well-stocked library and spotless corridors of Plainview-Old Bethpage High School. Ms. Atkinson is not sure.

But four years later, the 16-year old does know one thing: they could not have meant Roosevelt, where boarded-up houses dot the walk home from high school and people complain that their streets are last to be plowed by the town of Hempstead, where Roosevelt is the most troubled section.

"I think they set it up so that when a black family moves here, it ends up in Roosevelt," said Ms. Atkinson, a junior at Roosevelt High School. She glanced at a hole in her classroom ceiling where tiles had been ripped away. Graffiti scarred the walls. "I thought it was going to be a dream place," she said.

Drawn by the promise of escape from inner-city congestion and violence, more and more families like the Atkinsons are moving to America's

SOURCE: Diane Jean Schemo, "Persistent Racial Segregation Mars Suburbs' Green Dream," *The New York Times,* March 17, 1994. Copyright © 1994 by *The New York Times* Company. Reprinted by permission.

suburbs. Like the white middle class before them, they come for a home of their own, good schools, open spaces and relative safety, everything that the suburbs symbolize in the American narrative.

But segregation is not declining as black and Hispanic people move to the suburbs, according to John R. Logan, a sociologist at the State University of New York at Albany, who has studied segregation around 10 major cities. Nationally, 1 black person in 3 now lives in the suburbs, but even those with middle-class incomes usually end up in middle-class pockets of poorer neighborhoods.

Lily-white communities tend not to become integrated but to remain largely lily-white, with the addition of well-defined minority precincts. On Long Island, 95 percent of black residents are concentrated in 5 percent of the census tracts. According to census data, the average white person in Nassau County lives in a census tract in which only 8 percent of the residents are black or Hispanic. The average white child attends a school that is just 9 percent black. . . .

"Both within cities and suburbs, Hispanics and blacks are segregated, and they're forced to locate in the least desirable communities," Professor Logan said. "And I see no evidence that any change in civil rights laws or fair housing legislation is having any effect."

Of course, some blacks choose to live in black neighborhoods. Others opted for integrated areas that white flight has since rendered mostly black. Still others can afford only the cheapest suburban housing. But a great many blacks complain they are never shown the full range of housing choices or are discouraged from buying in predominantly white communities.

Once they arrive, blacks find that the suburban landscape and the suburban way of life increase racial isolation: The tendency to restrict parks, libraries and other amenities to local residents; to rely on cars rather than on mass transit, and to emphasize home rule in government promote a segregated existence, no matter what the intent.

While the Long Island suburbs, in their postwar expansion, were providing the blueprint for an America of the automobile age, the plan accepted white prejudices of the day, typically restricting the emerging communities to "members of the Caucasian race."

Federal laws now bar discrimination, but mechanisms of segregation endure. James Thomas landed in the Suffolk County hamlet of Bellport after a thwarted attempt to buy a house in white Port Jefferson 33 years ago. Mr. Thomas's mailman, who was white, offered to sell Mr. Thomas his Cape Cod in Bellport for $10,500. "You have to take where you can get," the retired factory supervisor said.

For 20 years, Bellport remained a "solid, good community." But what he thought was steady integration turned out to be a white hemorrhage. A decade ago, Mr. Thomas realized that the people moving in were no longer working class or middle class but getting by on government aid. Bellport became as blighted as any city neighborhood, its streets lined with prostitutes and certain corners given over to drug dealing.

Mr. Thomas looked across the hedges at a house that had burned down several months before: a jungle of exposed wires and half-fallen floors. For him, the delay in razing the house, since removed, was sure proof of the Town of Brookhaven's disregard for blacks. "You can't tell me that this would be left to stand this way in a white neighborhood," he said.

Services Dwindle

Whites who bought homes in the suburbs typically began a lifelong climb up the social and economic ladder. Many blacks are forced to watch their investment decline as whites flee, poorer minorities move in and services dwindle. Homeowners like Ed Larson of the North Amityville Taxpayers Association meet to enlist police against drug peddlers, prostitutes and street crime, problems that seldom preoccupy their white counterparts.

"If the American dream is to buy a house in the suburbs, send your kid to a good school and have some grass, yes, it's the American dream," said Hugh A. Wilson, director of the Institute for Suburban Studies at Adelphi University. "If it's also to do that in an integrated setting, then for blacks, it's not fulfilling the dream."

Some blacks complain that isolation feeds a quiet acceptance of racism. Alton Williams, first vice president of the Nassau County Guardians, which represents black police officers, said he was shocked to see a white supremacist flyer on another officer's bulletin board. It showed a smiling blond child with the caption "MISSING: A future for white children in America."

Melting Pot Goes Suburban, 2002

MAYNARD [, MA]—Fist-sized chunks of lamb and pork turned slowly over a crackling barbecue as Dennis Lima, co-owner of the new Rio Cafe on Main Street, patiently explained why thousands of Brazilian immigrants are bypassing Boston and heading straight to the suburbs of Middlesex County.

"Parking tickets. Cockroaches. People sleeping on the steps of the building. And expensive—very expensive," he said of his short time living in Boston, where immigrants have historically settled.

When he moved to Acton and later Boxborough, he said, "We could park. We have a pool. We have everything here."

Down the street in downtown Maynard, where Portuguese is heard more than English along Railroad Street and Florida Road, Americano Borges said Brazilian transplants snap up the Brazilian CDs, soaps, and food products he sells.

"I don't think people go to Boston," he said. "It's too far."

Whether Brazilians in Maynard, Turks in Methuen, Koreans in Newton, or Indians in Shrewsbury, the melting pot is increasingly a suburban phenomenon.

Across the country, immigrants are joining singles and the elderly in a continuing dispersal from cities, according to researchers at the Brookings Institution in Washington, D.C.—fueling a massive change in the demographics of areas long associated with subdivisions and country clubs.

The trend, supported by preliminary Census figures—with more detailed data set to be released by early summer—is so pronounced that immigrants in the suburbs are changing the terms of the debate on sprawl.

Free-market conservatives applaud how immigrants are reviving older suburban communities, and cite it as evidence that cities are no longer preferable, even among those who have traditionally settled there. But in another example of the shifting alliances in the politics of sprawl, those who want to slow immigration are trying to align themselves with environmentalists and smart-growth advocates—identifying immigrant-laden population growth as the most powerful force driving sprawl.

The increase of immigrants in the suburbs is leading to conflicted feelings among environmentalists and planners, similar to the discussion about the link between sprawl and housing for low-income families.

The source of that angst, say observers and immigrants who have settled in the Maynard–Acton–Hudson area, lies with two economic truths: The suburbs are where the jobs are; the more development is spread, the more opportunities there are to find affordable housing.

"The rents are low" compared with Allston–Brighton, Cambridge, or Somerville, said Lima, who opened Cafe Rio in December with Jonathan Wise, who he met while working at a Dunkin' Donuts in Acton.

The trade-off, Lima said, is that immigrants must buy a car, because there is virtually no public transportation.

But a 10-year-old car can be had for $500 down, through a network of car dealers that have sprung up in the area that specialize in helping Portuguese-speaking immigrants, Lima said. Many immigrants then carpool to get to jobs in maintenance or groundskeeping for high-tech firms along I-495, as cooks or waiters at suburban restaurants, as cleaners in suburban homes, or as employees of major retailers. "To start with, it's a matter of learning the English skills to work at the drive-through window," said Karen Pervier, coordinator of the Maynard Adult Learning Center, which includes instruction in English and has a waiting list of 300.

The process of finding those kinds of classes, a home, and a job is repeated over and over as friends and relatives join those who have established themselves. Yet today's suburban-oriented immigrants are less apt to confine themselves to one area, said Isabel Skoog, who assists immigrants as part of the South Middlesex Opportunity Council, a human services organization.

"They have a very good network, and information is passed on—they know where the services are and where their dollar will go the furthest," she said.

Accordingly, Portuguese-speaking immigrants have spilled from Hudson to adjoining towns, and from Framingham to Marlborough, where officials estimate there are 6,000 Brazilians and at least as many people from Russia, Southeast Asia, Mexico, the Caribbean, Peru, Ecuador, and Chile.

Marlborough, Chicopee, and Maynard are the melting-pot hot spots with the most rapidly diversifying populations, said Fatinha Kerr, executive director of Marlborough Community Services Inc.

In the area defined by the US Census Bureau as essentially Eastern Massachusetts, the foreign-born population grew by almost 300,000 from 1990 to 2000. Roughly 85 percent of that growth occurred in the areas around Boston, according to an analysis of the 1990 Census and the Census 2000 Supplemental Survey.

In a study of the Washington, D.C., metropolitan area, Audrey Singer, a researcher at the Brookings Institution's center for Urban and Metropolitan Policy, found that nearly 90 percent of recent immigrants headed straight for suburban communities. Immigrants are either settling in first- or second-ring suburbs surrounding cities in the Northeast, Singer said, or going to high-growth, low-density areas in the Southwest or West, such as Atlanta or Las Vegas.

Combined with other demographic changes—a Brookings study released last month found that singles and seniors outnumber traditional married couples in the suburbs—the choices being made by immigrants will radically change perceptions of suburbia, she said.

"There are huge implications, for schools, for housing, the labor market. There are some areas that aren't used to receiving immigrants. There can be conflict within neighborhoods," she said.

For Maynard, with a population of about 10,000, the influx of Brazilians is being viewed as a more positive development for a community with a history of economic ups and downs—as the latest phase of a continuing reinvention. The computer company Digital used the original woolen mill for its headquarters but then went out of business; the offices around the Clock Tower are just filling back to capacity with smaller firms. "Obviously there must be jobs around," said Maynard resident Roy Helander, a member of the Maynard Historical Society.

Maynard High School recently had all of its students research their family histories and then displayed the flags of their countries of origin in the school cafeteria. There were nearly 100.

Selectwoman Anne Marie Desmarais, who has lived in Maynard for 22 years, said she worries that "we're a bit thin on support services. We can't reach out like a big city can." She also believes that the traditionally quiet area can be "culturally and emotionally isolating," especially for women without job skills.

But, she said, the fact that immigrants would come to Maynard is heartening to many residents, and testament to how the community is more affordable than its neighbors Sudbury, Wayland, and Concord: "They wouldn't come here unless they felt welcome."

Chapter 13

The Black Struggle for Equality

Integrating Little Rock's Central High School, October 3, 1957.

Southern white educators, relying on the "separate but equal" doctrine announced in the 1896 *Plessy* v. *Ferguson* Supreme Court decision, insisted that their states could operate dual racial school systems. Consequently, segregated public education was the norm throughout the South. In the late 1930s, the National Association for the Advancement of Colored People (NAACP) began to attack racial inequality in American schools, at first suing communities that ran inferior schools for African-American children and students. The NAACP pointed out that schools for black children received far less funding than was allocated to white schools and were housed in inferior facilities. Feeling the pressure, some communities did begin to spend more for black education. Gradually, some southern state universities also began to admit limited numbers of African Americans to their graduate-level programs. But primary and secondary schools continued to be racially segregated into the early 1950s, and southern communities continued to spend considerably more for white schools than for blacks.

Finally, the NAACP assailed the "separate but equal" doctrine itself, claiming that racially segregated schools were inherently unconstitutional. In 1954 the Supreme Court, in a unanimous decision (*Brown* v. *Board of Education*) written by Chief Justice Earl Warren, agreed and overturned the *Plessy* v. *Ferguson* decision as it applied to education. But as William Doyle points out in his essay "Crisis in Little Rock," it was one thing to hand down a court decision and another for the states and local communities to enforce it. In 1957, a modest plan to introduce desegregation in Little Rock, Arkansas's Central High School led to a major crisis that engulfed a handful of black children, angry white mobs, Governor Orval Faubus, and the National Guard. Eventually the crisis forced a reluctant President Dwight Eisenhower to intervene on the side of desegregation and federal authority. The Little Rock conflict received major coverage in the nation's media, became the subject of a famous painting by Norman Rockwell, and helped win increased support for black civil rights outside the South. What do you think there was about this event that so stirred emotions throughout the nation? Based on what you have read in this essay, how would you evaluate Dwight Eisenhower's record on civil rights?

The first document, an account of growing up in the racially segregated South, is by African-American civil rights leader Hosea Williams. How do his experiences help explain why so many young African-American youth, like those in Little Rock, were willing to subject themselves to physical danger in order to achieve their full and equal rights as citizens?

As the second document illustrates, opposition to desegregation was by no means limited to street mobs. It is an excerpt from "The Southern Manifesto," signed by most southern members of Congress in 1956. Based upon what you have read, what is your opinion of the Manifesto's view of the "relations between the white and Negro races" during the ninety years prior to *Brown* v. *Board of Education?*

The last document is from a remarkable speech given by President Lyndon Johnson at Howard University, a historically black college in Washington, D.C. Johnson spoke following the passage of the 1964 Civil Rights Act, which provided for desegregation in public facilities, and on the eve of the enactment of the 1965 Voting Rights Act. While citing accomplishments in the area of civil rights legislation, the President argued that legal equality was not enough. What did Johnson see as obstacles yet to be overcome before achieving full equality and justice for African Americans? What relation, if any, do you perceive between the views set forth in this speech and proposals for affirmative action programs in the years ahead?

ESSAY

Crisis in Little Rock

William Doyle

> We could have another Civil War on our hands.
> —*President Dwight D. Eisenhower, cabinet meeting,*
> *March 1956*

Little Rock, Arkansas, September 8, 1957, 8:50 A.M.

A shy fifteen-year-old girl wearing bobby sox, ballet slippers, and a crisp black-and-white cotton dress stepped off a bus and walked toward Central High School, carrying a set of school books.

Elizabeth Eckford and nine other black students hoped to enter the all-white school today as part of a desegregation plan ordered by a federal judge. Because Eckford's family did not have a phone, she had missed the instructions to join the other students this morning, so she was walking toward the school completely alone.

Until today, Arkansas was making slow, peaceful progress toward integration. The state university was quietly desegregated in 1948, the state bus system had been integrated and black patrolmen were on the Little Rock police force. Several school districts were planning to accept black students this semester. In the wake of a lawsuit by the NAACP (National Association for the Advancement of Colored People), the Little Rock school board had approved a plan to gradually desegregate Central High, and ten volunteer students were selected to go in.

Through her sunglasses Eckford could see the school up ahead, and she was amazed at how big it was. She was so nervous, she hadn't slept at all the night before, so to pass the time she had read her Bible. She dwelled on the opening passage of the Twenty-seventh Psalm: "The Lord is my light and my salvation; whom shall I fear? the Lord is the strength of my life; of whom shall I be afraid?"

As she neared the school, the girl became vaguely aware of a crowd of white people swarming around her. Somewhere a voice called out, "Here she comes, get ready!" People started shouting insults. "Then my knees started to shake all of a sudden," Eckford later explained privately to Little Rock NAACP leader Daisy Bates, "and I wondered whether I could make it to the center entrance a block away. It was the longest block I ever walked in my whole life."

Eckford could see uniformed soldiers ringing the entrance and letting white students into the school, and she assumed they were supposed to protect her. But when she approached the entrance, one soldier waved her away. When she tried to move past another soldier, he and his comrades lifted their bayonet-tipped M-1 rifles and surged toward her to block her path.

The soldiers were Arkansas National Guardsmen, and their commander in chief was Democratic governor Orval Eugene Faubus, who had ordered the troops to block the black students at gunpoint. Faubus was a hound dog–faced populist who was born in a plank cabin in a remote Ozark forest near a place called Greasy Creek, and grew up trapping skunks to help his family scrape out a living. Until today, he was considered something of a moderate on racial issues. But Faubus was up for reelection, and sensing a rising white backlash to integration, he decided to become its champion.

When she faced the solid wall of soldiers, Elizabeth Eckford wasn't sure what to do, so she retreated back across the street and into the white mob. Voices called out, "Lynch her! Lynch her!" and "Go home, you burr-head!" She scanned the mob for someone who might help her and spotted an old woman who seemed to have a kind face. The woman spat on her. A voice from the mob announced, "No nigger bitch is going to get in our school. Get out of here!"

The chanting mob swelled toward five hundred. Behind Eckford, someone said, "Push her!" Eckford later explained that she was afraid she would "bust out crying," and she "didn't want to in front of all that crowd." Ahead of her, news photographers snapped photos of a young white student named Hazel Bryan screaming at Eckford behind her back, a searing image that would soon be flashed around the world. "I looked down the block and saw a bench at the bus stop," recalled Eckford. "I thought, 'If only I can get there I will be safe.' I don't know why the bench seemed a safe place to me but I started walking toward it."

Eckford made it to the bus stop and sat down with her head bowed, tightly gripping her books as news cameras whirred and snapped. Someone in the crowd said, "Get a rope and drag her over to this tree." Benjamin Fine, an education reporter from the *New York Times* who had been scribbling notes in his steno pad, sat down next to Eckford, wrapped his arm around her shoulder, and whispered, "Don't let them see you cry."

A furious white woman named Grace Lorch fought her way through the mob, and screamed, "Leave this child alone! Why are you tormenting her? Six months from now, you will hang your heads in shame." Lorch tried to enter a drugstore to call a taxi for Eckford, but the door was slammed in her face.

"She's just a little girl," Lorch declared to the mob as she moved next to Eckford to defend her. "I'm just waiting for one of you to dare touch me! I'm just aching to punch somebody in the nose!"

Eventually a bus came, Mrs. Lorch helped Eckford up the stairs, and the bus pulled away. Eckford got off at the school for the blind, where her mother taught, and ran to her classroom. "Mother was standing at the window with her head bowed," Eckford recalled, "but she must have sensed I was there because she turned around. She looked as if she had been crying, and I wanted to tell her I was all right. But I couldn't speak. She put her arms around me and I cried."

Minutes after Eckford was turned away, her colleagues, who with her would soon become world famous as the "Little Rock Nine," were refused admission as well: Melba Pattillo, Gloria Ray, Carlotta Walls, Minnijean Brown, Thelma Mothershed, Ernest Green, Jefferson Thomas and Terrence Roberts. A tenth black student who was turned back, Jane Hill, chose to return to all-black Horace Mann High School.

Over the next two weeks, frantic negotiations resulted in a summit conference between President Dwight D. Eisenhower and Governor Faubus at Ike's vacation retreat in Newport, Rhode Island, during which the president thought he'd made a deal with Faubus to deploy Arkansas National Guardsmen to protect the black students as they entered Central High. But on September 23, when the Little Rock Nine tried again to enter the school, Faubus ordered the National Guard instead to abandon the premises.

Escorted by Little Rock police, the Nine briefly made it inside the school and started their classes. But outside the building, a furious mob of more than one thousand white civilians was surging against barricades, threatening to overwhelm the police trying to hold them in check. A white woman cried out hysterically to the police, "They've got the doors locked. They won't let the white kids out. My daughter's in there with those niggers. Oh, my God, oh God!" Policemen lashed out with their billy clubs, knocking down two men in the mob. "Come out!" adults yelled to the white students. "Don't stay in there with those niggers!"

A pack of fifty white men peeled off down a side street to chase a tall black journalist named Alex Wilson, civil rights reporter for Defender Publications, a national chain of black newspapers. A voice warned, "Run, nigger, run!" The mob caught up with Wilson and attacked him from behind with their fists. A brick slammed point-blank into the back of his head, and he tumbled to the ground like a mighty tree. Wilson raised himself to a kneeling position, was kicked and punched, but still he rose, grasping his hat in his hand. He brushed off his fedora, recreased it, and resumed walking.

"Strangely, the vision of Elizabeth Eckford flashed before me," Wilson recalled soon after the attack. "I decided not to run. If I were to be beaten, I'd take it walking if I could—not running." He told his wife, Emogene, "They would have had to kill me before I would have run." Another brick scored a direct hit on the back of Wilson's head, but he kept walking. "I looked into the tear-filled eyes of a white woman. Although there was sorrow in her eyes, I knew there would not be any help."

In a frantic effort to take Wilson down again, a crazed-looking, stocky white man in coveralls jumped clear up onto Wilson's back and wrapped his arm around his neck in a choke hold, but the ex-marine Wilson shook him off. "Don't kill him," a voice in the crowd cautioned the mob. Finally Wilson reached his car and escaped.

In front of Central High, a white policeman named Thomas Dunaway suddenly flung his billy club to the street, threw down his badge, and walked away from the barricade. The crowd cheered him, and a young man yelled, "He's the only white man on the force!" A hat was passed around the crowd, and it soon filled up with two hundred dollars in donations for the officer.

Inside Central High School, police and school officials gathered the nine black students. Word was relayed from the mob that they would not storm the building if one black pupil was turned over to them, presumably to be torn to pieces or hung from a tree. Instead, the Little Rock police chief evacuated the Nine out a side door into police cars that blasted away from the school.

At 12:14 P.M., police lieutenant Carl Jackson faced the mob and announced through a loudspeaker, "The Negroes have been withdrawn from the school." Someone in the crowd replied, "That's just a pack of lies!" Then another shouted, "We don't believe you!" A Mrs. Allen Thevenet stepped out from the mob and offered to verify the claim. After a full tour of the building, Mrs. Thevenet marched to the loudspeaker, and proclaimed, "We went through every room in the school and there was no niggers there."

White supremacists across the South rejoiced. Integration at Central High had been defeated in barely half a day.

The next day, September 24, President Eisenhower was back at the White House, and he was furious. He was supposed to still be on vacation. Instead, the old general was sitting at his desk in the Oval Office, dripping with rage over the treachery of Orval Faubus. "He double-crossed me," fumed the president.

On the wall of the elliptical presidential office were two small paintings, one of Union general and U.S. president Ulysses S. Grant, the other of Confederate general and Southern demigod Robert E. Lee. They captured the paradox at the heart of the America Eisenhower led. Nearly a century after the Civil War, as the nation asserted global moral leadership and reached out to explore the heavens, millions of black Americans were effectively not citizens of the country in which they were born.

[handwritten margin note: paradox of Eisenhower American society]

That morning, the mayor of Little Rock had sent a desperate telegram to the president, who had been still savoring his relaxing vacation in Newport, Rhode Island. "The immediate need for federal troops is urgent," the mayor pleaded. "Situation is out of control and police cannot disperse the mob." Ike now feared a full-blown insurrection in the city.

The battle Eisenhower never wanted was hurtling toward him, and he was afraid it could tear the country apart. As his officials debated civil rights at a March 1956 Cabinet meeting, Eisenhower confessed, "I'm at sea on all this." He added, "Not enough people know how deep this emotion is in the South. Unless you've lived there you can't know. . . . We could have another Civil War on our hands."

On May 17, 1954, in its decision on *Brown v. the Board of Education of Topeka, Kansas,* the United States Supreme Court outlawed government-imposed segregation in public schools, but a year later the Court ruled that the order should be implemented not immediately, but "with all deliberate speed." This ambiguous phrase gave federal judges leeway to impose integration on varying timetables in different school districts, which delayed progress in some places well into the next decade.

Privately, Eisenhower disagreed with the *Brown* decision, and believed it could only be implemented slowly. "When emotions are deeply stirred," he wrote in July 1957 to his childhood friend Swede Hazlett, "logic and reason must operate gradually and with consideration for human feelings or we will have a resultant disaster rather than human advancement."

"School segregation itself," Ike pointed out, "was, according to the Supreme Court decision of 1896 [the *Plessy v. Ferguson* case], completely Constitutional until the reversal of that decision was accomplished in 1954. The decision of 1896 gave a cloak of legality to segregation in all its forms." People couldn't change overnight, Ike believed.

Dwight Eisenhower was a creature of forty years in the hermetically segregated U.S. military, and he personally had no quarrel with separation of the races. Although as president he quietly completed Harry S. Truman's 1948 order desegregating the armed forces and ordered the integration of public facilities in the nation's capital, not once in eight years in office did Ike publicly endorse the concept of integration. In that time he met with civil rights leaders on a grand total of one occasion—in a meeting that took less than an hour.

On the rare occasions he met with other black audiences, Eisenhower would sternly say, "Now, you people have to be patient." His attitude toward the black White House servants was "definitely not friendly" in the words of one of them, "the President hardly knew we were there." In private, he traded "nigger jokes" with his tycoon cronies.

Eisenhower appointed only one black person to his staff, and E. Frederic Morrow's experience as the first black White House official in history was pathetic. Promised a job during the 1952 campaign, Morrow showed up in Washington only to find the offer was withdrawn because White House employees threatened to boycott their jobs if he entered the building. The White House wouldn't return his calls.

Seventeen months later, an unemployed Morrow was offered temporary work in the Commerce Department. After he was finally moved to the

White House two years later to work on miscellaneous "special projects," he was ignored by Eisenhower and humiliated by most everybody else. He couldn't find anyone to be his secretary. Women entered his office only in pairs to avoid talk of sexual misconduct. Morrow was not formally appointed and sworn in until 1959, and he spent much of his time feeling heartsick and ridiculous as he traveled the country defending Ike's indifferent civil rights stand to black audiences.

At the final White House Christmas party, Eisenhower pulled Morrow aside to say he had called all his friends but no one would hire a Negro. "Literally, out on my ear," Morrow reported. "I was the only member of the staff for whom the president could not find a job." It took him three years to find one.

In the days after the *Brown* decision, the man who defeated Hitler was too timid to lift a finger as black Americans and federal courts launched probing assaults on segregation, and white supremacists counterattacked with speed, imagination, brutality, and a strategy of "massive resistance" to integration.

In 1955, when fourteen-year-old black Chicago boy Emmett Till was tortured and executed by a gang of Mississippi whites for allegedly whistling at a white woman, Ike ignored his mother's telegrams pleading for justice.

During the epic bus boycott triggered in 1955 by Rosa Parks to protest segregation in public transportation in Montgomery, Alabama, Eisenhower stubbornly sat on his hands. He even refused to oppose the state's plan to arrest the Reverend Martin Luther King, Jr., for leading the peaceful, entirely legal campaign. In February 1956 Eisenhower did nothing when white mobs went on a rampage at the University of Alabama and chased black applicant Autherine Lucy out of town.

On March 12, 1956, nearly one hundred senators and congressmen introduced a "Southern Manifesto," which rejected *Brown* and pledged "to use all lawful means to bring about a reversal of this decision which is contrary to the Constitution and to prevent the use of force in its implementation." Eisenhower had virtually no comment. Later that year, Texas governor Allan Shivers deployed Texas Rangers to block the federal court-ordered integration of Mansfield High School and Texarkana Junior College. Again Ike did nothing. The armies of white "massive resistance" grew stronger.

Even Dwight Eisenhower had his limits, though. He supported blacks' right to vote and was disgusted by Southern Democratic attempts to block it. On September 9, 1957, he signed the Civil Rights Act of 1957, the first federal civil rights legislation since Reconstruction.

The law empowered the federal government to enforce voting rights, but congressional Democrats, including Lyndon Johnson, John F. Kennedy, and the Southern bloc gutted the act by requiring that voting-rights offenses be prosecuted before jury trials, which guaranteed acquittals in the

South. Eisenhower issued a rare public statement on civil rights, saying that the jury-trial requirement of the Civil Rights Act would be "bitterly disappointing" to many millions of Americans who "will continue to be disenfranchised."

Eisenhower also took his constitutional obligations to uphold the laws very seriously, and the mob violence in Little Rock was giving them their first battlefield test.

On the flight from Newport back to Washington, he scribbled angrily on a notepad, "Troops—not to enforce integration but to prevent opposition by violence to orders of a court." Whatever his feelings on *Brown*, he felt, "there must be respect for the Constitution—which means the Supreme Court's interpretation of the Constitution—or we shall have chaos.

Now, at the White House, at 12:15 P.M. on September 24, Eisenhower called the Pentagon and ordered U.S. Army paratroopers of the 101st Airborne Division "Screaming Eagles" to seize Little Rock. "If you have to use force," Ike believed, "use overwhelming force and save lives thereby." Within hours, fifty-two planeloads of airborne infantry troops were racing westward from Fort Campbell, Kentucky.

Eisenhower was disgusted that he had to order troops into action on American soil, but he felt secure in his authority to do so. In his proclamation, which committed the troops, he invoked provisions of the U.S. Code, including Chapter 15 of Title 10, Section 332, which specified that "if rebellion against the authority of the United States" made it impossible to enforce the law, the president "may call into Federal service such of the militia of any state, and use such of the armed forces, as he considers necessary to enforce those laws or to suppress the rebellion." When the Supreme Court reviewed the principle in 1879, it ruled as follows: "We hold it to be an incontrovertible principle, that the Government of the United States may by means of physical force, exercised through its official agents, execute on every foot of American soil the powers and functions that belong to it."

Accompanied by wailing sirens and flashing headlights, federal paratroopers in sharply pressed olive-green battle fatigues jumped out of trucks and half-tracks and assumed dress formation around the Central High School perimeter, M-1 rifles slung on their shoulders and entrenching tools stuffed in their belts. One thousand soldiers were in place by nightfall.

On the morning of September 25, Major General Edwin Walker, in dress uniform, sped up to the school and took command. He was a general's general, a tall, lean Texan who had served under Eisenhower as a commando in Europe during World War II, fighting in the Anzio invasion and in the conquest of southern France. Walker flatly disagreed with this operation, believing that American troops had no business getting involved in domestic peacekeeping; that was the job of civilian police only. Privately, Walker offered his resignation, but Ike refused to accept it.

General Walker and his officers huddled over a battle map and aerial photos of the assault zone, reviewing the tactical plan: paratroopers lining the street at intervals of three yards . . . a detachment, with rifles, in the hallway outside every classroom . . . troops not to enter the classroom unless a teacher calls for help . . . all Negro troops to be kept out of sight at the Little Rock University Armory until further notice . . . any group of more than three adults within a mile of the school to be dispersed . . . civilians to be treated politely and addressed as "sir" and "ma'am" at all times.

At 8:00 A.M., pockets of sullen white onlookers gathered around the school. An otherworldly silence prevailed, soon pierced by bursts of radio traffic on the troops' walkie-talkies. An army helicopter appeared low in the sky, buzzing the area in search of trouble. A pink-shirted boy jeered at the troops. "Why don't you tin soldiers go home?"

Coy Vance, a white seventeen-year-old student planning to study medicine, declared, "I'm not going to school with niggers, because they are inferior to us." The boy vowed, "If I catch one, I'll chase him out of the school." Bonnie Vance, his sixteen-year-old sister, chimed in, "If they didn't have soldiers in the halls the niggers would get murdered." Senior Tommy Dunn speculated: "I think that if they get chased in the halls enough they will leave by themselves. Don't they know we don't want them?"

Major James Meyers called up an army mobile public-address system and announced, "You are instructed to go to your homes peacefully. Disperse and return to your homes." The crowd wouldn't budge. Soon two platoons of infantrymen dog-trotted in formation toward the two biggest crowd concentrations. "Back!" a soldier yelled. "Back on the sidewalk!"

A sergeant barked the command, "Bayonets at the back of their heads, move 'em fast!" The paratroopers advanced, bayonets pointed out, and began pushing the crowds down the side streets. Forty-seven-year-old railroad worker C. E. Blake stood his ground and tried to grab a paratrooper's rifle. The trooper quickly flipped his rifle around and punched Blake over the eye with the rifle butt, knocking him to the ground. Nearby, Paul Downs of Springfield, Arkansas, got jabbed in the arm with a bayonet when he didn't move fast enough.

General Walker dispatched army station wagons, jeeps with mounted turret guns, and trucks packed with bayonet-wielding troops to pick up the black teenagers at a designated group-pickup spot and drive to the school at high speed to avoid possible snipers, under the watchful gaze of an escort helicopter. Then he ordered the white students of Central High to an assembly. The astonished teenagers passed bayonet-wielding Airborne troops and filed into the auditorium for an address by General Walker. There was dead silence as Walker took the stage.

"As an officer of the United States Army," General Walker announced to the wide-eyed students, "I have been chosen to command these forces and to execute the President's orders. . . . We are all subject to all the laws

233

whether we approve of them or not, and as law-abiding citizens, we have an obligation in conscience to obey them. There can be no exceptions; if it were otherwise, we would not be a strong nation but a mere unruly mob.

"You have nothing to fear from my soldiers, and no one will interfere with your coming, going or your peaceful pursuit of your studies," the general concluded. "They are seasoned, well-trained soldiers, many of them combat veterans. Being soldiers, they are as determined as I to carry out their orders." Walker strode out of the hall.

At 9:20 A.M., shouts erupted outside the school, "There they come!" A U.S. Army station wagon raced through a security barricade up to the front entrance of Central High, flanked by two jeeps stuffed with helmeted troops. The black students got out of the wagon, six girls in brightly colored dresses and with books under their arms, and three boys in sport shirts, one swinging his books on a strap. The windows of the school were packed with white students quietly peering down at the historic tableau.

Thirty paratroopers formed a protective bubble around the black children as 350 soldiers stood at attention around the school. "Forward march," an officer called out. "We began moving forward," wrote Melba Pattillo. "The eerie silence of that moment would forever be etched in my memory. All I could hear was my own heartbeat and the sound of boots clicking on the stone. Everything seemed to be moving in slow motion as I peered past the raised bayonets of the 101st soldiers." That morning, Pattillo heard her colleague Minnijean Brown say, "For the first time in my life, I feel like an American citizen."

Many white Southerners reacted with horror at the spectacle, and Southern newspapers launched a chorus of outrage. Governor Faubus, now riding a wave of popular support in Arkansas for his defiance, said in a TV speech, "We are now an occupied territory." "In the name of God," he implored, "what's happening in America?"

In Marshall, Texas, a speaker at a Kiwanis meeting proclaimed the Little Rock event "the darkest day in Southern history since Reconstruction." The Kiwanians then refused to pledge allegiance to the American flag. Georgia's senator Herman Talmadge thundered, "The South is threatened by the President of the U.S. using tanks and troops in the streets of Little Rock. I wish I could cast one vote for impeachment right now." South Carolina's senator Olin Johnston proposed an even more radical step: "If I were Governor Faubus, I'd proclaim a state of insurrection down there, and I'd call out the National Guard and I'd then find out who's going to run things in my state."

President Eisenhower himself was defensive, knowing that while 75 percent of Northerners in a Gallup Poll thought his Little Rock operation was right, only 36 percent of Southerners did. "No one can deplore more than I do the sending of federal troops anywhere," he told a press conference after the deployment. At the same time, he pointed out, "the courts must be sustained or it's not America."

Inside Central High School, however, there were some hopeful signs. Melba Pattillo recalled entering her first class: "My heart skipped a beat as the classroom door closed behind me." Then she looked back and saw her bodyguard, a helmeted young soldier of the 101st Airborne, gazing through the door window, keeping watch over her. "Sunlight flooded into the room through a full bank of windows along the far wall," she wrote. "It was a beautiful morning."

During lunch, one of the black male students sat alone in the cafeteria with a glass of milk and a sandwich. Some white students nearby asked him, "Won't you join us?" The boy broke into an enthusiastic smile. "Gee, thanks," he replied. "I'd love to." They finished their meals together, eating and chatting.

The "Battle of Little Rock" was over nearly as soon as it started, without a single serious injury and without a shot fired.

DOCUMENTS

Growing Up Black in the South: A Remembrance, 1977

I was born in poverty. My mother was never married to my father, which was a stigma in the American society. . . . I was reared up in Decatur County, Georgia . . . that's southwest Georgia, and the racism of segregation was so prevalent until it was something that you had to notice, like black farmers couldn't plant tobacco. They didn't allow black men to plant tobacco, 'cause there's a lot of money in it. White people virtually owned black people . . . they'd concoct debts, like you get in jail, all the white man had to do, to come there, and the sheriff would let you out, and the white man tell the sheriff to tell you he paid a hundred dollars for you, but you didn't have to worry 'bout that hundred dollars long as you stay on his farm and work. If you ever left to go to Florida, he'd come get you, arrest you and bring you back. . . . There's a white man down there named Wonnie Miller. On the Wonnie Miller farm, all the blacks were born and worked and lived and died in poverty, and they worked like slaves from "cain't to cain't"— say, "Ya cain't see your hand before your face when you go out in the field, and ya cain't see your hand when you come in from the field," because it was dark each time. And Mr. Wonnie used to ride a big horse and never really worked, and he died a millionaire. All his children are rich. . . .

SOURCE: From *My Soul Is Rested,* by Howell Raines. Copyright © 1977 by Howell Raines. Used by permission of G. P. Putnam's Sons, a division of Penguin Group (USA).

We used to walk two and a half miles to school . . . the white kids always had a bus. No black kids were allowed to ride the bus, and I guess every day of my life—it looked like to me every day, probably just my imagination—those white kids would spit on us or throw rocks at us, holler, and call us "niggers." *Every* day. Pick at us, and I just knew that was not right.

In my early life once whites tried to lynch me about a little white girl that was from a very poor family that lived up there. Her father was a bum, wouldn't work; all he did was fish and hunt all the time, just like some of the black families. The word got around that I was havin' affair with the girl. This was a rumor, and they came to the house to lynch me . . . and my grandfather stood 'em off with a gun. We went over to white man's house, Mr. Wonnie Miller, who took the thing up and stopped the whites. . . .

The vast majority of blacks was reared in the same circumstances I was reared in. It's just hard for me to see how they can go along and take it. Then I educated myself and became a professional person. I thought you could escape black America by being educated and professional and being rich, and you just cain't do it.* . . .

I was paid well. I went right up, straight up the ladder. I was accepted, *I thought,* but what I really finally decided, I had hit that "nigger ceiling." They wasn't gonna let me go no higher. . . . I had more publication than all the white guys put together, except an old Ph.D. who had thirty years in the lab. So the assistant chief's job became open, and I thought sure they'd make me the assistant chief, because I thought they had accepted me as a scientist. And they gave the job to a white girl who knew very little chemistry, and that was a very hard pill for me to swallow. But you know the old thing 'bout how Jackie Robinson made it in baseball, the old poem, "Life Ain't Been No Christmas Day," and all this jazz, so I bought it and buckled my bed up: "After all, I'm black and she's white. My day comin'."

I remember one time after I bought this new home and new car. . . . You know, I was a social climbin', middle-class Negro. I guess I was the first black person in Savannah to have a zoysia lawn. I remember buying this grass from Sears and Roebuck, and had sodded my lawn, and I was out there one day tryin' to water it, and my hose would not stretch to sprinkle across the whole lawn. I had a big lot there. And I went back up to this new drugstore . . . gonna buy some hose connectors, an extension to a hose. . . . And I carried my two sons with me. They wasn't but about six and seven, six and eight years old then, and as we walked into this drug-

---

*Williams became a chemist with the U.S. Department of Agriculture Bureau of Entomology in Savannah.

store, it had a long lunch counter and these white kids were sittin' on these
stools, spinnin' around, eatin' hot dogs and drinkin' Co-cola.

And my boys started askin' me, "Daddy, let's get a sandwich and a
Coke." But I always will believe what they wanted to do was play on those
stools, and I said, "Naw, you cain't have a Coke and sandwich." And one of
'em started cryin'. And I said, "Well, you know, I'm gonna take you back
home and Momma'll fix you a hot dog and give you a Coke," and then both
of 'em started cryin'. And both of them just fell out in the floor, which was
very unusual for my kids to do me like that. And I remember stoopin' down
and I started cryin', because I realized I couldn't tell 'em the truth. The truth
was they was black and they didn't 'low black people to use them lunch
counters. So I picked the two kids up and went back to the car and I guess I
made 'em a promise that I'd bring 'em back someday. So that really got me
involved.

The Southern Manifesto, 1956

The unwarranted decision of the Supreme Court in the public school cases
is now bearing the fruit always produced when men substitute naked
power for established law.

The Founding Fathers gave us a Constitution of checks and balances because they realized the inescapable lesson of history that no man or group
of men can be safely entrusted with unlimited power. They framed this
Constitution with its provisions for change by amendment in order to secure the fundamentals of government against the dangers of temporary
popular passion or the personal predilections of public officeholders.

We regard the decision of the Supreme Court in the school cases as a
clear abuse of judicial power. It climaxes a trend in the Federal Judiciary undertaking to legislate, in derogation of the authority of Congress, and to en-
croach upon the reserved rights of the States and the people.

The original Constitution does not mention education. Neither does the
14th amendment nor any other amendment. The debates preceding the submission of the 14th amendment clearly show that there was no intent that it
should affect the system of education maintained by the States.

The very Congress which proposed the amendment subsequently provided for segregated schools in the District of Columbia.

When the amendment was adopted in 1868, there were 37 States of
the Union. Every one of the 26 States that had any substantial racial differences among its people, either approved the operation of segregated schools

SOURCE: Declaration of Constitutional Principles," *Congressional Record*, 84th Cong., 2d
sess., March 12, 1956, 4460–61.

already in existence or subsequently established such schools by action of the same law-making body which considered the 14th amendment.

As admitted by the Supreme Court in the public school case (*Brown* v. *Board of Education*), the doctrine of separate but equal schools "apparently originated in *Roberts* v. *City of Boston* (1849), upholding school segregation against attack as being violative of a State constitutional guarantee of equality." This constitutional doctrine began in the North, not in the South, and it was followed not only in Massachusetts, but in Connecticut, New York, Illinois, Indiana, Michigan, Minnesota, New Jersey, Ohio, Pennsylvania and other northern States until they, exercising their rights as States through the constitutional processes of local self-government, changed their school systems.

In the case of *Plessy* v. *Ferguson* in 1896 the Supreme Court expressly declared that under the 14th amendment no person was denied any of his rights if the States provided separate but equal public facilities. This decision has been followed in many other cases. It is notable that the Supreme Court, speaking through Chief Justice Taft, a former President of the United States, unanimously declared in 1927 in *Lum* v. *Rice* that the "separate but equal" principle is "within the discretion of the State in regulating its public schools and does not conflict with the 14th amendment."

This interpretation, restated time and again, became a part of the life of the people of many of the States and confirmed their habits, customs, traditions, and way of life. It is founded on elemental humanity and common-sense, for parents should not be deprived by Government of the right to direct the lives and education of their own children.

Though there has been no constitutional amendment or act of Congress changing this established legal principle almost a century old, the Supreme Court of the United States, with no legal basis for such action, undertook to exercise their naked judicial power and substituted their personal political and social ideas for the established law of the land.

This unwarranted exercise of power by the Court, contrary to the Constitution, is creating chaos and confusion in the States principally affected. It is destroying the amicable relations between the white and Negro races that have been created through 90 years of patient effort by the good people of both races. It has planted hatred and suspicion where there has been heretofore friendship and understanding.

Without regard to the consent of the governed, outside agitators are threatening immediate and revolutionary changes in our public-school systems. If done, this is certain to destroy the system of public education in some of the States. . . .

President Lyndon Johnson on Racial Equality, 1965

Our earth is the home of revolution.

In every corner of every continent men charged with hope contend with ancient ways in pursuit of justice. They reach for the newest of weapons to realize the oldest of dreams: that each may walk in freedom and pride, stretching his talents, enjoying the fruits of the earth.

Our enemies may occasionally seize the day of change. But it is the banner of our revolution they take. And our own future is linked to this process of swift and turbulent change in many lands. But nothing, in any country, touches us more profoundly, nothing is more freighted with meaning for our own destiny, than the revolution of the Negro American.

In far too many ways American Negroes have been another nation: deprived of freedom, crippled by hatred, the doors of opportunity closed to hope.

In our time change has come to this nation too. Heroically, the American Negro—acting with impressive restraint—has peacefully protested and marched, entered the courtrooms and the seats of government, demanding a justice long denied. The voice of the Negro was the call to action. But it is a tribute to America that, once aroused, the courts and the Congress, the President and most of the people, have been the allies of progress.

Thus we have seen the high court of the country declare that discrimination based on race was repugnant to the Constitution, and therefore void. We have seen—in 1957, 1960, and again in 1964—the first civil rights legislation in almost a century.

As majority leader I helped guide two of these bills through the Senate. And, as your President, I was proud to sign the third.

And soon we will have the fourth new law, guaranteeing every American the right to vote.

No act of my administration will give me greater satisfaction than the day when my signature makes this bill too the law of the land.

The voting rights bill will be the latest, and among the most important, in a long series of victories. But this victory—as Winston Churchill said of another triumph for freedom—"is not the end. It is not even the beginning of the end. But it is, perhaps, the end of the beginning."

That beginning is freedom; and the barriers to that freedom are tumbling. Freedom is the right to share, fully and equally, in American society—to vote, to hold a job, to enter a public place, to go to school. It is the right to be treated, in every part of our national life, as a man equal in dignity and promise to all others.

SOURCE: Text of President Lyndon Johnson's commencement address, Howard University, Washington, D.C., June 4, 1965. White House press release.

But freedom is not enough. You do not wipe away the scars of centuries by saying: Now, you are free to go where you want, do as you desire, and choose the leaders you please.

You do not take a man who, for years, has been hobbled by chains, liberate him, bring him to the starting line of a race, saying "you are free to compete with all the others," and still justly believe you have been completely fair.

Thus it is not enough to open the gates of opportunity. All our citizens must have the ability to walk through those gates.

This is the next and the more profound stage of the battle for civil rights. We seek not just freedom but opportunity—not just legal equity but human ability—not just equality as a right and a theory, but equality as a fact and a result.

For the task is to give twenty million Negroes the same chance as every other American to learn and grow—to work and share in society—to develop their abilities—physical, mental and spiritual, and to pursue their individual happiness.

To this end equal opportunity is essential, but not enough. Men and women of all races are born with the same range of abilities. But ability is not just the product of birth. It is stretched or stunted by the family you live with, and the neighborhood you live in—by the school you go to, and the poverty or richness of your surroundings. It is the product of a hundred unseen forces playing upon the infant, the child, and the man.

This graduating class at Howard University is witness to the indomitable determination of the Negro American to win his way in American life.

The number of Negroes in schools of high learning has almost doubled in fifteen years. The number of nonwhite professional workers has more than doubled in ten years. The median income of Negro college women now exceeds that of white college women. And these are the enormous accomplishments of distinguished individual Negroes—many of them graduates of this institution.

These are proud and impressive achievements. But they only tell the story of a growing middle class minority, steadily narrowing the gap between them and their white counterparts.

But for the great majority of Negro Americans—the poor, the unemployed, the uprooted and dispossessed—there is a grimmer story. They still are another nation. Despite the court orders and the laws, the victories and speeches, for them the walls are rising and the gulf is widening.

Here are some of the facts of this American failure.

Thirty-five years ago the rate of unemployment for Negroes and whites was about the same. Today the Negro rate is twice as high.

In 1948 the 8 per cent unemployment rate for Negro teenage boys was actually less than that of whites. By last year it had grown to 23 per cent, as against 13 per cent for whites.

240

Between 1949 and 1959, the income of Negro men relative to white men declined in every section of the country. From 1952 to 1963 the median income of Negro families compared to white actually dropped from 57 per cent to 53 per cent.

In the years 1955–57, 22 per cent of experienced Negro workers were out of work at some time during the year. In 1961–63 that proportion had soared to 29 per cent.

Since 1947 the number of white families living in poverty has decreased 27 per cent while the number of poor non-white families went down only 3 per cent.

The infant mortality of nonwhites in 1940 was 70 per cent greater than whites. Twenty-two years later it was 90 per cent greater.

Moreover, the isolation of Negro from white communities is increasing, rather than diminishing as Negroes crowd into the central cities—becoming a city within a city.

Of course Negro Americans as well as white Americans have shared in our rising national abundance. But the harsh fact of the matter is that in the battle for true equality too many are losing ground.

We are not completely sure why this is. The causes are complex and subtle. But we do know the two broad basic reasons. And we know we have to act.

First, Negroes are trapped—as many whites are trapped—in inherited, gateless poverty. They lack training and skills. They are shut in slums, without decent medical care. Private and public poverty combine to cripple their capacities.

We are attacking these evils through our poverty program, our education program, our health program and a dozen more—aimed at the root causes of poverty.

We will increase, and accelerate, and broaden this attack in years to come, until this most enduring of foes yields to our unyielding will.

But there is a *second* cause—more difficult to explain, more deeply grounded, more desperate in its force. It is the devastating heritage of long years of slavery; and a century of oppression, hatred and injustice.

For Negro poverty is not white poverty. Many of its causes and many of its cures are the same. But there are differences—deep, corrosive, obstinate differences—radiating painful roots into the community, the family, and the nature of the individual.

These differences are not racial differences. They are solely and simply the consequence of ancient brutality, past injustice, and present prejudice. They are anguishing to observe. For the Negro they are a reminder of oppression. For the white they are a reminder of guilt. But they must be faced, and dealt with, and overcome; if we are to reach the time when the only difference between Negroes and whites is the color of their skin.

Nor can we find a complete answer in the experience of other American minorities. They made a valiant, and largely successful effort to emerge from poverty and prejudice. The Negro, like these others, will have to rely mostly on his own efforts. But he cannot do it alone. For they did not have the heritage of centuries to overcome. They did not have a cultural tradition which had been twisted and battered by endless years of hatred and hopelessness. Nor were they excluded because of race or color—a feeling whose dark intensity is matched by no other prejudice in our society.

Nor can these differences be understood as isolated infirmities. They are a seamless web. They cause each other. They result from each other. They reinforce each other. Much of the Negro community is buried under a blanket of history and circumstance. It is not a lasting solution to lift just one corner. We must stand on all sides and raise the entire cover if we are to liberate our fellow citizens.

One of the differences is the increased concentration of Negroes in our cities. More than 73 per cent of all Negroes live in urban areas compared with less than 70 per cent of whites. Most of them live in slums. And most of them live together; a separated people. Men are shaped by their world. When it is a world of decay ringed by an invisible wall—when escape is arduous and uncertain, and the saving pressures of a more hopeful society are unknown—it can cripple the youth and desolate the man.

There is also the burden a dark skin can add to the search for a productive place in society. Unemployment strikes most swiftly and broadly at the Negro. This burden erodes hope. Blighted hope breeds despair. Despair brings indifference to the learning which offers a way out. And despair coupled with indifference is often the source of destructive rebellion against the fabric of society.

There is also the lacerating hurt of early collision with white hatred or prejudice, distaste or condescension. Other groups have felt similar intolerance. But success and achievement could wipe it away. They do not change the color of a man's skin. I have seen this uncomprehending pain in the eyes of young Mexican-American school children. It can be overcome. But for many, the wounds are always open.

Perhaps most important—its influence radiating to every part of life—is the breakdown of the Negro family structure. For this, most of all, white America must accept responsibility. It flows from centuries of oppression and persecution of the Negro man. It flows from the long years of degradation and discrimination which have attacked his dignity and assaulted his ability to provide for his family.

This, too, is not pleasant to look upon. But it must be faced by those whose serious intent is to improve the life of all Americans.

Only a minority—less than half—of all Negro children reach the age of 18 having lived all their lives with both parents. At this moment, today, little less than two thirds are living with both parents. Probably a majority of all Negro children receive federally-aided public assistance during their childhood.

The family is the cornerstone of our society. More than any other force it shapes the attitude, the hopes, the ambitions, and the values of the child. When the family collapses the child is usually damaged. When it happens on a massive scale the community itself is crippled.

Unless we work to strengthen the family—to create conditions under which most parents will stay together—all the rest: schools and play-grounds, public assistance and private concern—will not be enough to cut completely the circle of despair and deprivation.

There is no single easy answer to all these problems.

Jobs are part of the answer. They bring the income which permits a man to provide for his family.

Decent homes in decent surroundings and a chance to learn are part of the answer.

Welfare and social programs better designed to hold families together are part of the answer.

Care for the sick is part of the answer.

An understanding heart by all Americans is also part of the answer.

To all these fronts—and a dozen more—I will dedicate the expanding efforts of my administration. . . .

Beyond the law lay the land. It was a rich land, glowing with more abundant promise than ever man had seen. Here, unlike any place yet known, all were to share the harvest.

And beyond this was the dignity of man. Each could become whatever his qualities of mind and spirit would permit—to strive, to seek, and, if he could, to find his happiness.

This is American justice. We have pursued it faithfully to the edge of our imperfections. And we have failed to find it for the American Negro.

It is the glorious opportunity of this generation to end the one huge wrong of the American nation—and in so doing to find America for our-selves, with the same immense thrill of discovery which gripped those who first began to realize that here, at last, was a home for freedom.

All it will take is for all of us to understand what this country is and what it must become.

Chapter 14

The Sixties:
A Decade of Protest

Anti-Vietnam War protesters taunting military police, 1967.

The civil rights revolution that began in the 1950s erupted into a full-scale protest movement during the 1960s and eventually led to the enactment of the Civil Rights Act of 1964 and the Voting Rights Act of 1965, both of which greatly expanded the rights of African Americans. Largely rooted in the churches of the southern black community and appealing to black youth, the movement also attracted a substantial following among white students in the north. In the early 1960s, young men and women of both races headed south to aid in voter registration and to test segregation. They also joined protest marches to support African Americans' aspirations for equality.

The experiences of the students heightened their awareness of injustice in America and led them to question institutions on a broad scale. In addition to those institutions supporting racial discrimination and segregation, students closely scrutinized their own colleges and universities. The University of California became a center of turmoil as students protested against the numerous restrictions on political debate and student activism imposed by the administration at that campus. In the essay from Terry Anderson's *The Movement and the Sixties,*

Berkeley student leader Mario Savio states that he had gone to Mississippi to struggle for civil rights and was now engaged in "another phase of the same struggle." How would you characterize this new phase, and what do you think prompted it? Anderson also describes the free speech movement at Berkeley during the 1960s and how it escalated into a major confrontation between students and the university administration. What does Anderson consider to be the key issues during those hectic times? Anderson acknowledges that on many campuses dissatisfaction was strangely absent, that students were often "optimistic and comfortable." How was it possible for both student satisfaction and protest to exist in the same decade?

Some students were not content to limit their protests to racial discrimination and restrictions on speech on their campuses; they also objected to university rules and regulations on social behavior, such as drinking and sexual activity. Still others saw the university as only one institution in need of fundamental change. In 1962 Students for a Democratic Society (SDS) was formed. From an organizational meeting at the United Auto Workers's Port Huron center in Michigan, SDS issued the Port Huron agenda, calling for radical solutions to what they believed to be injustice in America. The first document is taken from this SDS statement. What are the main points of its critique of society? Most of these predominantly white students were privileged; how can you explain their discontent?

Terry Anderson notes at the end of his essay that unhappiness with the Vietnam War was a major factor in explaining the upheavals of the sixties, and that without the war the "sixties generation" might have taken a different shape. It is understandable why male students especially objected to the war, for they were faced with the draft and the possibility of being sent to fight, thousands of miles across the Pacific in a war in which they did not believe. But students were by no means the only Americans to oppose what many termed "Lyndon Johnson's war." Returning veterans organized Vietnam Veterans Against the War. The second document, a statement by veteran John Kerry who would become a U.S. senator from Massachusetts, speaks for these veterans. What was there about this war that led to such widespread disillusionment?

ESSAY

————•◦•————

The Movement and the
Sixties Generation

Terry Anderson

"Last summer I went to Mississippi to join the struggle there for civil rights," said Berkeley student Mario Savio in 1964. "This fall I am engaged in another phase of the same struggle, this time in Berkeley. In Mississippi an autocratic and powerful minority rules, through organized violence, to suppress the vast, virtually powerless majority. In California, the privileged minority manipulates the university bureaucracy to suppress the students' political expression."

That expression had been curtailed by the University of California as students arrived on the Berkeley campus for fall semester in September. As was typical for university officials during the cold war era, a dean simply informed all student organizations that from now on they were no longer permitted to set up tables on campus to promote "off-campus" causes such as civil rights, and this ban applied to the traditional area for such endeavors, a small strip of property at the campus's main entrance where Telegraph Avenue met Bancroft Way.

Activism had long since arrived in Berkeley. In 1958 students organized Towards an Active Student Community, which later became SLATE, and a few dozen began discussing civil rights, capital punishment, and nuclear disarmament. "For us," student Michael Rossman later wrote, "the discovery was of each other. We began to realize we were not alone."

In spring 1960 they acted, holding silent vigils at San Quentin to protest the execution of Caryl Chessman and picketing the House Un-American Activities Committee investigation of Communist activities in the Bay Area, a demonstration that led to Black Friday.* Activism increased, and by the 1963–64 academic year hundreds of students had become involved in civil rights demonstrations, picketing hotels, automobile dealerships, restaurants, and other businesses that had discriminatory employment practices. At Lucky food stores, activists held "shop-ins," filling grocery carts with food, and after going through the checkout line, saying, "Sorry, I forgot my money. If you would hire some Negroes I would remember it next time." They picketed the Oakland *Tribune*, whose conservative owner was on the

SOURCE: From *The Movement and the Sixties,* by Terry H. Anderson. Copyright © 1996 by Terry H. Anderson. Used by permission of Oxford University Press, Inc.
*In May 1960 a student protest against the House Un-American Activities Committee in San Francisco resulted in a violent confrontation between the police and the demonstrators. (Eds.)

university's board of regents, and in March the local campaign reached a crescendo when 2000 violated a court order restricting the number of protesters in front of the Sheraton Palace Hotel; police arrested 800.

Political debate also was mounting. The Republican convention was held during June 1964 in San Francisco and the candidacy of conservative Barry Goldwater inspired discussion as he faced Lyndon Johnson in the upcoming elections. Then, in August, just weeks before students returned to classes, President Johnson declared that North Vietnam had attacked U.S. ships in the Gulf of Tonkin. He asked for and received from Congress the Gulf of Tonkin Resolution, which stimulated more student debate about America's role in South Vietnam. And as fall semester began in September approximately fifty students returned from volunteer work during Mississippi Summer.* At Berkeley and at other universities many of these students were welcomed back to campus as "civil rights heroes."

The university administration apparently was under pressure by conservatives in the state, community, and on the board of regents to curb activism when they issued the political ban. The students' response was dramatic. On September 21 campus organizations of all political persuasions united—from the Young Socialist Alliance to Youth for Goldwater—and they violated the ban. Two hundred students picketed on campus with signs such as "UC Manufactures Safe Minds," "Ban Political Birth Control," and "Bomb the Ban." To most, the issue was freedom of speech. "We're allowed to say why we think something is good or bad," said activist Jackie Goldberg, "but we're not allowed to distribute information as to what to do about it. Inaction is the rule, rather than the exception, in our society and on this campus." The movement gained support, and a week later some students set up political tables. Administrators took down names, and ordered civil rights veteran Jack Weinberg to appear in front of a dean. He did the next day, but he was followed by 500 supporters who packed into the administration building, Sproul Hall, and stayed until early the next morning. University of California president Clark Kerr suspended eight activists, but that did not stifle dissent as it would have in the 1950s. It only increased ill will and resulted in more protest. "A student who has been chased by the KKK in Mississippi," said student Roger Sandall, "is not easily scared by academic bureaucrats."

The Free Speech Movement it was called, and along with the civil rights protests the previous spring it demonstrated the emergence of a new generation. "How proud I felt," wrote Berkeley student Sara Davidson. "I belonged to a great new body of students who cared about the problems of the world. No longer would youth be apathetic. That was the fifties. We were *committed*." . . .

---

*A campaign to encourage voter registration among blacks. (Eds.)

The role of the university in the first half of the 1960s . . . was not only to train students but to tame them to be conventional adults. To fit in, to become their parents. Students who did not play the game often were expelled or left in disgust; professors who did not teach the game usually were fired. Journalism major Phil Ochs at Ohio State was slated to become editor of the school paper, *The Lantern,* but faculty advisers rejected him because his views were "too controversial." He quit in his last year and became a folksinger. Illinois professor Leo Koch wrote in the *Daily Illini* that in his opinion premarital sex was all right for mature unmarried college students. The university president found the views "offensive and repugnant . . . contrary to the accepted standards of morality," and he fired Koch. For similar reasons St. John's University fired two dozen faculty members in 1966—none even received a hearing, for according to university rules the board of trustees could give or take away tenure at any time without explanation. *Newsweek* editorialized that "college must not abdicate its role in conserving, transmitting, and helping to mold both moral and intellectual values" of its students.

Yet many students by the mid-1960s had little desire to "be molded." This generation was different from older brothers and sisters who had been cowed by McCarthyism. That campaign was ancient history to them, hardly remembered and not taken seriously. Furthermore, these students had learned from the struggle. "If there is any one reason for increased student protest," a University of Utah journalist wrote, "it would probably be the civil rights movement. The movement . . . convinced many of them that non-violent demonstrations could be an effective device on the campus. It also served to make them more sensitive of their own civil rights." Problems in society had to be confronted and resolved, not blamed on imaginary subversives or outside agitators, and that called for student activism.

The reasons for student power were stated by the activists themselves in their campus papers and in new student undergrounds. This generation felt *in loco parentis* rules were absurd. Texas student Jeff Shero complained that campus regulations were "aimed at maintaining a 'proper image' for the University, rather than protecting girls." The young editor of *The Paper* declared "Michigan State is the Mississippi of American universities," protesting the administration's "closed-mindedness, intolerance and backwoods McCarthyism." The *New Orleans Freedom Press* proclaimed that student discontent resulted from "administrative restrictions on student autonomy," while University of Florida activists were blunt in their campus underground, *Freedom Forum:* "The American university campus has become a ghetto. Like all ghettoes, it has its managers (the administration), its Uncle Toms (the intimidated, status-berserk faculty), its raw natural resources processed for outside exploitation and consumption (the students)." Their demand highlighted the reasons for student power: "NO RESTRICTIONS MAY BE PLACED ON STUDENT DRINKING, GAMBLING, SEXUAL ACTIVITY, OR ANY SUCH PRIVATE MORAL DECISION."

The sixties generation began to confront its university administrations in 1964, politely demanding to be heard. During spring semester the administration at Brandeis consulted no one and then instituted new, stricter dorm visitation rules. That prompted several hundred students to stage a two-day demonstration, and the campus newspaper declared that such regulations "makes impossible any meaningful relationship between boy and girl." That fall semester, Syracuse University students approached their administrators with a simple request—they felt that holiday break, which began on December 23, was too close to Christmas. A few dozen students asked for more travel time to get home by Christmas Eve. After officials turned down all petitions, the students called a rally in December, and they were surprised when 2000 appeared. They demanded a speech from the chancellor, and he gave a short address, again saying no. As he ended his talk, some students jeered and booed, which shocked elders. "The students were supposed to show proper respect," a journalist wrote, "to know their place and keep it." Student activists, however, had a different interpretation. They wanted some role in the university. "If today's demonstration proves nothing else," the student paper editorialized, "we are not ones to be ignored or taken lightly."

Students at Berkeley certainly were not going to be taken lightly—they again challenged the ban on disseminating literature. On October 1, Jack Weinberg and others set up a few tables outside the administration building on Sproul Plaza and began passing out civil rights and political flyers. Before noon two university deans and a policeman approached Weinberg. "Are you prepared to remove yourself and the table from university property?" asked the dean. "I am not," replied Weinberg. After a brief discussion the official informed Weinberg of his arrest, and at this point several hundred students who were gathering for a free speech rally startled the officials by shouting, "Take us all, take us all!" Policemen drove a car onto the plaza and placed Weinberg inside, but suddenly someone shouted, "Sit down!" "I'm around the police car," recalled Michael Rossman. "I'm the first person to sit down. You will hear five hundred others who say that, and everyone is telling the truth." Students either laid or sat down around the car. They refused to move. The police could not drive their prisoner to jail as the crowd swelled to 3000. Mario Savio and many others climbed on top of the car and gave speeches, and later the crowd sang civil rights songs. They remained on the plaza all night. The next morning the area looked like a campsite, filled with sleeping bags, blankets, and even a pup tent. The crowd increased to 4000 that afternoon and President Kerr realized that the free speech issue was not going to disappear. After a thirty-hour sit-in, university administrators finally agreed to meet the activists.

To university officials, and to most citizens after the law and order 1950s, Berkeley had been reduced to chaos. Although campus rebellion would become common later in the decade, this was the first major eruption, and administrators responded forcefully. Under pressure from conservatives in the community and state government, they allowed 500 police officers to appear on campus minutes before they met activists. The police were armed with nightsticks, and the sight shocked students who never could remember a police army on campus and who felt that the incident was novel in American educational history. As police stood by, civil rights veterans taught nonviolent arrest tactics and urged those with police records or children to leave. Administrators had the support of California Governor Edmund G. Brown, a Democrat who stated that the demonstration was "not a matter of freedom of speech" but was an attempt by the students to use the campus illegally. "This will not be tolerated." He continued, "We must have—and will continue to have—law and order on our campuses."

Negotiations with Kerr continued for two hours, and then Savio and other students emerged from Sproul Hall. Savio climbed on the police car and announced that an agreement had been reached. A student–faculty committee would examine the free speech issue and make recommendations to the president. The university would not press charges against Weinberg or FSM leaders, and the eight students suspended earlier would have their case reviewed. Kerr seemed to support establishing a small free speech area at the campus's main entrance where Telegraph Avenue met Bancroft Way.

The October 2 agreement collapsed by November. The administration filled the committee with their own supporters, and then stalled for weeks. Meanwhile, Kerr took the issue to the press. Under pressure from conservative regents and politicians, the president attacked activists by raising the old bugaboos: "Reds on Campus," Kerr told the *San Francisco Examiner.* The article reported that the president "declared flatly that a hard core of 'Castro–Mao-Tse-tung line' Communists were in the crowd of demonstrators." The president then rejected political activity, provoking students to petition the regents and to set up tables on Sproul Plaza. The regents refused to hear the case, and on November 29 Kerr surprised students by announcing that the university was going to press new charges against FSM leaders Art Goldberg and Savio for their actions during the October 1 demonstrations. Charges included "entrapping a police car," "packing in" Sproul Hall, and, against Savio alone, biting a policeman "on the left thigh, breaking the skin and causing bruises."

The administration's behavior only alienated more students, irritated many professors, and fueled more protest as students and faculty began to feel that the university all along had been negotiating in bad faith. "The Administration sees the free speech protest as a simple problem of disobedience," proclaimed an FSM steering committee statement. "By again arbitrarily singling out students for punishment, the Administration avoids facing the real issues. . . . We demand that these new charges be dropped." Thousands of activists took those demands to Sproul Plaza on December 2, and Savio voiced the students' frustration by telling the crowd: "There is a time when the operation of the machine becomes so odious, makes you so sick at heart, that you can't take part; you can't even tacitly take part, and you've got to put your bodies upon the gears and upon the wheels, upon the levers, upon all the apparatus and you've got to make it stop."

"We Shall Overcome," sang Joan Baez, and others joined in as they moved toward Sproul Hall. "We'll walk hand in hand," for "the truth will make us free." The activists shut down the university administration— again they confronted the establishment.

Governor Brown responded immediately: "We're not going to have anarchy in California." He informed Kerr that force must be used to oust the students and ordered police to arrest activists who refused to leave the administration building. At about 4 a.m. some 600 policemen entered Sproul Hall and began arresting students, eventually about 770, in the largest mass arrest in California history. Some 7000 students remained on the plaza, and that morning they began picketing all entrances to the campus, handing out flyers:

IT IS HAPPENING NOW!

In the middle of the night, the police began dragging 800 of your fellow students from Sproul Hall. Sproul Hall was turned into a booking station; the University has become an armed camp—armed against its own students! . . .

Now the police take over.

Instead of recognizing the legitimacy of the students' demands, the administration is attempting to destroy the FSM. . . . The administration position is clear. It is saying "We decide what is acceptable freedom of speech on this campus. Those who disagree will be ignored; when they can no longer be ignored, they will be destroyed."

We have not been defeated by the University's troops! Our protest will continue until the justice of our cause is acknowledged. You must take a stand now! No longer can the faculty attempt to mediate from the outskirts of the crowd. No longer can students on this campus afford to accept humbly administrative fiat. Raise your voice now!

WE SHALL OVERCOME.

The faculty met, and after a long and heated discussion in their senate, they declared their position: Professors overwhelmingly voted to condemn the use of police on campus and to support the FSM. As faculty left the meeting, students cheered, and on December 4 both students and faculty held a huge rally on Sproul Plaza. Arrested activists had been released on

251

bail, many wore a large white "V" on black shirts, and they and several professors criticized Governor Brown, the regents, and President Kerr. Students declared a strike, and that week half the classes were canceled.

With business as usual disrupted, Kerr called a special meeting for December 7 at the Greek Theater. About 16,000 students, faculty, and staff gathered, and the president condemned the sit-in but offered clemency for all acts of civil disobedience before December 2 and stated that the university would abide by "new and liberalized political action rules" then being developed by the faculty senate. The speech sounded conciliatory, and as the president left the podium Savio began walking across the stage apparently to make an announcement. Before he reached the microphone, campus police astonished the crowd by grabbing the activist and dragging him backstage. When other activists attempted to help, the police wrestled them off the stage.

"The crowd was stunned," wrote participant Bettina Aptheker, "then there was pandemonium." Students cried out "We Want Mario! We Want Mario!" Kerr, realizing that the police were ruining his efforts to reach an understanding, quickly agreed to let Savio make his announcement—a rally would be held at noon. Nevertheless, most spectators remembered the incident and its inescapable symbolism: authorities physically preventing a student committed to free speech from speaking on his own campus. As Aptheker later wrote: "That episode more than any other single event revolutionized the *thinking* of many thousands of students."

The next day the faculty met and overwhelmingly passed a motion affirming that "speech or advocacy should not be restricted by the university." While the administration and regents discussed the motion during the next two weeks, the FSM invited CORE national director James Farmer to address a rally on December 15. The administration was conciliatory, informing students that Farmer could talk on campus, but FSM activists decided to hold a legal rally off campus as a token of good faith. Farmer told the crowd that the "battle for free speech" could not be lost, for that would "turn off the faucet of the civil rights movement." When someone charged that he was an "outside agitator," he replied, "Every housewife knows the value of an agitator. It's the instrument inside the washing machine that bangs around and gets out all the dirt."

The administration eventually decided to accept the faculty's liberalized political rules. On January 4, 1965, the Free Speech Movement held its first legal rally on Sproul Plaza. The FSM was a success, Savio told the crowd, because "it was so obvious to everybody that it was right."

The FSM raised a philosophical debate that divided many students and administrators: What is the nature of a public university? While Kerr thought of himself as a liberal and had been praised for his stand favoring academic freedom, he stated the usual reasoning of cold war culture. The "university is an educational institution that has been given to the regents as a trust to administer for educational reasons, and not to be used for direct political actions." FSM advocates and many professors disagreed, arguing that the mission of higher education was much broader. "The university is the place where people begin seriously to question the conditions of their existence and raise the issue of whether they can be committed to the society they have been born into," wrote Savio. At a public institution supported by all taxpayers, activists felt that discussion should not be reserved only for campus issues but should be open to all concerns of the Republic. Art Goldberg advocated making Berkeley "a marketplace of ideas" where citizens would be exposed to "new and creative solutions to the problems that every American realizes are facing this society in the mid-60s."

That idea was not original in 1964, for actually students had initiated free speech movements earlier at a few other campuses, including Ohio State and Indiana University. In March 1963 three students at Indiana, officers of the Young Socialist Alliance, sponsored a speech by a black socialist on the civil rights movement. In May, the county prosecuting attorney charged the students with violating the Indiana Anti-Communist Act, meeting with the purpose of "advocating the violent overthrow" of the governments of Indiana and the United States. The prosecutor also demanded that the university drop its recognition of YSA. "We may all be ten years away from Senator McCarthy," wrote one professor, "but I am ten blocks away from the office of the Prosecuting Attorney." Supporters of the three established the Committee to Aid the Bloomington Students, which eventually received assistance from 50 colleges in 15 states. Over 140 faculty members signed a statement that the indictment was not "motivated by zeal for law enforcement, but by a desire to dictate to Indiana University that it shall not permit the use of University facilities for the expression of ideas repugnant to the Prosecutor." The university president agreed, and state courts found the law unconstitutional: The faculty continued supporting the students and broadly defined the university as a community where "debate, disagreement and the sharp confrontation of opposing ideas is a vital part of the attempt to come closer to the truth."

The free speech episode at Indiana differed from that at Berkeley. The Indiana administration viewed the conservative attack as a threat to the institution, and eventually the president supported the First Amendment. If Berkeley administrators had subscribed to such views, the sit-in of Sproul Hall probably would have been avoided. Flexible officials could avoid most confrontations on campus—a point remembered by hundreds of successful university presidents throughout the 1960s.

Kerr and the regents could not overcome their authoritarian 1950s mentality. They treated the students like subordinates, gave orders to tuition-payers, which only increased resentment toward authority. Activists felt that "liberal" administrators, the "power elites" who ran the university in Berkeley, seemed more interested in maintaining the status quo than changing rules, even if those regulations denied rights guaranteed by the First Amendment of the U.S. Constitution. Looking back, Kerr's position was indefensible. During the 1950s he had supported academic freedom for professors, yet in 1964 his administration curtailed freedom of speech for students. Many students wondered, if they could not hand out political statements, if freedom of speech did not exist on a public campus, then where did it exist in the land of the free?

The administration brought on the crisis, handled it poorly, and lost to students. As in the civil rights struggle, the FSM students put another dent in the idea that those in charge should be in charge, that the older generation had some monopoly on determining the proper path for the present and future in America. "Don't trust anyone over thirty," said Jack Weinberg and others, meaning that the generation who grew up in the 1950s had a different view of the world than their parents. During cold war culture the older generation "told the truth" to students, but in the 1960s students were "discovering the truth" for themselves, and their younger siblings would continue the process throughout the decade. At Berkeley, the young began to realize that the older generation had no monopoly on truth or on virtue. Once students began to raise their voices and question policy, Michael Rossman wrote, then "the emperor had no clothes." President Kerr's decision to uphold an untenable regulation at Berkeley could be just as wrong as Chief of Police Bull Connor's enforcement of segregation rules in Birmingham.

The FSM was significant for many other reasons. Activists adopted a political style that reflected the ideas of the new left and some of the practices of SNCC.* Unlike traditional organizations or political parties, Berkeley students "worked through direct personal involvement in small autonomous interest groups. Our groups were ad hoc," Rossman recalled, "problem-orientated, flexible. They strove to govern themselves by participatory democracy, and to come to consensus on decisions." They also were pragmatic. "We were experimental social scientists, placing practice before theory. . . . We also were cheerful and funny, and made art as we went.

. . . [B]y the end of spring semester 1965 the climate on campus had shifted dramatically from the 1950s and early 1960s. "An End to Panty Raids," wrote a student at Kansas. The most important issues were civil and student rights; another continued that his generation was "fed up with their elders over such things as mass faceless education. . . . Students want to feel a sense of participation." With successes in the South and on their campuses, many students were optimistic about change, and as they became involved many began to think of themselves as part of a movement. "The thing for me right now is the movement," said Steven Block, an activist at Williams College. "That's an interesting word, if you think about it—

---

*At this stage in its history, the Student Nonviolent Coordinating Committee (SNCC) employed peaceful demonstrations to achieve civil rights goals. (Eds.)

movement. Because it is people in motion. It's not an end; it's not static. That's a very apt word for what we are doing."

The silent generation was history. *College Press Service* in December declared, "1964 Is Year of Protest on Nation's Campuses," and Professor Andrew Hacker called 1964–65 the "Year of the Demonstration." It was when compared with any time in memory.

But, more important, Hacker then placed the activists in context of the larger sixties generation. "Certainly, this year's protesters and demonstrators were not representative of their classmates, and it is instructive how quickly their ranks have tended to dwindle away after the first flamboyant outbursts. So long as a school will give an undergraduate his passport into the upper-middle-class without demanding more than . . . 15 weekly hours of studying, few are going to complain." Few indeed. Two years later, in 1967, professors Seymour Lipset and Philip Altbach flatly declared that it "should be made clear that . . . the scope of the American student 'revolution' has been greatly exaggerated by the mass media."

Newsweek confirmed such sentiments during spring 1965 when it conducted interviews and a poll of over 800 students at numerous universities. Over 90 percent expressed confidence in higher education, big corporations, and the federal government, while over 80 percent were satisfied with college and had positive views about the armed forces, organized religion, and the United Nations. When asked what students thought their lives would be like in fifteen years, most of them mimicked their older brothers: "I'll be secure, financially, married, have children, at least three," said one. Another aimed to be "upper middle class," and a third predicted, "I'll be living in a Long Island suburb." A journalist labeled the students "Flaming Moderates."

In mid-decade only a few students were activists while the larger sixties generation was comfortably moderate. A conservative student at the University of Miami wrote about the "deadly infection called student apathy" and referred to his campus as a "hotbed of apathy." Fraternities and sororities still dominated campus life, and a coed at Kansas as late as 1967 admitted that the biggest craze on her campus was "to get your boyfriend's fraternity sweater." Most college papers were similar to the *Daily Illini*, printing regular features like "The Party Line" which announced lavalierings, pinnings, engagements, and marriages. "I have respect for the ones who went to Mississippi or joined the Peace Corps, who committed themselves," said an English professor at Illinois in 1965, "but there are very, very few of them. Very few on this campus."

While some students had been provoked out of apathy by campus issues and civil rights, most of the sixties generation sitting in crowded classes during spring semester of 1965 were optimistic and comfortable—still best defined as the cool generation—mildly alienated from their parents' values and eager to sing along and "let the good times roll." *Time* surveyed the generation then and reported conformity: "Almost everywhere boys dress in madras shirts and chinos, or perhaps green Levis, all trim and neat. The standard for girls is sweaters and skirts dyed to match, or shirt-waists and jumpers plus blazers, Weejun loafers, and knee socks or stockings." At that time no one would have predicted that just two years away were the Summer of Love and the March on the Pentagon. Campus life that spring semester was cool, the good life. As the student body president of University of Texas said, "We haven't really been tested by war or depression. We live very much in the present because we don't have to be overly concerned about the future."

"There was that little conflict in Vietnam," Bob Calvert remembered, "but most of us in the movement felt optimistic during the summer of 1965." Indeed, most Americans felt that the nation was moving forward, and that mood was glowing in August when LBJ signed the Voting Rights Act. The president asked civil rights leaders to be present, and the signing ceremony included Bayard Rustin, Roy Wilkins, A. Philip Randolph, and Martin Luther King, Jr. LBJ had met with King the previous day and they discussed the remarkable advances during 1964 and 1965, not only in civil rights but also in the War on Poverty and Great Society programs—massive federal aid to education and job training, Headstart, Medicare, and Medicaid. King spoke of the president's amazing sensitivity to the difficult problems that Negro Americans face in the stride toward freedom," and at the signing celebration the president declared, "Today is a triumph for freedom as huge as any victory that's ever been won on any battlefield." The civil rights leaders proclaimed LBJ the "greatest President" for blacks, even surpassing Abraham Lincoln.

"There was a religiosity about the meeting," recalled a presidential aide, "which was warm with emotion—a final celebration of an act so long desired and so long in achieving." Now liberals could sit back in their easy chairs and relax. In spring 1964 a new president had made his pledge, had declared his vision of the future. "This nation, this people, this generation, has man's first chance to create a Great Society: a society of success without squalor, beauty without barrenness, works of genius without the wretchedness of poverty. We can open the doors of learning. We can open the doors of fruitful labor and rewarding leisure, of open opportunity and close community—not just to the privileged few, but, thank God, we can open those doors to *everyone.* Now, just fifteen months later, it seemed that the liberals were delivering. The civil and voting rights acts had outlawed racial discrimination in public accommodations, employment, and the vote, and social programs were beginning to help the poor—white and black—to share the American Dream. On that day in August, liberalism reached its zenith in the 1960s.

Then, during the next two years, President Johnson gave the sixties generation a reason to be concerned about the future—he massively escalated America's role in the Vietnam War. The cool generation became history.

What would have happened to the sixties generation without the experience of Vietnam? Certainly, many would have continued to support and some would have demonstrated for civil rights. Five years of the struggle meant that it had become part of the generation's consciousness, and students began demanding classes on black literature and history at universities such as Stanford, Cornell, and San Francisco State. The "movement" would have been remembered as the civil rights struggle and the rise of student power. Increasing enrollments meant that the university was going to continue evolving in size and in substance, and that students would continue demanding and supporting change. In spring 1966 Stanford activist David Harris won election as student body president by calling for student control of regulations, equal policies for men and women, option of pass-fail grades, legalization of marijuana, elimination of the board of trustees, and the end of all university cooperation with the Vietnam War. The next year students challenged campus rules and regulations at Brown, Cornell, Oregon, Washington, and administrators at the best institutions were moving toward adopting the suggestion of a committee at Wisconsin that advocated "withdrawal by the University from its *in loco parentis* activities." By mid-decade it also was clear that 1950s morality was cracking and that the younger generation was revolting against the values of Ma and Pa. Most of this quest would be superficial, beer bashes and bundling at the beach as the sixties became a party decade. But for a few others, the questioning of morals would lead them to substantial changes as they became part of an emerging counterculture. Finally, the massive size of the generation alone meant that it would have modified society, and thus would have made an impact.

What would have been remembered as the "sixties" without Vietnam? The Johnson administration would have continued civil rights legislation and Great Society programs, and along with the significant rulings of the Supreme Court of Chief Justice Earl Warren, the decade would have been taught today as another major reform era in American history.

Without the war, however, one wonders if the decade would have been as dramatic—would have been remembered as "the sixties." The decade had been a turning point for blacks since Greensboro in 1960.* For white students and their parents the decade began to take shape in 1964 and 1965 as the young began to exhibit their new values and make demands on their campus administrators. Then, between autumn 1965 and the end of 1967, the Johnson administration escalated American involvement in Vietnam—and for the entire nation the decade became "the sixties."

---

*It was in Greensboro, North Carolina, that black college students began the nonviolent sit-in movement to desegregate eating facilities in southern stores and restaurants. (Eds.)

DOCUMENTS

Port Huron Statement, 1962

Introduction: Agenda for a Generation

We are people of this generation, bred in at least modest comfort, housed now in universities, looking uncomfortably to the world we inherit.

When we were kids the United States was the wealthiest and strongest country in the world; the only one with the atom bomb, the least scarred by modern war, an initiator of the United Nations that we thought would distribute Western influence throughout the world. Freedom and equality for each individual, government of, by, and for the people—these American values we found good, principles by which we could live as men. Many of us began maturing in complacency.

As we grew, however, our comfort was penetrated by events too troubling to dismiss. First, the permeating and victimizing fact of human degradation, symbolized by the Southern struggle against racial bigotry, compelled most of us from silence to activism. Second, the enclosing fact of the Cold War, symbolized by the presence of the Bomb, brought awareness that we ourselves, and our friends, and millions of abstract "others" we knew more directly because of our common peril, might die at any time. We might deliberately ignore, or avoid, or fail to feel all other human problems, but not these two, for these were too immediate and crushing in their impact, too challenging in the demand that we as individuals take the responsibility for encounter and resolution.

While these and other problems either directly oppressed us or rankled our consciences and became our own subjective concerns, we began to see complicated and disturbing paradoxes in our surrounding America. The declaration "all men are created equal . . . " rang hollow before the facts of Negro life in the South and the big cities of the North. The proclaimed peaceful intentions of the United States contradicted its economic and military investments in the Cold War status quo.

We witnessed, and continue to witness, other paradoxes. With nuclear energy whole cities can easily be powered, yet the dominant nation-states seem more likely to unleash destruction greater than that incurred in all wars of human history. Although our own technology is destroying old and creating new forms of social organization, men still tolerate meaningless work and idleness. While two-thirds of mankind suffers undernourishment, our own upper classes revel amidst superfluous abundance. Although world population is expected to double in forty years, the nations still toler-

SOURCE: Students for a Democratic Society, Port Huron Manifesto, 1962.

258

ate anarchy as a major principle of international conduct and uncontrolled exploitation governs the mapping of the earth's physical resources. Although mankind desperately needs revolutionary leadership, America rests in national stalemate, its goals ambiguous and tradition-bound instead of informed and clear, its democratic system apathetic and manipulated rather than "of, by, and for the people."

Not only did tarnish appear on our image of American virtue, not only did disillusion occur when the hypocrisy of American ideals was discovered, but we began to sense that what we had originally seen as the American Golden Age was actually the decline of an era. The worldwide outbreak of revolution against colonialism and imperialism, the entrenchment of totalitarian states, the menace of war, overpopulation, international disorder, supertechnology—these trends were testing the tenacity of our own commitment to democracy and freedom and our abilities to visualize their application to a world in upheaval.

* * *

Some would have us believe that Americans feel contentment amidst prosperity—but might it not better be called a glaze above deeply felt anxieties about their role in the new world? And if these anxieties produce a developed indifference to human affairs, do they not as well produce a yearning to believe there *is* an alternative to the present, that something *can* be done to change circumstances in the school, the workplaces, the bureaucracies, the government? It is to this latter yearning, at once the spark and engine of change, that we direct our present appeal. The search for truly democratic alternatives to the present, and a commitment to social experimentation with them, is a worthy and fulfilling human enterprise, one which moves us and, we hope, others today. On such a basis do we offer this document of our convictions and analysis: as an effort in understanding and changing the conditions of humanity in the late twentieth century, an effort rooted in the ancient, still unfulfilled conception of man attaining determining influence over his circumstances of life.

Values

Making values explicit—an initial task in establishing alternatives—is an activity that has been devalued and corrupted. The conventional moral terms of the age, the politician moralities—"free world," "people's democracies"—reflect realities poorly, if at all, and seem to function more as ruling myths than as descriptive principles. But neither has our experience in the universities brought us moral enlightenment. Our professors and administrators sacrifice controversy to public relations; their curriculums change more slowly than the living events of the world; their skills and silence are purchased by investors in the arms race; passion is called unscholastic. The questions we might want raised—what is really important? can we live in a different and better way? if we wanted to change society, how would we do it?—are not thought to be questions of a "fruitful, empirical nature," and thus are brushed aside.

* * *

Men have unrealized potential for self-cultivation, self-direction, self-understanding, and creativity. It is this potential that we regard as crucial and to which we appeal, not to the human potentiality for violence, unreason, and submission to authority. The goal of man and society should be human independence: a concern not with image of popularity but with finding a meaning in life that is personally authentic; a quality of mind not compulsively driven by a sense of powerlessness, nor one which unthinkingly adopts status values, nor one which represses all threats to its habits, but one which has full, spontaneous access to present and past experiences, one which easily unites the fragmented parts of personal history, one which openly faces problems which are troubling and unresolved; one with an intuitive awareness of possibilities, an active sense of curiosity, an ability and willingness to learn.

This kind of independence does not mean egotistic individualism—the object is not to have one's way so much as it is to have a way that is one's own. Nor do we deify man—we merely have faith in his potential.

Human relationships should involve fraternity and honesty. Human interdependence is contemporary fact; human brotherhood must be willed, however, as a condition of future survival and as the most appropriate form of social relations. Personal links between man and man are needed, especially to go beyond the partial and fragmentary bonds of function that bind men only as worker to worker, employer to employee, teacher to student, American to Russian.

Loneliness, estrangement, isolation describe the vast distance between man and man today. These dominant tendencies cannot be overcome by better personnel management, nor by improved gadgets, but only when a love of man overcomes the idolatrous worship of things by man. As the individualism we affirm is not egoism, the selflessness we affirm is not self-elimination. On the contrary, we believe in generosity of a kind that imprints one's unique individual qualities in the relation to other men, and to all human activity. Further, to dislike isolation is not to favor the abolition of privacy; the latter differs from isolation in that it occurs or is abolished according to individual will.

We would replace power rooted in possession, privilege, or circumstance by power and uniqueness rooted in love, reflectiveness, reason, and creativity. As a *social system* we seek the establishment of a democracy of individual participation, governed by two central aims: that the individual share in those social decisions determining the quality and direction of his life; that society be organized to encourage independence in men and provide the media for their common participation. . . .

The Students

In the last few years, thousands of American students demonstrated that they at least felt the urgency of the times. They moved actively and directly against racial injustices, the threat of war, violations of individual rights of conscience and, less frequently, against economic manipulation. They succeeded in restoring a small measure of controversy to the campuses after the stillness of the McCarthy period. They succeeded, too, in gaining some concessions from the people and institutions they opposed, especially in the fight against racial bigotry.

The significance of these scattered movements lies not in their success or failure in gaining objectives—at least not yet. Nor does the significance lie in the intellectual "competence" or "maturity" of the students involved—as some pedantic elders allege. The significance is in the fact that the students are breaking the crust of apathy and overcoming the inner alienation that remain the defining characteristics of American college life.

If student movements for change are still rarities on the campus scene, what is commonplace there? The real campus, the familiar campus, is a place of private people, engaged in their notorious "inner emigration." It is a place of commitment to business-as-usual, getting ahead, playing it cool. It is a place of mass affirmation of the Twist,* but mass reluctance toward the controversial public stance. Rules are accepted as "inevitable," bureaucracy as "just circumstances," irrelevance as "scholarship," selflessness as "martyrdom," politics as "just another way to make people do what you want, and an unprofitable one, too."

Almost no students value activity as citizens. Passive in public, they are hardly more idealistic in arranging their private lives: Gallup concludes they will settle for "low success, and won't risk high failure." There is not much willingness to take risks (not even in business), no setting of dangerous goals, no real conception of personal identity except one manufactured in the image of others, no real urge for personal fulfillment except to be almost as successful as the very successful people. Attention is being paid to social status (the quality of shirt collars, meeting people, getting wives or husbands, making solid contacts for later on); much, too, is paid to academic status (grades, honors, the med school rat race). But neglected generally is real intellectual status, the personal cultivation of the mind.

"Students don't even give a damn about the apathy," one has said. Apathy toward apathy begets a privately constructed universe, a place of systematic study schedules, two nights each week for beer, a girl or two, and

*A popular dance during the 1960s (Eds.)

261

early marriage; a framework infused with personality, warmth, and under control, no matter how unsatisfying otherwise. . . .

The academic life contains reinforcing counterparts to the way in which extracurricular life is organized. The academic world is founded on a teacher-student relation analogous to the parent-child relation which characterizes *in loco parentis*. Further, academia includes a radical separation of the student from the material of study. That which is studied, the social reality, is "objectified" to sterility, dividing the student from life—just as he is restrained in active involvement by the deans controlling student government. The specialization of function and knowledge, admittedly necessary to our complex technological and social structure, has produced an exaggerated compartmentalization of study and understanding. This has contributed to an overly parochial view, by faculty, of the role of its research and scholarship, to a discontinuous and truncated understanding, by students, of the surrounding social order; and to a loss of personal attachment, by nearly all, to the worth of study as a humanistic enterprise.

There is, finally, the cumbersome academic bureaucracy extending throughout the academic as well as the extracurricular structures, contributing to the sense of outer complexity and inner powerlessness that transforms the honest searching of many students to a ratification of convention and, worse, to a numbness to present and future catastrophes. The size and financing systems of the university enhance the permanent trusteeship of the administrative bureaucracy, their power leading to a shift within the university toward the value standards of business and the administrative mentality. Huge foundations and other private financial interests shape the under-financed colleges and universities, not only making them more commercial, but less disposed to diagnose society critically, less open to dissent. Many social and physical scientists, neglecting the liberating heritage of higher learning, develop "human relations" or "morale-producing" techniques for the corporate economy, while others exercise their intellectual skills to accelerate the arms race.

Vietnam Veterans Against the War, *1971*

. . . [S]everal months ago in Detroit we had an investigation at which over 150 honorably discharged and many very highly decorated veterans testified to war crimes committed in Southeast Asia, not isolated incidents

SOURCE: Hearings Before the Committee on Foreign Relations, U.S. Senate, 92nd Cong., 1st sess., 1971. Document from Bibliobase®, edited by Michael Bellesiles. Copyright © by Houghton Mifflin Company. Reprinted by permission.

but crimes committed on a day-to-day basis with the full awareness of officers at all levels of command.

It is impossible to describe to you exactly what did happen in Detroit, the emotions in the room, the feelings of the men who were reliving their experiences in Vietnam, but they did. They relived the absolute horror of what this country, in a sense, made them do.

They told the stories [of] times they had personally raped, cut off ears, cut off heads, taped wires from portable telephones to human genitals and turned up the power, cut off limbs, blown up bodies, randomly shot at civilians, razed villages in fashion reminiscent of Genghis Khan, shot cattle and dogs for fun, poisoned food stocks, and generally ravaged the countryside of South Vietnam in addition to the normal ravage of war, and the normal and very particular ravaging which is done by the applied bombing power of this country. . . .

We who have come here to Washington have come here because we feel we have to be winter soldiers now. We could come back to this country; we could be quiet; we could hold our silence; we could not tell what went on in Vietnam, but we feel because of what threatens this country, the fact that the crimes threaten it, not reds, and not redcoats but the crimes which we are committing that threaten it, that we have to speak out. . . .

I would like to talk to you a little bit about what the result is of the feelings these men carry with them after coming back from Vietnam. The country doesn't know it yet, but it has created a monster, a monster in the form of millions of men who have been taught to deal and to trade in violence, and who are given the chance to die for the biggest nothing in history; men who have returned with a sense of anger and a sense of betrayal which no one has yet grasped. . . .

In our opinion, and from our experience, there is nothing in South Vietnam, nothing which could happen that realistically threatens the United States of America. And to attempt to justify the loss of one American life in Vietnam, Cambodia, or Laos by linking such loss to the preservation of freedom, which those misfits supposedly abuse, is to us the height of criminal hypocrisy, and it is that kind of hypocrisy which we feel has torn this country apart. . . .

We found that not only was it a civil war, an effort by a people who had for years been seeking their liberation from any colonial influence whatsoever, but also we found that the Vietnamese whom we had enthusiastically molded after our own image were hard put to take up the fight against the threat we were supposedly saving them from.

We found most people didn't even know the difference between communism and democracy. They only wanted to work in rice paddies without helicopters strafing them and bombs with napalm burning their villages and tearing their country apart. . . .

We rationalized destroying villages in order to save them. We saw America lose her sense of morality as she accepted very coolly a My Lai* and refused to give up the image of American soldiers who hand out chocolate bars and chewing gum. . . .

Now we are told that the men who fought there must watch quietly while American lives are lost so that we can exercise the incredible arrogance of Vietnamizing the Vietnamese. . . .

. . . Each day to facilitate the process by which the United States washes her hands of Vietnam someone has to give up his life so that the United States doesn't have to admit something that the entire world already knows, so that we can't say that we have made a mistake. Someone has to die so that President Nixon won't be, and these are his words, "the first President to lose a war."

We are asking Americans to think about that because how do you ask a man to be the last man to die in Vietnam? How do you ask a man to be the last man to die for a mistake? . . .

We wish that a merciful God could wipe away our own memories of that service as easily as this administration has wiped their memories of us. But all that they have done and all that they can do by this denial is to make more clear than ever our own determination to undertake one last mission, to search out and destroy the last vestige of this barbaric war, to pacify our own hearts, to conquer the hate and the fear that have driven this country these last 10 years and more, and so when, in 30 years from now, our brothers go down the street without a leg, without an arm, or a face, and small boys ask why, we will be able to say "Vietnam" and not mean a desert, not a filthy obscene memory but mean instead the place where America finally turned and where soldiers like us helped it in the turning. . .

---

*My Lai refers to the village in which American soldiers killed many innocent Vietnamese civilians. (Eds.)

Chapter 15

The Revival of Feminism

Feminist leaders Bella Abzug and Betty Friedan join a women's rights parade in Houston, Texas, circa 1977.

When women gained the vote in 1920, the women's movement that had long sought this goal—dating back to the mid-nineteenth century—became dormant for several decades. Yet that victory by no means marked the end of the struggle for equality of opportunity and treatment for women. The franchise gained women entry to the voting booth, but few won elective office. Women still found most of their employment opportunities in the traditional, low-paying, "feminine" occupations, and their wages typically ranged lower than those of men with similar experience, education, skill, and responsibility. Moreover, during the Great Depression, married women discovered that many employers hesitated to hire them, insisting that men be given preference for available jobs.

Economic discrimination had much to do with the emergence of a new wave of feminism beginning in the 1960s, but there were other factors as well. In the essay "Feminism's Second Wave: The Opening Salvos," author Flora Davis points to wide-ranging discontent among airline stewardesses during the 1950s and early 1960s. *Stewardess,* rather than today's term, *flight attendant,* was the designation of the then almost totally feminine occupation. What were the major issues in the women's struggle with their airline employers? What tactics proved most significant in determining the final outcome? Can you think of other occupations, usually low-paid, that are dominated by women?

In 1923, a group of women led by Alice Paul had proposed an equal rights amendment (ERA) to the Constitution designed to ensure sexual equality. The idea lay quiescent for nearly half a century until the resurgence of the women's movement in the 1960s. By 1970, the ERA had again become a live issue. The first document is a statement in support of the amendment before a Senate committee by the well-known feminist writer and editor Gloria Steinem. To what extent and in what ways might the ERA affect the conditions that Steinem describes?

In 1972 Congress approved the ERA by the necessary two-thirds margin, and opinion polls indicated support for the amendment by a vast majority of the American public. Nevertheless, the amendment failed to receive ratification by the required three-quarters of the states. Opposition centered in the South, several western states, Missouri, and Illinois.

The defeat of the ERA, although a major setback, did not fatally injure the women's movement. A growing number of women ran for and were elected to office. In 1976, 21 women held seats in the United States Congress. Twenty years later, 55 women were in Congress, and both United States senators from California were women. In 1984, for the first time, a woman, Geraldine Ferraro, was selected as a vice-presidential candidate.

Encouraged by the spirit of feminism and aided by civil rights legislation, favorable court decisions, and government-directed affirmative action programs, increasing numbers of women entered traditionally male occupations. Since 1980 women have outnumbered men in undergraduate colleges and universities, and they have been increasing their presence in graduate schools. Women received 14.3 percent of the Ph.D.s granted in 1970, but by 1994 the figure had reached 38.5 percent. In 1960, only 6.8 percent of physicians were women, but in the academic year 1997–1998, 42.6 percent of medical students were women, thus ensuring that they would be a strong presence in the practice of medicine in the new millennium. The change among lawyers was even more startling. In 1960 women won only 2.5 percent of the law degrees granted that year, but by 1994 the figure was 43 percent. However, as the decade of the 1980s came to an end, men continued to earn more than women, and the plight of mothers in single-parent households remained difficult, with many living in poverty.

In addition to the ERA, abortion became a highly controversial issue after 1973. The Supreme Court in *Roe* v. *Wade* (1973), parts of which are included in the second document, paved the way for the legalization of abortion in many states that had formerly imposed severe limits on the procedure. What did the justices say about the right to privacy and how it affected abortion? Did the Court suggest that abortion was an absolute right? The last document is a statement by President George H. W. Bush to a group of prolife (antiabortion) marchers in the nation's capital. What possibilities for compromise, if any, do you see on this issue?

ESSAY

Feminism's Second Wave:
The Opening Salvos

Flora Davis

The women's movement, as reincarnated in the 1960s, is often called the "second wave" of feminism, to distinguish it from the "first wave," which arose during the nineteenth century and won the vote for women in 1920. The wave analogy is helpful because it underscores the fact that the women's movement didn't die after 1920, though it did lose much of its momentum. The analogy also reminds us that major social changes tend to happen in waves. First, there's a lot of intense activity and some aspects of life are transformed; then, when the public has absorbed as much as it can stand, reaction sets in. Stability reigns for a while, and if there's a strong backlash, some of the changes may be undone. Eventually, if vital issues remain unresolved, another wave of activism arises. . . .

The turbulent, affluent, optimistic 1960s provided an unusually hospitable climate for feminism. The civil rights movement had broken new ground and a number of related social movements sprang up in its wake. One of them was the women's movement. Like a brush fire in a dry season, it ignited simultaneously in two different places: among older, liberal women and among the young radicals of the New Left.

Throughout the sixties, the women's movement grew steadily, but most Americans were barely aware of what was happening. Then in the early 1970s, feminism exploded across the national scene as groups of activists cropped up almost everywhere. Often, women coalesced around a single issue, pouring their efforts into a rape hotline, a battered women's shelter, or some other highly focused project.

At the same time, a broad-based right-wing backlash began to build, fueled by white male resentment at the challenges from feminists and from

SOURCE: "Feminism's Second Wave: The Opening Salvos," from *Moving the Mountain: The Women's Movement in America Since 1960*, by Flora Davis, p. 6, 15–25. Copyright © 1991 by Flora Davis. Published by Simon & Schuster. Reprinted by permission of Curtis Brown, Ltd.

the civil rights movement. When conservatives won the White House in 1980, feminists were thrown on the defensive; for the next decade, they had to fight to hang onto the ground they'd already gained. They lost some battles and won others, and overall, progress for women stalled. Nevertheless, new feminist groups kept emerging, many of them now being formed by women of color. Going into the 1990s, the women's movement was bigger, stronger, and more diverse than ever.

Between 1960 and 1990, feminists achieved half a revolution. Laws were passed, court decisions were handed down, and sex discrimination was officially prohibited; women were elected to office, grudgingly accepted into male occupations, and promoted to positions that women had never held before. New terms entered the nation's vocabulary: People spoke of "sexism" and "male chauvinism." Probably, the movement's single greatest achievement was that it transformed most people's assumptions about what women were capable of and had a right to expect from life.

The Battle with the Airlines

The story of how airline stewardesses forced American airlines to change unfair work rules is the perfect introduction to the second wave. By throwing into sharp relief the old attitudes to women and the impact those attitudes had on people's lives, it shows just how far women have come. The activists involved were few in number, and they challenged just one aspect of the pervasive problem of sex discrimination. That was typical of the second wave and illustrates the point that social transformations, like jigsaw puzzles, are put together one piece at a time.

The battle with the airlines spanned a crucial period in the history of the women's movement. Stewardesses fought to be treated as workers, rather than as sex objects, at a time when the term "sex object" hadn't yet been invented. The work rules they challenged decreed that to keep their jobs they must remain single, and they were fired the minute they married. Many airlines fired them, in any case, as soon as they turned thirty-two, while others set the limit at thirty-five. Women much over the age of thirty were no longer considered attractive enough to fly for an airline. It hadn't even occurred to most Americans that the system was unfair, and that made changing the rules an uphill fight in a way it wouldn't have been a few years later.

The stewardess unions actually began their campaign before the second wave, at a time when few people had any interest in women's rights. When the women's movement caught up with them, union leaders used its impetus, and as they did, they quickly came to identify themselves as feminists fighting sex discrimination, not just as unionists confronting management.

At one time or another, stewardess unions at most of the major airlines joined the struggle to change the work rules. There was some communication between union leaders, but they never really made a coordinated effort.

Instead, the battle was fought simultaneously on many different fronts by different groups. The women who worked for American Airlines belonged to a union called ALSSA—the Air Line Stewards and Stewardesses Association—and their campaign was typical.

The Age and Marriage Issues

In the hierarchy of "glamour" jobs open to white women in the early sixties, stewardesses ranked right after movie stars and models.* In fact, for every woman hired as a stewardess, more than a hundred applicants were turned away. Those who were chosen embodied the American image of the wholesome girl-next-door.

As the airlines saw it, these "girls" would fly for a few years, then leave the job to marry and settle down. In the midsixties, stewardesses lasted 32.4 months, on the average, less than three years. "If that figure ever got up to thirty-five months, I'd know we're getting the wrong kind of girl. She's not getting married," a personnel manager for United Airlines said solemnly in 1965.

In the early 1960s, the social pressure to marry was relentless. The average woman became a wife at age twenty, younger than in any generation since the turn of the century. Seventy percent of American women made it safely to the altar before they were twenty-four, and a woman still unmarried at the advanced age of twenty-five was considered an "old maid." She was pitied, and people wondered what was wrong with her that no man had asked her to be his wife. Most stewardesses themselves assumed when they were hired that they'd marry within a few years. In fact, at American Airlines the gold wings presented to a woman after five years of flying were known as "your failure pin," because they signified that she had so far failed to marry.

By becoming a stewardess, an adventurous young woman had a chance to travel and meet interesting people in the time warp between the end of her schooling and the beginning of marriage. And the job was said to be good experience for marriage. At the airline training schools the women learned safety procedures, but also took classes in make-up, grooming, and social skills, "the perfect course for being a perfect hostess at home," according to one stewardess. (At American, the school was known irreverently as "the charm farm.")

Although most stewardesses seemed to love their jobs, they lived with more restrictions than the most overprotected teenager. They were told how long to wear their skirts and their hair and how high their heels could be. They could be fired for gaining too much weight. Girdles were generally required and supervisors did "touch checks" to make sure employees were

---

*Stewardesses (also called air hostesses) became known as flight attendants during the 1970s, as men began to be hired for the job.

wearing them. In addition, the women were paid so little that home was often a small apartment shared with as many as half a dozen other stewardesses.

Almost from the beginning, most airlines expected their stewardesses to resign when they married. Age didn't become an issue until the early 1950s, when American Airlines became the first company to retire the women as soon as they reached their midthirties. To get the union to agree to the age limit, management negotiators exempted those already working for the company. They stipulated that only women hired after November 1, 1953, would be forced to retire at thirty-two.

Dusty Roads got in under the wire. So did Nancy Collins, who would become the union's master executive chairman (equivalent to being its president) in the early sixties. They led the long struggle to get the airline to lift the age restriction, because both felt a moral issue was involved.

As the 1950s wore on, more and more airlines routinely dismissed stewardesses for growing too old. By 1965, fifteen of the thirty-eight U.S. airlines were doing it. "I was twenty-eight when we fought the age issue, and I was absolutely hysterical," said Lynda Oswald, who was with American Airlines. "I was trying to prepare myself for another job, but when I tried to get into a university, they wouldn't accept me as a part-time student. The whole climate was catch-22."

Yet many stewardesses saw nothing wrong with the airlines' regulations, and union leaders found it hard to marshall support. Roads recalled that "some of our own flight attendants would say, 'I don't think you should fly when you're fat or old.'" Younger women weren't interested in the age issue. "When you're twenty, you don't believe you're ever going to be thirty-two," Roads observed drily. Older women, as their thirty-second birthday approached, often cast about desperately for a ground job with the company. Reluctant to antagonize management, most "retired" from flying without a protest. As for the marriage regulation, many women did marry and kept their marriage a secret. At one point, airline officials estimated that 30 to 40 percent of stewardesses were secretly married.

In short, the battle with the airlines was fought by a minority of activists who were willing to take risks. Most of the women who ultimately benefited from their efforts were initially too timid or indifferent to take part, or actually opposed any change in the status quo. That was the case with the first challenges to sex discrimination in many occupations.

In defending their regulations, the airlines talked a lot about the image of a stewardess as a young, single woman, and the importance of maintaining that image. However, the union's leaders were well aware that, as Collins put it, "Ninety percent of this had to do with economics." Money was usually the bottom line when employers discriminated against women. In their stewardesses, the airlines had the ideal work force. Few stayed long enough to earn more than beginners' wages, and the savings on fringe benefits must have been considerable. What other company could guarantee health insurers a group of insurees who would never be older than thirty-two?

In the beginning, ALSSA's leaders believed their problem was unique; they didn't see it as part of a pattern of discrimination against women. Dusty Roads's eyes were opened in the late fifties. She had a good friend, Ann Cooper Penning, who was administrative assistant to Congresswoman Martha Griffiths, a Michigan Democrat. Roads recalled that "I was telling Annie about things the airlines did, and she said, 'You've got to be kidding me. I can't wait to tell this to Martha.' Eventually, I met Martha." Before that, Roads had more or less accepted the way stewardesses were treated. "But Martha was so upset about it," she said. From conversations with Griffiths, Roads came to realize that sex discrimination was widespread.

"The Old Broads' Bill"

At that point, there seemed to be two possible strategies open to the stewardesses. They could try to persuade the airlines at the bargaining table to drop the age and marriage regulations, or they could push for legislation.

Stewardess leaders tried bargaining first. However, they got minimal support from male union colleagues. All the stewardess unions were actually subunits of huge, male-dominated unions, and the union men were mostly blue-collar males who had come up the hard way. In dealing with the stewardesses, they were protective but autocratic. They had traditional ideas about a woman's role and little sympathy for women's issues.

Without the support of male unionists, the stewardesses were unable to get rid of the age and marriage restrictions. It was also clear that no airline was likely to give up these money-saving measures as long as other airlines were still taking advantage of them. Thus, in the early sixties, Collins and Roads tried to solve the problem by getting Congress to pass a law.

By that time, Roads was ALSSA's official, if unpaid, lobbyist. She was chosen for the job in 1958 because she was flying in and out of Washington, D.C., regularly, was dating a congressman, and could count Congresswoman Griffiths as a friend. Roads did her lobbying on her own time between flights. She had no trouble getting appointments with male members of Congress; she was a stewardess, and the men simply assumed that she would be young and attractive. Once through the door, she could often interest them in her union's case against the airlines.

Roads's efforts resulted in one early attempt to pass a law against the airlines' restrictions, but it was a piece of legislation few were comfortable with. Was it fair for Congress to target one industry and forbid one or two specific practices? "They didn't know how to go about this," said Roads. "To introduce a bill that would keep a company from firing anybody at the age of thirty-two was kind of preposterous. It was a very narrow attack on a very broad issue, which was age discrimination or discrimination against women. Eventually, the bill became a joke—they called it 'the old broads' bill.'"

In 1963, Collins and Roads decided to go public with their problem. They held a press conference at the Commodore Hotel in New York City. Collins wanted stewardesses there in significant numbers, to prove a lot of them cared about the age issue, but it wasn't easy to find women who were willing to take a public stand and risk their jobs.

Once again, the aura of glamour that came with the stewardess job paid off. Many newspapers sent reporters and photographers, and after Roads pointed out that four of the stewardesses in the room were actually over thirty-two—hired before November 1953, they couldn't be fired—one photographer seized the chance to set up a picture that ultimately appeared in papers across the country. It showed nearly a dozen uniformed women, shoulder to shoulder and displaying quite a lot of leg, over a caption that in many cases invited readers to guess which of the women were over thirty-two. Columnist Art Buchwald maintained that older stewardesses were better cooks and were just as attractive—missing the point, that the women had a right not to be fired arbitrarily. Collins and Roads were willing to be patronized as long as they got the story out. The press conference produced sheaves of clippings, but there was still no progress on the age issue.

In 1964, stewardess unions filed a complaint against American and TWA with the New York State Commission for Human Rights. New York and some other states had laws against discrimination because of age, but had nothing on the books as yet about sex discrimination.

Congress, too, was concerned about just treatment for older workers. On September 2, 1965, women from several airlines appeared before a House Labor subcommittee to talk about the age issue; other stewardesses, many in uniform, were in the audience to show support. One of the congressmen on the committee seemed to think it funny that attractive women in their thirties were talking of discrimination because of age. Representative James H. Scheuer, a Democrat from New York, turned to the stewardesses and asked them to "stand up, so we can see the dimensions of the problem."

Colleen Boland, then head of ALSSA, testified that an airlines executive had explained the age regulation this way: "It's the sex thing. Put a dog on an airplane and twenty businessmen are sore for a month." Representative Scheuer gallantly replied, "I would oppose with my dying breath the notion that a woman is less beautiful, less appealing, less sensitive after thirty. . . . " Nancy Collins said, "In those days, we felt we were being patted on our little heads about 90 percent of the time."

The congressional hearing brought no visible progress, and in New York the age discrimination case dragged on through hearings and appeals. It wasn't until early 1968 that the state's five-man Appellate Court ruled unanimously against the stewardesses on the grounds that the age law was intended to apply only to those between forty and sixty-five.

Though the stewardesses' glamour image gave them advantages in pressing their case, they were very much aware of the way society devalued older women. Once a woman was no longer young and sexually appealing to men, she had lost whatever leverage she originally had.

The EEOC: Reluctant Enforcer

In 1964, as part of a landmark civil rights bill, Congress banned sex discrimination by employers and created a new federal agency, the Equal Employment Opportunity Commission (EEOC), to enforce the law. The stewardess unions were quick to seize the chance it offered them, and when the EEOC officially opened its doors in the summer of 1965, two American Airlines stewardesses were among the first people through them.

"We got there so early, we had to help unpack the typewriters; they were still in boxes," said Dusty Roads.

With Roads that day, ready to sign a sex discrimination complaint, was Jean Montague, who was due to be fired by American because she would soon turn thirty-two. The women assumed that, thanks to the section of the new civil rights law known as Title VII, the airlines would have to mend their ways. "We were naive," Roads admitted later.

The EEOC staffer who handled their complaint that day was an African-American woman. At first she couldn't see how young, educated, white women could possibly be victims of discrimination, but she soon got into the spirit of the thing. "Do they fire pilots at thirty-two?" she asked Roads. "Do they fire flight engineers?" When Roads assured her the airlines didn't, she said with relish, "Go get 'em." That's just what Roads and her union did.

However, it took almost a year before the EEOC finally held a hearing on the women's charges in May 1966. Afterward, Roads couldn't be certain how the session had gone, but it was clear that at least one of the five commissioners, Aileen Hernandez, was sympathetic. In an unexpected way, Hernandez played a key role in the stewardess story. She resigned from the EEOC in October that year, disillusioned because the Commission was so reluctant to act on women's issues. Later, she recalled that "Commission meetings produced a sea of male faces, nearly all of which reflected attitudes that ranged from boredom to virulent hostility whenever the issue of sex discrimination was raised." Hernandez noted that the EEOC's priority was race discrimination—but apparently only as it affected black *men*. She was particularly frustrated by the long delay in ruling on complaints brought by stewardesses. At the time she resigned, there were ninety-two such cases pending, and some were more than a year old.

Hernandez resigned on October 10, giving a month's notice. On the last weekend in October, a brand-new feminist organization, NOW (the National Organization for Women), held its founding conference. Afterward, the women issued a press release. Among other things, it backed the stewardesses; it also announced that Hernandez had been elected executive vice-president of NOW, subject to her consent. According to Hernandez, her election was "a charitable, but unauthorized gesture," apparently intended to express support for her decision to resign from the EEOC.*

On November 9, the day before Hernandez's resignation was to take effect, the Commission finally ruled that company policies setting age limits for stewardesses amounted to sex discrimination. Just two weeks later, the airlines won a temporary court order which blocked the ruling on the grounds that Hernandez had a conflict of interests, because presumably she was a member of NOW. In an effort to prove she was, they had a federal court subpoena Betty Friedan, NOW's newly elected president, and Muriel Fox, who was in charge of public relations, and dragged them into court in New York City on Christmas Eve, while on the West Coast Hernandez was subpoenaed in the same way. A lawyer for the airlines demanded that Friedan produce a list of NOW's members; she declined. "We had all agreed to keep the membership list of NOW secret," Friedan wrote later, "for in those early days no one was sure she wouldn't be fired or otherwise excommunicated for belonging to an organization to overthrow sex discrimination."

In February 1967, a federal district court judge issued an injunction that, in effect, erased the EEOC decision on the age question because of Hernandez's supposed conflict of interests. The Commission and the stewardesses had to begin all over again with hearings.**

Meanwhile, the unions were trying to end the marriage restriction, working on it as a separate issue from the age limit. The airlines resisted, maintaining that married women would miss work too often and would gain weight. (Some supervisors apparently believed that with marriage a woman inevitably became plump and docile.) Eventually, the unions brought marriage-regulation complaints, too, to the EEOC. In June 1968, the agency finally announced in a case involving an American Airlines stewardess that the marriage restriction violated Title VII. In the meantime, unions at other airlines had been able to resolve the marriage issue at the bargaining table.

There was still no word from the EEOC about the age restriction, and ALSSA was soon deep in contract negotiations with American with the age limit a key issue. "We were ready to roll on a strike then," said Roads. "I called Martha and said, 'If you know anyone on the Commission, call them and tell them that if they would just make a decision, there wouldn't have to be a strike.'"

Griffiths made the phone call, and on August 10, 1968, the EEOC finally released new guidelines that barred the airlines from dismissing stewardesses

---

*In 1970, Hernandez succeeded Betty Friedan as president of NOW.

**NOW ultimately did help the stewardess unions a great deal by persistently lobbying the EEOC on their behalf.

for being overage. The following day, ALSSA reached agreement with American on a new contract, and, as Nancy Collins put it, "The age and marriage issues just faded into the woodwork."

From the time the women filed their complaint with the EEOC in July 1965, more than three years had passed; it had been five years since Roads and Collins staged their press conference. However, the struggle wasn't over yet. Some stewardesses took the airlines to court, because they not only wanted to return to their jobs but they wanted back pay and accumulated seniority. There were many individual suits as well as class-action suits. The stewardess unions also challenged the airlines successfully on the question of whether a woman should be allowed to return to her job after having a baby.

Throughout the sixties, class and race were invisible elements in the struggle between women and the airlines, for the unions never addressed the fact that women of color and white women from working-class backgrounds were seldom hired as stewardesses. At the time, most white feminists saw "women's issues" solely in terms of white women's issues—and were unaware that that was what they were doing. The second wave's size and scope were limited as a result.

The Aftereffects

In tackling the age and marriage restrictions, stewardesses assaulted some of society's ingrained assumptions: that marriage was all women really wanted; that it was perfectly natural to judge a woman solely on her looks; and that men somehow had a right to the services of women—and if it could be arranged that the women doing the serving were young, single, and attractive, so much the better.

Lynda Oswald said, "I think many of us who were stewardesses during the 1960s suffered deep psychological scars. We still have a terror of age and of being discarded because our skin isn't quite smooth enough any more."

Roads, Collins, and other activists improved the lot of most women and men who were subsequently hired as (gender-neutral) "cabin crew." In 1985, flight attendants kept their job, on the average, for ten years; they were now required to retire at age seventy; and some long-term employees were making more than $40,000 a year.

There were other, less tangible gains as well. As they stood up for their rights, the stewardesses found that their image of women and of themselves changed profoundly. A story Roads liked to tell summed up the difference. A male passenger once complained to her, "I don't know why you girls should object to being called 'girls.'"

"That's because you don't know the difference between a girl and a woman," she told him. "A 'girl' is somebody who rents an apartment. A 'woman' owns a house."

In 1991, Dusty Roads and Nancy Collins were still flying. Their names weren't likely to be the first to pop into anyone's mind during a discussion of the women's movement, but their victory was typical of the second wave. American women owed the progress they made largely to thousands of unknown activists like Roads and Collins, who tackled a small piece of the overall problem of sex discrimination. Social change advanced like an incoming tide at many different points simultaneously.

DOCUMENTS

In Support of the ERA, 1970

My name is Gloria Steinem. I am a writer and editor. I have worked in several political campaigns, and am currently a member of the Policy Council of the Democratic National Committee.

During twelve years of working for a living, I've experienced much of the legal and social discrimination reserved for women in this country. I have been refused service in public restaurants, ordered out of public gathering places, and turned away from apartment rentals; all for the clearly-stated sole reason that I am a woman. And all without the legal remedies available to blacks and other minorities. I have been excluded from professional groups, writing assignments on so-called "unfeminine" subjects such as politics, full participation in the Democratic Party, jury duty, and even from such small male privileges as discounts on airline fares. Most important to me, I have been denied a society in which women are encouraged, or even allowed, to think of themselves as first-class citizens and responsible human beings.

However, after two years of researching the status of American women, I have discovered that I am very, very lucky. Most women, both wage-earners and housewives, routinely suffer more humiliation and injustice than I do.

As a freelance writer, I don't work in the male-dominated hierarchy of an office. (Women, like blacks and other visibly-different minorities, do better in individual professions such as the arts, sports, or domestic work; anything in which they don't have authority over white males.) I am not one of the millions of women who must support a family. Therefore, I haven't had to go on welfare because there are no day care centers for my children while I work, and I haven't had to submit to the humiliating welfare inquiries

SOURCE: Testimony of Gloria Steinem, U.S. Congress, Senate Committee on the Judiciary, Subcommittee on Constitutional Amendments, Hearings, *The "Equal Rights" Amendment*, 91st Cong., 2d sess., 1970, 335–37.

about my private and sexual life, inquiries from which men are exempt. I haven't had to brave the sex bias of labor unions and employers, only to see my family subsist on a median salary 40 percent less than the male median salary.

I hope this committee will hear the personal, daily injustices suffered by many women—professionals and day laborers, women housebound by welfare as well as suburbia. We have all been silent for too long. We won't be silent anymore.

The truth is that all our problems stem from the same sex-based myths. We may appear before you as white radicals or the middle-aged middle class or black soul sisters, but we are *all* sisters in fighting against these outdated myths. Like racial myths, they have been reflected in our laws. Let me list a few:

That Women Are Biologically Inferior to Men

In fact, an equally good case can be made for the reverse. Women live longer than men, even when the men are not subject to business pressures. Women survived Nazi concentration camps better, keep cooler heads in emergencies currently studied by disaster-researchers, are protected against heart attacks by their female sex hormones, and are so much more durable at every stage of life that nature must conceive 20 to 50 percent more males in order to keep some balance going.

Man's hunting activities are forever being pointed to as tribal proof of superiority. But while he was hunting, women built houses, tilled the fields, developed animal husbandry, and perfected language. Men, being all alone in the bush, often developed into a creature [*sic*] as strong as women, fleeter of foot, but not very bright.

However, I don't want to prove the superiority of one sex to another. That would only be repeating a male mistake. English scientists once definitively proved, after all, that the English were descended from the angels, while the Irish were descended from the apes: it was the rationale for England's domination of Ireland for more than a century. The point is that science is used to support current myth and economics almost as much as the church was.

What we do know is that the difference *between* two races or two sexes is much smaller than the differences to be found *within* each group. Therefore, in spite of the slide show on female inferiorities that I understand was shown to you yesterday, the law makes much more sense when it treats individuals, not groups bundled together by some condition of birth.

A word should be said about Dr. Freud, the great nineteenth-century perpetuator of female inferiority. Many of the differences he assumed to be biological, and therefore changeless, have turned out to be societal, and have already changed. . . .

277

That Women Are Already Treated Equally in This Society

I'm sure there has been ample testimony to prove that equal pay for equal work, equal chance for advancement, and equal training or encouragement is obscenely scarce in every field, even those—like food and fashion industries—that are supposedly "feminine."

A deeper result of social and legal injustice, however, is what sociologists refer to as "Internalized Aggression." Victims of aggression absorb the myth of their own inferiority, and come to believe that their group is in fact second-class.

Women suffer this second-class treatment from the moment they are born. They are expected to be rather than achieve, to function biologically rather than learn. A brother, whatever his intellect, is more likely to get the family's encouragement and education money, while girls are often pressured to conceal ambition and intelligence, to "Uncle Tom."

I interviewed a New York public school teacher who told me about a black teenager's desire to be a doctor. With all the barriers in mind, she suggested he be a veterinarian instead.

The same day, a high school teacher mentioned a girl who wanted to be a doctor. The teacher said, "How about a nurse—"

Teachers, parents, and the Supreme Court may exude a protective, well-meaning rationale, but limiting the individual's ambition is doing no one a favor. Certainly not this country. It needs all the talent it can get.

That American Women Hold Great Economic Power

Fifty-one percent of all shareholders in this country are women. That's a favorite male-chauvinist statistic. However, the number of shares they hold is so small that the total is only 18 percent of all shares. Even those holdings are often controlled by men.

Similarly, only 5 percent of all the people in the country who receive $10,000 a year or more, earned or otherwise, are women. And that includes all the famous rich widows.

The constantly-repeated myth of our economic power seems less testimony to our real power than to the resentment of what little power we do have.

That Children Must Have Full-Time Mothers

American mothers spend more time with their homes and children than those of any other society we know about. In the past, joint families, servants, a prevalent system in which grandparents raised the children, or family field work in the agrarian systems—all these factors contributed more to child care than the labor-saving devices of which we are so proud.

The truth is that most American children seem to be suffering from too much Mother, and too little Father. Part of the program of Women's Liberation is a return of fathers to their children. If laws permit women equal work and pay opportunities, men will then be relieved of their role as sole breadwinner. Fewer ulcers, fewer hours of meaningless work, equal responsibility for his own children: these are a few of the reasons that Women's Liberation is Men's Liberation, too.

As for the psychic health of the children, studies show that the quality of time spent by parents is more important than the quantity. The most damaged children were not those whose mothers worked, but those whose mothers preferred to work but stayed home out of role-playing desire to be a "good mother."

That the Women's Movement Is Not Political, Won't Last, or Is Somehow Not "Serious"

When black people leave their nineteenth-century roles, they are feared. When women dare to leave theirs, they are ridiculed. We understand this, and accept the burden of ridicule. It won't keep us quiet anymore.

Similarly, it shouldn't deceive male observers into thinking this is somehow a joke. We are 51 percent of the population, we are essentially united on these issues across boundaries of class or race or age, and we may well end by changing this society more than the civil rights movement. That is an apt parallel. We, too, have our right wing and left wing, our separatists, gradualists, and Uncle Toms. But we are changing our own consciousness, and that of the country. [Friedrich] Engels noted the relationship of the authoritarian, nuclear family to capitalism: the father as capitalist, the mother as means of production, and the children as labor. He said the family would change as the economic system did, and that seems to have happened, whether we want to admit it or not. Women's bodies will no longer be owned by the state for the production of workers and soldiers: birth control and abortion are facts of everyday life. The new family is an egalitarian family.

Gunnar Myrdal noted thirty years ago the parallel between women and Negroes in this country. Both suffered from such restricting social myths as: smaller brains, passive natures, inability to govern themselves (and certainly not white men), sex objects only, childlike natures, special skills and the like. When evaluating a general statement about women, it might be valuable to substitute "black people" for "women"—just to test the prejudice at work.

And it might be valuable to do this Constitutionally as well. Neither group is going to be content as a cheap labor pool anymore. And neither is going to be content without full Constitutional rights.

Finally, I would like to say one thing about this time in which I am testifying.

I had deep misgivings about discussing this topic when National Guardsmen are occupying our campuses, the country is being turned against itself in a terrible polarization, and America is enlarging an already inhuman and unjustifiable war.* But it seems to me that much of the trouble this country is in has to do with the Masculine Mystique; with the myth that masculinity somehow depends on the subjugation of other people. It is a bipartisan problem: both our past and current Presidents seem to be victims of this myth, and to behave accordingly.

Women are not more moral than men. We are only uncorrupted by power. But we do not want to imitate men, to join this country as it is, and I think our very participation will change it. Perhaps women elected leaders—and there will be many more of them—will not be so likely to dominate black people or yellow people or men; anybody who looks different from us.

After all, we won't have our masculinity to prove.

A Woman's Right to Abortion, 1973

We forthwith acknowledge our awareness of the sensitive and emotional nature of the abortion controversy, of the vigorous opposing views, even among physicians, and of the deep and seemingly absolute convictions that the subject inspires. One's philosophy, one's experiences, one's exposure to the raw edges of human existence, one's religious training, one's attitudes toward life and family and their values, and the moral standards one establishes and seeks to observe, are all likely to influence and to color one's thinking and conclusions about abortion.

In addition, population growth, pollution, poverty, and racial overtones tend to complicate and not to simplify the problem.

Our task, of course, is to resolve the issue by constitutional measurement, free of emotion and of predilection. We seek earnestly to do this, and, because we do, we have inquired into, and in this opinion place some emphasis upon, medical and medical-legal history and what that history reveals about man's attitudes toward the abortion procedure over the centuries. . . .

It perhaps is not generally appreciated that the restrictive criminal abortion laws in effect in a majority of States today are of relatively recent vintage. Those laws, generally proscribing abortion or its attempt at any time during pregnancy except when necessary to preserve the pregnant woman's life, are not of ancient or even of common-law origin. Instead, they derive from statutory changes effected, for the most part, in the latter half of the nineteenth century. . . .

The Constitution does not explicitly mention any right of privacy. In a line of decisions, however, the Court has recognized that a right of personal

SOURCE: *Roe* v. *Wade* (1973)
*In 1970, many colleges were centers of the struggle for civil rights for women and minorities and the anti-Vietnam War movement. (Eds.)

privacy, or a guarantee of certain areas or zones of privacy, does exist under the Constitution. . . .

This right of privacy, whether it be founded in the Fourteenth Amendment's concept of personal liberty and restrictions upon state action, as we feel it is, or, as the District Court determined, in the Ninth Amendment's reservation of rights to the people, is broad enough to encompass a woman's decision whether or not to terminate her pregnancy. The detriment that the State would impose upon the pregnant woman by denying this choice altogether is apparent. Specific and direct harm medically diagnosable even in early pregnancy may be involved. Maternity, or additional offspring, may force upon the woman a distressful life and future. Psychological harm may be imminent. Mental and physical health may be taxed by child care. There is also the distress, for all concerned, associated with the unwanted child, and there is the problem of bringing a child into a family already unable, psychologically and otherwise, to care for it. In other cases, as in this one, the additional difficulties and continuing stigma of unwed motherhood may be involved. All these are factors the woman and her responsible physician necessarily will consider in consultation.

On the basis of elements such as these, appellant and some amici argue that the woman's right is absolute and that she is entitled to terminate her pregnancy at whatever time, in whatever way, and for whatever reason she alone chooses. With this we do not agree. Appellant's arguments that Texas either has no valid interest at all in regulating the abortion decision, or no interest strong enough to support any limitation upon the woman's sole determination, is unpersuasive. The Court's decisions recognizing a right of privacy also acknowledge that some state regulation in areas protected by that right is appropriate. [A] State may properly assert important interests in safeguarding health, in maintaining medical standards, and in protecting potential life. At some point in pregnancy, these respective interests become sufficiently compelling to sustain regulation of the factors that govern the abortion decision. The privacy right involved, therefore, cannot be said to be absolute. . . .

We, therefore, conclude that the right of personal privacy includes the abortion decision, but that this right is not unqualified and must be considered against important state interests in regulation. . . .

The appellee and certain amici argue that the fetus is a "person" within the language and meaning of the Fourteenth Amendment. In support of this, they outline at length and in detail the well-known facts of fetal development. If this suggestion of personhood is established, the appellant's case, of course, collapses, for the fetus's right to life is then guaranteed specifically by the Amendment. The appellant conceded as much on reargument. On the other hand, the appellee conceded on reargument that no case could be cited that holds that a fetus is a person within the meaning of the Fourteenth Amendment.

The Constitution does not define "person" in so many words. Section 1 of the Fourteenth Amendment contains three references to "person." The first, in defining "citizens," speaks of "persons born or naturalized in the United States." The word also appears both in the Due Process Clause and in the Equal Protection Clause. "Person" is used in other places in the Constitution. . . . But in nearly all these instances, the use of the word is such that it has application only postnatally. None indicates, with any assurance, that it has any possible prenatal application.

All this, together with our observation, supra, that throughout the major portion of the nineteenth century prevailing legal abortion practices were far freer than they are today, persuades us that the word "person," as used in the Fourteenth Amendment, does not include the unborn. . . .

President George H. W. Bush Opposes Abortion, 1989

Good afternoon, ladies and gentlemen. This is George Bush in the Oval Office.* And before you begin your march today, on this first Monday of my Presidency, I wanted to take just a few brief moments to restate my firm support of our cause and to share with you my deep personal concern about our American tragedy of abortion on demand.

We are concerned about abortion because it deals with the lives of two human beings, mother and child. I know there are people of good will who disagree, but after years of sober and serious reflection on the issue, this is what I think. I think the Supreme Court's decision in *Roe* versus *Wade* was wrong and should be overturned. I think America needs a human life amendment. And I think when it comes to abortion there's a better way: the way of adoption, the way of life.

I know that this morning several of your leaders had a meeting in the White House with Vice President Quayle. I know, too, that you and hundreds of thousands with you across the country have raised a voice of moral gravity about abortion, a voice of principle, a voice of faith, a full voice that properly asserts and affirms the basic dignity of human life. I'm confident that more and more Americans every year—every day—are hearing your message and taking it to heart.

And, ladies and gentlemen—and, yes, young people as well—I promise you that the President hears you now and stands with you in a cause that must be won.

God bless you all, and God bless life.

SOURCE: *Weekly Compilation of Presidential Documents*, George Bush, January 23, 1989.
*The President spoke at 12:05 P.M. from the Oval Office at the White House via an electronic communications link with the rally site. Participants had gathered on the Ellipse for a march to the Supreme Court on the occasion of the sixteenth anniversary of the Court's decision of *Roe* v. *Wade*, which legalized abortion.

Chapter 16

The New Immigration

Carnival time in Miami's Little Havana.

Immigration in the past four decades has been changing the social demography of the United States. Large numbers of Asians, Latinos, and Africans have been arriving. In no American city can the social changes due to immigration be seen more clearly than in Miami. The essay "The Creation of Cuban Miami" tells of the impact of the wave of Cuban immigrants to that city since the triumph of Fidel Castro in 1959. The communist revolution led by Castro prompted hundreds of thousands of Cubans to flee. At first the elite of Cuban society headed for Florida, but they were followed by the middle class and then in 1980 by many working-class Cubans. Why did so many Cubans decide to settle in Miami, even after initially going to other places in the United States? What has been the impact of these immigrants, both economically and politically, on the character of Miami?

The immigration of so many non-Europeans was made possible because of the elimination of discriminatory laws. A significant change occurred in 1965, when Congress overhauled the immigration system. In place of small quotas for Asians and Africans, the new law gave every nation the same quota. The first document, by Senator Edward Kennedy, points to a new perspective on immigration.

In what ways did the proposed bill, which was later passed, reflect the social climate of the 1960s and the domestic policies of the Johnson administration? What fears regarding the new immigration policy did the senator seek to assuage in his speech?

Though the discriminatory provisions of immigration laws were eliminated in the 1965 legislation, annual immigration quotas meant that not all potential immigrants were able to obtain visas. Consequently, undocumented immigrants made up a substantial number of newcomers. An amnesty for undocumented persons in 1986 granted about three million of these immigrants the right to legalize their status. But many in foreign lands still desired to come to the United States, and if they could not gain legal entrance, they chose to enter without proper papers. The Bureau of the Census estimated that in 2000 there were nearly 9 million undocumented immigrants living in the United States. The second document is a statement by Miguel Torres, an undocumented immigrant. Compare his experiences with those of the Cubans as described in the essay. How do you account for the differences?

While Cubans have settled in Florida, other Hispanics have been heading for Texas, New York, and California. So great has this migration been that the 2000 census revealed that Latinos now outnumber blacks. Of course, Hispanics in the United States represent the cultures of several nations, with Mexicans constituting about two-thirds of the Latino immigrant population. In recent years, Hispanics have been moving to states and towns where few had gone before. The third document from *Hispanic* magazine discusses such settlement in North Carolina. What drew the first of these migrants to that state, and what led to the subsequent rapid growth in North Carolina's Hispanic population?

Newcomers to the United States in the last four decades have come from all over the world. Asians, benefiting from changes in immigration laws, represented more than 40 percent of all immigrants arriving in the 1980s and 1990s. They have grown from less than 1 percent of our nation's population to 4 percent. More blacks have immigrated from Africa and the West Indies during the last forty years than during the entire era of slavery. The final document, a report from the *Wall Street Journal,* discusses the workplace of an Illinois corporation that employs 1,200 workers who speak no less than twenty languages. A similar story could be related of public schools in cities impacted by immigration. How does the plant manage such a diverse workforce? What are the implications of such diversity for the future of American society?

ESSAY

The Creation of Cuban Miami

Guillermo J. Grenier and Lisandro Perez

Greater Miami has experienced a quarter-century of profound changes that have transformed the city from a midsized tourist haven into a socially and economically complex metropolis. The history of Miami since the early 1960s has been driven by one particular phenomenon: immigration. Dade County's history can be divided into two basic chapters: before the immigrants and after the immigrants. . . .

The very creation of Miami hinged on the actions of northern retirees. In the 1880s, Henry Flagler, millionaire partner of John D. Rockefeller in Standard Oil, moved to Florida for his health and found a new career as a railroad and real estate magnate. A decade later he was persuaded to extend his rail line from Palm Beach to Biscayne Bay by Julia Tuttle, a widow from Cleveland who had relocated to a 600-acre tract on the northern bank of the Miami River where it flows into the bay. It is the core of downtown Miami today.

The railroad provided the necessary transportation link to fuel the local economy. In those early days, Bahamian immigrants provided the local unskilled labor, outnumbering Black Americans who came to Miami primarily from northern Florida and Georgia. When Miami was incorporated in 1896 with a petition bearing 368 signatures, only about 200 residents of the locality were White. The new city's promoters solicited the remainder of the signees among the local Black residents, primarily immigrants from the Bahamas.

The enfranchisement of Blacks did not last long. The city officials elected as a result of the process of incorporation were White. Since the Bahamians considered themselves the social equals of Whites, it was important for the new city leaders to impress upon local Black citizens the appropriate behavior standards of "southern Negroes."

Decades before Disney World, the state's laissez-faire policies gave northern entrepreneurs license to create fantasy real estate and resort ventures. Venetian and Spanish-style housing developments sprang up, while the indigenous mangrove coast was plowed away to make room for luxury hotels and wide beaches. Without the trees to hold the sand, the ocean washed it away. The hotel proprietors arranged for sand to be pumped back onto the beaches.

SOURCE: Silvia Pedraza and Ruben Rumbaut, eds., *Origins and Destinies: Immigration, Race, and Ethnicity in America*, 360–372. Copyright © 1996. Reprinted with permission of Wadsworth, a division of Thomson Learning: www.thomsonrights.com. Fax (800) 730-2215.

Miami experienced dizzying growth between 1910 and 1925. Its population grew from 5,000 to 146,000 and the development of Miami Beach began full throttle upon completion of a causeway across the bay. By the early 1920s, the planned residential community of Coral Gables, surrounded by lush, tropical vegetation, was constructed and the doors of the University of Miami were opened.

The boom came to an abrupt end in 1926, when a major hurricane devastated the city, followed by years of financial crisis and the Great Depression. By the mid-1930s, the local economy had begun to recover and a significant influx of Jewish working-class and middle-class migrants from cities in the Northeast led to the proliferation of distinctive small hotels and apartments in what became the Art Deco district of south Miami Beach.

World War II began the next development boom that picked up steam in the 1950s. Many servicemen and women stationed in south Florida during the war decided to stay. Refugees from northern winters opted for Florida on an ever-larger scale, and the popularization of air travel brought Miami vacations within reach of growing numbers of Americans across the country. Most of the large hotels of Miami Beach (including the Fontainebleau, opened with great fanfare in 1954) date from this era. Between 1940 and 1950 the population of metropolitan Miami (Dade County) nearly doubled, rising from 268,000 to 505,000; by the 1960s it had reached nearly 1 million.

As Miami acquired the dimensions of a large metropolis, its economy began to diversify, and it took on an increasingly important role as a port city in the commerce between the United States, the Caribbean, and Latin America. Miami's image as a tropical paradise for tourists had faded by the 1960s. Eventually, tourists to Florida preferred Walt Disney World, the fantasy creation near Orlando in Central Florida. Meanwhile, those seeking sun and sea vacations increasingly found them further south in the Bahamas, Jamaica, Puerto Rico, and Yucatán.

Even before the massive arrival of Cubans in the early 1960s, the influx of northern "Anglos" (as non-Hispanic Whites are called in Miami) had slowed to a trickle, becoming negative after 1970. The next wave of Miami's development would be spurred by migration from Latin America, especially from Cuba.

Before the 1960s, Miami's population consisted largely of Black and White southern migrants and their descendants, transplanted northerners (including many Jews), and Bahamian and other Caribbean Blacks and their descendants. . . . In the past twenty-five years, however, a very large number of Latin Americans and a substantial Haitian population added to the mix with dramatic impact.

Cubans fleeing Castro's Cuba, Miami's principal immigrant group, began arriving in significant numbers in the early 1960s, following the 1959 Cuban Revolution and the failure in 1961 of the Bay of Pigs invasion. The

U.S. government encouraged and aided the flow. . . . While significant numbers of Cubans settled in New York and New Jersey, Miami was the preferred destination of the vast majority, making Cubans Miami's most visible minority. Their numbers were considerably increased by the Mariel boatlift of 1980, which brought 125,000 Cubans to the United States, the majority of whom settled in Miami. In 1990, there were 953,400 persons of Hispanic origin or descent in Dade County, representing slightly more than 49 percent of the entire metropolitan population. Cubans accounted for about 59 percent of Miami's Hispanics. . . .

Southern Florida now has the highest proportion of foreign-born residents of any U.S. city. The two largest incorporated areas within Greater Miami occupy, nationally, the first and second positions in the percentage of their residents who were born in a foreign country. Hialeah, a working-class suburb of Miami that has received large numbers of Cubans since the 1960s, is by far the most populated area by immigrants in the entire nation: 70.4 percent of its population was reported in 1990 to be foreign-born. The city of Miami, second in the nation, had a proportion of 59.7 percent foreign-born.

In contrast to the growth of the foreign-born and Latin population, the White non-Hispanic population has been decreasing, in relative terms, since 1960, and in absolute terms since 1970. From a peak in the 1950s of 85 percent, it is expected to decline by the year 2000 to around 30 percent of the total, barely more than the figure for Blacks. The decline is evident throughout the metropolitan area, including the suburbs and Miami's elite residential areas.

Miami has always been a service-centered economy, but after the arrival of the Cubans, the focus of those services shifted from tourism to Latin America. Beginning in the 1960s, Miami came to displace New Orleans as the country's principal trade entrepôt with that region. By 1980, 100 multinational corporations had their Latin American headquarters in Miami and Miami stood second only to New York as an international banking center. By the mid-1980s, Miami International Airport was the ninth-busiest airport in the world in passengers and the sixth largest in air cargo tonnage. About 160,000 workers, one-fifth of its labor force, were directly or indirectly employed in airport and aviation activities. By the late 1980s, Miami's industrial profile was similar to other newer American cities in which the economy was led by services, wholesale trade, finance, insurance, and real estate.

The existence of the Cuban enclave played a pivotal role in Miami's economic transformation. Cubans frequently headed the import and export companies, the banks that financed the transactions, and the transportation and service companies that moved goods and services. Over 25,000 Hispanic businesses exist in Dade County, the vast majority of which are small enterprises that have been described as the true engines of

Miami's economic growth. . . . But many of the most powerful economic corporations are also Latin-owned and operated. While Miami holds only 5 percent of the U.S. Hispanic population, it has close to half of the forty largest Hispanic-owned industrial and commercial firms in the country. By the mid to late 1980s, 40 percent of Miami's banks were owned by Latins . . . , as were numerous Latin insurance companies, shipping firms, and innumerable import and export establishments. Some of the most important developers are Latins, one of which became the first Latin to head the Greater Miami Chamber of Commerce.

The city's emergence as the "capital of the Caribbean" has reinforced these trends in immigration. Miami now is the most desired migration point of many Latins, especially the elite and middle classes of the Caribbean and Central America. In the late 1980s, . . . a broader, working-class flow emerged, first from Nicaragua, then from other Central American nations as well as Colombia, the Dominican Republic, and Puerto Rico. Meanwhile, the frustration of democracy in Haiti increased migration pressures there, despite U.S. policies designed to repress the Haitian flow.

This transformation of Miami's demographic profile got under way precisely when Black Americans were beginning to achieve the civil rights that had been denied them since the city's founding at the end of the last century. The new White immigrants, the Cubans, soon received the benefits of being a minority. While Blacks have experienced some progress, the White Cuban immigrants leaped over Blacks, quickly garnering the political and economic gains that still elude Black Americans. Meanwhile, the response by many Anglos has been to abandon the city. "White flight" decreased the number of non-Latin Whites in Dade County by 24 percent between 1980 and 1990.

Much of this decline is attributable to the decrease in the elderly population, once so characteristic of the greater Miami area. In 1980 the elderly comprised 52 percent of the population of Miami Beach, the highest proportion for any city of comparable size in the United States. Although Miami Beach had been founded by wealthy White Anglo-Saxons, with anti-Semitic restrictions in housing, hotels, and private clubs that persisted for several decades, the retirement wave made it the most Jewish of American cities as well. By 1950, the population of Miami Beach was half Jewish; by 1970, the proportion had reached 80 percent.

All this began to change in the 1970s, in the context of a stagnant tourist economy and the diversion of the retirement flow to other parts of Florida. By 1980, the Jewish component of the population had declined to 66 percent, falling even more steeply thereafter to reach 40 percent in 1990. The decline of the elderly component of the population was just as rapid, dropping to 30 percent in 1990. . . .

. . . The rise of Cuban Miami as the largest concentration of Cubans in the United States—and the third largest Hispanic community in this country, after New York and Los Angeles—effectively starts in 1959 with the exodus from the island that resulted from the social transformations effected by the Cuban Revolution. Prior to that time, Miami, largely because of its youth and weak economic structure, was never the principal destination of Cuban immigrants to the United States. Sizable Cuban communities thrived in New York, Key West, New Orleans, and Ybor City, on the outskirts of Tampa, in the nineteenth century. New York was still the premier destination for migrants from the island in the period between World War II and the rise of Fidel Castro's government.

This pattern of migration started changing with the creation of rail and highway links between Miami and Key West and their extensions to Havana by way of regular ferry service. Air service between Miami, Key West, and Havana dates back to the 1920s and represents a pioneering effort in the history of passenger aviation. Those transportation links served to make Miami the principal staging area for the increasingly close relationship developing between Cuba and the Florida peninsula. In the year 1948, for example, Cuba led all countries in the world in the volume of passengers exchanged with the United States. . . .

While Miami did not have the employment opportunities Cuban immigrants required during the first half of the twentieth century, it did receive those seeking refuge from the shifting fortunes of the island's turbulent political history. Two deposed Cuban Presidents, Gerardo Machado (in 1933) and Carlos Prío Socarrás (in 1952), made their homes in Miami. A prominent Cuban politician of the 1940s built Miami's baseball stadium. Even Fidel Castro spent time in Miami in the 1950s.

As leader of the 1959 Revolution, Castro initiated a process of change that, in its rapidity and pervasiveness, alienated large sectors of the Cuban population . . . and contributed to the creation of Cuban Miami. . . .

The concentration of Cubans in Miami, starting in the mid-1970s, was first preceded by their intentional dispersion throughout the United States. The Cuban Refugee Program was established in February 1961 as a federal effort to provide assistance in handling the large influx of people coming from Cuba. One of its purposes was to ease the demographic and economic pressures that the influx was exerting on south Florida. A resettlement program was established through which families arriving from Cuba were given assistance if they immediately relocated away from Miami. According to a Cuban Refuge Program Fact Sheet . . . , 300,232 persons were resettled away from Miami between February 1961 and August 1978, approximately 64 percent of all Cubans then arriving in the United States. The bulk of the resettled Cubans went to New York, New Jersey, California, and Illinois. In 1965, 42 percent of the Cuban population in the United States lived in Dade County; in 1970, 40 percent. Resettlement reached its peak in the late 1960s. Thus, contrary to the experience of most immigrant groups for whom concentration in a city or region formed part of the process of adjustment to the

United States, Cubans underwent a process of intentional dispersion early in their history of immigration.

In the mid-1970s, however, a process of concentration in Miami was well under way as many resettled Cubans decided to make their home in southern Florida. By 1980, the U.S. census found about 52 percent of all U.S. Cubans living in Greater Miami. The concentration of Cubans in south Florida increased during the 1980s as the majority of the *Marielitos* settled in Miami, where they could find employment in a familiar cultural environment. By the 1990 census, 57 percent of all U.S. Cubans lived in Dade County. The process of concentration in Miami is likely to continue in the 1990s due to the aging of the large middle-aged cohort that left Cuba during the early 1960s and were resettled away from Miami.

In the mid-1990s, the "open arms" U.S. policy toward Cuban migrants shifted dramatically. The massive exodus of rafters in the summer of 1994, initiated by the Cuban government's decision not to impede their departure, prompted the United States to intercept vessels on the high seas and send their occupants to detention camps outside the United States. The attorney general vowed that the detained Cubans would never enter this country. In May 1995, in the interest of ending the indefinite detention of more than 20,000 Cubans at the Guantànamo Naval Base, the United States announced that the detainees would be processed for admission to the United States. However, recognizing the prevailing anti-immigration sentiment, the move was balanced with an unprecedented announcement: future rafters would be intercepted and returned directly to Cuba, under the terms of an agreement reached with the Cuban government. The only way Cubans will be allowed to enter the United States from Cuba will be through the normal visa application process conducted by the U.S. Interest Section in Havana. At least 20,000 people will presumably be admitted every year through that process.

Cuban migration to the United States will continue, but the exile era has officially ended. Cubans are no longer recognized as refugees by the U.S. government. The newly established policy for their admission into this country does not differ in any essential way from the policy toward other nationalities: one enters only through the regular visa process; those attempting to enter without authorization will be returned. In effect, there has been, for the first time, a normalization of one aspect of U.S.–Cuba relations.

. . . Today persons of Cuban origin represent Miami's largest ethnic group. Cubans account for 56 percent of Greater Miami's foreign-born population and a majority of all Hispanics in the area. About 29 percent of Dade County's 1990 population was of Cuban birth or descent.

The demographic importance of the Cuban presence in Miami is evident in a myriad of ways. The "Cubanness" of the area is manifested not only in demonstrable terms, such as economic activities and cultural events, but also in its more intangible "ambience." Rieff, a New Yorker who has written on Miami, noted that Cubans have largely taken control of the "atmosphere" of the city. . . .

More than thirty years after the start of the exodus, today Cubans have a sense of "rootedness" in Miami. Miami is the capital and mecca of Cubans in the United States. As Rieff . . . expressed it, "Cubans are probably the only people who really do feel comfortable in Dade County these days. . . . Miami is their town now." Nearly 70 percent of the Hispanic population of Greater Miami, Cubans can be found throughout most of the metropolitan area. Generally the heaviest concentrations of Hispanics within the county are found along a belt running west from downtown (which is located east of Biscayne Bay) all the way to the western edges of the metropolitan area.

Since the 1960s the settlement of Cubans along this belt has proceeded from east to west, emanating largely from the area known as "Little Havana," which is located within the city of Miami, some twelve to fifteen city blocks directly west of downtown and stretching west along Calle Ocho for about fifteen city blocks.

Middle-income Cubans, and especially professionals, are now hard to find in Little Havana. As with so many other immigrant groups, their upward mobility has taken them to more suburban areas. The current residents of Little Havana are likely to be blue-collar and service workers, the elderly, the poor, and recent immigrants, including other Latin American immigrants. . . .

A strong and diversified entrepreneurial activity is responsible for the enclave's most important overall feature: institutional completeness. Cubans in Miami can, if they wish, literally live out their lives within the ethnic community. The wide range of sales and services, including professional services, available within the community makes that possible.

Three factors have been identified as promoting Cubans' economic and political activity in Miami: (1) structural factors arising from the human capital Cubans brought with them and their geographical concentration in Miami . . . , (2) the role of the U.S. government in providing aid to the arriving Cuban refugees . . . ; and (3) the creation of a collective Cuban-American political identity arising from the interplay of the U.S. state and Cuban exile counterrevolutionary organizations.

The favorable reception by the U.S. government entailed a "direct line" for Cuban exile leaders to the centers of political power in Washington. Unlike other immigrant and ethnic minorities who struggled painfully for years or even generations to gain access to the corridors of power, Cuban leaders accessed it almost from the start. This window of opportunity greatly boosted the Cubans in the 1960s and the Miami economy in general. Waves of Cuban immigrants stimulated demand and received substantial subsidies from the federal government. With a high rate of labor force participation, especially among women, the Cubans also contributed significantly to productivity growth. The 1973 to 1974 recession even had an indirect benefit for Cubans. Construction, one of the growth sectors during the boom, almost completely collapsed, spurring many American residents to flee Dade County. In the subsequent recovery of the late 1970s a de facto segmentation of the industry emerged, with Latins becoming the leaders in home construction and Anglos maintaining dominance in large-scale commercial construction. This division reflected an even more important development within the community, the emergence of the Cuban enclave. . . .

. . . During the 1980s Cubans in Miami were able to establish pivotal local power, exercised through an increasing number of elected officials and organizations such as the Cuban American National Foundation, the Latin Builders Association, the Hispanic Builders Association, and the Latin Chamber of Commerce. By the late 1980s, the City of Miami, Hialeah, Sweetwater, West Miami, and Hialeah Gardens all had Cuban-born mayors. The city manager and the county manager were Cubans. Cubans controlled the City Commission and constituted more than a third of the county delegation to the state legislature. After Claude Pepper died, a Cuban woman, Ileana Ros-Lehtinen, won his U.S. House of Representatives seat. Most recently, Lincoln Díaz-Balart, a Cuban-born politician elected to the state legislature in the mid-1980s, joined Ros-Lehtinen as the second Cuban American from Miami in Congress. Nowhere else in America, nor even in American history, have first-generation immigrants so quickly and so thoroughly appropriated political power.

Perhaps for this reason, no aspect of Cuban Miami attracts more national and international attention than its politics. Even after more than thirty years, Miami remains a community of exiles, largely preoccupied with the political status of the homeland. At the same time, however, Miami's Cubans demonstrated a strong participation in the U.S. political system at the local and state levels.

. . . Although the enclave favors the retention of the culture of the homeland, delaying the process of acculturation, it is unlikely that Cubans in the United States will be an exception to the usual intergenerational shift toward greater acculturation and assimilation. English is the principal language among Cubans who have lived all or most of their lives in the United States. Sharp intergenerational differences exist among Cubans in Miami, with alienation between parents and children usually found in Cuban families with interactional problems. . . . An important focus of these intergenerational tensions are the conflicting value orientations with respect to dependence and independence. . . . Cuban culture foments the continued dependence of children on their parents, even in the teenage years and beyond. Cuban children, however, are more likely to have internalized the norms of independence commonly found in U.S. society. One adaptation that reduces intergenerational tension is "biculturality," by which each generation adjusts to the other generation's cultural preferences: "parents learn how to remain loyal to their ethnic background while becoming skilled in interacting with their youngsters' Americanized values and behaviors, and vice versa." . . .

DOCUMENTS

"Favoritism Based on Nationality Will Disappear," 1965

Mr. [Edward] Kennedy [of Massachusetts]. Mr. President, the bill we are considering today accomplishes major reforms in our immigration policy. This bill is not concerned with increasing immigration to this country, nor will it lower any of the high standards we apply in selection of immigrants. The basic change it makes is the elimination of the national origins quota system in line with the recommendations of the last four Presidents of the United States and Members of Congress from both parties.

For forty-one years the immigration policy of our country has been crippled by this system. Because of it we have never been able to achieve the annual quota use authorized by law. We have discriminated in favor of some people over others, contrary to our basic principles as a nation, simply on the basis of birth. We have separated families needlessly. We have been forced to forgo the talents of many professionals whose skills were needed to cure, to teach, and to enhance the lives of Americans.

The present law has caused thousands of instances of personal hardship, of which every senator is aware. Several times Congress has tried to correct the twisted results of the national origins system through emergency legislation. Six times between 1948 and 1962 laws were passed for the admission of refugees. Four times between 1957 and 1962 we have made special provisions for relatives of American citizens or orphans. In addition, each year we are called upon to consider thousands of private bills to accommodate persons caught in the backwash of this origins system. . . .

The new policy in the bill before us was developed under the administration of President Kennedy by experts both in Congress and the executive branch. Extensive hearings were held both last year and this, in the Senate and the House. The Senate Immigration Subcommittee has sat regularly since last February. We have heard over fifty witnesses. I can report, Mr. President, that opposition to this measure is minimal. Many of the private

SOURCE: U.S., Congress, Senate, *Congressional Record,* 89th Cong., 1st sess., 111, September 17, 20–22, 1965, 24225–29 passim, 24231–33 passim, 24446–51 passim, 24467–68 passim.

organizations who differed with us in the past now agree the national origins system must be eliminated.

The current bill phases out the national origins system over a three-year period. Beginning July 1, 1968, our immigration policy will be based on the concept of "first come, first served." We no longer will ask a man where he was born. Instead we will ask if he seeks to join his family, or if he can help meet the economic and social needs of the Nation. Favoritism based on nationality will disappear. Favoritism based on individual worth and qualifications will take its place. . . .

. . . The percentage increase that immigration will represent is infinitesimally small. This legislation opens no "floodgate." Rather it admits about the same number of immigrants that current law would allow, but for the national origins restriction.

Another fear is that immigrants from nations other than those in northern Europe will not assimilate into our society. The difficulty with this argument is that it comes 40 years too late. Hundreds of thousands of such immigrants have come here in recent years, and their adjustment has been notable. At my request, many voluntary agencies that assist new immigrants conducted lengthy surveys covering people who have arrived since the late 1940's. The results would be most gratifying to any American. I have only found five cases of criminal complaints involving immigrants in our studies of many thousands. Unemployment rates among these people are much lower than the national average; business ownership between 10 percent and 15 percent higher; home ownership as high as 80 percent in one city and averaging about 30 percent elsewhere. . . .

In whatever other definition we wish to give to assimilate, we would find our new residents doing well. Family stability is found to be excellent; cases of immigrants on public welfare are difficult to find; 85 to 95 percent of those eligible have become naturalized citizens, and so forth.

The fact is, Mr. President, that the people who comprise the new immigration—the type which this bill would give preference to—are relatively well educated and well to do. They are familiar with American ways. They share our ideals. Our merchandise, our styles, our patterns of living are an integral part of their own countries. Many of them learn English as a second language in their schools. In an age of global television and the universality of American culture, their assimilation, in a real sense, begins before they come here.

Finally, the fear is raised that under this bill immigrants will be taking jobs away from Americans at a time we find it difficult to lower our unemployment rate below 4 percent. Mr. President, I have already described the more stringent controls that this bill gives to the Secretary of Labor to insure against any adverse effects of immigration on American labor. I would also point out that this measure has the complete support of the AFL–CIO; support that would not be forthcoming if the fear of job loss for Americans were real. . . .

An Undocumented Mexican Immigrant:
Miguel Torres, 1977

Miguel Torres is a slight, shy youth of twenty with a pale skin and El Greco features. He works in a mushroom plant in California. He has entered the United States illegally four times in the past year, and he has been caught three times. He told his story through a trusted interpreter.

I was born in a small town in the state of Michoacán in Mexico. When I was fifteen, I went to Mexico City with my grandmother and my mother. I worked in a parking lot, a big car lot. People would come in and they'd say, "Well, park my car." and I'd give them a ticket and I'd park the car and I'd be there, you know, watching the cars. I got paid in tips.

But I wanted to come to the United States to work and to earn more money. My uncle was here, and I thought if I could come to him, I could live with him and work and he would help me.

It's not possible to get papers to come over now. So when I decided to come, I went to Tijuana in Mexico. There's a person there that will get in contact with you. They call him the Coyote. He walks around town, and if he sees someone wandering around alone, he says, "Hello, do you have relatives in the United States?" And if you say yes, he says, "Do you want to visit them?" And if you say yes, he says he can arrange it through a friend. It costs $250 or $300.

The Coyote rounded up me and five other guys, and then he got in contact with a guide to take us across the border. We had to go through the hills and the desert, and we had to swim through a river. I was a little scared. Then we come to a highway and a man was there with a van, pretending to fix his motor. Our guide said hello, and the man jumped into the car and we ran and jumped in, too. He began to drive down the highway fast and we knew we were safe in the United States. He took us to San Isidro that night, and the next day he took us all the way here to Watsonville. I had to pay him $250 and then, after I'd been here a month, he came back and I had to give him $50 more. He said I owed him that.

I was here for two months before I started working, and then my uncle got me a job, first in the celery fields picking celery, washing it, packing it, and later picking prunes. Then, all of a sudden, one day the Immigration showed up, and I ran and I hid in a river that was next to the orchard. The man saw me and he questioned me, and he saw I didn't have any papers. So they put me in a van and took me to Salinas, and there was some more illegals there and they put us in buses and took us all the way to Mexicali near the border. We were under guard; the driver and another one that sleeps

SOURCE: Joan Morrison and Charlotte Fox Zabusky, *American Mosaic: The Immigrant Experience in the Words of Those Who Lived It,* 347–49. Copyright © 1980 by Joan Morrison and Charlotte Fox Zabusky. Currently available in paperback from the University of Pittsburgh Press. Reprinted with permission of John Ware Literary Agency.

while one drives. The seats are like hard boards. We'd get up from one side and rub, you know, that side a little bit and then sit on the other side for a while and then rub that side because it's so hard. It was a long trip.

When we arrived in Mexicali, they let us go. We caught a bus to Tijuana, and then at Tijuana, that night, we found the Coyote again and we paid him and we came back the next day. I had to pay $250 again, but this time he knew me and he let me pay $30 then and $30 each week. Because he knew me, you know. He trusted me.

We came through the mountains that time. We had to walk through a train tunnel. It all lasted maybe about three hours, through the tunnel. It was short; for me it was short. We're used to walking, you know. Over in Mexico we have to walk like ten miles to go to work or to go home or to go to school, so we're used to walking. To me it was a short distance to walk for three hours. And after we got out of the tunnel, we got into a car; and from there, from the tunnel, we came all the way into Los Angeles. That was the second time. We didn't see any border patrol either time.

The second time I was here for three months. My uncle managed to get me a job in the mushroom plant. I was working there when the Immigration came. There's this place where they blow air between the walls to make it cool and I hid there. And I was watching. The Immigration was looking around the plant everywhere. There was another illegal there, and he just kept on picking the mushrooms. He'd only been back a couple of days himself. The Immigration walked over there, and that kid turned around and looked at the Immigration and said, "What's the matter? What happened?" And the Immigration looked at him and said, "Oh, nothing," and the kid kept right on picking mushrooms. Yet he was an illegal! He knew how to act, play it cool. If you just sit tight they don't know you're illegal.

Well, the Immigration looked between the walls then and he caught me again. That was the second time. They put handcuffs on me with another guy and we were handcuffed together all the way from California to Mexicali.

Altogether I've been caught three times this year and made the trip over here four times. It's cost me one thousand dollars but it's still better than what I was making in Mexico City.

It's the money. When you come back here you get more money here than you do over there. Right now, the most that I'd be getting in Mexico would be from 25 to 30 pesos a day, which is maybe $2.00, $2.50. And here, with overtime, sometimes I make $150 a week. Things are expensive here, but it's expensive over there, too. And I like the way people live here. All the—what do you call it—all the facilities that you have here, all the things you can get and everything.

The boss at the mushroom factory doesn't ask for papers. He doesn't say anything about it. The last time, he hired me back as soon as I got back here, without any questions.

I learned to hide my money when the Immigration catch me. You know, if you have a lot on you, they take you fifteen or twenty miles from the border in Mexico. But if you have just two dollars or so, they let you go right in Tijuana. Then it's easier to come back. You can just walk right down the street and find the Coyote or someone like him. A man I know was hitch-hiking along the road near San Diego and someone picked him up and it was the Immigration man who had just brought him back to Mexico! The Immigration laughed and said, "You got back faster than I did." Of course, he took him back to Mexico again then. But that man is back in Watsonville now, working in the brussels sprouts. It takes a longer time for the Immigration to catch us than it does for us to come back. [*Laughs.*]

I'd like to be able to stay here, to live here and work; but the only way now is to find someone that'll say, "Well, I'll marry you, I'll fix your papers for you." There's a lot of them who do that. I'd be willing to if I could find someone that would do it for me. You pay them, you know. You don't sleep together or even live in the same house, but they marry you. A long time ago you could fix up papers for your nephew or brother, a friend, a cousin. It was real easy then. But now it has to be close relations: mother, father, wife, son, or daughter. My uncle can't do it for me. The only way I could do it would be if I could marry an American citizen.

I'd like to learn English because it would be easier for me. There is a night school here, but I don't like to go because after work I like to go out and mess around and goof off. [*Laughs.*] Maybe I'll go later. If I could just learn a tiny bit of English, you know, I could turn around and tell the Immigration, "What's the matter with you? What do you want?" and I wouldn't be recognized as an illegal.

The Hispanic Boom, 2002

On a gray Sunday morning, the Iglesia Cristiana Wesleyana in Kernersville, North Carolina, is filled with families sitting on blue-cushioned pews under the glare of fluorescent lights. At the pulpit, a small wooden cross adorning the wall behind him, Pastor Fermín Bocanegra, a small man who speaks with big, passionate gestures, greets his congregation in Spanish. Toddlers play in the aisles as Bocanegra prays out loud, and asks the congregation to join him. He prays that no one will lose his job. He prays that no one's car will break down. And he asks for everyone to remember that no matter how bad things may seem, they were worse where they came from.

Bocanegra, who came to North Carolina from his native Peru in 1968 to attend college, was once lonesome for the sound of Spanish voices. Today,

SOURCE: Jane Kitchen, "The Hispanic Boom," *Hispanic* (January–February, 2002), 32–34. Reprinted with permission from *Hispanic* Magazine.

he ministers to more than 300 families, a small section of North Carolina's growing Hispanic population. In the past 10 years, North Carolina has seen a 394 percent increase in its Latino population, making it one of the fastest-growing states for Hispanics in the country. The congregation of the Iglesia Cristiana Wesleyana, the majority of whom are recent Mexican immigrants, mirrors the state's Hispanic population, which is 65 percent Mexican. In fact, according to Nolo Martínez, director of Hispanic Affairs for the Office of the Governor, the Mexican population in North Carolina is growing at 600 percent, faster than anywhere else in the country.

The first generation of Hispanics to come to North Carolina were single males, who worked in the agriculture industry. "It was a temporary mission to send money home," says Martínez. Now the new population is more permanent. "Families have joined those single males," he says, "everyone from wife to grandpa."

As the population has grown, Hispanics have branched out to work in other areas of the economy—jobs that don't necessarily require proficiency in English, such as manufacturing, textiles, and construction. And as more Hispanics have landed those jobs, word has gotten out that there is work in North Carolina.

Roberto Camacho, 28, came to the United States four years ago from Mexico, but has only been in North Carolina three months. He moved to Charlotte from New York after he heard about a construction job from his cousin-in-law. Today, he is working for Formco Concrete Forming helping to build a new science building at the University of North Carolina, Greensboro. He gestures to the men around him. "Everybody here is from Mexico," he says. "Everybody here came here because they heard from someone else [that there were jobs]."

Greg Troutman, 22, a supervisor at Formco and an American who's been working construction since he was 14, says he has definitely seen an increase in the number of Hispanics, especially in the past four years. "These guys will work," he says. "You can't get [Americans] black or white to work, but these guys will work."

The demand for workers, and particularly construction workers, has grown with the increase in the overall population in North Carolina, ranked the ninth fastest-growing state in the 2000 Census; its total population increased 21.4 percent between 1990 and 2000. Hispanic workers have become vital to North Carolina's economy and workforce; 95 percent of the construction jobs in Charlotte, and 90 percent of the construction jobs in Raleigh, are held by Hispanics, according to Martínez.

"Originally, they took the jobs no one else wanted," says Claudia Main, a member of the Hickory Community Relations Council. Main says Hickory has attracted Hispanics for jobs in textiles, fiber-optics and furniture manufacturing.

Mark Sills, executive director of Faith Action, a non-profit advocacy group in Greensboro, tells the story of a man who traveled to North Carolina from where he'd been working in Alabama. "He spent his last penny getting a bus ticket to Greensboro because he heard there was work," Sills says. "Word has been out all over the country—and I mean that literally— that there are jobs here."

But the job growth in North Carolina may be slowing for Hispanics. With recent downturns in the economy, Sills anticipates a slowing of the growth in the Hispanic community statewide, but not a shrinkage.

"The population that is already here has put down roots," he says. "They've purchased homes, started businesses." Add to this the fact that borders are now more tightly regulated than ever, and many people—both documented and undocumented—who would normally head home in times of economic slowdown are staying, Sills says, because they're afraid they won't be able to come back.

And those who are staying are contributing to the growth. The 2002 Latino Legislative Agenda report, put out by El Pueblo, a non-profit community-based organization in Durham, suggests that because so many Hispanic women in North Carolina are at peak childbearing age, the potential for population increase is "enormous." Experts at Faith Action estimate the Hispanic population in 2001 to have climbed 28 percent from the 2000 Census figures, which Sills says is due to both new births and new arrivals.

But despite the tremendous growth, North Carolina's Hispanic population is only 4.7 percent overall, still nowhere near states like New York (15.1%), Florida (16.8%), Texas (32%) or California (32.4%). But it is the growth that's caught some North Carolinians off-guard.

"The problem is that North Carolina wasn't prepared for such a huge increase in the Hispanic population," says Cristina Roche, a board member of the Hispanic League of the Piedmont Triad, and a native of Argentina. "We never thought we'd have to learn a second language. [Hispanics] were always here, but in the form of migrant workers. Now, they're in the hospitals, having babies, getting sick. They're in the workforce—they're starting their own companies."

Roche, a middle-school Spanish teacher, recently started her own company, Language Links, which provides Spanish lessons to the corporate world. She works with companies like Sara Lee, a major employer in the Piedmont Triad area of North Carolina, who want to train employees supervising a large number of Hispanic workers. At first, Roche held on to her middle-school teaching job, but as the demand for her corporate language classes grew, she soon realized it was a full-time venture. Today, she employs four Spanish teachers, and has recently branched out to teach classes outside of the corporate world, which are frequented by policemen, health-care workers—anyone exposed to Spanish-speaking populations.

North Carolina's Hispanic population is also very young; one-third are under 18. In the Winston-Salem Forsyth County School System, María Zazzarino coordinates the Newcomer Center, opened in 2000 with a federal grant in response to the increased number of Limited English

Proficient (LEP) students that area was seeing. The first year they were open, the Newcomer Center enrolled 1800 students in the 68 schools in the system. "People wanted to help [the parents]," says Zazzarino, "but often they couldn't—they didn't have anyone who could communicate with them."

Back at the basement of the Iglesia Cristiana Wesleyana, Pastor Bocanegra holds free dental clinics after Sunday services. He got a good deal on dental chairs and equipment from a retiring dentist, turned a former women's restroom into an X-ray room, and found local dentists to donate their time. But because none of the volunteer dentists speak Spanish, Bocanegra often runs back and forth, translating for the patients. Last week, he says, they saw 43 patients and he translated for all them.

Still, Bocanegra doesn't plan to stop there. He hopes to open a daycare, build a soccer field, provide pre-natal and pediatric care, and start a family resource center for the area's Hispanics. His vision, he says, "is not just to preach, but to change their life."

And life is changing for both Hispanics and non-Hispanics in North Carolina. The state has recently seen its first Latino elected to municipal office. John Herrera, founder of El Pueblo and co-founder of the Latino Community Credit Union was recently elected to the Carrboro Board of Aldermen, and is the highest-ranking elected Latino Democrat in North Carolina. "I want Latino kids in North Carolina to start thinking of having the privilege of dreaming," he says. "Now, our kids can dream of being senators, or even President."

Multiculturalism in the Workplace, 1998

MORTON GROVE, Ill.—Draped from the ceiling in 3Com Corp.'s sprawling modem factory in this Chicago suburb is a sign of the times: 65 different national flags, each representing the origin of at least one person who has worked here since it opened 2½ years ago.

The plant employs 1,200 people, the vast majority immigrants. They speak more than 20 languages, including Tagalog, Gujarati and Chinese. English, of varying degrees, ties them together.

"If there's a problem, I call over somebody who speaks the person's language to help," says Thai Chung, a 33-year-old refugee from Vietnam who manages Line 12, one of a dozen assembly lines.

That doesn't always work. A few days ago, Mr. Chung, a wiry man who spends much of his day striding up and down his line, wanted a janitor to clean up some grease. He spoke to him in English but obviously wasn't understood even after repeating himself slowly. He thought the man might be Polish; so he enlisted Vesna Stevanovic, one of the assemblers on his line. But she's from Serbia and couldn't speak to him, either. "I'm not even sure he's Polish," says Ms. Stevanovic, gazing over the frames of pink eyeglasses. "I don't know what he is."

The janitor eventually got the message. Nobody knows how. Stella Foy, a gruff 57-year-old Chicago native who also works on the line, says simply: "Around here, you point a lot."

Many factories, as they hire more immigrants, are being plunged into an industrial Tower of Babel. Earlier waves of immigrants tended to have more in common, such as the East Europeans who flocked to the steel mills a century ago. Now factories, running faster and using increasingly complex equipment, might seem to need such commonality among their workers more than ever.

. . . Churning out modems around the clock, 3Com's workers could hardly be more diverse. Urbane Asians with multiple college degrees work alongside people only recently arrived from Central American villages. Serbs work with Bosnian Muslims, as well as Iraqis, Peruvians and South Africans. Managers think at least a third of their workers wouldn't mind if asked to work Christmas—as they were two years ago—because they don't celebrate it.

Overcoming language barriers is just one of the challenges. Some immigrants come from countries where you seldom say "please," and certainly not to someone you consider your social inferior. That aloofness can cause hurt feelings. The factory also has its own hierarchy, based largely on language ability and background. Those who speak the best English and are the best educated are the most upwardly mobile.

Saji Korah is one of them. "I have a bachelor's degree in economics from India and an associate's degree in computer programming," the 34-year-old says in crisp English. Yet his job today, riveting brackets onto circuit boards, could be done by someone far less educated.

It's monotonous, and he makes it clear he has no intention of doing such work for long. He is going to school part time for yet-another degree, in computer-information systems. He dreams of becoming one of the plant's roving technicians.

Asked whether he has problems communicating with less-well-spoken colleagues, he says, "Sometimes, I have trouble following their pronunciations." Standing nearby, Suresh Patel says he has trouble, too, but mainly in understanding American-born workers. "Sometimes, they talk too fast," he explains. . . .

The factory doesn't have much choice but to hire a lot of immigrants. Many native-born Americans wouldn't consider taking the often-tedious entry-level jobs. But for John Phan, a 35-year-old who came from Vietnam a decade ago speaking little English, operating a machine on Line 12 is a step

301

up. He makes $10.05 an hour, compared with $7.50 an hour he previously earned at a plastics factory.

Mr. Phan's English is heavily accented, and he admits he sometimes can't understand co-workers. But that hardly matters; he seldom has to talk. He knows when a machine is running low on components, for instance, because a white light flashes on a pole jutting up from the top of it. One machine even talks to him: "Be careful, the feeder section may move," coos a soothing female voice, just before a big metal rack known as a feeder automatically shifts out into the corridor. "These machines are very smart," he says.

Those at the plant with good English and ambitious to advance can choose from an array of training courses beyond the basics needed for their immediate jobs. The courses cover everything from leadership skills to how to run a chip shooter. Workers can even take a course on drawing up an instructional sheet similar to those hanging over their workstations; they practice by writing one for making a peanut-butter-and-jelly sandwich. Training also relies heavily on lots of illustrations and on-the-job practice.

Hattie Curry is one of the few Americans on Line 12. A native of North Carolina, she started working for the company seven years ago, before this plant opened; the company, acquired by 3Com last year, was then known as U.S. Robotics.

Ms. Curry notes the increase in immigrants at 3Com and says working with them hasn't always been easy for her. "Before I worked here," she says, "I hadn't been around a lot of foreign people; I didn't understand their ways." As a newcomer, she thought some with more skills were reluctant to train her and tried to block her advancement. "Now, I know that's just their way," she says. "They don't mean to be mean." But she has changed her own style: "I handle them more firmly now; I've become stronger."

Yet despite all the blending of people on the factory floor, it stops in the lunchroom. From a corner table, three Indian women look over the rest of the big dining area. A table near the checkout is occupied almost entirely by African-American women. The table next to them, by Indian men. And so it goes around the room. "We share our food," says Jashwanti Bodhanwala, a mother of two who has been in the U.S. for 23 years, as if that entirely explains the apartheid-style dining.

One thing the lunch groups do is to facilitate gossip. The room is one of the few places, besides the outdoor smoking areas, where people relax and swap rumors.

Ms. Bodhanwala tugs off a piece of moist, spicy Indian flatbread, and spoons onto it a lump of homemade mango chutney from a plastic container. Asmabahen Patel, sitting opposite her, offers some mustard pickles. "Of course, if you weren't here," says Ms. Patel, gazing at a reporter, "we'd be speaking Gujarati."

PART II

Suggestions for Further Reading

Some of the changes in American society during the 1920s are covered in Lois Banner, *The American Beauty: A Social History Through Two Centuries of the American Idea, Ideal, and Image of the Beautiful Woman* (1983), and William Leuchtenburg, *Perils of Prosperity, 1914–1932* (1958). A good study on Prohibition is Andrew Sinclair, *Era of Excess: A Social History of the Prohibition Movement* (1964). On the Ku Klux Klan, see Kenneth Jackson, *The Ku Klux Klan in the Cities, 1915–1930* (1967), and David Chalmers, *Hooded Americanism: The First Century of the Ku Klux Klan* (1965). Information about the Klan and bigotry can also be found in David Bennett, *The Party of Fear: From Nativist Movements to the New Right in American History* (1988). Paula Fass, *The Damned and the Beautiful: American Youth in the 1920s* (1977), is valuable, as is J. Stanley Lemons, *The Woman Citizen: Social Feminism in the 1920s* (1973). A classic study of that era is Helen Merrill Lynd and Robert S. Lynd, *Middletown: A Study of Contemporary American Culture* (1929). On gay and lesbian history, see George Chauncey, *Gay New York: Gender, Urban Culture, and the Making of the Gay Male World, 1890–1940* (1994), and Lillian Faderman, *Odd Girls and Twilight Lovers: A History of Lesbian Life in Twentieth-Century America* (1991).

On the Great Depression, a good introduction is Robert S. McElvaine, *The Great Depression: America, 1929–1941* (1984). Also of use are Caroline Bird, *The Invisible Scar: The Great Depression and What It Did to American Life, From Then Until Now* (1966); Donald Worster, *Dust Bowl: The South Plains in the 1930s* (1979); and William Leuchtenburg, *Franklin Roosevelt and the New Deal* (1963). For women during the 1930s, see Susan Ware, *Holding Their Own: American Women in the 1930s* (1982). On blacks, see Nancy Weiss, *Farewell to the Party of Lincoln: Black Politics in the Age of FDR* (1983). A good picture of life in one American community can be found in Robert Lynd and Helen Lynd, *Middletown in Transition: A Study in Cultural Conflict* (1937). Information on workers during the Great Depression and after can be found in Robert H. Zieger, *American Workers, American Unions, 1920–1985* (1986). Another good book on the Great Depression is James Goodman, *Stories of Scottsboro: The Rape Case That Shocked 1930s America and Revived the Struggle for Equality* (1994). Especially good are Lizabeth Cohen, *Making a New Deal: Industrial Workers in Chicago, 1919–1939* (1990), and Neil Foley, *The White Scourge: Mexicans, Blacks and Poor Whites in Texas Cotton Culture* (1997).

America during World War II has received increasing attention. For introductions see William O'Neill, *A Democracy at War* (1993), and Peter Lingeman, *Don't You Know There Is a War On?* (1970). Another general work is Richard Polenberg, *War and Society* (1972). On Japanese Americans, see Peter Irons, *Justice at War* (1983), and Roger Daniels, *Concentration Camps, U.S.A.* (1970). On women during the war, see D'Ann Campbell, *Women at*

War with America: Private Lives in a Patriotic Cause (1984); Maureen Honey, *Creating Rosie the Riveter: Class, Gender and Propaganda During World War II* (1984); Leisa D. Meyer, *Creating GI Jane: Sexuality and Power in the Women's Army Corps During World War II* (1996); and Ruth Milkman, *Gender at Work: The Dynamics of Job Segregation During World War II* (1987). The experience of gay men and women is told by Allan Berube, *Coming Out Under Fire: The History of Gay Men and Women in World War II* (1990), while the battle experience is covered in Gerald F. Linderman, *The World Within the War: America's Combat Experience in World War II* (1997). A revisionist account of the war is Michael C. Adams, *The Best War Ever: America and World War II* (1994).

For changes during the war and after, see Kenneth Jackson, *Crabgrass Frontier: The Suburbanization of the United States* (1985), and Gavin Wright, *Old South, New South: Revolutions in the Southern Economy Since the Civil War* (1986). On suburbs, see Herbert J. Gans, *Levittowners: Ways of Life and Politics in a New Suburban Community* (1982); Gwendolyn Wright, *Building the Dream: A Social History of Housing in America* (1981); and William Dobriner, *Class in Suburbia* (1963). Elaine May, *Homeward Bound: American Families in the Cold War* (1988), attempts to trace the impact of the cold war on families. Also useful are Arlene Skolnick, *Embattled Paradise: the American Family in an Age of Uncertainty* (1991), and Donald Katz, *Home Fires: An Intimate Portrait of One Middle-Class Family in Postwar America* (1992). For a view of city life in contrast to suburbia, see Thomas J. Sugrue, *The Origins of the Urban Crisis: Race and Inequality in Postwar Detroit* (1997).

The civil rights movement is covered in Harry Ashmore, *Civil Rights and Wrongs: A Memoir of Race and Politics, 1944–1994* (1994). Another overall view is Harvard Sitkoff, *The Struggle for Black Equality, 1954–1992* (1993). On the background of the *Brown* v. *Board of Education* decision, see Richard Kruger, *Simple Justice: The History of Brown* v. *Board of Education: Black America's Struggle for Equality* (1976). A moving biography of Martin Luther King Jr. is Stephen Oates, *Let the Trumpet Sound: The Life of Martin Luther King* (1982). The process of ghettoization is discussed in Nicholas Lemann, *The Promised Land: The Great Black Migration and How It Changed America* (1991), and Arnold Hirsch, *Making the Second Ghetto: Race and Housing in Chicago, 1940–1960* (1983). A controversial book about black progress is William Wilson, *The Declining Significance of Race: Blacks and Changing American Institutions* (1978). Wilson's *The Truly Disadvantaged: The Inner City, the Underclass, and Public Policy* (1987) centers on poverty. An attempt to look at black progress is Reynolds Farley, *Blacks and Whites* (1984), while the National Research Council publication *A Common Destiny: Blacks and Whites in American Society* (1989) is filled with information. Two newer accounts of the civil rights movement are Robert Weisbort, *Freedom Bound: A History of the Civil Rights Movement* (1989), and Taylor Branch, *Parting the Waters: America in the King Years, 1954–1963* (1988). For women and the civil rights movement, see Belinda Robnett, *How Long? How Long? African American Women in the Strug-*

gle for Civil Rights (1997). A view of race relations at the end of the 1990s is David K. Shipler, *A Country of Strangers: Blacks and Whites in America* (1997). Overall views of American racism include Philip A. Klinder with Rogers Smith, *The Unsteady March: The Rise and Decline of Racial Equality in America* (1999); Manning Marable, *Race, Reform and Rebellion: The Second Reconstruction in Black America, 1945–2000* (2000); Adam Fairclough, *Better Day Coming: Blacks and Equality, 1890–2000* (2001); and William O'Brien, *The Color Law: Race, Violence and Justice in the Post–World War II South* (1999).

For the 1960s, the standard treatment of the Vietnam War is George Herring, *America's Longest War: The United States and Vietnam, 1950–1975* (1996). See also Lauri Umansky, *Motherhood Reconsidered: Feminism and the Legacies of the Sixties* (1996); David Burner, *Making Peace with the 60s* (1996); and Paul Berman, *A Tale of Two Utopias: The Political Journey of the Generation of 1968* (1996).

For American women in recent years, the best introduction is William Chafe, *The American Woman: Her Changing Social, Economic, and Political Role, 1920–1970* (1972). Jacqueline Jones, *Labor of Love, Labor of Sorrow* (1985), is also useful, as is Alice Kessler-Harris, *Out to Work* (1982). Also helpful are Sara Evans, *Personal Politics: The Roots of Women's Liberation in the Civil Rights Movement and the New Left* (1979); Carol Stack, *All Our Kin: Strategies for Survival in a Black Community* (1974); and Susan Estabrook Kennedy, *If All We Did Was to Weep at Home: A History of White Working-Class Women in America* (1979). Jane Mansbridge, *Why We Lost the ERA* (1986), centers on the ERA; Susan Hartman, *From Margin to Mainstream: American Women in Politics Since 1960* (1989), discusses politics. A useful history of American women is Sara Evans, *Born for Liberty: A History of Women in America* (1989). Susan Faludi, *Backlash: The Undeclared War Against American Women* (1991), covers recent developments, especially in the media.

On recent immigration, Ronald Takaki, *Strangers from a Different Shore: A History of Asian Americans* (1989); Roger Daniels, *Asian America: Chinese and Japanese in the United States Since 1850* (1988); and Peter Kwong, *The New Chinatown* (1986) are useful regarding Asians. General information can be found in Alejandro Portes and Ruben G. Rumbaut, *Immigrant America: A Portrait* (1990), and David M. Reimers, *Still the Golden Door: The Third World Comes to America* (1992). On Miami, see Alejandro Portes and Alex Stepick, *City on the Edge* (1993). On Hispanics, consult Roberto Suro, *Strangers Among Us: How Latino Immigration Is Transforming America* (1998). On Mexican women, see Vicki L. Ruiz, *From Out of the Shadows: Mexican Women in Twentieth Century America* (1997). A general account of immigration since 1920 is Elliott Robert Barkan, *And Still They Come: Immigrants and American Society, 1920–1990s* (1996). Manuel G. Gonzales, *Mexicanos: A History of Mexicans in the United States* (1999), covers Mexican immigration, while Elliot Robert Barkan, ed., *A Nation of Peoples: A Sourcebook on America's Multicultural Heritage* (1999), contains a wealth of information.